OCUP 2 Certifica

OCUP 2 Certification Guide

Preparing for the OMG Certified UML 2.5 Professional 2 Foundation Exam

Michael Jesse Chonoles

MORGAN KAUFMANN PUBLISHERS
AN IMPRINT OF ELSEVIER

Morgan Kaufmann is an imprint of Elsevier
50 Hampshire Street, 5th Floor, Cambridge, MA 02139, United States

Copyright © 2018 Elsevier Inc. All rights reserved.

No part of this publication may be reproduced or transmitted in any form or by any means, electronic or mechanical, including photocopying, recording, or any information storage and retrieval system, without permission in writing from the publisher. Details on how to seek permission, further information about the Publisher's permissions policies and our arrangements with organizations such as the Copyright Clearance Center and the Copyright Licensing Agency, can be found at our website: www.elsevier.com/permissions.

This book and the individual contributions contained in it are protected under copyright by the Publisher (other than as may be noted herein).

Designations used by companies to distinguish their products are often claimed as trademarks or registered trademarks. In all instances in which Morgan Kaufmann Publishers is aware of a claim, the product names appear in initial capital or all capital letters. Readers, however, should contact the appropriate companies for more complete information regarding trademarks and registration.

UML is a trademark of Object Management Group, Inc. in the United States and/or other countries.

Notices
Knowledge and best practice in this field are constantly changing. As new research and experience broaden our understanding, changes in research methods, professional practices, or medical treatment may become necessary.

Practitioners and researchers must always rely on their own experience and knowledge in evaluating and using any information, methods, compounds, or experiments described herein. In using such information or methods they should be mindful of their own safety and the safety of others, including parties for whom they have a professional responsibility.

To the fullest extent of the law, neither the Publisher nor the authors, contributors, or editors, assume any liability for any injury and/or damage to persons or property as a matter of products liability, negligence or otherwise, or from any use or operation of any methods, products, instructions, or ideas contained in the material herein.

British Library Cataloguing-in-Publication Data
A catalogue record for this book is available from the British Library

Library of Congress Cataloging-in-Publication Data
A catalog record for this book is available from the Library of Congress

ISBN: 978-0-12-809640-6

For Information on all Morgan Kaufmann publications
visit our website at https://www.elsevier.com/books-and-journals

Publishing Director: Jonathan Simpson
Acquisition Editor: Jonathan Simpson
Editorial Project Manager: Lindsay Lawrence
Production Project Manager: Punithavathy Govindaradjane
Cover Designer: Victoria Pearson

Typeset by MPS Limited, Chennai, India

Contents

FOREWORD xi

ACKNOWLEDGMENTS xv

Chapter 1 What is OCUP 2? 1
    1.1 The OCUP Programs 1
        1.1.1 OMG Certified UML Professional 1 1
        1.1.2 OMG Certified UML Professional 2 2
        1.1.3 Why Does OMG Offer It? 2
        1.1.4 Why Should You Take It? 2
    1.2 The Levels 3
        1.2.1 Foundation Level 4
        1.2.2 Intermediate Level 5
        1.2.3 Advanced Level 6
    1.3 What Do You Get If You Pass? 6
    1.4 Taking the Exam 7
        1.4.1 Signing Up for the Exam 7
    1.5 How to Prepare 8
        1.5.1 Cheating 9
        1.5.2 Coverage Map 10
    1.6 What an Exam Is Like 11
        1.6.1 Exam Structure 12
        1.6.2 Question Structure 13
    1.7 How We Wrote the Examinations 14
        1.7.1 Team 14
        1.7.2 Review Process and Criteria 15
        1.7.3 Beta Review and Criteria 15

Chapter 2 What is UML? 17
    2.1 What Does UML Stand for? 17
        2.1.1 How is UML a *Language*? 17
        2.1.2 How is UML a *Modeling* Language? 18
        2.1.3 How is UML a *Unified* Modeling Language? 21
    2.2 UML Goals 23
        2.2.1 The Original Goals of UML 23
        2.2.2 Updated Goals for UML 24

  2.3 What is the Object Management Group (OMG)?..........................26
    2.3.1 The Standards-Making Process of OMG..........................26
    2.3.2 The History of UML..28
  2.4 Modeling..29
    2.4.1 What Kind of Modeling..29
    2.4.2 Purposes for UML Modeling..30
    2.4.3 Principles of Modeling..37

Chapter 3 Questions for Chapter 2..43
  Answers for Chapter 2..46

Chapter 4 The Organization of UML...55
  4.1 The UML 2.5 Specification..55
    4.1.1 Target Audience..55
    4.1.2 The Document Layout..55
  4.2 The Language Definition—The Clauses..56
  4.3 The Subclauses...58
  4.4 The Abstract Syntax...59
  4.5 The Layered Metamodel..60
  4.6 Diagrams..65
    4.6.1 Structure Diagrams..67
    4.6.2 Behavior Diagrams...68
    4.6.3 General Diagram Features..68

Chapter 5 Questions for Chapter 4..75
  Answers for Chapter 4..79

Chapter 6 Objects and Classes..89
  6.1 Finding Objects and Classes..89
    6.1.1 Attributes..93
    6.1.2 Operations..94
    6.1.3 Referring to a Member Feature..96
    6.1.4 Static Features...96
  6.2 Types...97
    6.2.1 Class Versus Datatype...98
    6.2.2 Primitive Types..98
    6.2.3 Enumerations..99
    6.2.4 DataTypes..101
  6.3 Modifiers..104
    6.3.1 Derived Properties...104
    6.3.2 Default Value...105
    6.3.3 Protecting from Change..106
    6.3.4 Parameter Direction..107
  6.4 Assigning Value...109
    6.4.1 Literals..109
    6.4.2 Instance Specifications...110
    6.4.3 Expressions...111

Chapter 7 Questions for Chapter 6 115
Answers for Chapter 6 119

Chapter 8 Packages and Namespaces 129
    8.1 Package Notation 129
        8.1.1 Packages and Their Contents 129
        8.1.2 Diagrams of Packages 131
        8.1.3 Uniform Resource Identifiers 132
    8.2 Packages and Visibility 133
        8.2.1 Package Member Visibility 133
        8.2.2 Inner and Outer Names 135
        8.2.3 Namespaces and Distinguishable Names 137
    8.3 Packages and Their Contents 138
        8.3.1 Package Dependencies 140
        8.3.2 Specific Elements from Other Packages 140
    8.4 Package Stereotypes 144
        8.4.1 Packages and Models 144
        8.4.2 Miscellaneous Stereotypes of Packages 147

Chapter 9 Questions for Chapter 8 149
Answers for Chapter 8 154

Chapter 10 Finishing the Static Model 163
    10.1 Multiplicity 163
        10.1.1 Representing the Multiplicity of Attributes 163
        10.1.2 Representing Argument Multiplicity 167
        10.1.3 Multiplicity Properties and Collection Types 168
        10.1.4 Discontinuity 170
    10.2 Associations 172
        10.2.1 Attribute and Role Adornments 172
        10.2.2 Reading Associations 175
        10.2.3 Associations and Datatypes 178
        10.2.4 Links and Instances 179
        10.2.5 Composition and Aggregation 179
    10.3 Generalization, Specialization, and Inheritance 183
        10.3.1 Reflexive Structures Using Generalization 186
        10.3.2 The Process 187
        10.3.3 Polymorphism 187

Chapter 11 Questions for Chapter 10 191
Answers for Chapter 10 196

Chapter 12 Use Cases 207
    12.1 Finding Use Cases 207
        12.1.1 Naming Use Cases 208
        12.1.2 Actors 210

		12.1.3	Subject	214
		12.1.4	Other Use Cases	215
	12.2	Simplifying Use Cases		217
		12.2.1	Generalization	217
		12.2.2	Include	219
		12.2.3	Extend	220
		12.2.4	Owners	223
		12.2.5	Use Case Diagrams	224

Chapter 13 Questions for Chapter 12 227
Answers for Chapter 12 233

Chapter 14 Behavior: Sequence Diagrams 243
    14.1 Sequence Diagram History 243
    14.2 Lifelines 243
    14.3 Messages 245
        14.3.1 Synchronous Messages 245
        14.3.2 Asynchronous Messages 247
    14.4 Time & Occurrences 247
    14.5 Execution Specification 253
    14.6 Sequence Diagrams 255
    14.7 Practical Sequence Diagrams 256

Chapter 15 Questions for Chapter 14 259
Answers for Chapter 14 263

Chapter 16 Behavior: Activity Diagrams 271
    16.1 What is an Activity Diagram? 271
        16.1.1 Activity Diagram History 271
        16.1.2 Single Token Diagrams 277
        16.1.3 Concurrent (Multi-Token) Diagrams 278
        16.1.4 Consuming Tokens 281
        16.1.5 Joining at an Action 283
    16.2 Timers and Timing Events 284
    16.3 Object Flows/Edges 287
    16.4 Advanced Topics 289
        16.4.1 Weights 289
        16.4.2 Stream 289
        16.4.3 Send/Receive Messages/Events 290
        16.4.4 Local Pre/Postconditions 291
    16.5 Activity Diagrams 292
        16.5.1 Activities 293
        16.5.2 Invoking an Activity 294
        16.5.3 Calling an Operation 294

Chapter 17 Questions for Chapter 16 297
Answers for Chapter 16 303

Chapter 18 Behavior: State Machine Diagrams.. 313
    18.1 What is a State and State Machine.. 313
        18.1.1 States and Modes 315
        18.1.2 Differences Between States 316
        18.1.3 Qualitatively Different States................................... 316
        18.1.4 Naming States 317
        18.1.5 Overlapping States 317
        18.1.6 Finding States 319
    18.2 Transitions... 321
        18.2.1 Events 321
        18.2.2 Simple State Machine 322
        18.2.3 Guard Conditions 324
        18.2.4 Transition Effect 326
        18.2.5 Transition Syntax 327
        18.2.6 Ongoing Behavior 328
        18.2.7 State Setup and Teardown....................................... 329
        18.2.8 Exit/Entry Action Equivalents 330
        18.2.9 Completion 331
        18.2.10 Internal Transitions 331
    18.3 State Machine Processing... 333
        18.3.1 Run-to-Completion... 333
        18.3.2 States and Pseudostates 335
        18.3.3 Types of Transitions 337
        18.3.4 State Diagrams and Machines 338
        18.3.5 Hierarchy of States... 339
        18.3.6 States Contours 340
    18.4 State vs Activity Semantics 342

Chapter 19 Questions for Chapter 18 343
Answers for Chapter 18 348

INDEX **359**

Foreword

We at OMG approached the task of updating our established and venerable OCUP exams and certification program with some trepidation. We recognized the popularity and standing of the original OCUP program in the industry but, when we had originally laid out its coverage some years back, its position as our first certification program rendered us a bit timid so we restricted its content to materials in our specification document. Emboldened by the acceptance of this program, however, when we followed up with certification exams in our other fields we went beyond the BPMN, BPMN 2, and SysML specifications to test modeling skills in their domains and, for some exams, extend into subtopic areas beyond the scope of our specifications. With this experience, we felt confident in extending the OCUP 2 coverage beyond the specification that defines the UML model elements to cover software *modeling* skills and knowledge—i.e., how to *use* UML to model software effectively, and reap the benefits of the modeling step that should start the work of every substantial software project.

In addition to this expanded point of view that emphasizes modeling over language detail, OCUP 2 extends beyond UML at the beginning of the Foundation level where it covers "Why we model"—and (in a portion not included in this book, of course) at the end of the Advanced exam where it devotes several sections to metamodeling including the MOF, fUML (Semantics of a Foundational Subset for Executable UML Models), and Alf (Action Language for Foundational UML). If you are a UML guru, or you aspire to become one, you should know what these specifications are and how they are used, so the OCUP 2 Advanced exam covers them at about that level. Let this be something that you look forward to as you climb the OCUP 2 certification levels!

The references for "Why we model," all papers downloadable free, cover a range of aspects of modeling under titles that reflect their practicality: *The*

Value of Modeling; Why Model; Business Modeling: A Practical Guide to Realizing Business Value; and *Why Domain Modeling*. We expect that many OCUP 2 exam candidates will learn from these papers and, in future when a project leader or supervisor asks "Why should we take the time to model this? We can just start coding now!", these developers will have a ready answer.

But what about the UML coverage itself? The UML experts who wrote the OCUP 2 examinations, who mapped the program's topical coverage before they set about writing the exam questions, wanted to tailor each level to a role or set of roles in the industry so that certified candidates (that's you, soon!) and the people who hire them (hiring managers, or companies offering contracts) know why they should prefer these OCUP 2-certified candidates. In fact, our role analysis extended beyond developers to consider stakeholder roles—i.e., model *users*—in parallel to the roles defined in our SysML certification program which names its foundation level "Model User." There is a chart of the roles that we consider on the OCUP 2 website's index page (http://www.omg.org/ocup-2/index.htm).

On the basis of this role analysis, the authors of the OCUP 2 program set its coverage by topic and level to reflect industry usage: For the Foundation level, they selected these diagram types: Class, Object, and Package on the structural side; Sequence, Activity, State Machine, and Use Case on the behavioral. These depict the features that architects and developers need to visualize as they design and implement real, practical, everyday systems.

However, when you look into the UML specification document, you discover that its presentation is not arranged by diagram type. Instead, the spec defines UML *elements* in an order that builds in functionality and, necessarily because of the language's structure, in complexity as well. (Element and Relationship are defined first, e.g., the spec pointing out that they provide the basis for all other modeling concepts in UML.) And the presentation of each major element or type—e.g., Classifier or Behavior—occupies a full section of the specification that commingles aspects used in basic, intermediate, and advanced levels of modeling.

So, if you have examined the OCUP 2 coverage maps (and you should!), including the Foundation *supplementary* coverage map along with the Intermediate and Advanced, you know that we split individual UML model elements into parts that fit naturally (well, as naturally as practical) into the three levels of the OCUP 2 program—Foundation, Intermediate, and Advanced. While this had the advantage of yielding three exams that each fit into an industry niche, the price for this was that the content for each level was distributed—scattered, really—throughout the UML specification document.

Thus this book. It is much easier to have one person chase down the scattered Foundation level UML treasures and collect them into one tome than for each candidate to do it individually and, if a particularly knowledgeable person does it, he can couple an explanation to each exposition where it will be most helpful. Even more helpful would be a set of sample exam questions at the end of each chapter—don't you think?

The author of this book, Michael Chonoles, is this particularly knowledgeable and helpful person. He has participated in OMG's UML standardization process since it began back in the 20th century. He wrote questions for both the original OCUP program and the current OCUP 2 and is already a coauthor of two books on UML modeling including the popular *UML For Dummies*. In this book, he describes the UML elements covered in the OCUP 2 Foundation exam, explains how each is used, and includes after each chapter an additional chapter of sample exam questions.

That, of course, makes this a rather remarkable book. Why? Recall that the authors of the OCUP 2 program set the coverage of the three levels to each correspond—in topic and detail—to an industry niche. That means the OCUP 2 Foundation level exam covers the UML model elements and attributes that beginning model builders and serious model users need to know about. So, as you prepare yourself for OCUP 2 Foundation level certification by studying from this book, you also build your modeling knowledge and improve your modeling skills, improving your performance at work and this, of course, is what we at OMG had in mind from the beginning.

Let me personally wish you the best as you prepare to enhance your career by achieving OCUP 2 Foundation level certification as you build your UML modeling knowledge and skills. I know you will be proud to display the OCUP 2 Certified logo on your business card and resume, and I hope that you will extend your certification to OCUP 2 Intermediate and, if you are a technical manager or aspire to be the UML guru at your company, perhaps Advanced as well.

Jon Siegel, Ph.D.
Vice President, Technology Transfer
and Director, Certification
OMG

Acknowledgments

I need to thank several people for their help, including my parents for moral inspiration. So thanks Mom and Dad. My son, Zev Chonoles, also helped with encouragement, technical advice, and competition. (I'm getting this book done before he gets his PhD in mathematics). I also need to thank Dr. Pat Loudis, who helped by being my friend and not my doctor. Dr. Jon Siegel, OMG's Vice President in charge of the OCUP 2 program, gets the credit for getting me motivated, giving technical advice, and proofreading, and for running an excellent certification program. Of course, any remaining technical errors are my own. I also need to acknowledge the good people at Change Vision, who are sponsoring my work at OMG and let me use their quality Astah modeling tool on many of the diagrams in this book.

You've bought this book and studied hard—Now take the exam!

We at OMG think that your dedication deserves a reward so, to encourage you to take the OCUP 2 Foundation Exam that you've studied so hard for, we're giving you a coupon code good for a 10% discount on your Pearson VUE exam fee!

When you register for your exam at http://pearsonvue.com/omg/ and get to the page **Checkout—Step 3: Enter Payment**, click on **Add Voucher or Promo Code** and enter this code: VdaVQMcPya6U. This code will work only once on your account, so study hard and plan to do well the first time you take the exam!

Best wishes for a successful OCUP 2 Foundation Level certification from the author, Michael Chonoles, and the OMG Certification Team!

CHAPTER 1

What is OCUP 2?

1.1 THE OCUP PROGRAMS

1.1.1 OMG Certified UML Professional 1

In 2003, the Object Management Group (OMG) established a certification program for users of UML, based on the UML standard then undergoing finalization, UML 2.0. The certification program was a three-level program called the OMG Certified UML Professional (OCUP).

The program was very successful, and many candidates took and passed the examinations[1]. Since the OCUP program was created, tens of thousands of candidates have taken the examinations and have been certified. These certificate holders come pretty evenly from countries around the world and every continent (except Antarctica). No single country dominates[2].

Unfortunately, some candidates thought that the original examinations were overly focused on the UML 2.0 specification and metamodel, and not sufficiently on more practical aspects of UML modeling. The candidates that passed certainly knew their UML, but some good modelers may have failed because they were not sufficiently familiar with the UML specification documents. The UML specifications, then, as now, are formal documents with a syntax and terminology of their own and are not intended for the practical modeler. These documents are more appropriate for tool vendors, language designers, and chief modelers or methodologists tailoring UML for a project.

---

[1] "OMG does not publish the number of candidates who take their exams, but they have said in the past that several tens of thousands of UML modelers hold the various levels of OCUP and OCUP 2 certifications", Jon Siegel, Ph.D., Vice President, (OMG) Technology Transfer and Director, Certification. Jan 2016.
[2] Jon Siegel, Ph.D., Vice President, (OMG) Technology Transfer and Director, Certification. Jan 2016.

1.1.2 OMG Certified UML Professional 2

By 2013, with the development of UML 2.5, which entailed a significant restructuring and simplification of the UML specifications (e.g., merging the two documents; Infrastructure and Superstructure into one document) the certification examinations needed to change. No longer could the test depend in any way on the original 2.0 UML specifications and metamodel[3]. Moreover, by the time of UML 2.5, significant changes had occurred to UML that needed to be included in any certification program. This time, taking advantage of the need to rewrite, now the examinations do not rely on specific knowledge of the format of the UML specification or the metamodel, except where relevant to the practical application of modeling. Of course, the certification examinations ultimately rely on the content of the UML 2.5 Specification, because the specification defines UML.

The first exam in the OMG Certified UML Professional 2 (OCUP 2) series, the Foundation Level, came out in 2014. The next exam, the Intermediate Level, will be available in 2016. The final exam, the Advanced Level, will be available in 2017.

1.1.3 Why Does OMG Offer It?

I asked Jon Siegel, Ph.D., Director of the Certification for OMG (and Vice President, Technology Transfer) why OMG offers the OCUP 2 program. Here is his answer.

> Certification Program benefits an organization's standard in many ways. Most fundamentally, it creates a population of trained, identifiable practitioners. Hiring managers charged with introducing UML modeling to a company will favor these candidates because their knowledge level is certified, but companies with established UML modeling groups benefit as well. The program also forms the focus of an "ecosystem" of support as training courses (taught in-person or online), books, and ancillary material are produced and published. Working together, all of these factors encourage the spread of usage of a standard. This has certainly been the case for UML, OCUP, and OCUP 2.[4]

1.1.4 Why Should You Take It?

Candidates take the certification examinations for two kinds of reasons: To impress others, and to prove something to themselves. The others you might try to impress, include your current boss, future hiring bosses, and project/team leaders looking to fill a position, or contracting, and outsourcing

---

[3] Because OMG discarded the two-document approach to the UML specification, and by restructuring and combining them into much simpler document, all the original references were obsolete.
[4] Jon Siegel, Ph.D., Vice President, (OMG) Technology Transfer and Director, Certification. Jan 2016.

agencies looking to hire. In some cases, a particular level of certification may be required for a job or appointment. Many companies have programs or study groups that sponsor (and pay for) the examinations for their employees. A few universities are considering the idea of adding certifications to their degree requirements.

Some candidates feel a strong sense of accomplishment when they become certified and try to get as many certifications as possible.

Candidates also learn from their examination results report, which specifies in what UML topic areas they are strong and in what topic areas they are weak. A good diagnostic evaluation of their skills is very useful. Many candidates can use a realistic evaluation; people often have significantly overvalued or undervalued their abilities.

Though a candidate will learn much from the examination results report, most of the learning arises from studying for the exam. UML 2.5 is very large and complex. With just 90 questions per exam, we can only test a small percentage of the UML language. The learning of UML comes from studying the topics not by sitting for the examination.

POINTS TO REMEMBER

- The OCUP programs have been very popular and successful.
- The OCUP 2 program replaces the OCUP 1 program.
  - OCUP 2 is based on UML 2.5; OCUP 1 was based on UML 2.0
  - OCUP 2 is more focused on modeling than OCUP 1, which was more focused on the specification structure.
- Becoming OCUP 2 certified demonstrates to your employers, peers, and yourself, that you are competent in UML 2.5 modeling.
- The learning that you undergo by certification is in the studying, not in the test taking.

1.2 THE LEVELS

The OCUP 2 Certification program has three levels of certification: Foundation, Intermediate, and Advanced. We determined what should go in each level by examining UML 2.5 training programs, industry hiring requirements, project requirements, and UML tools capabilities. The team of experts developing the OCUP 2 program includes UML book authors, UML trainers, both in-house and independent, people working on the UML specifications, senior project leaders, and methodologists for UML-using projects.

Each level builds on knowledge of the previous levels though most material is only tested on one exam. You cannot get the Advanced certification by just

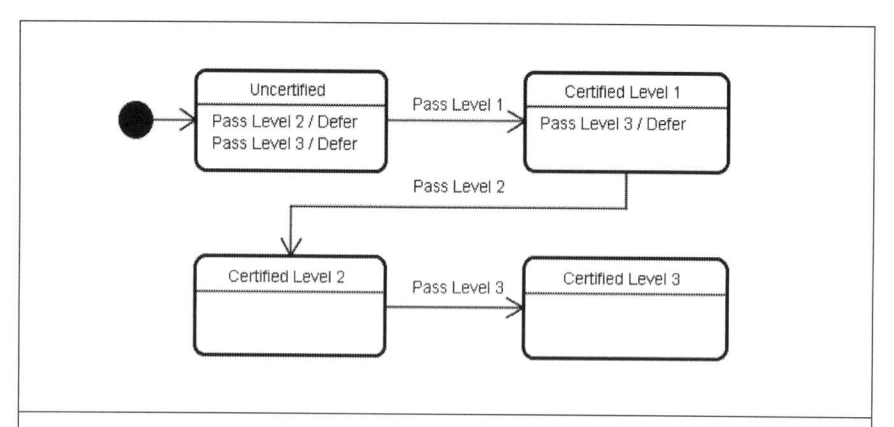

```
                    ┌──────────────────────┐                    ┌──────────────────────┐
                    │     Uncertified      │   Pass Level 1     │   Certified Level 1  │
       ●───────────▶│ Pass Level 2 / Defer ├───────────────────▶│ Pass Level 3 / Defer │
                    │ Pass Level 3 / Defer │                    │                      │
                    └──────────┬───────────┘                    └──────────────────────┘
                               │ Pass Level 2
                               ▼
                    ┌──────────────────────┐   Pass Level 3     ┌──────────────────────┐
                    │  Certified Level 2   ├───────────────────▶│   Certified Level 3  │
                    └──────────────────────┘                    └──────────────────────┘
```

This is a small State Machine diagram for a Candidate, showing how the Certification Levels work.

The normal flow is that a candidate starts out as Uncertified. When the event of Pass Level 1 occurs, they move to the state of being Certified Level 1, and likewise to Certified Level 2 and Level 3 on the relevant events.

The only tricky spot is if the Candidate passes the exams out of order. If the Candidate passes Level 2 before Level 1 (or Level 3 before Level 1 or Level 2), the State Machine DEFERS the event. When the Candidate reaches the next state, the State Machine reapplies any deferred events, again deferring any remaining out-of-order events. Therefore, if the Candidate passes level 2 first, nothing happens. If the Candidate later passes Level 1, the Candidate moves into Certified Level 2 by quickly going through the state of being Certified Level 1.

We will cover this material in more detail later.

FIGURE 1.1
State machine diagram for passing exams and certifications.

passing the Advanced Exam; you need to pass the earlier exams also. We show this in the UML state machines diagram of Fig. 1.1.

Here is how we determined the contents of the levels.

1.2.1 Foundation Level

For example, looking at the Foundation Level, we examined the hiring requirements for entry-level UML modelers (UML model builders) and other people on a team that are required to read UML Models, (i.e., UML model users). Some projects do not put UML skills into their hiring requirements; instead, they send their developers to take an "Introduction to UML" course (usually three to four days long). If UML material did not fall into the prerequisites for real jobs, or if it did not fall into a typical "Introduction to UML" curriculum, it was not placed in the Foundation Level exam.

We also looked at tool support. If popular UML tools do not commonly support a notation, we did not include the notation, though the concept might still make it into the exam.

With the level of knowledge and skill tested at the OCUP 2 Foundation Level and a corresponding amount of industry experience, a UML model user will be well equipped to read and understand the diagrams he or she encounters in work situations. It will help the Model User, as a stakeholder checking that a design expressed in UML satisfies requirements, or as a coder responsible for implementing that functionality following the structure and design depicted in the model[5]. We also target other model users, including Managers, Requirements Engineers, Configuration Management Practitioners, Software Quality Assurance Engineers, Testers, Documentation Specialists, and similar people working on or with a project.

Similarly, a UML Model Builder will be prepared to work alongside others in a modeling team as the group prepares a model for presentation to stakeholders or implementers. Equipped with the foundation defined by this level, the model builder will also be prepared to study, practice, and move up to the OCUP 2 Intermediate certification—A level better aligned with the design and development skill set that the model builder uses in his or her work[5].

We also included the basics principles and purposes of modeling. We realize that if Model Users and Model Builders do not understand the motivation for making models, they may not completely buy-in to modeling nor sustain the modeling effort.

The OCUP 2 Foundation certification is a prerequisite for receiving the higher level certifications.

1.2.2 Intermediate Level

In constructing the Intermediate Level of UML 2.5 Certification, we looked at the requirements for independent working on a UML project, or as a supervisor of a small modeling team. We also checked against what is often called "Advanced UML" training courses, five to eight days long. If some topic was not commonly taught in such curricula, nor used on the majority of projects, nor supported by UML tools, it was deemed too advanced for Intermediate Level and left for the Advanced Exam. Familiarity with items on the Intermediate Level examination and several years of industry experience allows a Model Builder to read, interpret, construct, and work with complex UML models.

The OCUP 2 Intermediate certification is a prerequisite for receiving the Advanced Level certification.

---

[5] Modified from OMG. http://www.omg.org/ocup-2/exam-info.htm. Last updated 2/11/2015.

1.2.3 Advanced Level

In constructing the Advanced Level of UML 2.5 Certification, we looked at the requirements for a Modeling Lead on a large UML project, making decisions on the types of modeling for the project to use. With the appropriate level of industry experience, these people, who may be called Methodologists, often advise management on the role and extent of modeling.

We also checked against semester-long Advanced UML training courses and the most advanced UML training books. If no UML tools support a notation, we may still filter the topic. The Advanced Level certificate holder should be able to tailor UML for a project's needs. We have also included material on metamodeling covering the MOF and, at an awareness level, the uses of two members of OMG's metamodel-linked family of specifications: fUML (Semantics of a Foundational Subset for Executable UML Models) and Alf (Acton Language for Foundational UML). Including these other standards will ensure that the certificate holder can function at this Advanced Level.

POINTS TO REMEMBER

- There are three levels of the OCUP 2 Certification Program: Foundation, Intermediate, and Advanced.
    - Each level is a prerequisite for being certified at the next higher level.
- The Foundation certification is aimed at
    - Model Builders who wish to become a competent part of modeling team on a project.
    - Model Users who need to understand the typical models produced on a project.

1.3 WHAT DO YOU GET IF YOU PASS?

After taking the examination, the screen will display your score. Therefore, you will know whether you have passed immediately. You will receive a printed examination results report indicating the number of incorrect answers per topic area. This information is very useful, even if you have passed, as it identifies your weaker areas in UML, which could help guide you in future modeling efforts, and in taking the next level exam.

In a month's time after passing, OMG will send a congratulation letter, and a certificate, that is suitable for framing. You will also get instructions and permission to download an icon that you can put on email or business cards. See Fig. 1.2.

You will also be able to enter your name, and optional contact information (e.g., company and address) in the OMG Certified Professionals Directory, where it can be searched for by prospective employers, friends, etc. To search for your own entry, just go to http://www.omg.org/cgi-bin/searchcert.cgi.

FIGURE 1.2
OCUP 2 Foundation Level icon.
OMG Certification Directory, Jan 2016.

In addition, you will earn the respect and admiration from your peers, by demonstrating your knowledge and perseverance.

1.4 TAKING THE EXAM

1.4.1 Signing Up for the Exam

To schedule an exam, go to the Pearson Vue's OMG site by visiting http://www.pearsonvue.com/omg/ and then selecting OMG. On the right of the screen, you can create an account if you do not already have one. If this is your first OMG exam at Pearson Vue, you need to make an account before you can schedule an exam.

When you select the examination, please make sure you select OMG-OCUP2-FOUND100. You will need to schedule the exam appointment several business days in advance. This rule also applies to canceling an appointment. It may also be difficult to find an open appointment slot at a location nearby on the day you want. Some facilities are not open on weekends, and weekends are the most desired time as most candidates work or go to school. If you go to the wrong exam, arrive more than 15 minutes late, or your ID is insufficient, you will not be able to get your money back.

The examination is $200 (US) in English-speaking countries for the 120-minute exam. Most local currencies are also accepted. In non-English-speaking countries, you will have an extra half-hour to take the exam; the cost is $210 or equivalent in the local currency. You might wish to contact your employer as many of them have bought (at a discount) a set of exam vouchers that they can make available to their candidates free or at a reduced price. The voucher is often part of an in-house training program[6]. If you are an employer or training company, consider sending an email to OMG at certificationinfo@omg.org asking about their quantity discount voucher program.

Please arrive at least 30 minutes before the scheduled time to allow adequate time to sign-in. You will have to plan for traffic conditions and weather. You will need two valid forms of ID with signature; at least one of the two must have your photo.

You will not be able to bring anything in, except for necessary eyeglasses. Do not bring in bags, books, notes, cell phones, Google Glasses, watches, or wallets. Most examination sites have lockers. However, they do not all do so, so call the site in advance, or work out an alternate approach.

They will have surveillance of the candidates including their hands, for example, at least, one proctor per 15 candidates and/or video surveillance. If you get nervous while taking tests or while being watched, you may have difficulty in these exams.

Remember to have plenty of sleep and eat before the exam. Try not to drink too much as bathroom access may be limited.

POINTS TO REMEMBER

- Do not be late to your test appointment. You should be aiming to arrive at least 30 minutes early to handle the paperwork.
- You will not be allowed to bring anything into the examination room.
- Have two forms of valid ID with signatures, one, at least, showing your photo.
- Have plenty of sleep before the exam.

1.5 HOW TO PREPARE

I would love to say that all you need to pass the examination in this book. Unfortunately, this is not true. You will also have to study.

---

[6]From a company's perspective, the cost of the voucher is much more cost-effective than sending the employees to a course. This is especially true as the employees do the studying for the certification exam on their own time and they do not miss any work.

You will probably need to have access to the UML 2.5 (or later) specification. The most recent specification will be found at http://www.omg.org/spec/UML/Current. The specification was not written to study from, but if, while reading this book or other study sources, you find questions that your study material cannot answer, the specification holds the final answer.

There is also additional useful background material at http://www.uml.org/index.htm#UML2.0. The detailed coverage map is at http://www.omg.org/ocup-2/coverage-map-found.htm. There is a supplemental coverage map that gives more detail at http://www.omg.org/ocup-2/coverage map-found-suppl.htm.

Unfortunately, there are no other books (at the time of this writing) that are aimed directly at passing the OCUP 2 exam. Books written for passing the OCUP 1 exams, while very good for that purpose, will not be helpful for OCUP 2, because the focus of the exams has changed (from spec focused to modeling focused). Still good books on the modeling of UML 2 may be helpful to you on modeling UML 2.5, because the changes between UML 2 and UML 2.5 are not sufficiently significant, especially at the Foundation Level.

Some useful material books and articles can be found after the coverage map at http://www.omg.org/ocup-2/coverage-map-found.htm[7].

One approach might be to use this book by going through each chapter in detail, taking the sample tests as they appear. Then after finishing the book and feeling comfortable with the material, go back through only the sample tests, with a timer, given yourself about 80 seconds per item. When the time is up, score your results. If you have more than 66.7% correct, you might be ready to take the actual certification examination. Of course, it is best to try to prepare to get a much higher score, for more confidence in becoming certified, and for better UML skills in application.

1.5.1 Cheating

There are several (>5) websites that claim to offer examination questions from OCUP 2 and OCUP 1, usually for about $90.00 ± $30.00. After investigating these sites, I cannot recommend them. Here are some of the problems I have found.

1. Most do not have any questions ready for OCUP 2. They will take your money but will say that they will send the questions to you when they become available.
2. Most items are text-based questions. The real examination requires reading UML diagrams and choosing among them.

---

[7] This includes my book, Chonoles, Michael and Schardt, James. *UML 2 for Dummies*, Wiley 2003 [ISBN 978-0-7645-2614-5]. I can't resist the plug.

3. Several of the sites use exactly the same questions as each other. Perhaps these are the same organization using different names.
4. About 10% of the questions in their free demos have the wrong answer specified.
5. If they did have the actual questions, I would imagine that these examination organizations and their candidates would be under legal investigation.
6. Any employer would be able to detect quickly that you really did not know UML.
7. It would be cheating.

Other forms of cheating, such as taking an exam by proxy or sharing of results while taking the exam are increasingly being addressed by the exam vendors, in this case of OCUP 2, Pearson Vue. They are randomly taking the candidate's electronic photo and signature, detecting electronically phone signals, randomizing the question order, inserting traceable false questions, performing statistical analysis of candidate's answers, and other unrevealed techniques to prevent cheating and brain dumping. If you are caught cheating, you may be banned for life from Pearson Vue certification exams.

1.5.2 Coverage Map

The topic areas and diagrams covered in the Foundation Exam and their percentages of questions on the test are shown in Table 1.1. The detailed coverage map for the Foundation Examination can be found at OMG's website for OCUP 2, http://www.omg.org/ocup-2/coverage-map-found.htm. There is a supplemental coverage map that gives more detail at http://www.omg.org/ocup-2/coverage-map-found-suppl.htm.

Table 1.1 Topic Areas on Foundation Exam

Topic Area	% Of Exam	Approximate Number of Questions
Why we model includes motivation, types of models, and their benefits	15	13–14
Class diagram	25	22–23
Object diagram	5	4–5
Package diagram	5	4–5
Use case diagram	5	4–5
Activity diagram	20	18
Sequence diagram	15	13–14
State machine diagram	10	9

We use that coverage maps and the actual test contents to guide the rest of this book. You can be very confident that if it is on the exam, it will be covered in this book. However, some useful material that did not make it into the examinations, such as the background material found in this chapter will also be here.

POINTS TO REMEMBER

- Study hard.
- Do not cheat.

1.6 WHAT AN EXAM IS LIKE

The Foundation Exam has 90 computer-based questions. The computer monitor will be at least 17 inches and have no working USB ports. It will be using the latest Windows Operating System and software.

A candidate will have 120 minutes to take the exam in English-speaking countries. This time restriction means that a candidate has, on average, $1.\overline{33}$ minutes (80 seconds). When we wrote the questions, we kept this average time firmly in mind. Though there are some very rare exceptions, we constructed the questions to avoid requiring calculations, counting, logic problems, for example, nothing that would soak up time without testing the foundational knowledge of UML and modeling. For inhabitants of non-English-speaking countries, the candidates get an additional 30 minutes (for a total of 150 minutes) for the exam or $1.\overline{66}$ minutes per question (100 seconds) for an extra $10 US[8].

The room should be quiet, smoke-free, and comfortable. Please complain if there is disturbing noise (e.g., nearby construction). If you will need medical accommodation, please contact the site in advance.

Passing is 60 correct questions (66.7%). You will not receive partial credit, and your score is only available to you (not your boss, not your friends, nor future employers). You would get the same certificate if you got 60 questions right (66.7%) or 90 questions right (100%). Best of all, there is no penalty for guessing.

No matter how you look at it, there is not much time to take the test; most candidates report feeling a little bit rushed. However, all but the slowest

---

[8] It should be automatic to get the extra time in a non-English-speaking country, but it is worth checking with Pearson Vue. If you are a resident of French-speaking Quebec, you must request the half-hour accommodation.

candidates will finish in time. Good time management skills may be necessary to do well. One common approach is to skip any question that is taking you too long. Certainly, if you do not have any idea, you can skip it and get back to it later. If you can eliminate some of the DISTRACTORS, (choices that are meant to *distract* you from the correct answer), you can consider guessing. You will not be allowed to bring anything into the exam room (that means, for example, no paper, pencils, pens, cell phones) so you cannot record which items you guessed at, however, the test exam software will let you mark questions to come back to if you have time.

I recommend skipping any questions that you cannot get down to two choices. If it is a choice of two, and you are not making progress, just guess. If you reach the end of the exam, go back to the questions you skipped and give them another crack. On your second pass, you might want to guess when you are down to three choices. If you ever get to 5–10 minutes left, go back and guess at each item you still have skipped. Of course, if you have time, go back and check all your answers, paying attentions to those you marked as guessed.

If you do have time to check your questions, do not hesitate to switch your choice if it seems good to do so. It is a myth that one's first choice is always the best. Studies show that most changes are for the better. As test item writers, we try to make the distractors plausible but still definitely incorrect. A candidate's first attraction to a distractor is often an instinctive reaction that after careful evaluation of all the choices may be better changed[9].

If you are taking the examination in Japan in Japanese, OMG is not the direct sponsor as it is in the rest of the world. The UML Technology Institute (UTI) is OMG's partner and offers all the Japanese-language OMG exams in those locations. Please contact them at http://www.umlcert.org/ or http://www.umlcert.org/en/ for scheduling and other details. If you still want the English Language exam, even in Japan, you can contact Pearson Vue for scheduling.

1.6.1 Exam Structure

We develop multiple sets of questions. Each set has 90 questions. When you first take the exam, Pearson Vue assigns you an exam at random. If you fail and then retake the exam, you will get a different exam, so remembering particular questions will not help. There is a minimum waiting period of 30 days to take an exam again after failing. If you pass, you will not be allowed to take it again, as there is no benefit to improving your score.

---

[9]Benjamin, L. T., Cavell, T. A., & Shallenberger, W. R. (1984). Staying with the initial answers on objective tests: Is it a myth? *Teaching of Psychology*, 11(3), 133–141.

The questions are always ordered by topic area, though, within the topic area, the questions are randomized for each examination instance. The ordered topic areas and their weightings are shown in Table 1.1. However, each item may assume that you have some of the knowledge of the rest of the exam. Therefore, a question on Sequence Diagrams can assume that you have some knowledge of Classes, Object, or Activities. A question on Class Diagrams can assume that you have foundational knowledge of Object, Package, or Sequence Diagrams. This cross-usage prevents a strategy that has the candidate concentrating exclusively on a few sections that add up to more than 60 questions (passing). For example, if you decide to learn nothing about Class Diagrams, but study the rest, you will still find classes used in the remaining questions. True, the focus on the remaining questions will be on their own topic areas, but they are free to use classes and class diagrams as needed.

1.6.2 Question Structure

Using the terminology of the exam makers the Foundation Exam has 90 ITEMS. Most people would call them QUESTIONS, but every specialty field has its own terminology, including that of test construction. All the ITEMS are multiple choice format questions. The items usually have four alternatives, of which one is the KEY (the correct answer), and the rest are DISTRACTORS (so-called because they are meant to distract you from the key) though there may be much more than three distractors. The options may be UML diagram fragments and/or textual choices.

Each item has a STEM, which is the prompt. The STEM may have two parts, an optional SCENARIO and a QUESTION, which tells you what to look for in the answer. The scenario may describe a set of circumstances or show you a UML diagram fragment. The QUESTION is often a real question, ending with a "?" (e.g., "Which choice is correct?"). Alternatively, it may be a directive (e.g., "Choose the correct option below."). The choices themselves are either CHOICES or OPTIONS. For a UML Class diagram that describes the Item structure graphically, look at Fig. 1.3.

POINTS TO REMEMBER

- There are multiple versions of the exam.
- The test has eight ordered topic areas, though the items are randomized within them. See Table 1.1 Topic Areas on Foundation Exam.
- All the questions are multiple choice, with only one correct answer, and three or more distracting alternatives.
- None of the items is in a fill-in-the-blank format.
  - The stems all end in a complete sentence with no missing words.
- The stem (setup) for an item will end with a question (which choice is correct?) or directive (Select the correct choice.) and may have a textual or diagrammatic scenario to setup the item.

- The examination is pass-fail. If you get 60 items or more right, you pass.
- Good time management will be essential; use your 120 minutes well.
- If you skip a question, you may mark it to go directly back to it later.
- You are not penalized for guessing.

1.7 HOW WE WROTE THE EXAMINATIONS

Learning how we constructed the examinations will help you to know what to expect in the structure, format, and quality of the examination items.

1.7.1 Team

Under the leadership of Jon Siegel, Ph.D., Director, Certification, the team of 15 or more experts first determined the coverage map for the OCUP 2 Foundation Level and the outlines of the higher level coverage maps. Then the experts (including UML book authors, UML trainers, people working on the UML specifications, senior project leaders, and methodologists for UML-using projects) split the coverage maps into about 30 assignments and volunteered for their favorite parts until all the exam was assigned.

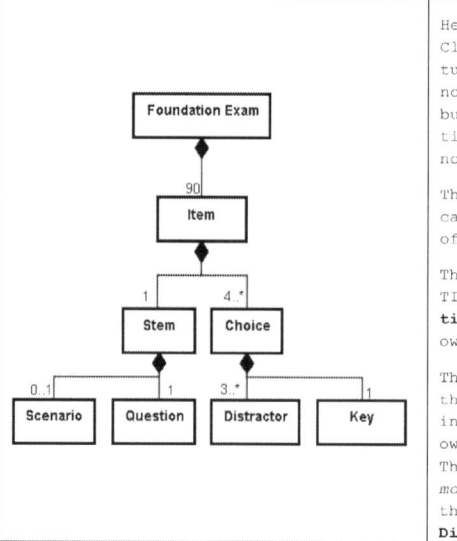

Here is a little example of a UML Class diagram, which shows the structure of this exam. We will cover the notation in detail later in Chapter 5, but following the principle that repetition helps in learning, we show this now.

The boxes represent classes, in this case, things of interest in the domain of the **Foundation Exam**.

The solid diamond represents COMPOSITION, which indicates that the **Foundation Exam** owns **Item**, which in turn, owns **Stem** and **Choice**, and so on.

The numbers represent MULTIPLICITY, the number of instances that the owning class owns (e.g., **Foundation Exam** owns 90 **Items**, and **Item** owns 1 **Stem**). The 3..* and 4..* indicates *three or more* and *four or more* respectively so that a **Choice/Option** has three or more **Distractors**.

FIGURE 1.3
Class diagram showing Foundation Exam structure.

Hired Psychometricians, experts in fair test construction, gave us a short course on how to use our test-writing tool and the criteria for writing a good item.

Then we each wrote the items. We paid extra attention to those features of UML 2.5 that have recently changed from previous versions of UML or to the common errors that beginning students often make.

1.7.2 Review Process and Criteria

Each item was reviewed by our team leader for being within the coverage map and conformity to the standard formatting, construction, and basic psychometric rules. After any needed modification, we agreed and went to a team-based review.

The filtering criteria the team-based review looked concentrated on the item having exactly one answer and being on the Foundational Level—Not too hard and not too easy. We looked to eliminate tricky questions, questions that would take too long, methodology-based questions, or involving logic interpretation. Such items do not test the essence of modeling.

If we made changes to an item, we sent it back through the process.

The psychometricians also reviewed the items keeping only those properly constructed and fair.

1.7.3 Beta Review and Criteria

After we vetted the items, we tried a Beta Test. We establish a Beta program where we collect information on the UML experience of the Candidates. We have many people taking all the questions that we have written and that have survived so far. The purpose of the Beta test is to have questions taken by candidates of varied abilities and the results examined to see if any questions need to be eliminated. More than enough people took the beta test to provide statistically reliable information.

A detailed statistical analysis of the beta results was used to identify items that were too easy (e.g., too many got correct) or too hard (e.g., too few got correct). We also separated items with similar statistical properties onto different versions of the exams, allowing that a candidate should get the same score no matter which exam Pearson Vue assigned them.

We also look at questions that the most experienced candidates get wrong as this could indicate something tricky in the question. Questions with wrong answers that are equally distributed among the distractors probably indicate something that is not known by the candidates; however, if one particular wrong answer predominates, we look to see if this choice could be justified or the item could be misleading.

Next, we look at each exam, keeping in mind a reasonable pass-fail ratio and setting a rational passing grade. The background of the beta participants also factors into these calculations. We expect senior people with many years of UML experience to pass, and Beta candidates with no UML experience at all to have a higher rate of failure. By eliminating the harder or easier items, we get down to 90 questions on each exam.

A committee of UML modeling domain experts set the CUT SCORE (passing grade) by using an established formal psychometric procedure. This ensures that industry experience is properly incorporated into the cut score and that the results are valid as well as useful.

POINTS TO REMEMBER

- Many experts review every item (question) several times from both UML and authorship perspectives.
- Every item has exactly one reasonable answer, reviewed many times.
- Items are not intended to be tricky; they should just test the candidates' knowledge of UML 2.5.
    - Few negatively worded items. (Which choice is NOT correct)
    - No logic problems (A and not B, B and not A, both A and B).
- We use psychometricians to check out the items to ensure that they obey good test design principles.
- The Beta exam filters out items that are too easy or too hard.
    - If a candidate gets an item wrong, it is probably not because it was too tricky or because it had multiple answers; we would have filtered it out earlier.

CHAPTER 2

What is UML?

2.1 WHAT DOES UML STAND FOR?

If you are looking at this book, you probably have an idea of what UML is and maybe what it is for. However, just because you have some idea, you may not have a good or accurate idea, for many people have misconceptions. UML winds up being hard to define and is subject to many false impressions and false hopes.

Let us first examine the name "UML". UML is an initialism that stands for the **U**nified **M**odeling **L**anguage. I hesitate to tell you what some people think it stands for so as not to contaminate your memory with the mistakes made by nonexpert users of UML[1].

2.1.1 How is UML a *Language*?

Is it a language like English, Python, or Klingon?

UML is a graphical language suitable for pen and pencil, whiteboard, PowerPoint presentations, printed or electronic documentation, diagraming tools, or specially purposed computer-based UML modeling tools. Because of this broad range of target media, the UML STANDARD intentionally does not require any use of color or shading.

Some of the UML tools allow for color, shading, or even a sort of pseudo-3D effect, but they have options to turn off these features. A consideration is not only in the drawing of the UML DIAGRAMS but also is in the reading of them; upwards of 9% of the male population has genetically impaired color vision.

UML has all of the typical parts of a language, including the features necessary to construct a book, from parts of speech to chapters (see Table 2.1).

---

[1] There are at least 75 expansions of UML found on the Internet, including universal modeling language and unified markup language. Don't remember these.

OCUP 2 Certification Guide. DOI: http://dx.doi.org/10.1016/B978-0-12-809640-6.00003-9
© 2018 Elsevier Inc. All rights reserved.

Table 2.1 Mapping Written Languages to the Unified Modeling Language

Language	UML
Book	Model
Chapter	Package
Paragraph	Diagram
Sentence	Relationship
Parts of speech	Element types
Word	Element
Grammar	Syntax
Character set	Notation
Meaning	Semantics

This hierarchical capability allows UML to be very expressive and adaptable for many purposes as is English. Because of this mapping to written languages, UML is more like English than Python.

However, UML is an intentionally constructed language, and in that way, it is more like Python than like English. Moreover, UML is most expressive when talking about software systems, and in that way, UML is also more like Python than English. But, as an inherently visual, graphic language, UML is more like electronic circuit diagrams, architectural blueprints, or process flowcharts than any spoken or programing language.

Like both Python and Klingon, UML has a dedicated community and is fun to use.

POINTS TO REMEMBER

- UML is an expressive, intentionally constructed language for the purpose of software modeling.
- UML is a graphical language, not a spoken language.
  - Capable of being created by hand or with dedicated software tools
  - Doesn't require the use of color or of shading
- UML has syntax (grammar), notation, and semantics (meaning).

2.1.2 How is UML a *Modeling* Language?

Moreover, although UML has the necessary structure to construct a book, it is not about writing books. UML is not intended to write books. People who use UML can model the structure of a book, but not write them. However, some tools can read a UML model to generate documentation in book form, which is very useful on projects with documentation requirements.

2.1 What Does UML Stand for?

UML is a language; specifically, it is a "MODELING" language. UML allows you to build models, a reflection of something in the real world or a reflection of something in a planned world. These models can be examined to determine how the modeled system may behave or how it is structured, showing essential features, design decisions, and architecture. As an example of a UML Modeling diagram, see Fig. 2.1 for a sample SEQUENCE DIAGRAM.

UML models show some details of the things in a system or domain of interest and their properties, relationships, and behaviors. The things being modeled can be physical or conceptual, but they cannot be amorphous.

For example, in the airline domain, the modelable things could include aircraft, passengers, airports, seats, routes, and reservations. We could model repairs, seatbelts, and safety reports if they were of interest, but we would

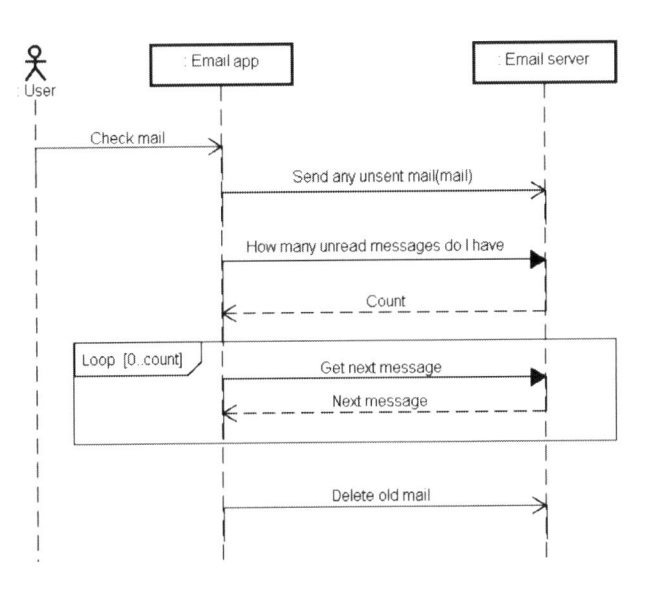

In this simple Sequence diagram, we show a typical interaction involving email.

The participants in this interaction include the user (the stick figure), the email app and the email server.

After the user initiates the behavior with the Check Mail message, the email app starts an interaction with the email server; sending any unsent messages, retrieving a new message count, retrieving all the new messages, and then deleting any old mail.

The behavior that this diagram shows should be understandable. The fine details of the notation (e.g., arrowhead and line style) are not necessary to understand the basic information.

FIGURE 2.1
Sample UML Sequence diagram showing email processing.

find it difficult to model "safety." Similarly, it would be difficult to model friendship, world peace, or harmony, unless we could concretize them and make them something that can be pointed to or counted. The things that you can model are those things with crisp boundaries, and their associated properties, relationships, and behaviors.

The things in a UML model should be items of interest to you or your project. There are many modelable things in an airline domain, such as the parts of a plane, e.g., the individual bolts and rivets. If you were interested in the construction of an aircraft or producing a bill of materials for a jet, you might go down to that level of detail. However, if you were interested in the problem of scheduling flights, you might instead include pilots, crew, runways, hubs, and schedules. If instead you were interested in the ticketing or reservation systems, you might model fare classes, codes, tickets, flight capacity, upgrades, and boarding class zones.

In any domain, there are just too many possible things to model. The basic guide is to model what is useful and relevant to your understanding of how things work or what you have to build. Anything more, you will be wasting your time and your project's money.

If there are parts of the domain or solution space that are well understood and known by everyone, you may find it best to concentrate on those areas that most unusual or most uncertain. It is here where the power of UML in helping you to understand the possibilities and communicating your decisions becomes most valuable. On the other hand, depending on the objective, it may be necessary to model everything to the same level of detail, for example, if you wish to produce complete documentation, to generate automatically complete code from the model, or to perform some other automated model transformation.

You will find UML to be different from other modeling languages, primarily in power and scope. For example, Flowcharts are typically limited to showing control flow, processing steps, and input-output. The UML equivalent, ACTIVITY DIAGRAMS, can show these, but also can show concurrency, interrupts, and data flow on the same diagram. On other diagrams, UML also can show structural information (CLASS DIAGRAMS), state-event responses (STATE MACHINE DIAGRAMS), and message exchange (Sequence diagrams) that Flowcharts cannot do at all. Another modeling language, EXPRESS, can display most of the core UML structural information, but only for the context of database design. It also can't model any of the behavior features that UML can. Most of the Structured Analysis/Structured Design (SA/SD) diagram notations suffer from similar limitations.

The modeling language that is most similar to UML is the IDEF (Integration Definition) family of modeling languages. IDEF has 16 diagram types that cover similar territory to UML, but it also appears to be limited in modeling states and message exchange. IDEF also suffers from being associated with the US military, whereas UML is sponsored by large software companies such as IBM and Microsoft. IDEF also is hindered by having weaker cross-diagram integration, lack of support for object-oriented concepts, and weaker and fewer tools.

POINTS TO REMEMBER

- UML can model real or planned systems. It can capture
  - the system's features and characteristics.
  - the structure, behavior, and relationship of the system's elements.
  - the purposes, architecture, design decisions for the system.
- You can model things with crisp boundaries and their properties, relationships, and behaviors.
- Limit your modeling to interesting and relevant things.
- UML is more powerful and popular that other software modeling languages, such as Flowcharts, SA/SD, and IDEF.

2.1.3 How is UML a *Unified* Modeling Language?

Before UML was created, there were over 50 object-oriented notations and methodologies[2] competing for market and mind share. This plethora of notations significantly impeded the growth of object-oriented languages and tools. Most companies would not invest their money in an object-oriented tool, and most programers would not invest their time in object-oriented training if they could not be sure that the investments would remain useful for, at least, a few years. Each company and project would use a different favorite approach and tooling, but no investment was portable nor were they stable. In such circumstances, tool and training vendors could not build on previous work nor advance the state of the art. Each could be a notational dead end.

The first object-oriented modeling languages began to appear between the mid-1970s and the late 1980s as various methodologists and gurus experimented and proposed different approaches to capturing the ideas of object-oriented analysis and design. In addition, for each approach, there were rabid followers, causing a series of "method wars".

As there was no clear dominant modeling language, users and companies had to choose from among many modeling languages with small differences, but similar expressive power. The modeling languages shared a set of commonly accepted concepts, but each language expressed them slightly

---

[2]Rational Software Corp. *et al. Proposal to the OMG's Analysis and Design Task Force: Part I—UML Definition Jan 13 1997* (Rational Software Corp., 1997). pp. 2–3. Members of OMG companies can see an electronic copy at http://www.omg.org/members/cgi-bin/doc?ad/97-01-02.pdf.

Table 2.2 The Major Sources of UML (The Three Amigos)

Source Method	Proponent	Strengths	Exemplary Notation
Object Modeling Technique—OMT	Jim Rumbaugh of General Electric, then Rational Software Corp	Excellent for conceptualization, analysis, and data intensive systems	OMT (box)
Booch Method	Grady Booch then Rational Software Corp	Enabled design, architecture, and construction detail	Booch (cloud) [a]
Object-Oriented Software Engineering—OOSE	Ivar Jacobson of Objectory, then Rational Software Corp	Use-case oriented approach providing excellent support for business engineering, user perspectives, and requirements analysis	OOSE (actor and ellipse)

[a] There was a fierce partisan controversy over whether cloud icons (from the Booch Method) or box icons (from OMT) should be used for classes in the unification. They announced their decision to use boxes by both Grady Booch and Jim Rumbaugh singing a version of Joni Mitchell's "I've looked at clouds from both sides now" tailored to the situation.

differently. This lack of agreement discouraged users and companies from entering the object technology market, but no one language had significantly furthered the power of modeling.

By the mid-1990s, second and third generations of these modeling approaches were beginning to evolve, with borrowings of each other's techniques. The numbers started to winnow down to popular methods, Object Modeling Technique (OMT), Booch, and Object-Oriented Software Engineering (OOSE). As these progressed, they were also increasingly incorporating features from each other. In 1994, under the auspices of the Rational Software Corporation, Grady Booch and Jim Rumbaugh starting work on unifying their methods. This effort produced the 0.8 draft of the *Unified Method* in October 1995. Soon, Ivar Jacobson joined the unification effort. These leading proponents, Jim Rumbaugh, Grady Booch, and Ivar Jacobson, were often called the "THREE AMIGOS"[3].

UML benefits from using the Class Diagrams and most notations from OMT, the ability to capture design detail from the Booch Method, and the use-case oriented capabilities from OOSE (see Table 2.2).

As they worked on the integration of their methods, they realized that though it may be possible to integrate their methods into a method framework[4], it would not have the significant buy-in that an integrated notation alone would have. Different domains have different methodology needs. Consider that shrink-wrapped commercial software, business IT systems,

---

[3] It is unclear how well they actually got along with each other.
[4] Ultimately, their integrated methodology became the Rational Unified Process (RUP).

medical equipment software, and hard-real-time avionics all need to have different development processes.

To get the widest possible input, the Three Amigos made some decisions that have held throughout the development of UML:

- *Change from a Unified **Method** to a Unified **Modeling Language***. Thus, UML is a language but not a method or methodology. UML works with any approach and in any industry.
- *Make UML nonproprietary*. Thus, no company owns UML. Any vendor can make a UML modeling tool.
- *Propose UML to the Object Management Group (OMG) as a possible standard*. Thus, UML is a standard managed by OMG, an industry consortium and is available for anybody to use free of charge.
- *Work with a team, the UML Partners*. The UML Partners included Digital Equipment Corp., Hewlett-Packard, i-Logix, Intellicorp, IBM, ICON Computing, MCI Systemhouse, Microsoft, Oracle, Rational Software Corp., Texas Instruments, and Unisys. Today, anyone can help in maintaining UML by joining OMG and participating in the UML REVISION TASK FORCE (UML RTF[5]) at OMG. Thus, UML has had and continues to have many contributors.

POINTS TO REMEMBER

- UML is a nonproprietary approach.
- The OMG maintains the UML standard.
- Many contributors and methodologists have combined to produce a unified language.
- UML is method-independent and favors no methodology.

2.2 UML GOALS

2.2.1 The Original Goals of UML

When the Three Amigos and the UML Partners made their first proposal of UML to OMG, they established four goals for UML[6], which remain goals for UML.

1. To model systems (and not just software) using object-oriented concepts
2. To establish an explicit coupling to conceptual as well as executable artifacts

---

[5] At the time of this writing, the UML Revision Task Force (RTF) is working on UML 2.6.
[6] Rational Software Corp. *et al. Proposal to the OMG's Analysis and Design Task Force: Part I—UML Definition Jan 13, 1997* (Rational Software Corp., 1997). pp. 3. Members of OMG companies can see the electronic copy at http://www.omg.org/members/cgi-bin/doc?ad/97-01-02.pdf.

3. To address the issues of scale inherent in complex, mission-critical systems
4. To create a modeling language usable by both humans and machines

By the time UML reached version 1.3 in March 2000, UML was aimed at all types of systems. It became a language for analyzing, specifying, visualizing, designing, constructing, and documenting the artifacts of software-intensive systems, as well as for business modeling and other nonsoftware systems and domains.

UML continues to represent a collection of the best engineering and modeling practices that have proven successful in the making of large and complex systems. As such, UML incorporates a wide assortment of powerful object-oriented techniques, such as Generalization, inheritance, and abstraction, because these techniques are useful in many system approaches. Likewise, UML integrates powerful nonobject-oriented modeling techniques, such as composition, data and control flows, and state machines, because you may also want to use these techniques in many systems approaches. When modeling with UML, invariably one uses both object-oriented and nonobject-oriented approaches in the same model.

POINTS TO REMEMBER

- UML supports the entire lifecycle of development, from conceptualization and analysis, through architecture and design, to construction and documentation.
- UML is for modeling systems, not just software.
- UML works for small and large systems.
- UML is meant to be understandable by humans and by software tools.
- UML unites both object-oriented and nonobject-oriented approaches in developing systems.
  - You can use UML for traditional, object-oriented, and mixed systems.

2.2.2 Updated Goals for UML

The goals for UML version 1.3 grew to include the original goals and the following additions and clarifications[7]. These new goals have been implicitly continued for the remaining versions of UML.

1. Provide users with a ready-to-use, expressive visual modeling language to develop and exchange useful models.
2. Furnish extensibility and specialization mechanisms to extend the core concepts.

---

[7] Object Management Group, *OMG Unified Modeling Language Specification, v 1.3* (OMG March 2003). pp. 1–4.

3. Support specifications that are independent of particular programing languages and development processes.
4. Provide a formal basis for understanding the modeling language.
5. Encourage the growth of the object tools market.
6. Support higher-level development concepts such as components, collaborations, frameworks, and patterns.
7. Integrate best practices.

In support of these additional goals, UML has grown to incorporate the following features:

- UML supports an interchange method using XMI (XML METADATA INTERCHANGE) that allows UML tools to exchange models.
- It also incorporates a profile and stereotype capability that allows a project or team to tailor UML for their own needs. Languages derived from UML serve specialty markets, such as Systems Engineering Modeling Language (SysML) for Systems Engineering Modeling and SPEM for Software Process Engineering Modeling.
- Over the time of development of UML, several different programing languages have risen and fallen in popularity, so UML is now also programing language independent.
- The UML specification uses a formal metamodel to capture the abstract syntax.
- Many UML tools now exist, arising from many parts of the world (including the US, United Kingdom, EU, France, Austria, Germany, Lithuania, China, Japan, and Australia), competing at different price points and capabilities. The tools support additional languages, such as Portuguese, Spanish, Russian, and Korean.
- UML now supports higher-level organization concepts, including collaborations, composite structures, hierarchical state machines and reuse, and components.

POINTS TO REMEMBER

- UML tools use XMI to exchange models.
- A project or team may tailor UML for their own purposes using profiles and stereotypes.
- UML is the basis for several derivative languages in specialty fields, sharing technology, and infrastructure.
- As UML is independent of the choice of a programing language; you can use UML with a variety of programing languages.
- UML has a formal METAMODEL that defines the abstract syntax (grammar).
- An extensive international selection of tools exists that support UML.

2.3 WHAT IS THE OBJECT MANAGEMENT GROUP (OMG)?

Founded in 1989, the OMG is an international, open membership, not-for-profit consortium for the purpose of developing and maintaining technology standards, including UML and allied standards. At present, OMG has more than 400 members, including vendors, end-users, academic institutions, and government agencies. OMG members include organizations that represent software end-users and participants in many vertical markets (e.g., finance, healthcare, automotive, insurance, aerospace, and defense). Member organizations include those with one employee to thousands of employees. Although the member's gross revenue and level of participation factor into the OMG dues, each member gets one vote, so that every member organization—Whether small or large—Has a real say in the decision-making process. OMG meets quarterly in different locales around the world.

OMG is divided into two Technology Committees (TCs), Platform Technology Committee and Industry (Domain Technology Committee), and an ARCHITECTURE BOARD (AB) that handles standards that cross the two TCs. The AB also reviews all proposed standards for compatibility with existing standards and quality criteria. The committees are subdivided into Task Forces (TFs), Special Interest Groups (SIGs), and Subcommittees (SCs). Only active TFs can initiate a new standard. UML is under the purview of the ANALYSIS & DESIGN TASK FORCE (ADTF).

2.3.1 The Standards-Making Process of OMG

The process of developing a standard within OMG is somewhat complex. You can see a simplified Activity Diagram showing the process in Fig. 2.2. A TF produces a Request for Proposal (RFP) for a new standard, which includes a set of minimum requirements and desired features. One or more potential submitters accept(s) the RFP and submit(s) a Letter of Intent (LOI) to OMG. The LOI guarantees that a submitter will produce a working implementation of their proposal if it is accepted, ensuring that OMG standards and not shelf-ware, that they will be commercially available and viable.

The submitter or team of submitters submits the standard to the TF, which evaluates it. If there are problems with the submission, or if there are competitive submissions teams, the TF can recommend revisions. Often the teams decide to collaborate, taking the best from each submission. The TF vote guarantees that there are sufficient interest and agreement in the submissions, that the submission meets the requirements, and that there are no strong opposing opinions.

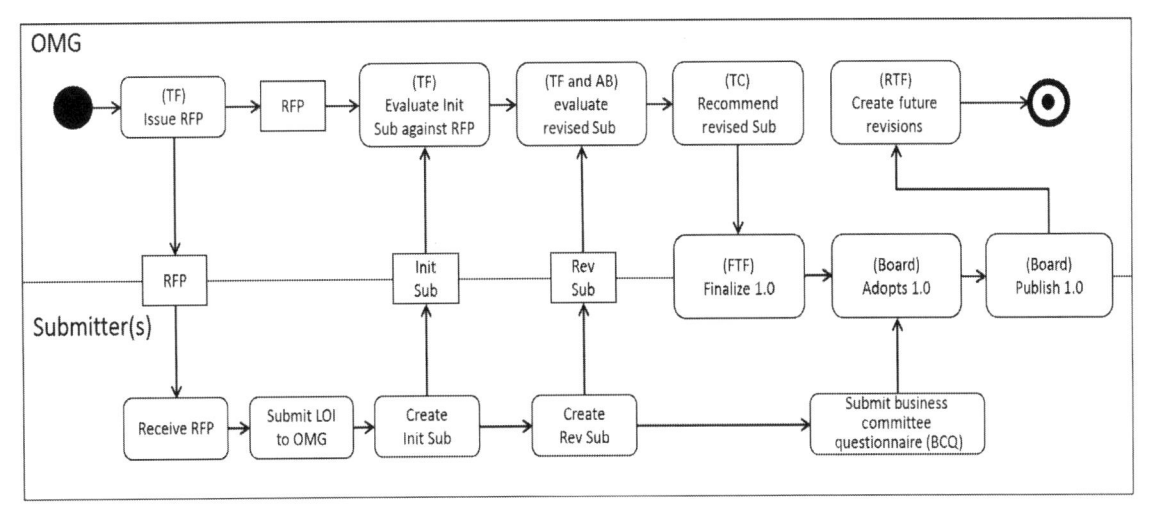

FIGURE 2.2
Simplified Activity Diagram of OMG standard process.
This diagram uses the UML Activity Diagram format to present a very simplified version of the OMG standardization process. The boxes represent the object/data that the processes produce; the arrows represent the control/data flow; the round-tangles represent the process steps. The bullet (*bullet*) indicates the start of the process, whereas the bullseye (◎) indicates the end. Because of the size limitations, the detail of the decision-making in this diagram is elided.

After the TFs approves a submission, a series of higher gates within OMG need to recommend the standard. After recommending the standard, OMG creates a Finalization Task Force (FTF) to fix any remaining issues that might inhibit publication. Eventually, the OMG Business Committee and Board adopt the standard. The series of gates evaluate the proposed standard for compatibility with existing OMG and outside standards, the viability of the business proposition, the commitment of at least one company to producing and marketing an implementation, and any intellectual property restrictions that might stand in the way of widespread adoption.

During the FTF, OMG grants the original submitters veto power over any change that might interfere with their commitments to produce a commercial implementation. For UML, the veto gave the original submitters a respite from having the standard change underneath them while they developed products though still letting the FTF incorporate changes based on problems found during the implementations.

Even before the standard becomes formally adopted, anyone can identify issues they that they believe need to be fixed (e.g., bugs, typos, inconsistencies) or improved. After OMG adopts the standard, OMG creates a RTF to address any remaining open issues. Each RTF has about a year to produce a revision (which gets a version number, e.g., x.1, x.2...). As long as the standard is active and there are open issues, OMG has an ongoing RTF to handle the issues.

OMG only allows an FTF or RTF to make fixes (bugs, typos, inconsistencies), not major improvements to a standard. If significant improvements are required, the whole process starts again with an RFP containing the new or modified requirements. Thus, an RTF-produced version is mostly compatible with previous versions of the standard, whereas a new version has more leeway in making changes. The new versions get an increment of the number before the point, so UML 1.5 became 2.0 after a major revision.

OMG submits many of its specifications to become ISO standards using the ISO Joint Technical Committee on Information Technology 1 (JTC-1) Publicly Available Specifications (PAS) process. The PAS process allows ISO to respond to a market need by bringing in outside standards that are the work of industry consortia (such as OMG, for whom the PAS process was originally created). This allows OMG specifications to become ISO standards without starting from scratch as an ISO standard, bypassing much (but not all) of that time-consuming process, and preventing divergence of the OMG and ISO versions. ISO reserved the ISO/IEC 195xx series of standards to be those from OMG.

2.3.2 The History of UML

UML went through this process, and had developed UML 1.1 (1997), 1.3 (1999), 1.4 (2001), 1.5 (2003). Most UML books in the market are still on UML 1.4. Unfortunately, this makes them inappropriate for studying for the UML 2.5 exam (OCUP 2).

OMG, using the ISO PAS process, submitted the 1.4.2 version of UML to ISO's JTC-1 Committee on Software and Systems Engineering (SC-7). They approved it as ISO/IEC 19501:2005.

By 2000, it was clear that some significant changes were necessary, including a reformulation based on Petri nets for Activity Diagrams rather than on state machines, better descriptions of behavior in general, and a more formal approach to specifying the abstract syntax. At this point, the ADTF voted to issue an RFP for UML 2.0[8].

UML 2.0 used two documents to describe the standard: A UML INFRASTRUCTURE document and a UML SUPERSTRUCTURE document. UML 2.0 versions came as

---

[8]Object Management Group, Request For Proposal (RFP) UML 2.0 Superstructure (OMG, 2000), see http://www.omg.org/cgi-bin/doc?ad/00-09-02.pdf.

UML 2.0 (2005), 2.1.1 (2007), 2.1.2 (2007), 2.2 (2009), 2.3 (2010), 2.4 (2011), 2.4.1 (2011).

Again, OMG submitted the 2.4.1 version to ISO JT1-SC7, who approved it as ISO/IEC 190504-1/2:2012.

Version 2.5 is officially a minor revision to the UML 2.4.1 specification based on meeting the UML Specification Simplification RFP ad/09-12-10. This simplification process recombined the Infrastructure and Superstructure back into one document that was significantly simpler and better organized.

The changes from 2.0 to 2.5, while incremental at each version, have also made the early 2.0 books and training material obsolete. Therefore, we have the need for a new certification program.

Work has started on UML 2.6 as part of the normal RTF cycle.

For details on the history of UML and its documents got to http://www.uml.org/. Anyone can submit issues against the UML specification by using the form at http://www.omg.org/report_issue.htm.

POINTS TO REMEMBER

- UML is an OMG standard with a history from 2007.
- Beware, UML 1.4 books or original OCUP study material will NOT help you pass OCUP 2.
- UML is now on version 2.5
  - A UML RTF is working on UML 2.6.
  - OMG limits the changes from UML 2.5 to 2.6 to minor cleanups, clarifications, and bug fixes.
- The Platform Committee's ADTF is responsible for UML.
- Anyone can identify issues with UML.

2.4 MODELING

2.4.1 What Kind of Modeling

UML was designed for modeling software-intensive systems and the domains in which such systems must work. However, you can model anything of interest that has crisp boundaries (and their properties, relationships, and behaviors). As UML is aimed at software-intensive systems, it assumes that time, messages, and behavior is (mostly) discrete.

Although analog systems, biological systems, and environmental systems may have structures capable of being modeled, UML should not be your first choice for modeling them. For example, the parts of a circuit could be modeled, their electric properties could be modeled, the connections among them could be modeled, but UML would not be the language to model Kirchhoff's circuit laws or Maxwell's equations. Instead, consider using SPICE[9] for circuit simulation or SysML[10] for systems engineering problems.

As with any modeling, you need to consider the target audience. UML is mostly understandable by technical and business people, but it does need some training. (I would recommend this book, of course.) UML was developed so that typical stakeholders, who may have various skills and interests, would understand the kind of diagrams that they would be normally shown. If you overload a stakeholder-targeted diagram with all the possible detail that it could contain, almost no one would understand it afterward, possibly even including you. Make the model and diagrams as simple as possible, while reserving its full explanatory power for the uses for which you have the need, always keeping the audience in mind[11].

If you are aiming to build a business or commercial IT software system, UML would be the language to use. If you are modeling a business process with rules, there are specialty languages similar to UML that tend to more interpretable by business types, such as the Business Process Modeling Notation.

POINTS TO REMEMBER

- UML is designed for discrete software-intensive systems and their domains.
- You can model things with crisp boundaries and their properties, relationships, and behaviors.
- Biological systems, analog systems, and business processes may be modeled better with other approaches.
- Most stakeholder groups can understand shared UML diagrams made with the intent of sharing.

2.4.2 Purposes for UML Modeling

We have already mentioned some of the purposes for which people employ UML modeling. In this section, we attempt to elaborate on them. As shown in Table 2.3, key modeling purposes include Analysis, Design, Implementation, and Communication. Each of these purposes has different

---

[9]SPICE (Simulation Program with Integrated Circuit Emphasis) is a general purpose, open source, analog electronic circuit simulator.
[10]SysML (Systems Engineering Modeling Language). Though based on UML, SysML has better abilities to model continuous and analog behavior.
[11]"Everything Should Be Made as Simple as Possible, But Not Simpler" Attributed to Albert Einstein.

Table 2.3 Common Purposes for UML Modeling

Key Purpose	Types of Supportive Modeling
Analysis	Domain analysis
	Use Case analysis
	Requirements analysis
Design	Conceptualization
	Architecture
	Detailed design
Implementation	Implementation by hand
	Automatic code generation
	Simulation/execution
	Reverse engineering
	Round Trip Modeling
	Debugging
Communication	To humans
	To other tools

types of modeling that might support that purpose. On a typical project, only some of these modeling types will be necessary, and they might have different formal definitions. However, you should know the general information on the types and purposes of modeling.

When using these different types of models on a project, consider that the models need to share common elements and definitions. The underlying model database will help to enforce this for you.

2.4.2.1 Analysis

ANALYSIS covers modeling of the things in the real world to improve understanding of where you are starting. It also includes modeling of what is wanted, but not how those things should be done. How they are to be done is design. The separation of design from analysis allows a new design to be supplied for the same analysis model, if, for some reason, the original design did not work, or if there are more than one competitive design team.

Domain Analysis: The modeling of the DOMAIN, the things in the real world to understand how the current system or legacy system works, possibly to extract the essentials to incorporate eventually into a replacement system. The current system may be entirely mechanical or manual. Domain analysis modeling is usually done with the idea that the existing stakeholders and users can review the model to determine its faithfulness to the actual system. Thus, the terminology used matches the legacy system's terminology so the current users and stakeholders can understand the model. As these models emphasize the things in the real world and not software constructs, they will concentrate on Class, State Machines, and possibly Sequence diagrams, with attention to definitions of the terms used. These models tend to emphasize simplicity and accuracy to maximize communication.

Use Case Analysis: USE CASE ANALYSIS concentrates on the purposes for which the existing users use or future users plan to use the system. Such modeling utilizes Use Case diagrams though other diagrams may be used as supplements. The Use Case analysis produces informal requirements for the planned system, which can be converted into formal requirements if the project requires such formality.

The Use Case analysis is a bridge between the users (called Actors) and the modelers to determine the needs that the system must satisfy. Therefore, Use Case analysis must also use the terminology of the users, so that missing needs can be identified by them.

Requirements Analysis: Requirements analysis starts with externally given requirements or in lieu of requirements, a problem statement. By examining the input text, it is possible to identify the nouns and verbs and create mapping objects and behaviors in your evolving model. This underlining-the-nouns approach sounds simplistic; in practice, it requires significant sophistication to do this well. However, it may be a good way to start modeling if the input is of high quality. In this approach, the models should use the requirements terminology because the interested stakeholders tend to be the authors of the requirements document. This approach tends to concentrate on Class, State Machines, and Activity Diagrams.

POINTS TO REMEMBER

- Analysis modeling captures what the current world has and what is needed, without making any design decisions.
- Domain analysis captures the significant things in the world in a way that both the team and the interested stakeholders can review and criticize.
- Use Case analysis captures the functionality and needs that the users of the new system want to have the system do. It also is done in a way that the both the team and interested users can review and criticize.

2.4.2.2 Design

Design covers modeling of the things in the solution world that you have chosen, the approaches you are going to take, the decisions you have made, based on your understanding of the analysis products. Taking the analysis products as input, Design covers the modeling of the additional things that you have chosen to be part of the solution, the approaches you are going to take, the patterns you are going to repeat, and the decisions you have made, all to meet the users' needs and system requirements.

CONCEPTUALIZATION: Covers the high-level design approaches to how the system will work, including the major systems and subsystems that will need to be made. Often the major principles of architecture are also covered. As the conceptualization effort reveals the basic solution approaches, conceptualization is often used to produce a better estimate of the cost and schedule for the project. In this type of model, all of the UML diagrams may be used, though the detail is light, to convey the approach without getting lost in the weeds.

ARCHITECTURE: Covers the modeling necessary to convey the organization and associated principles of the new system. The UML models will need to cover the structure, behavior, and other VIEWS of the system. Specialty views are common, for example, a Security View would encompass the set of UML diagrams that cover how the system's security will work. Other views may need to be constructed, such as how the system will be installed, upgraded, turned off, disposed of, upgraded, maintained, or replenished. These views are usually tailored to a particular community of interest.

Architecture models can include all of the diagrams in UML, but may only show the information supporting the current view. Architecture models need to support reasoning about the structure and behavior of the system, so that changes, when made, will be consistent with the overall architecture. Patterns specifying the how the elements interact with each other, such client-server, peer-to-peer, or layers, would be captured as part of the architecture model, so that reviewers will know the approaches being taken, and the later implementer can use the pattern when needed.

Detailed Design: Covers the remaining details necessary to specify the solution, following the architectural decisions made previously. The target of the models made during detailed design are the developers themselves so that the diagrams can be considerably more detailed. They typically include composite structure diagrams, communication, component, and deployment diagrams to an extent not done earlier.

POINTS TO REMEMBER

- Design modeling captures what the new system will have and how it will work.
- Conceptualization captures high-level design decisions on how the system will be made.
- Architecture captures the general arrangement of how the system's structure and behavior will work. It will show patterns of structure and behavior that will be repeated throughout. Architecture views will often be tailored to specific interested communities.
- Detailed Design capture the entire planned solution.

2.4.2.3 Implementation

Implementation modeling covers supplying the model details necessary to convert the model to an executable system. Supplying more detail will give you more control over what is done, but it may have an impact on the schedule and cost.

By Hand Generation: When the conversion will be done by hand, sufficient details need to be present to convey to the programer the programing constructs that will be necessary to employ. However, because many parts of the system may be implemented similarly, such detail may only be necessary to specify once.

Automatic Code Generation: However, to convert automatically a system, the modeling will usually need to be detailed everywhere. It may also need to include specific hints or annotations that will guide the automatic tools in choosing a correct and efficient programing construct (e.g., the correct containment class or error handling approach). Depending on the target programing language, the UML used for automatic code generation may need to avoid certain modeling constructs. To specify the necessary details of behavior, the UML model will often need to have additional annotations of code in the target language. It is also possible to generate automatically databases and user interfaces from suitably annotated models.

Direct Simulation or Execution: In some cases, it is possible that the UML model can be simulated or executed directly. Models that support this approach usually require similar features that automatic code generation requires, but even more detail needs to be supplied, and there are more limitations on the UML used. Often, the UML model will need to have an implementation independent action language added to specify the details of required behavior.

Reverse Engineering: When a team has existing code, but they wish to understand it better, possibly to make changes, they can try reverse engineering, that is, automatically generating the model from code. Of course, sloppy code will generate a sloppy model, so that hand editing and rearranging the model will probably be necessary. Reverse engineering capabilities exist for most common programming languages.

Round Trip Modeling: Some tools also allow an incremental approach, allowing a "model-a-little code-a-little" approach. This step-by-step approach enables the modeler to see the code automatically generated, modify the code, and regenerate the model based on the code changes, keeping the model and code in sync, and all the screen at the same time. Or the implementer can make changes directly to the model and immediately see the consequences to the code. The code will contain annotations that instruct the reverse engineering portion what it should do to convert the model back to the original, minimizing unintentional model changes while reverse engineering.

Debugging: In some tools, when simulating, executing, or round-trip modeling, it is possible to step through the behavior diagrams. For example, in Fig. 2.1, the messages on the diagram would be highlighted as they were being sent, under a pace being controlled by the user. If an error occurs, you can inspect the properties of the variables and classes involved and perhaps reset them.

POINTS TO REMEMBER

- Depending on your tool, it may be possible automatically to generate code, database, and user interface from some models.
- Reverse engineering of poorly structured code will produce poorly structured models.
- Round Trip Modeling keeps the model and code in sync.
- The more detail you supply in your implementation models, the more control you have over the final product, but it will take longer to produce the model.

2.4.2.4 *Communication*

All modeling is about communication, whether to a human or to an automatic transformation tool (e.g., a code generator). Most of the time, the communication is to humans: Yourself, the team, stakeholders, the users, clients, regulators, or posterity. The communication targets include, besides the current developers, the current and future developers, engineers, testers, and maintainers.

Communication to Humans: When communication is the goal, diagrams are the medium. Automatic transformation tools work on the models but humans use diagrams. Diagrams aren't necessary in UML. If you don't want humans to look at your work, you can delete all of the diagrams, leaving the underlying model intact. The diagrams are just views into the model. A model is really just a repository for all the model elements within the system, a database following the UML grammar. The diagrams are different perspectives of the same reality, the same database. Diagram elements, the things you place on a diagram, may be used to create a model element if it does not already exist but they ultimately are just representations of the model element. Multiple diagrams may contain the same element, show different aspects or detail of the same diagram element. They are the same model element, which you can show by changing some property of the underlying model element; all the diagrams will change to reflect the new reality (see Fig. 2.3). In fact, the same element can appear multiple times on the same diagram or on multiple diagrams.

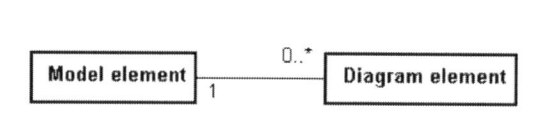

```
                                    We will explain the no-
                                    tation used here in more
                                    detail in the chapter on
                                    class diagrams, but for
                                    now, you can read this
              0..*                  in      two       ways.
Model element ─────── Diagram element Left→Right,   it  reads
              1                     that every Model Element
                                    can have zero or more
                                    Diagram    Elements   and
                                    Right→Left,  it   reads
                                    that every Diagram Ele-
                                    ment must have exactly
                                    one Model Element.
```

FIGURE 2.3
The relationship between model and diagram elements.

The power having more than one diagram element for a model element, potentially on many diagrams, allows the modeler to make several diagrams with overlapping content, each tailored to a different purpose, and audience. It is good practice to document the purpose and audience on the diagram, perhaps in the diagram name. By capturing the information explicitly, it will help to remind you of the goals as you produce the diagram and keep you focused. When the goals of the diagram are kept in mind, you can expect better review and feedback, better agreement with your plans, and better follow through on your intent.

You may wish to construct more than one level of diagrams for the same audience, the first, a high-level diagram showing an overview, and other diagrams showing more detail. If you have more than one level of diagrams, capture the level with the other information.

One special purpose of diagraming, often forgotten, is communicating to your future self. Many people find that if they look at code that they wrote a year later, they forgot all the details of how it works. Diagrams can be the same. Avoid tricky diagrams and place comments on any diagram that does something unusual.

Another special purpose of diagraming is that of training new people on the project, either new programmers, maintenance staff or users. Particularly in these cases, consider the needs and ability of audience when you determine how to diagram.

Documentation is a special type of communication with humans. Documentation may be required on a project, but even if not required, it is generally a good idea to document, especially for projects with a long-expected lifespan. A company can expect to change tools and technologies over a 10-year period. Though the UML notation may stand the test of time, the tool format may not. Keeping a paper copy or PDF will help the information to be available for future maintenance and modification.

When producing documentation, consider typical features, such as a table of contents, indices, cross-references, and detailed explanations.

Communication to Other Tools: There are several reasons to use UML models to communicate with other tools. We covered many of them in Section 2.4.2.3, Implementation on Implementation Modeling, such as automatically generating code, generating a database, simulation, or execution. These could be done within the modeling tool, or they may be done by exporting the model to some other tools. UML supplies a standard model-interchange mechanism that supports model exports and imports to other tools. A SIG at OMG called the Model Interchange SIG, tests tools interoperability using this mechanism, called XMI (XML-based Metadata Interchange).

If a tool supports XMI, it can export to another UML tool, or to a tool that uses XMI for model input, e.g., a tool calculating model metrics. There are stand-alone tools that accept XMI, evaluate the UML package contents and cross-package dependencies, and suggest moving elements from one package to another to improve encapsulation.

POINTS TO REMEMBER

- Diagrams are meant to be seen by some reviewer. Keep in mind the diagram's goals.
  - Purpose
  - Level
  - Audience
- More than one diagram element can represent the same model element, each showing a different perspective or detail.
- Be liberal with your comments and notes to explain your diagrams.
- A UML model is just a database of related model elements, following the UML syntax rules, with a unified purpose.
- UML tools use XMI to exchange models.

2.4.3 Principles of Modeling

There are principles of modeling that are necessary to observe to get good results. We have already discussed several in passing. In this section, we will expand a bit on these principles. We will be elaborating on them later throughout the book.

Table 2.4 Sample Risks Mitigated by Modeling

Modeling	Risk to Mitigate
General	Not all parts of team have a common understanding of what needs to be done
Domain	Development team doesn't understand the world in which their system will live
	Stakeholders do not know if you understand the situation
Use Case	Development team does not understand what the users want
	Users do not trust you to understand all their needs
Conceptualization	Development team and stakeholders might not agree on where the system is going or how much it will cost
Specialty	Development team is missing the solution for a problem, e.g., safety, security, reliability, system upgrades
Architecture	Development team may choose inconsistent solutions to solving system-wide problems

2.4.3.1 Risk Mitigation

Software development is fundamentally risky. Only about 39% of recent projects succeeded by being delivered on time and on budget, with the required features and functionality[12]. If a project takes on modeling into their lists of tasks, it is because modeling offers significant benefits. Modeling is only done to reduce some perceived risk (see Table 2.4). If making the model or drawing, the diagram does not address some problem or risk, are you really sure that you need it. This is a way of determining that the effort is useful.

Determining the risk you are addressing by a diagram is often part of identifying the purpose, level, and audience, and may be placed on the diagram to focus your efforts along with the other fields.

2.4.3.2 Information Hiding and Simplicity

An importance principle of modeling is to limit the amount of detail to the minimum necessary. A 1:1 map of a town would not be useful, not only would it be too complicated, but also it would be too difficult to fold. It is better to have several maps, each with its own intent, than putting it all together into one. Imaging one map of the roads, one map for the utilities, one map for the political subdivisions, one map for the school districts, i.e., one map for one purpose. Things are much simpler if you have the content of the map (or diagram) bound by a single purpose. This leads us to put the purpose on the diagram to focus your attention. You might want an

---

[12]The Standish Group, The Chaos Manifesto (The Standish Group International, Incorporated, 2013) pp. 1, https://www.versionone.com/assets/img/files/CHAOSManifesto2013.pdf.

overview map, so that you can tie the separate maps together, but single purpose maps and diagrams are much simpler and more useful than unfocused diagrams.

All the maps discussed above need to limit the amount of detail on the map to make them most useful. You need to abstract the essential features to map or model them and hide (or ELIDE[13], i.e., suppress) the unnecessary or irrelevant detail, because unnecessary detail is potentially confusing. It has to be possible to see the forest, without getting lost in the trees. This ABSTRACTION is a very powerful technique, and it has direct UML support and is a common object-oriented technique as well.

Related to abstraction is INFORMATION HIDING. You can determine what to not show, by determining what your users should not depend upon. If our electric utility map had the brand name and rating of every wire in the town indicated, as soon as there was some sort of repair, the map would become obsolete. If you do not want your diagram users to depend on every detail shown, then do not show the detail. You move to be visible the core abstractions of the features you need to share, and apply information hiding to the minor features that may change, that aren't necessary to understand how the major features work.

To give a software example, you may wish to say that you sort some list of objects; reviewers would need to know that that is your intention. However, you may need to suppress or ELIDE the detail of whether you are using a heap sort, a quicksort, a bubble sort, an insertion sort or some other type of sort. In this way, you are free to change your mind if you realize that for your circumstances a different sort would be better. For example, some of the sorts are consider "stable", in that they maintain the relative order of records with equal keys, and some sorts are not stable in this way. If users knew your intention of which sort algorithm you were planning to use, they could depend on its stability (or lack thereof) preventing you making changes without affecting them.

ENCAPSULATION is a technique where details that you need to hide (because of information hiding), but co-depend on each other, are placed together. Therefore, if one detail has to change, everything that depends on it is placed nearby so that they can change at the same time. Therefore, if you do have to change something the related changes don't propagate throughout the system, but are limited to one diagram and a limited number of elements.

---

[13] ELIDE is a term commonly used in UML modeling for the suppression on a diagram of known information that remains in the model. It is thought that the popularity of the term is due to frequent use by Grady Booch.

2.4.3.3 Whole-Part Relationships

In UML modeling as in object-oriented methodology, you will often find that you model a whole object that is made of many parts, but that you can apply operations to the whole that also apply to the parts. Therefore, if you buy, drive, or steal a car, you are also buying, driving, and stealing the engine, the chassis, the wheels, in fact, all the parts of the car. UML supplies several techniques that support specification of the whole-part structures within the model. COMPOSITION is a strong whole part relationship, where the part normally cannot exist without the whole and the part cannot be part of more than one whole at a time. Physical whole-part relationships are usually compositions. An engine can only be part of one car at a time. AGGREGATION is a weaker form, where the part can be part of many wholes. For example, a student could be part of more than one school.

2.4.3.4 Classification and Generalization

In UML modeling as in object-oriented methodology, you will often find that you model individual things, but then also model a more abstract, generalized version of those things. You can look at the individuals and develop a class that abstracts out the common properties of interest. You can look individual books in a library, examine their features, behaviors, and relationships, and devise a class of books that supports their individual features. The book you are reading has a title, number of pages, publisher, etc. After a while, you discover that all books have those same features, so you create a class of **Books** with those features. This is CLASSIFICATION. We call an individual book an INSTANCE of the class **Book**. Making a new INSTANCE of a **Book** is INSTANTIATION.

Among future reflection, you realize that the library also lets you borrow Movies and make an appropriate class of Movies. Movies have a title, runtime, publisher, etc. An individual movie is an instance of the class **Movie**.

If you wish to go further, you can make a class of **Borrowable Materials** that includes both **Books** and **Movies**. Place the common features of these two classes, **Books** and **Movies**, in the more general class, **Borrowable Materials**, while we leave the specific features in the **Book** and **Movie** classes. We call the abstraction process of making a common class for the common features Generalization. The opposite direction of making a specific version of a general class we call SPECIALIZATION. Specialization and Generalization are inverse relationships.

When Generalization and Specialization are involved, it is usually possible for any instance of the specialized classes to be used wherever an instance of the general class is needed. All the features of the generalized class are also available on the specialized class, so if you want the features of the general, you will also find them on the specialized. This if often called SUBSTITUTION. Therefore, any specific book or movie is also an instance of **Borrowable Material**.

POINTS TO REMEMBER

- Modeling and Diagraming should address one or more project risks.
- Abstraction allows you to make simpler models by showing only the essentials.
- Information hiding suppresses unnecessary details and prevents unwanted dependencies.
- Encapsulation prevents changes to details from propagating.
- Sometimes, the whole can represent the sum of the parts.
- Classification is the process of abstracting the common features from a set of individuals and making a class. The individuals are then instances of that class.
- Generalization is the process of abstracting the common features from a set of classes.
- Specialization is finding additional classes that are versions of a general class.
- Instances of a specialized class are also instances of the generalized class, allowing for substitution.
- Eliding is the suppressing of unneeded detail on a diagram element while keeping it hidden in the model.
- Composition and Aggregation are whole-part relationships. Composition is the stronger of the two, allowing only one owner at a time.

CHAPTER 3

Questions for Chapter 2

1. What does the initialism UML stand for?
   A. Universal Modeling Language
   B. Unified Modeling Language
   C. University of Massachusetts, in Lowell, where UML was invented
   D. Unified Markup Language
   E. Unified Marxist—Leninist Party, the radical first proponents of UML
2. What is the body that is responsible for the UML standard?
   A. W3C
   B. IEEE
   C. OMG
   D. CCITT/ITU-T
   E. EXPRESS/STEP
3. For what type of systems is UML primarily intended?
   A. Software-intensive systems
   B. Systems Engineering systems
   C. Business systems
   D. Interactive systems
   E. Mechanical/Analog systems
   F. Collaborating Smart Phone Apps
4. If a project is using a structured decomposition approach to development, how should UML be used?
   A. Don't use UML. It is only for object-oriented approaches.
   B. Use the structured decomposition approach during analysis using DF/CF diagrams and switch to an object-oriented approach during design and implementation using UML.
   C. Use fUML for the functional parts and UML for the object-oriented parts.
   D. There is no problem in using UML for everything.

5. What are some of the basic UML diagrams?
   A. Class diagrams, Sequence diagrams, and Use Case diagrams
   B. Block diagrams, Parametric diagrams, and Internal Block diagrams (IBD)
   C. Mind Map diagrams and Goal-Structure Notation diagrams (GSN)
   D. Class diagrams, Sequence diagrams, and Collaboration diagrams
   E. Data Flow diagrams (DFD), Control Flow diagrams (CFD), and Entity-Relationship diagrams (ERD)
   F. Fishbone (Ishikawa) diagrams and Bowtie diagrams
6. In the context of UML, what is the most common purpose of modeling?
   A. To get to try on and show off new clothes
   B. To support automatic code generation
   C. To produce executable models
   D. To capture and communicate analysis and design
   E. To meet contractual needs
7. Why type of modeling is most appropriate to determine if you understand the users' needs correctly?
   A. Domain Modeling
   B. Use Case Modeling
   C. Conceptualization Modeling
   D. Architecture Modeling
8. What is the organization within OMG that is responsible for UML?
   A. The Analysis & Design Task Force (ADTF)
   B. The Modeling Interchange Task Force (MITF)
   C. The Domain Technology Committee (DTC)
   D. The Business Subcommittee (BSC)
9. How is UML a language?
   A. One can use UML to write books.
   B. There are many dialects of UML.
   C. UML has syntax, notation, and semantics.
   D. It is a programming language similar to Python.
10. What is the best argument for making your UML models and diagrams as simple as possible?
    A. It is cheaper to make simpler models.
    B. Simpler diagrams and models allow the modeler and the diagram consumer to concentrate on the essential features without distraction.
    C. Simpler diagrams look and print better.
    D. The value of a model is inversely related to its complexity.
11. What is the best reason that projects take on the extra work of making models?
    A. Modeling makes it appear that you are making progress.
    B. Management requires modeling.

C. Modeling reduces the risk of system development.
D. Modeling can help in code generation.
12. Why type of UML diagram would be most appropriate to capture the order of messages being sent and received among a group of participants?
   A. Class Diagrams
   B. Use Case Diagrams
   C. State Machine Diagrams
   D. Sequence Diagrams
13. What is the purpose of Domain Modeling?
   A. To understand the magnetic field regions
   B. To understand the authorities involved in the system's internet presence
   C. To understand the goals of the users
   D. To understand the architecture of the system
   E. To understand the existing environment or legacy system for your problem
14. What modeling principle supports substituting members of one class for another class?
   A. Encapsulation
   B. Information Hiding
   C. Behavior Modeling
   D. Risk Mitigation
   E. Generalization
15. What type of relationship does a car form with a tire?
   A. Composition
   B. Aggregation
   C. Generalization
   D. Encapsulation
   E. Classification
16. What is the standardized mechanism to exchange UML models?
   A. GEDCOM
   B. MIWG
   C. RDF
   D. XML
   E. XMI
17. What is the UML relationship between both myCar and yourCar and the class **Car**?
   A. They are generalizations of the class **Car**.
   B. They are models of the class **Car**.
   C. They are examples of the class **Car**.
   D. They are specializations of the class **Car**.
   E. They are instances of the class **Car**.

18. What must a nonempty UML model contain?
    A. A model must contain diagram elements.
    B. A model must contain diagrams.
    C. A model must contain model elements.
    D. A model must contain XMI.
19. What does abstraction mean in the context of UML modeling?
    A. Abstraction means to model at the lowest possible level.
    B. Abstraction means to model at the highest possible level.
    C. Abstraction means to create a summary diagram as an abstract of the model.
    D. Abstraction means to hide unnecessary detail.

ANSWERS FOR CHAPTER 2

1. What does the initialism UML stand for?
    A. Universal Modeling Language
    B. **Unified Modeling Language**
    C. University of Massachusetts, in Lowell, where UML was invented
    D. Unified Markup Language
    E. Unified Marxist–Leninist Party, the radical first proponents of UML

    Discussion:
    Because UML is never pronounced as a word, but only pronounced as individual letters ("U", "M", "L"), many would feel that it is more appropriate to consider UML as an initialism rather than an acronym.
    A and D—Common internet explanations, by those who do not know the correct expansion.
    C and E—Common internet hits, but not related.

    As with much of the OCUP 2 exams, getting the correct answer requires knowledge or very lucky guessing. As A, B, and D are plausible answers, but A and D are just distractors (false answers), guessing from among these three will give you only a 33% chance of getting it correct. If you have no idea at all, guessing will give you a 20% chance of getting it correct. Always try to eliminate one or more answers before guessing.

    Also, A and D are common misconceptions. The test may use common misconceptions or errors as distractors to distinguish the successful candidates from dilettantes.

    In addition, note that C and E are not only wrong but accompanied by false explanations that make them sound slightly more plausible. This additional information is often the sign of a false answer, but not always, as additional information may be attached to the correct answer also.

2. What is the body that is responsible for the UML standard?
   A. W3C
   B. IEEE
   C. **OMG**
   D. CCITT/ITU-T
   E. EXPRESS/STEP

   Discussion:
   A, B, and D—Incorrect. These are all standards bodies with different portfolios
   E—Is also incorrect. EXPRESS is a data modeling language that is part of the STEP standards family (Standard for the Exchange of Product model data). The family is under ISO control as ISO 10303. EXPRESS is ISO 10303-11.
   Another standards body, ISO, is not on the list because some of the UML standards are sent to ISO for further approval. When ISO approves a UML standard, it is identical to the OMG version. When we made these tests, we tried to be careful to exclude distractors that are in some circumstances also correct. Thus, there should be only one correct answer and no partial credit. We also left out ANSII, though it does not approve the UML standard, you can order the ISO version through them, so to be safe, we didn't list ANSII.
   By the way, if you order your copy of the UML standard from ISO, it will cost you money, perhaps as much as $400. If you download it from OMG, it is free.

3. For what type of systems is UML primarily intended?
   A. **Software-intensive systems**
   B. Systems Engineering systems
   C. Business systems
   D. Interactive systems
   E. Mechanical/Analog systems
   F. Collaborating Smart Phone Apps

   Discussion:
   Although UML will be helpful in all the options, there may be better choices. For example, UML treats the world as discrete, so that System Engineering and Mechanical Analog Systems may not be best modeled with UML. Instead, consider using the Systems Engineering Modeling Language (SysML) or something similar for B and E.
   UML would be very useful for Business IT systems, but the business community has their own notation tailored to be understood by the Business community. Instead, consider using the Business Process Modeling Notation (BPMN).

Collaborating Peer-to-Peer systems will be helped by using UML, but no modeling approach appears to be most suitable. Instead, consider simulation-based models. The in-development AgentML may be suitable when it becomes available.

All the above-mentioned languages are managed and maintained by OMG. SysML and BPMN both have standardized certification exams similar to OCUP 2.

4. If a project is using a structured decomposition approach to development, how should UML be used?
   A. Don't use UML. It is only for object-oriented approaches.
   B. Use the structured decomposition approach during analysis using DF/CF diagrams and switch to an object-oriented approach during design and implementation using UML.
   C. Use fUML for the functional parts and UML for the object-oriented parts.
   D. **There is no problem in using UML for everything.**

   Discussion:
   Although UML 1.x was originally designed for object-oriented systems, it has evolved to be successful for all types of systems design, for example, object-oriented, functionally oriented, structural decomposition, and hybrid systems. So choosing A or B indicates an outdated understanding of UML.

   Switching an approach in the midst of development is unnecessary, and risky, so B and C are incorrect.

   The language fUML is a formalized version of UML suitable for execution. It is not a functional version of UML, so C is also incorrect.

   If you use UML with plans to use a non-object-oriented programming language, the simplest way of doing this would be to use UML for everything but avoid using the few object-oriented features of UML that may be difficult to translate into code when doing design-level or implementation-level models.

5. What are some of the basic UML diagrams?
   A. **Class diagrams, Sequence diagrams, and Use Case diagrams**
   B. Block diagrams, Parametric diagrams, and Internal Block diagrams (IBD)
   C. Mind Map diagrams and Goal-Structure Notation diagrams (GSN)
   D. Class diagrams, Sequence diagrams, and Collaboration diagrams
   E. Data Flow diagrams (DFD), Control Flow diagrams (CFD), and Entity-Relationship diagrams (ERD)
   F. Fishbone (Ishikawa) diagrams and Bowtie diagrams

Discussion:
A—Correct. These are three of the most popular UML diagrams. They are included in the OCUP 2 Foundation exam. B, C, D, E, and F—These are all diagrams used elsewhere.
B—The Block, Parametric, and Internal Block diagrams are diagrams in the Systems Engineering Modeling Language (SysML).
C—These additional diagrams approaches are used by other tools, e.g., Astah. Many tools implement diagram extensions, but they are not part of the standard.
D—Collaboration diagrams were part of UML 1.x. They are now called Communication diagrams. Choosing this answer indicates an outdated knowledge.
E—These diagrams were popular in structured analysis and database tools.
F—These diagrams are used for certain Risk Management methods.

6. In the context of UML, what is the most common purpose of modeling?
   A. To get to try on and show off new clothes
   B. To support automatic code generation
   C. To produce executable models
   D. **To capture and communicate analysis and design**
   E. To meet contractual needs

   Discussion:
   A—This is a throwaway here based on a different meaning of the word "modeling."
   B and C—Possible reasons to use UML but are relatively rare.
   D—This the most common purpose of creating UML models.
   E—Modeling to meet contractual purposes appears to be common, but such modeling is intended ultimately to capture and communicate project information, perhaps for the client of the system.

7. Which type of modeling is most appropriate to determine if you understand the users' needs correctly?
   A. Domain Modeling
   B. **Use Case Modeling**
   C. Conceptualization Modeling
   D. Architecture Modeling

   Discussion:
   A—Domain modeling checks that you understand the domain, the existing world surrounding your problem
   B—Use Case Modeling explores the users' goals and needs. It is written using their terminology to elicit feedback
   C—Conceptualization modeling shows the general approach taken for the system solution
   D—Architecture Modeling establishes the system architecture

8. What is the organization within OMG that is responsible for UML?
   A. **The Analysis & Design Task Force (ADTF)**
   B. The Modeling Interchange Task Force (MITF)
   C. The Domain Technology Committee (DTC)
   D. The Business Subcommittee (BSC)

   Discussion:
   B—There is no MITF; however, there is a Model Interchange Special Interest Group (MISIG) that works on making tests that can be used to verify that the tools can exchange models, including UML and SysML models.
   C—The ADTF is part of the Platform Technology Committee not the Domain Technology Committee
   D—The Business subcommittee works to guarantee that adopted standards have commercial implementations

9. How is UML a language?
   A. One can use UML to write books.
   B. There are many dialects of UML.
   C. **UML has syntax, notation, and semantics.**
   D. It is a programming language similar to Python.

   Discussion:
   A—You can write books on UML (this is one), and UML can automatically generate documentation with the proper tools, but you can't write books in UML
   B—UML does not have separate dialects. It does have versions. Currently, UML is on version 2.5
   D—UML is not a typical text-based programming language. In some circumstances, it can generate executable code in languages such as Python. You can also directly simulate a limited subset of UML.

10. What is the best argument for making your UML models and diagrams as simple as possible?
    A. It is cheaper to make simpler models.
    B. **Simpler diagrams and models allow the modeler and the diagram consumer to concentrate on the essential features without distraction.**
    C. Simpler diagrams look and print better.
    D. The value of a model is inversely related to its complexity.

    Discussion:
    The value of a model depends on how effectively the model coveys the necessary information. Generally, simpler models can communicate more effectively.
    A and C—Are true but are not great reasons
    D—This is wrong.

11. What is the best reason that projects take on the extra work of making models?
    A. Modeling makes it appear that you are making progress.
    B. Management requires modeling.
    C. **Modeling reduces the risk of system development.**
    D. Modeling can help in code generation.

    Discussion:
    A and B—Possibly true, but not a good reason
    D—True, but not the best reason.
       We are looking for the best reason. Reasons that are based on deception or authority are never the best reasons in the exam.

12. Why type of UML diagram would be most appropriate to capture the order of messages being sent and received among a group of participants?
    A. Class Diagrams
    B. Use Case Diagrams
    C. State Machine Diagrams
    D. **Sequence Diagrams**

    Discussion:
    A—Class Diagrams are static structure diagrams
    B—Use Case Diagrams show the needs of the users (Actors)
    C—State Machines Diagrams show how the states of an object change over time.
    D—Sequence Diagrams specialize in capturing the order of message exchange.

13. What is the purpose of Domain Modeling?
    A. To understand the magnetic field regions
    B. To understand the authorities involved in the system's internet presence
    C. To understand the goals of the users
    D. To understand the architecture of the system
    E. **To understand the existing environment or legacy system for your problem**

    Discussion:
    A and B—Different meaning for Domain than the UML meaning.
    C—This describes Use Case modeling, a different type of modeling,
    D—This describes Architecture modeling, a different type of modeling.

14. What modeling principle supports substituting members of one class for another class?
    A. Encapsulation
    B. Information Hiding

C. Behavior Modeling
D. Risk Mitigation
E. **Generalization**

Discussion:
A—Encapsulation is an approach for information hiding that limits the scope of changes.
B—Information Hiding hides information not needed at this time or that might cause unwanted dependencies.
C—Behavior Modeling is useful, but not related to substitution.
D—Risk Mitigation is a general goal of all modeling.

15. What type of relationship does a car form with a tire?
    A. **Composition**
    B. Aggregation
    C. Generalization
    D. Encapsulation
    E. Classification

    Discussion:
    A—Composition is the strong form of a whole-part relationship.
    B—Aggregation supports sharing of parts by more than one owner. A tire can only be part of ONE car.
    C—Generalization is the abstraction of common features from multiple classes.
    D—Encapsulation is the colocation of codependent information.
    E—Classification the abstraction of common features from instances.

16. What is the standardized mechanism to exchange UML models?
    A. GEDCOM
    B. MIWG
    C. RDF
    D. XML
    E. **XMI**

    Discussion:
    A—GEDCOM is a standard genealogy database interchange format.
    B—MIWG (Model Interchange Working Group) is responsible at OMG for testing tool compliances to XMI.
    C—RDF (Resource Description Framework) is a W3C specification. It can be used to exchange data among tools but is not tailored for UML.
    D—XML (Extensible Markup Language) is a W3C specification useful in transferring document and other data structure. XMI is based on XML.
    E—XMI (XML Metadata Interchange) is the OMG standard based on XML and tailored to support the transfer of UML and similar models.

17. What is the UML relationship between both myCar and yourCar and the class **Car**?
    A. They are generalizations of the class **Car**.
    B. They are models of the class **Car**.
    C. They are examples of the class **Car**.
    D. They are specializations of the class **Car**.
    E. **They are instances of the class Car**.

    Discussion:
    A—Generalizations are relationships among similar classes
    B—A model is a collection or related UML elements.
    C—This is true, but example is not a UML relationship.
    D—Specializations is the inverse relationship to Generalization, it is a relationship among classes,
    E—Correct.

18. What must a nonempty UML model contain?
    A. A model must contain diagram elements.
    B. A model must contain diagrams.
    C. **A model must contain model elements.**
    D. A model must contain XMI.

    Discussion:
    A and B—Usually, the diagrams and the diagram elements are stored in the model, but they are not necessary.
    C—Correct. Diagrams, diagram elements, and text are all optional.
    D—The internal representation of a model can be in any format, including XMI.

19. What does abstraction mean in the context of UML modeling?
    A. Abstraction means to model at the lowest possible level.
    B. Abstraction means to model at the highest possible level.
    C. Abstraction means to create a summary diagram as an abstract of the model.
    D. **Abstraction means to hide unnecessary detail.**

    Discussion:
    A—Abstraction means to be a higher level.
    B—You have to prevent being too high and missing necessary detail.
    C—This is the wrong meaning for abstract.
    D—This is the best answer.

CHAPTER 4

The Organization of UML

4.1 THE UML 2.5 SPECIFICATION

One of the big changes between the previous OCUP 1 Certification program and the current OCUP 2 Certification program is the deemphasis on what the SPECIFICATION contains and a new concentration on more practical UML modeling knowledge and skills. Still, there are things about the UML 2.5 specification that you will need to know, such as the UML diagrams types, and what you can find in the specification, how you can use it, and what information you will find on the certification exams. Moreover, even if it is not on the Foundational Examination, all this material will still be useful to you to become a successful UML modeler.

4.1.1 Target Audience

If you are reading this book, you will probably not be in the target audience for the UML specification. The specification is large[1], dense, complex, and formal. The target audience is tool designers, language designers, and project-tailoring methodologists. However, an occasional glance at the specification, along with limited expectations, may be useful for anyone interested in UML.

As the specification is complex and formal, this introduction to the specification may be difficult to follow. Unfortunately, many things in this chapter are on the OCUP 2 Foundation exam. We will highlight these important items in the occasional *Points to Remember* tables that you will find sprinkled through this chapter.

4.1.2 The Document Layout

The UML specification (the SPEC) lays out the formal definition of the UML 2.5 language. The major subdivisions of the UML specification are

---

[1] It has 752 pages of body matter and 42 pages of front matter. There is neither glossary nor index.

called CLAUSES[2], which are then divided into SUBCLAUSES, and so on. There are 22 Clauses and 5 ANNEXES. The document is almost 100% NORMATIVE, that is, part of the definition of UML 2.5. However, there is a small amount of implementation advice aimed at tool vendors and in some areas, the spec gives the tool vendors options on how to present the material. The leeway that is given to the tool vendors is in notation options.

The general format of the spec, including the division into clauses and subclauses, was chosen to be compatible with ISO. OMG submits the finalized specification to ISO for adoption as one of ISO's standards.

The general order is introductory material first (Clauses 1−6), followed by structural topics (Clauses 7−12), behavior (Clauses 13−17), some Supplement Modeling (Clauses 18−22).

As we wrote the spec to reduce forward references as much as possible, the order of the topics may not always appear logical. Sometimes, advanced topics, such as Templates, appear early to minimize these references.

For the UML 2.5 clauses and their relevance to the OCUP Foundation exam, see Table 4.1.

For the annexes, see Table 4.2. For a graphical view of the semantic areas, see Fig. 4.1.

4.2 THE LANGUAGE DEFINITION—THE CLAUSES

We[3] divided the specification into clauses, each representing a major topic area in UML 2.5. Table 4.1 indicates these 22 clauses. The clauses that represent language definition (Clauses 7−20) all share a similar structure.

> *Summary:* Each language definition clause begins with a brief summary, usually about one paragraph long, indicating the principles that bind all the clause's subclauses into a coherent whole.
> *Subclauses:* Then follow the subclauses, allocating the material of the clauses into separate sections.
> At the end of the clause, each UML language element identified in any of subclauses is defined. This material is divided into following three parts:
>> *Classifier Descriptions:* This shows the model elements and their properties. This material is generated automatically from the abstract syntax diagrams.

---

[2] A clause is what many people would call a section of the standard.
[3] I use "we" as I was a member of the UML Revision Task Force. However, I cannot take any credit (or blame) for most of the decisions, nor did I agree with them all.

Table 4.1 UML 2.5 Specification Clauses, Their Contents, and Diagrams Relevant to the OCUP 2 Foundation Exam

UML 2.5 Clause	Content if not Evident from the Name of Clause	Diagrams Covered
1. Scope		
2. Conformance		
3. Normative references		
4. Terms and definitions		
5. Notational conventions		
6. Additional information	Structure of the specification, BNF, abstract syntax	
7. Common structure	Root concepts, Templates, namespaces, types, multiplicity, constraints, dependencies	
8. Values	Literals, expressions, time, intervals	
9. Classification	Classifiers, features, properties, operations, instances	Object
10. Simple classifiers	Data types, signals, interfaces	
11. Structured classifiers	Classes, associations	Class, component, composite structure
12. Packages		Package, profile
13. Common behavior	Behaviors, events	
14. State machines	State machines, protocol state machines, alternate notation	State machine
15. Activities	Control nodes, object nodes, flows, executable notes, tokens	Activity
16. Actions	Actions, pins	
17. Interactions	Interactions, lifelines, messages, occurrences, fragments	Sequence, timing, interaction overview, communication
18. Use cases		Use case
19. Deployments		Deployment
20. Information flows		
21. Primitive types		
22. Standard profile		

This table shows the clauses of the UML 2.5 specification. For each clause, we show the content relevant to the OCUP 2 Fundamental Exam, when it not evident from the title of the clause. The diagrams discussed in each section are in the last column. We indicate the material that is not relevant to the Fundamental Exam in gray text.

Table 4.2 UML 2.5 Specification Annexes, Their Contents, and Diagrams Relevant to the OCUP 2 Foundation Exam

UML 2.5 Annex	Content if not Evident from the Name of the Clause	Diagrams Covered
A. Diagrams	Diagram headers and types. Diagram names	
B. UML diagram interchange		
C. Keywords	Reserved words: Their context and meaning	Multilevel
D. Tabular notations for sequence diagrams		Not on any exam
E. XMI serialization and schema	Used to exchange model	Not on any exam

FIGURE 4.1
Semantic areas of UML 2.5. *Source: UML 2.5 Specification Fig. 6.1 page 13.*

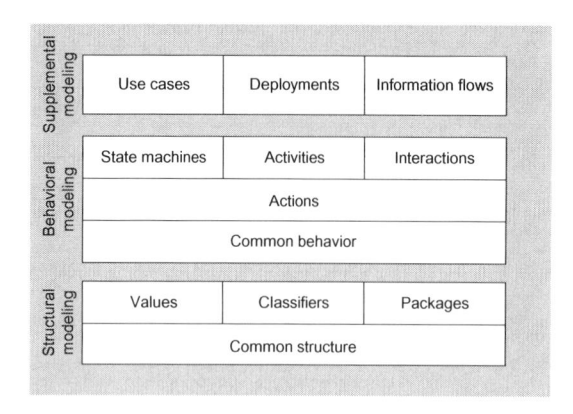

This diagram indicates the major semantic areas of UML 2.5 and their presentation order, starting at the bottom.

For example, within the specification, the Common Behavior material is built upon, and follows the Common Structure material, and Supplemental Modeling is built upon and follows both.

In the Foundational exam, you will not be responsible for either Deployments or Information Flows.

Their notation is rarely used by beginner modelers and is often omitted on projects.

Association Descriptions: This shows the relationships among the model elements and their multiplicities. This material is generated automatically from the abstract syntax diagrams.
Constraints: Any constraints on the model elements are stated in natural language and in the formal Object Constraint Language (OCL). OCL is a powerful language designed to express navigation within Meta Object Facility (MOF)-based languages and constraints among the elements.

4.3 THE SUBCLAUSES

For each subclause that defines part of the UML 2.5 language, there is a common structure to make the specification more useful in defining the language and more useful for the reader.

Summary: A brief informal description of the concepts described in that subclause. Each subclause covers a coherent set of concepts that is part of the clause. This makes them easier to discuss together.
Abstract Syntax: A formal diagram shows the UML elements of the subclause. Each UML element that is covered by the subclause has the element's properties and relationships indicated. This corresponds to the formal grammar of UML. See Section 4.4, The Abstract Syntax. The abstract syntax is independent of the notation.
Semantics: This section attempts to give meaning to the UML elements of this subclause, covering common real-world and runtime interpretations. Though UML follows no particular implementation approach or programming language, the semantics material gives examples, when

necessary for clarification. As the scope of UML is very wide, not every reader will recognize all of the most advanced examples.

When there are several possible interpretations for tools or users, the specification explains the available leeway.

Surface Syntax: Most of UML is visual. The standard visual or surface syntax for the elements that are defined in this subclause is shown with examples.

> *Notation:* For the elements that have a graphical appearance, the subclause then illustrates the standard notation and optional forms. The subclauses show the notation with examples.
>
> *Textual Syntax:* For the pieces of UML that are primarily textual or string-like in nature (such as names or multiplicity), this material shows the syntax that covers the textual format, usually in a variant of Backus—Naur Form (BNF). We'll give you a simple example of BNF in Section 4.6.3.2, *Diagram Frame and Header*.

After the material on each subclause, the clause continues with the *Element Descriptions* as described in Section 4.2, *The Language Definition—The Clauses*.

POINTS TO REMEMBER

- The UML 2.5 spec is divided into clauses, subclauses, and annexes.
- The spec covers structural, behavioral, and Supplemental modeling.
- The abstract syntax of UML shows the grammar of UML without regard to the notation.
- The UML semantics gives meaning to the UML elements.
- The notation is the standard visual surface syntax for the model elements.
- A variant of BNF is used to show the textual surface syntax.
- The OCL is used to express constraints.
- The XML Metadata Interchange (XMI) is the interchange format for UML models.

4.4 THE ABSTRACT SYNTAX

The abstract syntax of UML, which is the formal grammar for the UML 2.5 language, is specified as a set of formal diagrams using the MOF Version 2.5 modeling language[4]. The abstract syntax defines the set of UML modeling concepts, their attributes, and their relationships, as well as the rules for combining these concepts to construct partial or complete UML models[5].

For those of you who might worry that you will now have to learn a new modeling language, don't worry. The MOF as used in UML specification is a strict

---

[4]Object Management Group, *Meta Object Facility (MOF) Specification v 2.5*, (OMG June 2015). http://www.omg.org/spec/MOF/2.5/.

[5]Object Management Group, *OMG Unified Modeling Language Specification, v 2.5*, (OMG Sept 2013). §1 p. 1.

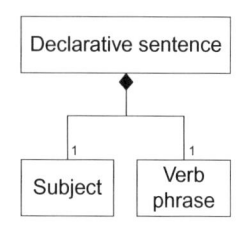

FIGURE 4.2

A metamodel for some English grammar.

subset of UML structural model notation. However, it does use some structural modeling features that would be in the OCUP 2 Advanced exam, which will not be covered in this book. Still, the basics of the abstract syntax diagrams used in the specification should be understandable by the time you finish the structural diagrams of this book, with the most-basic basics covered in this chapter.

Some of you may also wonder how UML can be used to define the grammar for UML. This "bootstrapping" technique is very common in the real world. For example, most grammarians write their English grammar books in English, and no one sees any conflict in this[6]. Also, most English dictionaries are in English. Many programing languages have compilers written in the language that they compile, and recursive mathematical functions (such as factorial![7]) can be defined using themselves. Still, it seems odd to many that we can make a model of UML in UML.

However, as we mentioned before, to pass the Fundamental exam, you may not even need to look at these MOF diagrams, though you need to know they exist, their purpose, and the essentials of how they work.

These diagrams depict the abstract syntax, the grammar of UML. They are "abstract" in that they would not need to change if the notation changes. This is similar to how the grammar rule of a natural language, such as English, is independent of the spelling or vocabulary.

As an example of the abstract syntax of English depicted in this manner using the MOF, see Fig. 4.2. The solid diamond indicates a COMPOSITION relationship, a WHOLE-PART relationship. The class at the diamond end, in this case, **Declarative Sentence**, is the whole, while the classes at the other ends are the parts. In this diagram, we are showing that an English **Declarative Sentence** has a **Subject** and a **Verb Phrase**. The numeral "1" at the ends of the composition is the MULTIPLICITY: A value of one indicates a mandatory part. Notice that, this sort of diagram does not indicate any order to the parts; a declarative sentence can have the subject first and then the verb phrase or in the other order.

4.5 THE LAYERED METAMODEL

One way that it becomes possible to have a model of a modeling language is to separate strictly the levels of discourse. We call a model of a modeling language a METAMODEL. Therefore, all the MOF models used to provide the formal abstract syntax for UML are metamodels. In philosophy and mathematics,

---

[6]There are formal grammars for English that use a specialty notation. However, they are more complicated and not well known. Using UML to describe itself rather than introducing an entire new language improves the usability and readability of the syntax.
[7]The Factorial function (!) is often defined as follows: $0! := 1; N! := N \times (N - 1)!$

this separation into levels is common to prevent malformed statements that can result in a paradox. Consider the levels shown in Table 4.3. These levels are often called layers.

Note that this section is both complex and confusing to many. When we talk to people about the metamodel, we are talking about a high-level model. They often claim to get a higher level headache, a "meta-muddle." At the end of the section, we will include a *Points to Remember* list that indicates the things you'll need to remember that will highlight the most important points.

If you were making a system for a Library, there could be at least three things called Books:

1. The physical books (M-1)
2. The books in the implementation (in the app, database table, runtime objects) (M0)
3. The class **Book** in the model (M1)

Table 4.3 The Levels of Metamodeling

Layer Name	Description	What You Can Do with It
Real World Layer M-1	**The real world** In the Library system, the physical books and patrons are the elements here	You can touch them
User objects layer M0	**The implementation world** Instances, database records, tables, executables are the elements here In a Library system, the books and the patrons in the Library database are level M0. Generally, there is one M0 object to represent the M-1 things	You can implement this layer
Model Layer M1	**The modeling world** Your model lives here and describes the things in the M0 layer Your model of the Library system is an M1 level description of the M0 implementation. The Book and Patron Classes live here	You can model in this layer
MetaModel Layer M2	**The metamodeling world** The elements in this layer are the elements of UML. The M1 level uses the M2 elements. Models at this level give the abstract syntax, the grammar of UML MOF. The METACLASSES Class and Object lives here	You can read the specification in this layer
MetaMetaModel Layer M3	**The meta-metamodeling world** This layer describes the MOF elements. The MOF is used to write the grammar of UML and several other OMG languages. The meta-metaclasses MOF Class and MOF object live here	Not much

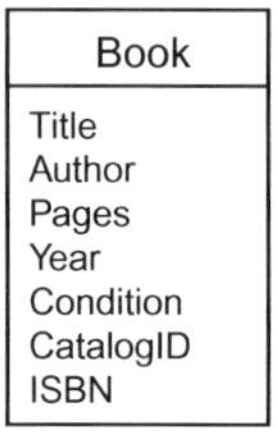

FIGURE 4.3

An initial cut at the book class.

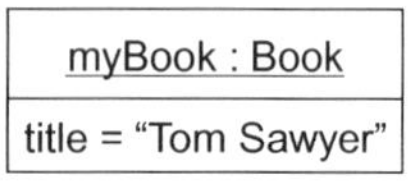

FIGURE 4.4

An initial cut at the book object.

This can get quite confusing. If you are talking to someone about the system and say, "*We need to make a change to allow senior citizens to borrow books for a longer time*", are you suggesting a change to the manual procedures, a change to the runtime software or app, or a change to your model, or perhaps a change to all of them?

Most experts consider it good practice to make clear which level you are talking about whenever a possibility of mixing the levels occurs.

Luckily while UML modeling, we rarely ever need to model the M-1 elements (the physical elements), but we might need to observe them and try to model their relevant properties.

For example, by looking at the physical books in the Library (the M-1 level) the properties (attributes) could include the title, author, number of pages, copyright year, condition, catalogID, ISBN, and perhaps even format, weight, and thickness. Business analysts spend much of their time observing the existing, legacy system to determine what properties and behaviors occur in the current world to determine how to automate or improve the current approach. This kind of analysis is a key part of domain analysis that is often done using UML. Domain analysis was previously discussed in Chapter 2, What is UML?.

Modeling rightfully uses real-world considerations to concentrate on the M1 level, where we would be creating classes. Later, we might convert these modeling (M1) classes (automatically or manually) to the M0 classes in the implementation.

We show an initial cut at the Book class in Fig. 4.3. The class symbol is a box with the name in the top COMPARTMENT. The properties of the class, called ATTRIBUTES, are in the next lower compartment. Can you think of other attributes of a book that might be relevant to a Library system[8]?

We cannot put an implementation level element (MO) into the model (M1), but we can show a representative example. Not only are there too many book records in the Book table of the database, but essentially a model-level element is not an implementation element. To distinguish the M0 objects from the M1 element version that represents them, we call the model versions, INSTANCE SPECIFICATIONS, though commonly we still call them OBJECTS.

In Fig. 4.4, we show an initial cut of a Book Object (instance specification). This object is an instance of the class Book. We show this by the placing the name of the object in a box ending with a reference to the Class name. The reference to the class is indicated as (": Book"). The whole string is

---

[8]I was considering, for example, replacement cost, reference (noncirculating flag), on-site/borrowed flag, overdue.

4.5 The Layered Metamodel

FIGURE 4.5
An instance and its class.

FIGURE 4.6
A class and its metaclass.

underlined to indicate that it is an object. As this book is written by me, I gave it the name myBook. Any name, including an empty name, is possible.

It is also possible to show some of the attributes of the class **Book** in the next compartment. You will find this useful because you can show the current values that the object has in these slots.

We draw such objects (instances) when we need to illustrate the participants of a scenario or collaboration for sample purposes. These diagrams are often useful to show examples to fellow workers or to help set up a test.

We can emphasize the relationship between the instance of a book and the **Book** class, by connecting them on a diagram. We use a dashed arrow pointing from the instance to the class. This arrow indicates a nonspecific DEPENDENCY. In this case, the object or instance DEPENDS on the class definition. We show this dependency in Fig. 4.5. On the right is the instance of the **Book** class. As the instance of a class depends on the definition of the class, the myBook instance depends on the definition of the **Book** class. The object may be connected with a dependency arrow (a dashed arrow) to emphasize this relationship. As the **Book** class may have a compartment showing its attributes, the myBook instance may also have a compartment showing their current values.

We can also represent in our models some M2 level elements. In fact, all the abstract syntax diagrams are metamodels of that level. Like a class, a metaclass is also shown in a class-like box with the name in the top compartment.

When we mix levels on the same diagram, we flag the elements with the level they come from. We place the terms «Metaclass» or «Class» above the names as shown in Fig. 4.6. This figure shows that a particular class, the **Book** class, which is the same class used as in Fig. 4.5, is also an instance of the Metaclass **Class**. We use both «Metaclass» and «Class» in this diagram because it is of mixed level.

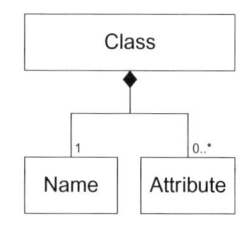

FIGURE 4.7
A partial metamodel for the UML class.

The terms enclosed in the "«" and "»" are called stereotypes[9]. They flag something in the model that is a special type of element.

The « and » are special characters called GUILLEMETS[10]. They are available in most character sets. For example, in Microsoft character sets as ALT + 174/ALT + 175 on the keypad. If you are typographically challenged, you can use the double angle brackets, that is, << and >> instead of « and ». Most UML tools will use the correct symbols, as does the UML specification.

We should flag both «Metaclass» and «Class» in this diagram because it is a mixed-level diagram, but such flagging is optional on single-level diagrams. In the abstract syntax diagrams within the UML specification, the «Metaclass» stereotype is omitted.

As an example of the abstract syntax of UML, we show, in Fig. 4.7, a partial definition of a UML **Class**. In this metamodel, we indicate that a **Class**, based on the multiplicities, must have a **Name** (1) and may have zero or more **Attributes** (0..*).

We can use stereotypes to identify the part of UML an element is. In English, we could imagine that a teacher of a class on UML might, while reviewing an exercise, say confusingly:

> **Class, I object, that object is really a class!**

However, we might clarify the sentence by flagging the part of speech of each tricky word.

> «collective noun of address» **Class, I** «active verb» **object,** that «noun» **object** is really a «noun» **class!**

We do not write this way in English or other natural languages because such clashes usually only occur in jokes or specially constructed sentences (like the one above). However, in UML, the notation is not always sufficiently precise to determine the part of UML (element type) that is being modeled. Therefore, tagging with a stereotype may be required. This becomes more important, as you will see if you read any advanced material, as it is possible to create a new element type in UML.

---

[9]In some contexts, they are not stereotypes, but keywords; the differences are subtle, but practically they both indicate a kind of the underlying element type.
[10]These signs are often called angle quotes, Latin quotation marks, or French quotation marks. Many other languages also use them to indicate quotations. Though they have no normal usage in English text, they are available in the standard symbol set.

POINTS TO REMEMBER

- The abstract syntax of UML uses MOF models to show the UML grammar.
  - These MOF models use a subset of UML structural diagrams.
  - As they are a level higher than normal UML models—They are metamodels.
- UML encloses stereotypes in guillemets (« and »).
  - Stereotypes indicate a special category of model element, a new term in the grammar, or to distinguish among similar-looking elements.
  - The boxes on the abstract syntax diagrams are «Metaclasses».
  - The elements of UML are instances of these «Metaclasses».
- It is confusing to mix meta-levels in a conversation or diagram.
- A solid diamond at the end of a line connecting classes indicates a composition relationship.
  - The diamond end indicates the whole; the other ends indicate parts.
  - A multiplicity of "1" indicates a mandatory participant.
  - A multiplicity of "0..*" indicates zero or more participants.
  - A multiplicity of "0..1" indicates an optional (zero or one) participant.
- The notation for a UML Class is a box with a mandatory compartment for the name.
  - An optional compartment can show the attributes of the class.
- The notation for a UML instance specification, commonly called an Object, is a box with a mandatory compartment for the name field.
  - The name field includes an object name, a ":", and the name of the instantiated class.
  - An optional second compartment can show the slots—The attributes and their current values.

4.6 DIAGRAMS

UML has 14 kinds of diagrams, divided into two convenient and conceptual groups: Structure and behavior. Each of the boxes in the tree-like Fig. 4.8 represents a diagram type in UML. As it is one of the first UML diagrams that you may have seen, we need to go over the meaning of the notation. Each box represents a class, that is, a type, a type of diagram. The concepts (Generalization and Specialization) were already introduced in Chapter 2, What is UML?. A hollow arrow points up from specific diagram types to a more general diagram type. This arrow is called a GENERALIZATION when you follow the arrow going up and SPECIALIZATION when you look toward the tail going down. Following a tree metaphor, the generalization arrow points to more central branches, and the box labeled diagram is the trunk of the tree. When you go down to the tail of the arrow, you are going down to smaller branches and pointing to the leaves at the lowest level.

When you travel up the tree, you can think of this best by reading it something like "A Class Diagram is a kind of Structure Diagram, which is a kind of Diagram." Similarly, "A Sequence Diagram is a kind of Interaction Diagram, which is a kind of Behavior Diagram, which is a kind of Diagram." Some people reading this prefer to use the words "sort of" or "type of" to "kind of."

FIGURE 4.8

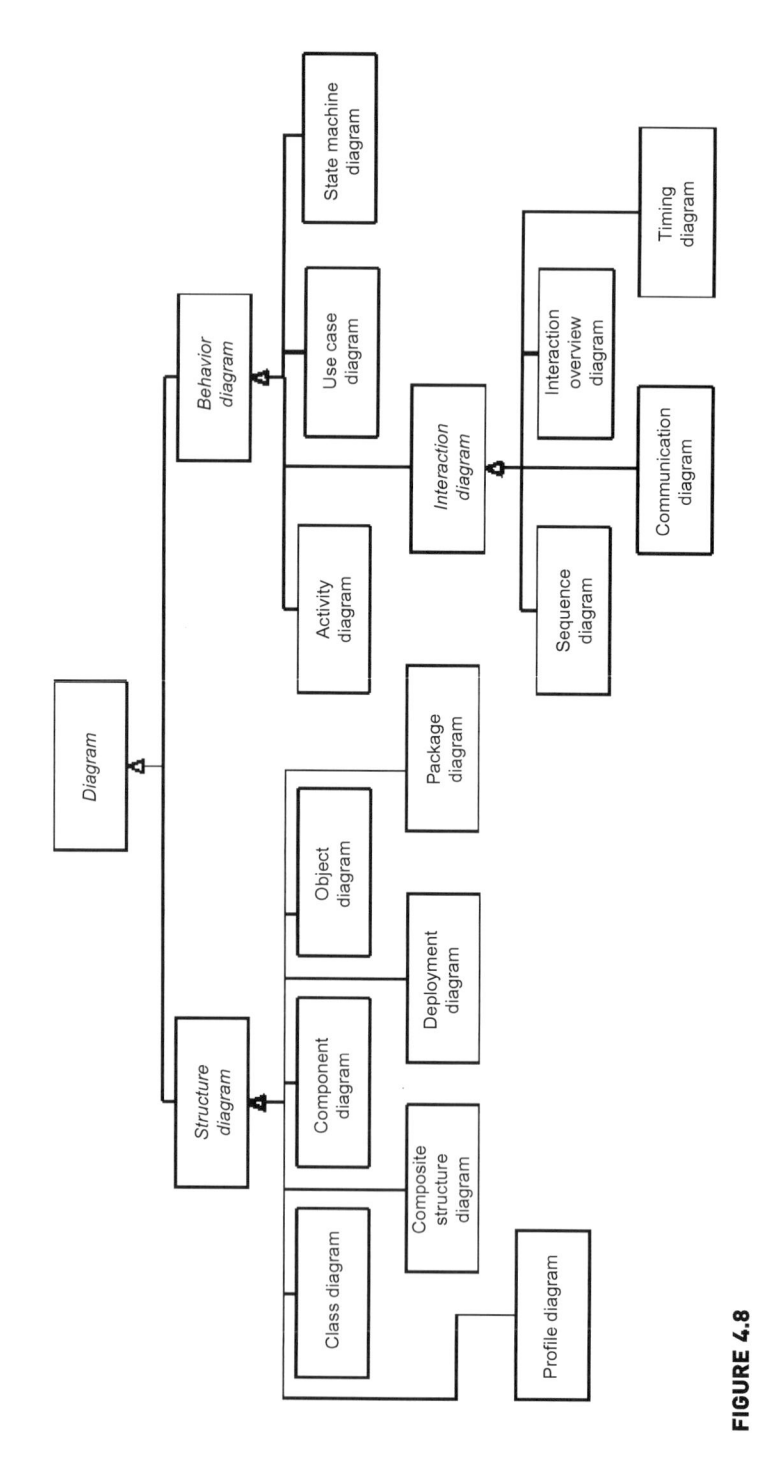

The taxonomy of UML diagrams. *Source: UML 2.5 Specification Fig. A.5.*

We introduced the topics of Generalization and Specialization earlier in Chapter 2, What is UML?. They play an important role in UML modeling.

When you travel down the tree toward the leaves, you find that there are multiple kinds of some of the diagrams. Fig. 4.8 shows that there are seven kinds of structure diagram. (Make sure you can see how this works.)

The boxes with their names in normal (roman) font are CONCRETE classes. Going left-to-right in Fig. 4.8, they are Profile, Class, Composite Structure, Component, Deployment, Object, Package, Activity, Use Case, State Machines, Sequence Communication, Interaction Overview, and Timing Diagrams. A concrete class is a class that may have individual instances—In this case; they may have diagrams of their specified type. A concrete class is a set that may contain individual elements. There are 14 concrete classes in the figure matching the 14 diagram types in UML 2.5.

The boxes with their names in italic font are ABSTRACT classes. (You should be able to find abstract classes in the figure.) These are branches that only split off into other branches, while not having any leaves themselves; that is, they are classes that can only contain other classes.

Don't worry if this sounds a bit confusing. We will cover the abstract—concrete distinction in more detail in the later chapters.

POINTS TO REMEMBER

- UML has 14 kinds of diagrams.
- There are two categories of UML diagrams: Structure and Behavior.
- A hollow arrow (generalization) points from the specific to the more general.
- Specialization (the other direction of a generalization) points to a special kind of the general.
- Abstract classes cannot have any individual elements, only other classes.
- Concrete classes may have individual elements.

4.6.1 Structure Diagrams

The UML structure diagrams show the static structure of the elements of the system being modeled. They depict those elements in a model independently of time[11]. We summarize the structure diagrams in Table 4.4.

The represent the meaningful and useful concepts that may exist in the real-world, in the software or hardware implementations, or only in the abstract

---

[11]Static diagrams may represent snapshots or values at a particular time.

Table 4.4 Structure Diagrams and What They Show

Structure Diagram	What the Diagram Depicts
Class	The elements or concepts of the system being modeled
Object	Instance specifications (objects) of some the classes, to illustrate examples elements and their connections
Composite structure	How the classes are assembled internally from other elements
Component	Deliverable elements in the working system and how they connect
Deployment	Architecture of the system's nodes or platforms and what runs or installs on what
Package	How the model is partitioned and worked
Profile	Extensions and tailorings to UML for the current project

or in the imagination. For example, a structure diagram for a library system might include elements that represent books, borrowings, due date algorithms, interlibrary loan (ILL) connections, patrons, and a credit authorization service for fines and fees. Structure diagrams do not show the details of dynamic behavior or of elements changing over time, which are reserved for the behavioral diagrams. However, structure diagrams are not isolated; they may indicate which behaviors, found on behavior diagrams, are exhibited by the elements of the structure diagrams.

4.6.2 Behavior Diagrams

Behavior diagrams show the dynamic behavior of the elements of a system. This can show their history over time, their collaboration, and their steps in algorithms and processes. For example, a behavior diagram for a library system might include use cases that show how the library can be used, the evolving state histories of a book (e.g., accessed, cataloged, borrowed, returned, loaned, and overdue), and the process steps involved in a borrowing or return. You would also use behavior diagrams to capture the scenarios and messages exchanged to create a borrowing or an ILL. Behavior diagrams are also not isolated as they generally show the static elements that participate, perform, or are affected by the behaviors they depict (Table 4.5).

4.6.3 General Diagram Features

In UML, there are some common diagram capabilities and features that are conveniently discussed here.

Table 4.5 Behavior Diagrams and What They Show

Behavior Diagram	What the Diagram Depicts
Use case	The behavioral goals that users wish the system to achieve for them
State machine	The history of the states and responses that an element goes through based on incoming events
Activity	Process steps and behaviors showing control and object flow
Interaction diagram	Interaction among participants
Sequence	A form of an interaction diagram that shows the exchange of messages among participants and their reactions, with an emphasis on peer-level interactions
Communication	A form of an interaction diagram that shows the exchange of messages among participants and their reactions, with an emphasis on the interaction within a composite structure or collaboration
Interaction overview	A high-level view of an interaction using combined activity and sequence diagram notation, with an emphasis on showing the control flow
Timing	A form of an interaction diagram emphasizing timing constraints

FIGURE 4.9
The relationship between model and diagram elements.

4.6.3.1 Views

A UML diagram is just a view into the model. A model element, such as a class, need not appear on any diagram. We have previously shown this relationship, but now we redraw it as a metamodel diagram in Fig. 4.9.

So not only may there be model elements that have no diagram elements, and therefore appear on no diagrams, but some model elements may appear on multiple diagrams, and can appear multiple times on the same diagram. Moreover, because they are views, they do not have to appear with the same amount of detail at each appearance. The underlying model element will be a cumulative union of all the matching diagram elements from all the diagrams. If you add detail to a matching diagram element, even if that detail appears on only one diagram, it becomes part of the underlying model element, and that detail is capable of being summoned up on each diagram that can display that detail.

The tools will allow you to delete detail from the diagram or from the model. Of course, if you delete the detail from the model, you will be updating all diagrams containing that element automatically to remain consistent with the underlying model element. So be careful, if you perform a delete on a diagram, you explicitly select the scope: Either diagram-element scope or model-element scope.

4.6.3.2 Diagram Frame and Header

Often in UML, we surround a UML diagram by a boundary box called a FRAME. For some diagram types, the frame has semantic meaning. In these diagram types, diagram elements may be placed on the frame or across the frame boundary for different meanings. In these diagram types, using the frame may be necessary to indicate some specific feature. However, except for this purpose, eliminating the frame is generally at the modeler's option.

Without the frame, the diagram often does not feel complete. In the OCUP 2 exams, as we often omit the frame because of space reasons, we usually refer to the remainder as a DIAGRAM FRAGMENT. Of course, everything relevant to answering the question is still in the diagram fragment.

When the diagram frame appears, we are required to have a diagram HEADER, which serves as the name for the diagram. Based on the UML Specification of Annex A, the diagram header is contained in a name tag, a rectangle with a cut-off corner (the lower right corner) forming an irregular pentagon (Fig. 4.10).

The format for the <heading>, given in BNF, is the following.

```
[<kind>]<name>[<parameters>]
<kind> ::= 'activity' | 'act' | 'class' | 'component' | 'cmp' |
'deployment' | 'dep' | 'interaction' | 'sd' | 'package' | 'pkg' | 'state
machine' | 'stm' | 'use case' | 'uc'
```

This syntax in BNF is subject to many rules; the example above has the following rules:

1. The angle brackets, "< >", indicate a field that the user can supply the contents.
2. Fields surrounded by square brackets, "[ ]", indicate that the field is optional.

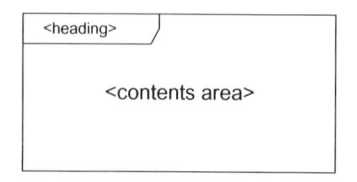

FIGURE 4.10
A UML diagram with <heading> and <contents area>. UML 2.5 Specification Fig. A.1.

3. The "∷ = " is an assignment statement defining a field by lower level fields for substitution.
4. Fields separated by vertical bars "|" are alternatives.
5. Terms surrounded by quotes are literals, and must be supplied as is. In the example, the literals are all **bold** face.

Therefore, the <kind> field is optional, but if used, it may be any one of the 15 listed possibilities. The <name> field is required, and the <parameters> field is optional.

The boundary box of the diagram represents the owning or containing model element. The heading of a diagram represents the <kind>, <name>, and <parameters> of the namespace enclosing or the model element owning or containing the element in the diagram's <contents area>. In the OCUP 2 Foundation exam, the <parameters> field will not be tested.

Many tools and users get confused and believe the bold <kind> field indicates the Diagram Kind. Thus, a diagram containing use cases and actors would be given the <kind> of **uc** based on this misconception. Unfortunately, this is wrong. Usually, a set of use cases would be kept in a package, so the correct <kind> field would be **pkg**. This approach is different from SysML, where the <kind> field indicates the kind of diagram.

The majority of structure diagrams and use case diagrams would have <kind> field of **pkg**. Because behavior diagrams work a bit differently, the <kind> of owning or containing model element tends to match the diagram type. There is still the confusion that interaction diagrams (sequence diagram, timing diagram, interaction overview diagrams, and communication diagrams) all use the <kind> field of **sd**.

We'll show examples of the basic format for a diagram header starting in Section 4.6.3.4, Namespace.

4.6.3.3 *Diagram Kind*

The Diagram Kind is still a useful concept, even if it is different from the <kind> field in the diagram header. If you know the kind of diagram, then you know what types of elements would be likely to appear on the diagram. This controls the editing palette that the tools will offer up for editing. If the majority of elements on a diagram are packages, then it is a package diagram. If the majority of elements on a diagram are classes, it is a class diagram. If the majority of elements are objects (instance specifications), then it is an object diagram. If there seems hard to decide, we generally go with the most inclusive, so we prefer to call a diagram a class diagram to calling it an object diagram if we can't decide.

It is always possible to put an object on a class diagram or a class on an object diagram and possible to put both objects and classes on a package diagram. As classes and objects can be stored in a package, all these diagrams are likely to have a <kind> field of **pkg**.

4.6.3.4 Namespace

What makes the given <kind> values the possible values? These are all namespaces in UML that are capable of holding other elements. A namespace is a software development concept. It is a set of unique names that identify entities. A namespace does not allow duplicate names. If a name appears more than once, it must refer to the same thing.

A package is a namespace. The symbol for a package is rectangle body with a tab in the upper left, which usually contains the name of the package, see Fig. 4.11. The elements inside the package cannot have clashing names. A class is also a namespace. It has a set of attributes (see the class symbol, **Book**, inside the figure), each with a name, and no duplicate names are allowed for the attributes.

A package is primarily an organization feature for a UML model. Consider it similar to a folder or directory in an operating system. These are also namespaces. The operating system will not allow you to have two files with identical names within the same directory/folder. A package will not allow two elements (of the same type) with the same name inside the package. If an element appears twice in a package, they are just representations of the same thing.

Modelers create packages for their namespace features, but they primarily create them for the same reasons developers create directories. They help to organize the project. They serve as configuration management structures. They can be used to assign work to teams, schedules, and limit the chance the modelers step on each other's work.

The above package could be converted into a diagram. In Fig. 4.12, we depict a class diagram (because the diagram depicts classes and objects) showing the contents of the package MyPackage. The <kind> field is **pkg** and the <name> field is MyPackage.

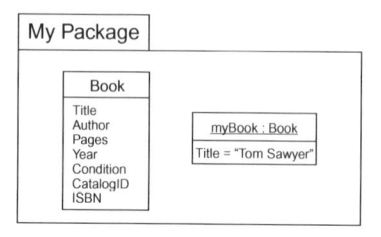

FIGURE 4.11
A package with a class and an object.

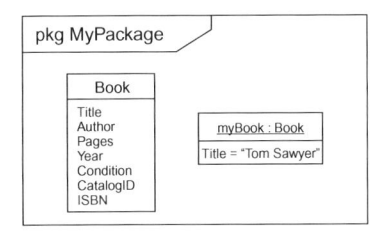

FIGURE 4.12
A class diagram showing the contents of a package.

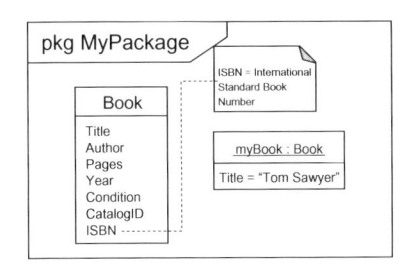

FIGURE 4.13
Class diagram with comment.

4.6.3.5 Comments
UML allows the modeler to add comments to a diagram or diagram fragment. The symbol for a comment, sometimes called a note-symbol, is a rectangle with a bent upper-right corner. The comment may be connected to the elements being annotated with a dashed line (not an arrow). In previous versions of UML instead of an arrowhead, there was a small circle. Now in UML 2.5, there is neither an arrowhead nor a circle (Fig. 4.13).

4.6.3.6 Constraints
A constraint is a rule that prohibits some potential values for a field. In UML, constraints can be added to many places on a diagram. One common way is to place the constraint inside a comment symbol. To identify it is a constraint the text of the constraint is surrounded by curly braces, {}.

The BNF for a constraint is as follows:

    <constraint> ::= '{' [<name> ':'] <boolean-expression> '}'

where <name> is the optional name of the Constraint.

    If the <name> field appears it is followed by the colon ':'.
    <boolean-expression> is the textual form for the Constraint. It is
    required to have either a true of false value when evaluated.
    The whole expression is surrounded by curly braces '{}'.

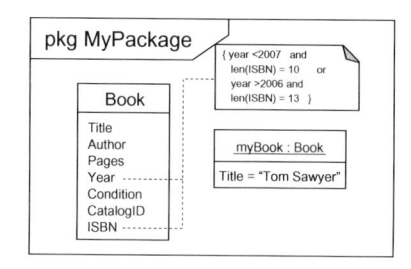

FIGURE 4.14
Class diagram with constraint.

The language for the constraint can be in the OCL, or in a programming-like syntax, or in mathematical-like syntax, or in natural language. We usually try to make it a true-false, Boolean expression, but if a natural language is used, it may be difficult to force it into that form.

In Fig. 4.14, we depict a constraint, using an unnamed Boolean expression. The constraint is on the length of the ISBN string, based on the publishing year of the book. As with a comment, we connect the constraint to all the elements that are involved. Here, we connect the constraint to year and to ISBN because the constraint uses both those fields.

POINTS TO REMEMBER

- An element can appear on as many diagrams as needed, including no diagrams, and multiple times on the same diagram.
  - The underlying model element is consistent with the union of the details of all its appearances.
- Deleting a diagram element or any of its features only changes the underlying model element if specifically requested.
- UML diagrams can be enclosed in a frame with a header.
  - The header is placed inside a pentagonal tab in the upper left.
  - The header has an optional <kind> field indicating the kind of the containing namespace.
  - The header also contains the <name> of the containing namespace.
- A namespace is a structure that enforces unique names on its contents.
- The most common namespace for structural diagrams (and use case diagrams) is the package (pkg).
- A package is an organizing namespace that has an upper-left named tab.
- Interaction diagrams use a <kind> of sd.
- The Diagram Kind is based on the diagram contents; the <kind> in the diagram header is the type of owning namespace.
- Diagrams can have comments and constraints which use a note shape with a folded down upper-right corner.
- Comments connect to the annotated elements and constraints connect to their constrained elements by a dashed line with no adornments.

CHAPTER 5

Questions for Chapter 4

1. How many UML 2.5 diagrams are there?
   A. 6
   B. 7
   C. 9
   D. 13
   E. 14
2. Besides OMG, which organization publishes the UML specifications?
   A. W3C
   B. IEEE
   C. ISO
   D. CCITT/ITU-T
   E. EXPRESS/STEP
3. Which diagram type is an Interaction Diagram?
   A. Activity Diagram
   B. Protocol State Machine Diagram
   C. Sequence Diagram
   D. State Machine Diagram
   E. Use Case Diagram
4. Why is the Metamodel considered an Abstract Syntax?
   A. Because all classes used in the metamodel are abstract
   B. Because the metamodel expresses syntax rules that apply no matter what surface notation or concrete syntax is used
   C. Because all classes in the specification, except for examples, are abstract data types
   D. Because it is written in MOF
5. What does the BNF used in the UML specification show?
   A. The BNF shows the surface syntax for textual fields.
   B. The BNF shows the Business Notation Format used within UML.
   C. The BNF shows unambiguously parsable textual fields.
   D. The BNF shows how the textual fields relate to the abstract syntax.

6. How does the UML specification indicate the abstract syntax?
   A. UML uses Extended Backus-Naur Form (EBNF).
   B. UML uses an LL(0) grammar.
   C. UML uses both UML structure and UML behavior diagrams.
   D. UML uses natural language English.
   E. UML uses a MOF metamodel.
7. What part of the UML specification defines the meaning of UML notation?
   A. UML expresses the meaning in UML.
   B. UML expresses the meaning in its abstract syntax.
   C. UML expresses the meaning in its concrete syntax.
   D. UML uses natural language to describe the semantics.
   E. UML expresses the meaning in BNF.
8. In the terminology of UML, what is a metamodel?
   A. The diagrams in a language
   B. A model of a modeling language
   C. A way of expressing the notation of UML
   D. The concrete syntax of UML
9. Which list contains only behavior diagrams?
   A. Communication, Component, Sequence
   B. Collaboration, Interaction, State Machine
   C. Sequence, State Machine, Timing
   D. Class, Component, Profile
   E. Component, Deployment, Use Case
10. What does the OCL used in the UML specification show?
    A. The syntax of calling objects
    B. The constraints embedded in the model
    C. The textual surface syntax
    D. The ISO change history of the document
    E. The format to exchange UML models
11. What is the XMI in the UML specification used for?
    A. The textual surface syntax
    B. The constraints embedded in the model
    C. To express models for interchange purposes
    D. The ITU format to express models
12. Which diagram emphasizes the exchange of messages or events among peer participants?
    A. Sequence
    B. State Machine
    C. Collaboration
    D. Timing

13. Examine the sample lines below.

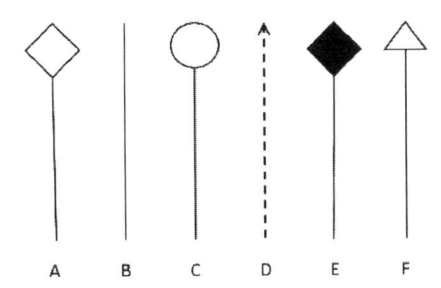

Which line indicates a *composition* relationship?
A. A
B. B
C. C
D. D
E. E
F. F

14. Which list contains only structure diagrams?
A. Communication, Component, Sequence
B. Collaboration, Interaction, State Machine
C. Sequence, State Machine, Timing
D. Class, Component, Profile
E. Component, Deployment, Use Case

15. Examine the sample lines below.

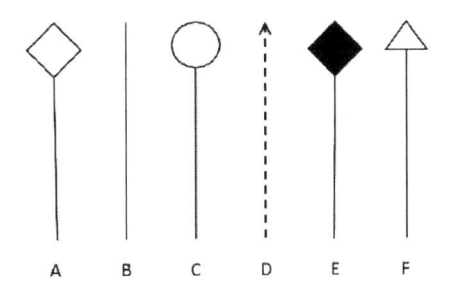

Which line indicates a *depends/dependency* relationship?
A. A
B. B
C. C
D. D
E. E
F. F

16. Examine the metamodel diagram below, where the multiplicities were replaced by ❶ and ❷ as placeholders.

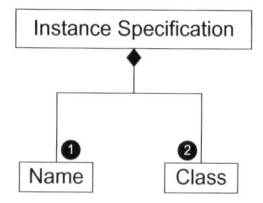

What multiplicity values should be used for ❶ and ❷ if we want the Instance Specification to be correct for UML, which states that the name is optional and there can be zero or more classes?

A. ❶ 1   ❷ 0+
B. ❶ 0..1 ❷ 0..*
C. ❶ 0..* ❷ 0,1,2,...
D. ❶ 0..1 ❷ 0..More
E. ❶ ?   ❷ 0..*
F. ❶ 0/1   ❷ 0..∞

17. The heading on a diagram is stored in what shape?
    A. A regular pentagon
    B. An irregular rectangle
    C. An irregular pentagon
    D. A tab

18. Which of the following diagrams contain a properly diagramed comment?

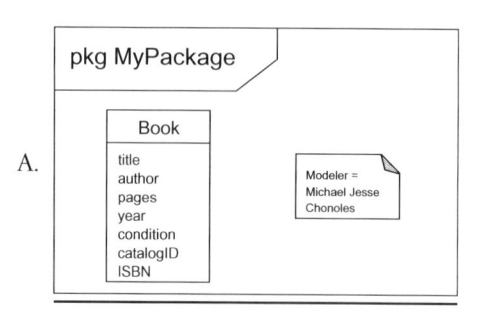

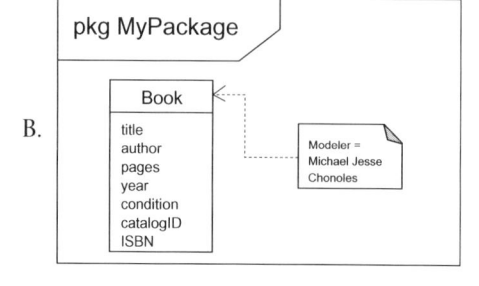

C.

[Diagram: pkg MyPackage containing Book class (title, author, pages, year, condition, catalogID, ISBN) with a dashed line to a note "Modeler = Michael Jesse Chonoles"]

D.

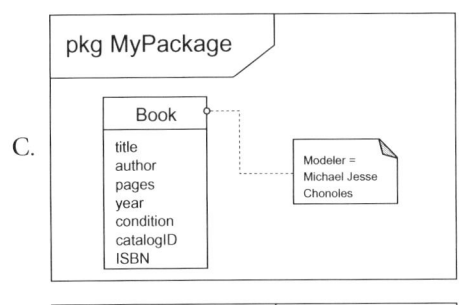

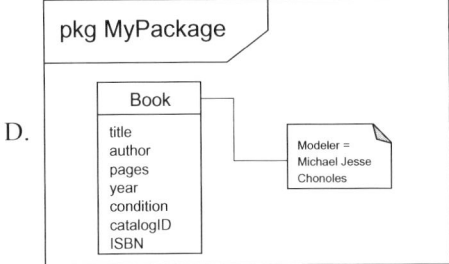

[Diagram: pkg MyPackage containing Book class (title, author, pages, year, condition, catalogID, ISBN) with a solid line to a note "Modeler = Michael Jesse Chonoles"]

ANSWERS FOR CHAPTER 4

1. How many UML 2.5 diagrams are there?
   A. 6
   B. 7
   C. 9
   D. 13
   E. **14**

   Discussion:
   A—No.
   B—No, the Foundation Exam only covers seven UML diagrams, though you need to know the names and purposes of them all. The seven covered diagrams are Activity, Class, Object, Package, Sequence, State Machine, and Use Case diagrams. Not all details or variants of these diagrams are covered on the first exam. The not yet-covered diagrams are Communication, Component, Composite Structure, Deployment, Interaction Overview, Profile, and Timing diagrams. Therefore, if you only counted the diagrams covered, you would get this wrong.
   C—No, there were nine diagrams in UML 1.x.
   D—No, there were 13 diagrams in UML 2.1.1.
   E—Yes, UML 2.2 added a 14th diagram, the Profile diagram.
   These test the currency of your knowledge.

2. Besides OMG, which organization publishes the UML specifications?
   A. W3C
   B. IEEE
   C. **ISO**
   D. CCITT/ITU-T
   E. EXPRESS/STEP

   Discussion:
   A, B, D, and E—Incorrect. These are all standards bodies with different portfolios
   C—Yes, ISO   JTC-1   SC-7 (International Organization for Standardization, Joint Technical Committee on Information Technology, Subcommittee on Software and Systems Engineering) also publishes the UML specifications. OMG, using the PAS process (Publically Available Specification), submits the UML specification for approval to become ISO specs, with numbers like ISO/IEC 1950xx:20yy.
   By the way, if you order your UML standard from ISO it will cost you much money, perhaps as much as $400. If you download it from OMG, it is free.

3. Which diagram type is an Interaction Diagram?
   A. Activity Diagram
   B. Protocol State Machine Diagram
   C. **Sequence Diagram**
   D. State Machine Diagram
   E. Use Case Diagram

   Discussion:
   A—No, an Activity diagram is a type of behavior diagram, but not an Interaction Diagram.
   B—No, a Protocol State Machine Diagram is a special type of State Machine Diagram. Despite the name, a Protocol State Machine diagram is not considered a separate diagram type. A State Machine Diagram is a behavior diagram, but not an Interaction Diagram.
   C—Yes, the Sequence Diagram is type of Interaction Diagram, which is a type of behavior diagram
   D—No, a State Machine Diagram is a behavior diagram but not an Interaction Diagrams
   E—No, a Use Case Diagram is a behavior diagram but not an Interaction Diagram

4. Why is the Metamodel considered an Abstract Syntax?
   A. Because all classes used in the metamodel are abstract
   B. **Because the metamodel expresses syntax rules that apply no matter what surface notation or concrete syntax is used**

C. Because all classes in the specification, except for examples, are abstract data types
D. Because it is written in MOF

Discussion:
A—No, they are not generally abstract in the typical meaning of abstract.
B—Yes, the Metamodel shows the required relationships among model elements, without specifying the necessary notation.
C—No, they are not abstract data types.
D—No, the MOF is a Meta-Object Facility, but not automatically a Metamodel because of it.

5. What does the BNF used in the UML specification show?
   A. **The BNF shows the surface syntax for textual fields.**
   B. The BNF shows the Business Notation Format used within UML.
   C. The BNF shows unambiguously parsable textual fields.
   D. The BNF shows how the textual fields relate to the abstract syntax.

   Discussion:
   A—Yes, many of the textual fields with UML have BNF to show you possible legal expressions.
   B—No, Business Notation Format begins with the initials BNF, but it is not an expression used within UML.
   C—No, There are no requirements that UML Textual notation is unambiguously parsable. For example, a modeler can use special characters within a property name, such as ":" for which the BNF indicates a special purpose (to precede the type of a property). This is, of course, very bad naming practice.
   D—No, the BNF only shows legal textual fields.

6. How does the UML specification indicate the abstract syntax?
   A. UML uses Extended Backus-Naur Form (EBNF).
   B. UML uses an LL(0) grammar.
   C. UML uses both UML structure and UML behavior diagrams.
   D. UML uses natural language English.
   E. **UML uses a MOF metamodel.**

   Discussion:
   A—No, UML uses BNF (not EBNF) to show the textual surface format.
   B—No, a LL(0) grammar is parsable by a LL(0) parser. It is a formal grammar that parses the token input from left to right. The zero indicates that it doesn't need to do any token look ahead. This does not describe the abstract syntax of UML, which UML does by MOF diagrams.

C—No, the abstract syntax only uses the MOF, which is a subset of UML structure diagrams.
D—No, the abstract syntax uses MOF diagrams, not English.
E—Yes, correct.

7. What part of the UML specification defines the meaning of UML notation?
   A. UML expresses the meaning in UML.
   B. UML expresses the meaning in its abstract syntax.
   C. UML expresses the meaning in its concrete syntax.
   D. **UML uses natural language to describe the semantics.**
   E. UML expresses the meaning in BNF.

   Discussion:
   A—No, the meaning of UML diagrams is in its relationship to elements outside of the model, either real-world or implementation elements. You can express the meaning of UML without some references to an external world.
   B—No, the abstract syntax is a grammar, and does not capture meaning.
   C—No, the concrete syntax, the notation or text, is just a notation on a diagram.
   D—No, the BNF is a type of grammar of the surface textual syntax, indicating legal strings.
   E—Yes, the UML specification uses natural language text (English) to explain the meaning along with examples.

8. In the terminology of UML, what is a metamodel?
   A. The diagrams in a language
   B. **A model of a modeling language**
   C. A way of expressing the notation of UML
   D. The concrete syntax of UML

   Discussion:
   A—No, the diagrams in a language is part of the notation.
   B—Yes, a model of a model. It expresses the abstract syntax or grammar of UML.
   C—No, the notation, is given in textual descriptions and in examples, not in a metamodel approach.
   D—No, the concrete syntax of UML is shown in notation and in BNF.

9. Which list contains only behavior diagrams?
   A. Communication, Component, Sequence
   B. Collaboration, Interaction, State Machine
   C. **Sequence, State Machine, Timing**
   D. Class, Component, Profile
   E. Component, Deployment, Use Case

Discussion:
A—No, behavior diagram, structure diagram, behavior diagram
B—No, not a current diagram type in UML—Though it was a behavior diagram in UML 1.x, behavior diagram, behavior diagram
C—Yes, behavior diagram, behavior diagram, behavior diagram
D—No, structure diagram, structure diagram, structure diagram
E—No, structure diagram, structure diagram, behavior diagram

10. What does the OCL used in the UML specification show?
    A. The syntax of calling objects
    B. **The constraints embedded In the model**
    C. The textual surface syntax
    D. The ISO change history of the document
    E. The format to exchange UML models

    Discussion:
    A—No
    B—Yes, UML uses the Object Constraint Language (OCL) to express constraints
    C—No, the textual surface syntax is shown in BNF
    D—No, the change history is captured by other means
    E—No, UML uses XMI (XML Metadata Interchange) to exchange models

11. What is the XMI in the UML specification used for?
    A. The textual surface syntax
    B. The constraints embedded In the model
    C. **To express models for interchange purposes**
    D. The ITU format to express models

    Discussion:
    A—No, the UML specification uses BNF to express textual surface syntax.
    B—No, the UML specification uses OCL to express constraints.
    C—Yes, the XML Metadata Interchange (XMI), an OMG standard, is used to exchange models. Some tools use XMI for their internal representation of the UML model
    D—No, the ITU is a telecommunications standards body.

12. Which diagram emphasizes the exchange of messages or events among peer participants?
    A. **Sequence**
    B. State Machine
    C. Collaboration
    D. Timing

Discussion:
A—Yes, a Sequence Diagram shows the Interaction of participants using message or events.
B—No, a State Machine diagram shows the life history of an object based on responses to incoming events.
C—No, a Collaboration is a special usage of a Composite Structure diagram, but it is not a diagram in itself. It can define the participants for a Sequence Diagram but does not show behavior. A Collaboration diagram was also the UML 1.x precursor to the current Communication diagram.
D—No, a Timing diagram emphasizes time and timing constraints.

13. Examine the sample lines below.

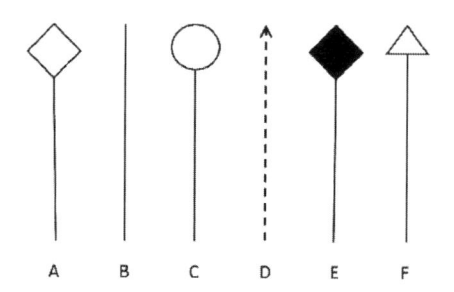

   A B C D E F

   Which line indicates a composition relationship?
   A. A
   B. B
   C. C
   D. D
   E. **E**
   F. F

   Discussion:
   A—No, this is an aggregation relationship.
   B—No, this is an association.
   C—No, this is a provided interface.
   D—No, this is a dependency relationship.
   E—Yes, a solid diagram indicates a composition relationship, with the diamond end indicating the "whole" side and the unadorned end indicating the "part" side.
   F—No, this is a generalization/specialization relationship.

14. Which list contains only structure diagrams?
    A. Communication, Component, Sequence
    B. Collaboration, Interaction, State Machine
    C. Sequence, State Machine, Timing
    D. **Class, Component, Profile**
    E. Component, Deployment, Use Case

Discussion:
A—No, behavior, structure, behavior
B—No, not a current diagram type in UML—Though it was a behavior diagram in UML 1.x, behavior, behavior
C—No, behavior, behavior, behavior
D—Yes, structure, structure, structure
E—No, structure, structure, behavior

15. Examine the sample lines below.

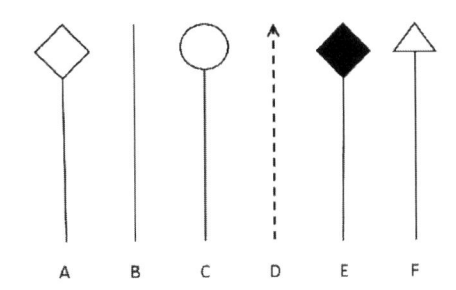

Which line indicates a *depends/dependency* relationship?

A. A
B. B
C. C
D. <u>D</u>
E. E
F. F

Discussion:
A—No, this is an aggregation relationship
B—No, this is an association
C—No, this is a provided interface
D—Yes, this is a dependency relationship. It usually has an arrow at one end
E—No, a solid diagram indicates a composition relationship, with the diamond end indicating the "whole" side and the unadorned end indicating the "part" side
F—No, this is a generalization/specialization relationship

16. Examine the metamodel diagram below, where the multiplicities were replaced by ❶ and ❷ as placeholders.

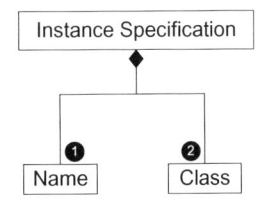

What multiplicity values should be used for ❶ and ❷ if we want the Instance Specification to be correct for UML, which states that the name is optional and there can be zero or more classes?

A. ❶ 1 ❷ 0+
B. ❶ 0..1 ❷ 0..*
C. ❶ 0..* ❷ 0,1,2,...
D. ❶ 0..1 ❷ 0..More
E. ❶ ? ❷ 0..*
F. ❶ 0/1 ❷ 0..∞

Discussion:

To summarize what we have covered so far, a multiplicity range is expressed by LowValue. HighValue. If the LowValue is the same as the HighValue, you only need to show one value. The * indicates "or more" or "unlimited"

Some of the common multiplicities are:
  1 Mandatory   0..1 Optional   1..* One or more   0..* Zero or more

A—No, ❶ mandatory (1)   ❷ not legal notation
B—Yes, ❶ optional (0..1)   ❷ zero or more (0..*)
C—No, ❶ zero or more (0..*) ❷ not legal notation
D—No, ❶ optional (0..1)   ❷ not legal notation
E—No, ❶ not legal notation   ❷ zero or more (0..*)
F—No, ❶ not legal notation   ❷ not legal notation

17. The heading on a diagram is stored in what shape?
    A. A regular pentagon
    B. An irregular rectangle
    C. **An irregular pentagon**
    D. A tab

    Discussion:
    A—No, a regular pentagon has all the sides equal in length.
    B—No, I'm not sure what an irregular rectangle would be. Is a regular rectangle a square?
    C—Yes, it's a 5-sided shape.
    D—No, a tab is used to contain the name of a package.

18. Which of the following diagrams contain a properly diagramed comment?

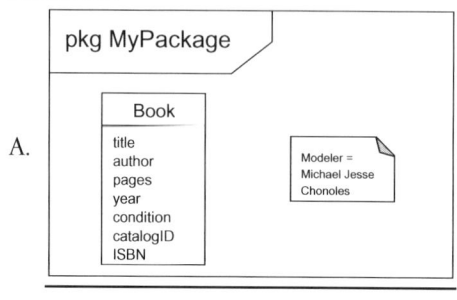

    A.

B.

[Diagram: pkg MyPackage containing Book class (title, author, pages, year, condition, catalogID, ISBN) with a dashed annotation line ending in an arrowhead connecting to a note "Modeler = Michael Jesse Chonoles"]

C.

[Diagram: pkg MyPackage containing Book class (title, author, pages, year, condition, catalogID, ISBN) with a dashed annotation line ending in a circle connecting to a note "Modeler = Michael Jesse Chonoles"]

D.

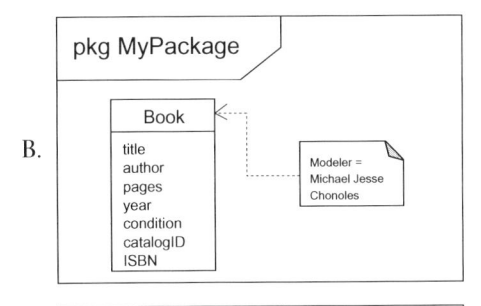

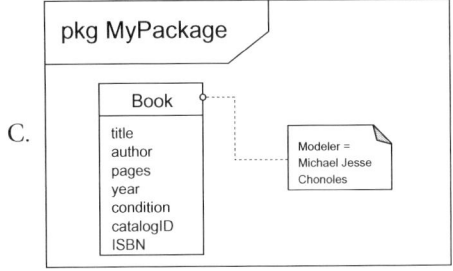

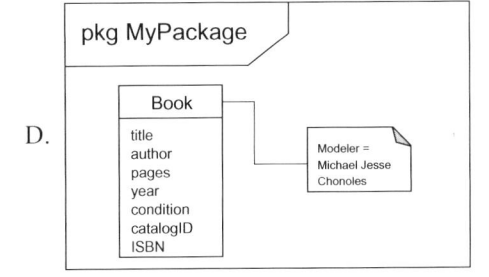

[Diagram: pkg MyPackage containing Book class (title, author, pages, year, condition, catalogID, ISBN) with a solid annotation line connecting to a note "Modeler = Michael Jesse Chonoles"]

Discussion:
Remember, this applies to constraints also.
A—Yes, the annotation line is optional, especially if the comment applies to the entire diagram.
B—No, there is no arrowhead on the annotation line.
C—No, the circle at the end of the annotation line is obsolete
D—No, the annotation line, if it is used, is a dashed line.

CHAPTER 6

Objects and Classes

6.1 FINDING OBJECTS AND CLASSES

Classes are the most common UML modeling element on all projects. The other modeling elements describe some behavior, internal structure, arrangement, relationships, or organization of one or more classes from various perspectives.[1]

In the implementation layer, it is the objects that do the work, but even there, the classes define features, (properties and behaviors) that the OBJECTS exhibit. We sometimes think of classes as factories or prototypes from which you can generate objects. A class might define Library Patron in a system for a library. We would then say that a **Library Patron** has the properties (ATTRIBUTES) of name, physical address, email address, and date of birth. At run time, when we create an instance of **Library Patron** from the class definition, we have the opportunity to give values to these attributes fields for the instance. We call the fields that hold the values in the object, SLOTS.

Classes can be also thought of as the common denominator to a *set* description. In a nonmathematical sense, a set is a collection of elements that have something in common. Each of the set's elements is objects. A set of **US Presidents**, contains the instances of George Washington, Thomas Jefferson, and Abraham Lincoln (among others), with some fields of name, birthdate, year elected, and political party. Each element of the set, that is, each object, would have values for those fields. A class can also be regarded as a database table with associated field definitions. Each object would be an instance of a

---

[1]This is a historical legacy based on the primacy of object-oriented methodologies. Most popular OOPL support this strongly-typed paradigm, e.g., Ada, C++, C#, Java, Objective-C, and Python. Some OOPL do not use classes, or focus less on classes; these are weakly, dynamically typed, or prototype-based languages. Of course, some of OOPLs use many different object-oriented approaches. UML can work with most, though it appears to be more natural with strongly typed, class-focused programing languages.

row (also called a record) of the table, with values allowed for each field. In these cases, each field name indicates an attribute.

With classes being the fundamental elements in UML and many object-oriented programing languages (OOPL), we need to know how to find the classes that will be useful to create. To do that properly, we need to identify the things that these classes will be the pattern to make, that is, the objects.

In some cases, the choice of objects is relatively easy. By investigating the real world, we can note the relevant real-world objects, usually obvious because we can point to them, manipulate them, and name them. In a library, each book has properties, such as a name, author, publisher, copyright, and catalog number. Each book is distinguishable from other books, even if they have identical properties, for each book has a separate existence for the others.[2] We can manipulate each book. Each book can be borrowed, returned, recalled, destroyed, accessioned,[3] and deaccessioned.

Objects that aren't physical may be harder to identify. Through a process of REIFICATION[4] (making something a thing), we can look at some persistent relationships as objects also. Consider a borrowing, it has a book, a patron, a due date as properties and has its own unique identity, and it can be created or removed.

Some of the features that make for a successful candidate object are as follows:

- Relevant to the problem at hand
- Can be pointed to, literally or figuratively
- Crisp boundary/distinguishable from others
- Has intrinsic identity
- Has some form of persistence
- Nameable with a singular noun or noun phrase
- Has properties, but is not a property itself
- Has behavior, but is not a behavior itself
- Can be created, destroyed, or manipulated

---

[2] There is a philosophic principle, called Leibniz's Law, or the *principle of the indiscernibility of identicals*, which claims that to be separate objects, there must be at least one property that is different between them. Generally, we assume that the location in space (or in computer memory) is different for otherwise identical objects. This sort of consideration is rarely necessary to consider by real modelers.
[3] Accessioning is the act of recording the addition of a new item to a collection, such as a library, museum, gallery, or archive. Every added item must be accessioned and the data entered in the accession list. Each accessioned item usually gets a unique number indicating the order of accessing. In some libraries with closed stacks, the items are stored in accession order. Deaccessioning is the process of selling or otherwise disposing of an item from a collection. After being accessioned, an item may be catalogued. The catalogue usually contains the accession number.
[4] On the basis of the pattern of the word deification, reification means "making into a thing."

We will discuss some of these in more detail later. However, remember that it is always possible to contrive circumstances where apparent violations of the guidelines might make sense. It is your job as a modeler to determine if this is one of the rare justifiable cases.

From the sample, exemplar objects we find in the real world or legacy system we can select some relevant ones and group them by commonality by looking at the features that are relevant to our project or domain. We call these natural groupings classes. So examining the lending library, we might group them into books, videos, library cards, patrons, and librarians. These are the candidate classes of our system.

Some people recommend reading the PROBLEM STATEMENT or the REQUIREMENTS of the project and underlining all the nouns and noun phrases, and starting with that list as the candidate objects or classes. This approach might work if you are part of a team working on an entirely new project with no preexisting system or domain experts. Realistically on many real projects, with a multiple of pages in the problem statement, this approach can be a bit unwieldy, but choosing the key nouns in the system description can be a good start.

When we are looking at a collection of exemplar objects, we usually have no problem finding useful classes. This process is called CLASSIFICATION and appears to be innate in humans. We know better because these features are not salient in a lending library context. Somehow, we detect the books and videos do not behave differently in any relevant way depending on their color or the initials of their publisher.[5]

The criteria that we gave earlier are still practical. A good class is a singular noun and not a mass noun (or noncountable noun). If we say, "a house is made of bricks," the individual bricks are objects and could be named or counted, and the class they fall into is **Brick**. On the other hand, if we insist that "a house is made of brick," we are using the mass noun brick, which is a property, as when we say that we have a "brick house." For consistency, we say that the class is **Brick** and not Bricks, always sticking to the singular form. A class name is usually bold, singular, and beginning with a capital letter.

A class and its objects must represent things that have a crisp boundary and that are distinguishable from others. In most systems, clouds or drops of water do not make good objects because they merge on contact. Similarly, abstractions, such as friendship, do not make good classes because it is hard to point to it.

---

[5]This problem of how this done relatively consistently by humans has been discussed since Plato. Think of it as a miracle that makes analysis work.

Not all salient singular distinguishable nouns should be in your first list of objects and classes. Consider moments in time: noon, conception, particle decay. They are not objects; they are not persistent, they are events. Therefore, if we underlined nouns to start our work off, the events would be a separate category that we identify. These will be useful later in behavior diagrams, such as state machines.

A noun phrase may be a good candidate class or for a separate subclass. We did this with diagrams as we depicted previously in Fig. 4.8. A **Class Diagram** is a separate class as is **State Machine Diagram**. Not all noun phrases are good candidates for objects. For example, consider that a **Reference Book**,[6] is a separate subclass of book because it has different behaviors (e.g., it cannot be borrowed) and would be a good candidate, but a Borrowed Book is really a Book that is in the state of *being borrowed*. Put this phrase aside for later consideration as a possible state for a book to be in a state machine.

Sometimes the record of an event is necessary to track or manipulate and has properties of its own. Therefore, despite these being events or operations, we convert them to objects so they can be manipulated, though we probably keep them also in the model as events and as operations. We mentioned that this was possible with **Borrowing**. The process of treating a nonobject as an object is REIFICATION[7]. Reification is very common when an event or operation creates a persistent relationship between two objects. A purchase at a supermarket, a marriage, and a person joining the library (becoming a patron) are all events or operations that need to be tracked with objects, of the class of: **Purchase**, **Marriage**, and **Membership**.

If you find roles that people play in your understanding of the problem, place them aside for later consideration as Actors in the Use Case diagram. If there are properties of the roles that need to be tracked, such as `fullName`, or `memberID`, this is a sign that these roles should be considered as both classes and actors.

POINTS TO REMEMBER

- An object or instance is a relevant, nameable entity with crisp boundaries and intrinsic identity.
  - An object is distinguishable from other entities.
  - An object may be created, destroyed, or manipulated.

---

[6]In many lending libraries, there is category of books called reference books that do not circulate. They are usually oriented to research, expensive, and limited to only be used on the library premises.
[7]Based on the pattern of the word deification, reification means "making into a thing".

- A class represents a noun or noun phrase that names a potential group of objects.
  - Finding the class from the objects is a process called classification.
  - Finding an object from the class is a process called instantiation.
- One way of finding objects and classes is to read the problem statement or the project requirements and select the relevant nouns or noun phrase.
  - Include persistent records or history of events or behaviors as potential classes.
  - Put the mass nouns, roles, points in time, and conditions aside for later considerations as attributes, actors, messages and events, and states.

6.1.1 Attributes

When we find a class that we like, we place it in our model. We do this typically by placing it on some diagram in the standard box-shaped form. When placed on a diagram, the first compartment of the display of the class is the Name of the class. The name compartment is required in all displays of the class. Below the name compartment is the attribute's compartment. The attributes are the properties of the class in which we are interested. As the class's display element is part of the view, we can omit the attribute compartment from the diagram, though the associated attributes are still there in the model. We can omit from the attribute compartment, any of the attributes if we wish because perhaps only some attributes are relevant to the current view. If we wind up omitting all the attributes, we might as well even omit the entire attribute compartment for that class from the diagram.

An attribute is typically also a noun, but it is a property and usually not an independent entity. For example, the copyright year is not an independent thing, it is a property of a book. These properties are things that you could imagine asking an instance for the current value. "O[8] currentBook, what is your title?" A request for the current value of an attribute that doesn't change anything is called a QUERY. You may ask the currentBook to change a value of a property for you, "O currentBook, please change your status to Overdue."

In Fig. 6.1, we depict four views of the same Book class. The first view shows four attributes (title, author, year, and accessionNo). Attributes generally start with a lower-case letter.[9] Each of these attributes is typed either as a String or as an Integer. The TYPE follows the attribute name and usually begins with an initial capital. If the type appears, the ":" is required to precede the type name for parsing.

---

[8]"O" is the English vocative indicator of direct address, used before the name or noun phrase identifying the being or thing you are addressing. It does not mean the same things as "Oh" which is an exclamation or sound of interruption.

[9]There are some exceptions. If the name of an attribute is an abbreviation that is normally capitalized, it may acceptable to start the attribute with a capital. For example, ISBN, an attribute of the Book class, is probably best spelled ISBN and not iSBN.

Book	Book	Book	Book
Title: String Author: String Year: Integer accessionNo: Integer	Title: String Author: String Year: Integer ...	Title: String Author: String Year: Integer	attributes Title: String Author: String Year: Integer

FIGURE 6.1
Four views of the same class.

The third view has the `accessionNo` attribute elided, so that it must have been suppressed in the view. The second view uses an ELLIPSIS (...). This is an explicit mark that there is at least one elided item. I call it the Nah-Nah symbol because it teases that we have something in the model that we are not going to show you here. When the ... appears, it must be the last or only item in the list.

In the fourth view of the `Book` class, we again show only three attributes, but we have also given the compartment its proper name, "attributes." Compartments have specific names, but they are optional to show. When compartment names appear, they are lower-case, centered, and plural.

If any of these symbols appear on the same diagram or elsewhere in the same namespace, they refer to the same **Book** class, which has, at least, four attributes in the model. On the basis of previous occurrences of the **Book** class in earlier chapters, we have at least five missing attributes that are not shown in any of these views.

6.1.2 Operations

Operations are relevant behaviors that instances of the class can be asked to do, endure, initiate, or relevant behaviors that can be done on (or to) the book. If we are looking at the Problem Statement, we are looking for verbs.

For the `Book` class in the Library, beginning modelers often choose operations such as `read()`, `open()`, V, and `turn page()`. This is not completely wrong; it is natural as these are behaviors that people can do to a book in the library. However, we can perform these behaviors on any book, anywhere. Moreover, they do not change any interesting state of the book or anything else in the context of the library. Take a moment to consider what behaviors of *interest* in a lending library that a book can do, endure, or initiate.

As a `Book` is not an active class, that is, it does not do anything by itself, we need to look at behaviors that people or other active classes can do to the `Book`. A possible list would likely include `checkout()`, `reserve()`, and `accession()`. In addition, from my experience in modeling, I can tell you that whenever you have an operation, look for variations on that operation, such as, the opposite or negation of the operation. Therefore, we would want to

Book	Book	Book	Book
check-out()	operations	check-out(bdate, borrower)	check-out(bdate:Date, borrower:Member): Date
return()	check-out()	return(rdate)	return(rdate:Date): Cost
reserve()	return()		
cancelReserve()	...		

FIGURE 6.2
The book class with operations.

include besides `checkout`, `reserve`, and `accession`, the operations of `return`, `cancel reserve`, and `deaccession`.

In object-oriented theory, as the METHODS (the behaviors behind the operations) are owned by the class and are internal to the class, calling an operation on an object is a request and not a command. The methods do not appear on the class diagram, though they may be explored in detail on a behavior diagram.

Beneath the attribute compartment is another compartment for operations. Operations are usually depicted beginning with a lower-case letter and a trailing "()." The () may contain the operation's ARGUMENTS (called PARAMETERS within UML). In Fig. 6.2, we show four different views of the `Book` class with operations. In all these views, we have elided the attributes compartment.

In the first view, we show the four interesting operations.

In the second view from the left, we display the operations compartment name, "operations" and use the ellipses, to indicate some operations are missing.

In the third view, we display the ARGUMENTS or PARAMETERS for the operations. When a Book is checked-out, we need to collect the `bdate` (borrowing date) and `borrower`. When a `Book` is returned, we do not need to know who returned it, just the `rdate` (return date).

In the rightmost view of the `Book`, we supply types for the arguments. Both `bdate` and `rdate` are of type `Date`, and the borrower argument is of type `Member` (a member of the library). We also show the return values for these operations. When a `Book` is checked-out, we are returned a `Due Date` of type `Date`. If the `Book` was overdue when we return the `Book`, a `Cost` is calculated, usually a per day fine. Return types, as any types when they are used, are preceded by a ":" and both follow the operation string.

In UML, if we want to show that nothing is returned, we don't put any ":<Type>" after the operation definition (for example, no null type). Though not part of UML because it would be programing language dependent, it is often possible to add type modifiers related to pointers, such as "*" and "&," depending on the tool. UML also does not distinguish between passing values *byVal* or *byRef*.

6.1.3 Referring to a Member Feature

Sometimes, if there are many elements with same named attribute, it becomes difficult to refer to the correct one. This could be in speech or in writing a constraint on the value. Imagine that there is a `Video` class that also has a `year` attribute. If we want to refer to the `year` attribute on `Book`, we would say "`Book.year`." To refer to the `year` attribute on the `Video` class, we would say "`Video.year`." If we want to refer to the slot on a book instance, we would use the name of the object, for example, "`myBook.year`" or "`myVideo.year`."

This "." notation is similar to what is used in many programing languages and is part of the Object Constraint Language (OCL). It is part of the path identification string used as a naming scope operator.

This the exact approach also used to refer to a behavioral member of a class. If we wanted to refer to the operation, `borrow()`, that might appear on both the `Book` and `Video` class. We would refer to the operation as "`Book.borrow()`" and "`Video.borrow()`." If we wanted to invoke the borrow operation on the `myBook` instance or on the `myVideo` instance, we would, in a similar manner, use `myBook.borrow()` and `myVideo.borrow()`.

6.1.4 Static Features

By default in UML, all features are considered to be instance scoped. If you refer to an attribute, you can get the value that the instance has, `myVideo.date` retrieves the value the `myVideo` instance holds for `date`. To borrow a book, you use `myBook.borrow()` and the operation applies to the `myBook` instance.

You can also specific that a feature is a classifier-scoped feature. This means that the value is defined once for the class. For a static attribute, this can be thought of as each instance of the class always sharing the same value. Alternatively, the class has a separate location for itself containing the attribute and value. A static operation is an operation that applies to the class as a whole. We show static (class-scope) by underlining the feature.

In Fig. 6.3, we depict both a static attribute (numPatron) and a static operation (incrementnumPatron). We would imagine in a fully detailed Patron, the incrementnumPatron would be called during the creation of a new **Patron**.

Patron
+name: FullName -numPatron: Integer = 0
-incrementnumPatron() ...

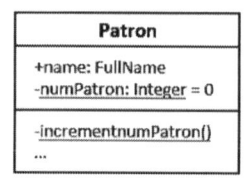

FIGURE 6.3

Static attributes and operations.

Thus, the value of `numPatron` would be the total count of the number of **Patrons** in the library.

The underline is an example of an attribute and operation adornment.

POINTS TO REMEMBER

- Properties of a class are called attributes.
  - They are displayed beneath the name compartment in an "attributes" compartment.
  - The form an attribute takes is <attributeName> : <Type> though just using the <attributeName> is sufficient.
  - An attribute is usually followed by ":" and the type of the attribute usually capitalized.
  - Each attribute on a class enables a slot for values on every instance (object) of the class (except for static attributes).
- Behaviors of a class are called operations.
  - They are displayed beneath the attributes compartment in an "operations" compartment.
  - The algorithm for the operation is called a "method." It does not appear on a class diagram but may be shown in an activity or other behavior diagram.
  - An operation can have parameters, also called arguments; they follow the same syntax that an attribute uses.
  - An operation should always contain a "()" to indicate where the parameters should be shown, even if there are none.
  - The operation may have a return type, at the end of the definition. The return type is a trailing ":" followed by the type name.
- Attributes and operations of a class are both called features.
  - A feature may be elided and suppressed from any or all diagram.
  - A compartment may be elided, though if both attributes and operations appear they must appear in that order.
  - The last feature in a compartment being displayed can be replaced by "...," which indicates that there are elided features elsewhere.
  - You can refer to a feature by specifying the <className>.featureName.
- Features are normally instance scoped, meaning that instances have slots for their values and that operations work on the instance.
- To indicate class scope, the feature is underlined. The attribute value is shared by the instances and the operation works on the class.

6.2 TYPES

A type specifies a set of values that an element can have. This set can be potentially infinite in size, such as when we talk about `Integers`. Alternatively, it can be limited in size such as when we talk about `Boolean`, which has only two values, `True` and `False`. We have used the data types of `Integer`, `String`, `Date`, and `Cost`. Classes are also types, because our class of `Book` (or `Video`) defines a set of possible books or videos. Each instance of `Book` must be compatible with the defined attributes and would have slots for values of these attributes. `Member` is also a type, as a class is a type.

6.2.1 Class Versus Datatype

Sometimes, there is confusion about whether something is a class or a dataType. They are both types, but they do behave differently. The major difference being IDENTITY.

Imagine having two identical books, with all their attributes being the same; we would still say that we have two books. This one, and that one. We say that objects/class instances have their own inherent identity. With dataTypes, the identity resides in the value. Two copyright years with the same value are the same, because their values are the same. This becomes apparent as it applies to copying and comparing. If we had the two identical books and compared them, we would still say that they are *different* books However, if we compare two identical copyright years, we would say they are the *same* year.

Two items with the same cost have identical costs, but the changing one of the costs does not change the other cost. Their identity was contingent and not inherent.

6.2.2 Primitive Types

A type specifies a set of values that an element can have. We have used the data types of Integer and String. Classes are also types because our class of Book (or Video) defines a set of possible books or videos. Each instance of Book must be compatible with attributes defined and would have slots for values for these attributes.

There are a small number of primitive types defined in UML that might be useful to know. We show them in Fig. 6.4. Some tools will also offer Date and Time as primitive types.

These UML types are not meant to match any particular programing language type. An Integer is not four bytes, two bytes, or eight bytes. It is arbitrarily long. A Boolean is not 1, 4, or 8-b long. It is not 0 or 1. It is True or False. A String is also arbitrarily long and is not null terminated, nor does it begin with a length field.

Of course, any physical implementation of the types must match some physical reality. The modeling tools offer programing-language packages that will supply additional types that match the programing language of your choice. For example, if you choose C++, you probably will be offered int, char,

«primitive» Integer	«primitive» String	«primitive» Boolean	«primitive» Real

FIGURE 6.4
UML primitive types.

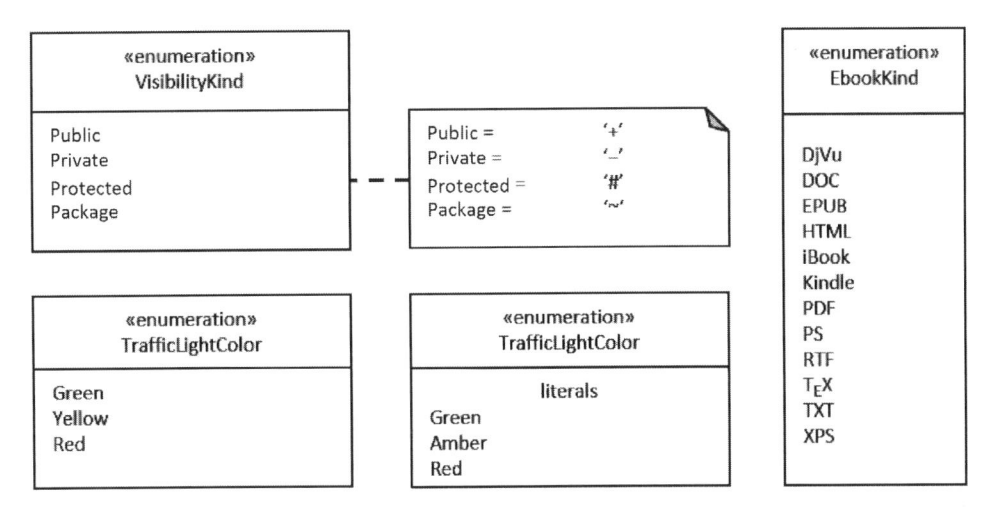

FIGURE 6.5
Sample enumerations.

`bool`, `float`, each taking up the standard number of bytes in C++. If you choose a different language package, you will be offered a different choice.

If you do not choose but later try to automatically generate code from the model, most tools will choose the closest match in the target language.[10] It might be best to do your modeling with the built-in types and have the tool do the translation at code-generation time, as this is the most portable approach. One of the advantages of modeling with UML is that you can target different implementation languages without changing the model.

6.2.3 Enumerations

Enumerations are finite-valued dataTypes.[11] Each possible value of the Enumeration type is one of the user-defined literals associated with the dataType. In Fig. 6.5, we show some sample enumerations. A common enumeration, that of `TrafficLightColor` is shown in both a US and UK style. UML uses the `VisibilityKind` to identify the visibility of attributes and operations. The `EbookKind` is a useful library domain enumeration for electronic books. The standard name for the compartment showing the enumeration literals is "literals."

---

[10]Many tools will allow you specify rules on how to make the choices of target types when implementing.
[11]It is certainly conceivable to have infinitely valued enumerated dataTypes. In UML, we treat them as infinite subsets of Integers (positive integers, negative integers, natural numbers...). We cannot construct our own infinite enumerations.

Table 6.1 UML Visibility Notation

Symbol	Visibility Kind	Description
+	Public	The member value/behavior may be seen or invoked by anyone
−	Private	The member is accessible only from within an instance of the class
#	Protected	Private, but instances of specializations of the class can also access
~	Package	Private, but peer elements in the same package can also access

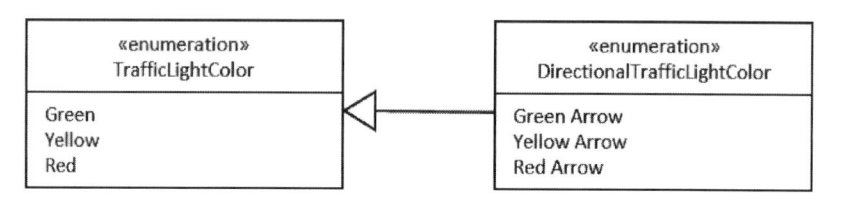

FIGURE 6.6
Inherited enumerations.

The note attached to the VisibilityKind indicates the standard symbols used in UML to identify the visibility of the feature. In a class diagram, a member, i.e., an attribute or operation, would be preceded by one of the listed symbols to indicate the visibility, as described in Table 6.1.

The VisibilityKind indicator is an example of an adornment for attributes or operations.

In the UML specification, all the enumeration type names end with "Kind," such as shown with VisibilityKind in Fig. 6.5. We followed that reasonable convention with our own enumerations, but you may follow your own approach if you want. In the figure, we included both TrafficLightColorKind and TrafficLightColourKind, to support both US and UK style traffic signals. Enumeration literals have identity only within the enumeration. If you tried to test for equality between both the traffic light Green values, you may or may not get them to show as equal, or you might just receive a type error. If you wish to refer to each color independently, you use the "." naming scope operator, as shown below.

$$\text{TrafficLightColorKind.Green} \neq \text{TrafficLightColourKind.Green} \quad (6.1)$$

Enumerations can participate in generalizations. Examine Fig. 6.6. How many literals does the DirectionalTrafficLightColor have?[12]

---

[12]Six, as there are three inherited values (green, yellow, and red).

Enumeration literals are immutable. We cannot change the value of any of the literals, so they cannot appear on the left-hand side of an assignment statement or as the return or output value of an operation. However, they can be used to set the value of an attribute or variable, or tested for in/equality (as shown in Eq. 6.1).

We do not worry about the internal representation of the enumeration literals. They could be strings, integers starting with one, or integers starting with zero, or something else. Some tools may allow you to specify values or an order to the literals for code generation, but that is not part of current UML.

6.2.4 DataTypes

Having just these few primitive types and enumerations to use is very limited. UML offers up the ability to build additional types based on the primitives. These look like classes except that they use the keyword «dataType» In Fig. 6.7, we show two dataTypes that we have constructed. We also used the " + ," public visibility, to indicate that the properties and operations of the dataType are visible outside of the dataType.

We have also added some operations to the Date datatType, to support adding days to the current date, and for comparing dates. The first operation addToDate(days:Integer) doesn't need a return type, because it updates the Date dataType value in place.

We have seen constraints in an attached note before. In Fig. 6.7, we placed constraints on the same line as the constrained property. We can also place them in a separate compartment called "constraints."

In all cases, constraints are enclosed in "{}." The constraints in Fig. 6.7 are not in the standard Boolean form, but the approach is common (and legal)

«dataType» Date
+year: Integer {>1910} +month: Integer {1..12} +day: Integer {1..31}
+addToDate(days: Integer) +deltaDays(aDate: Date): Integer +isBigger (aDate: Date): Boolean +isSmaller (aDate: Date): Boolean

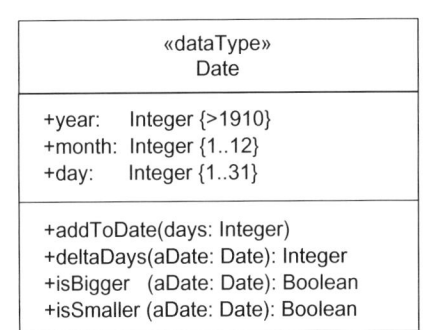

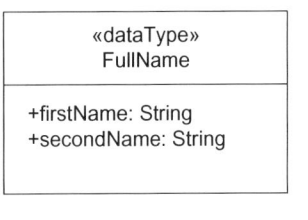

«dataType» FullName
+firstName: String +secondName: String

FIGURE 6.7

Two useful dataTypes.

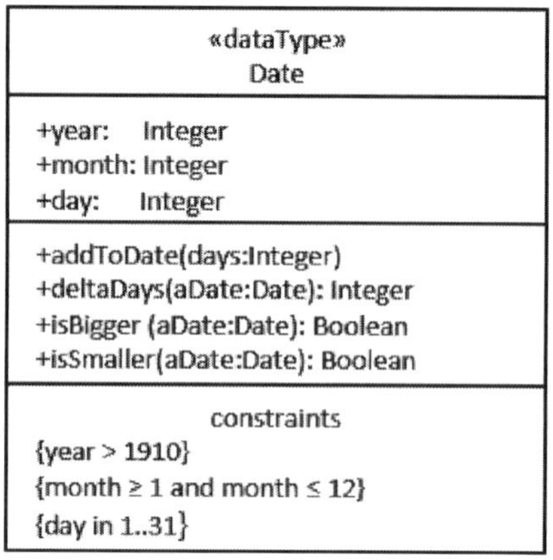

```
         «dataType»
            Date
+year:   Integer
+month:  Integer
+day:    Integer
+addToDate(days:Integer)
+deltaDays(aDate:Date): Integer
+isBigger (aDate:Date): Boolean
+isSmaller(aDate:Date): Boolean
         constraints
{year > 1910}
{month ≥ 1 and month ≤ 12}
{day in 1..31}
```

FIGURE 6.8
Constraints compartment.

when there is not enough space. To the right and in Fig. 6.8, we use the formal format.

{year > 1910}.

{month ≥ 1 and month ≤ 12}

{day in 1 ... 31}

The ".." is the standard way the UML represents an INTERVAL, from low to high.

6.2.4.1 Abstraction

A good type (dataType or class) supports an ABSTRACTION. In this context, an abstraction is a single concept that has been cleansed of physical or implementation details and using INFORMATION HIDING hides those details to prevent misuse or exposure of the details. Keeping the details hidden, by using techniques such as ENCAPSULATION, will encourage portability and clear thinking.

For example, if were to create a **Stack** class, perhaps implemented with a list internally, we would not want a user to be able to *set* or *get* at any element of the list other than the one designed at the top, see Fig. 6.9.

Some modelers will stereotype a dataType as an `AbstractDataType` (or ADT). This is not part of the standard (and not part of the test), but it is useful. An «`AbstractDataType`» declares that you have provided or prohibited all needed operations to maintain the consistency of the type. An ADT has some mathematical or architectural ABSTRACTION in mind.

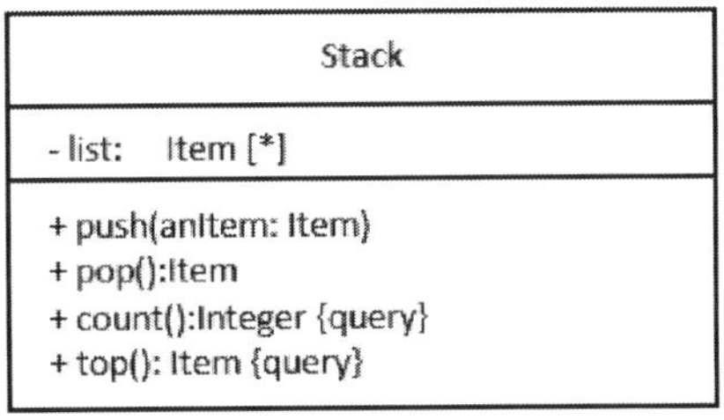

```
            Stack
  ─────────────────────────
  - list:   Item [*]
  ─────────────────────────
  + push(anItem: Item)
  + pop():Item
  + count():Integer {query}
  + top(): Item {query}
```

FIGURE 6.9
A stack.

In the stack above, the implementation approach, a list, is hidden from the outside and only "safe" operations are defined. This would prevent examining or changing Items within the stack, because it would violate the Stack abstraction.

POINTS TO REMEMBER

- Both classes and dataTypes are types. Both can contain attributes and operations.
- Instances of a class have intrinsic identity, though instances of a dataType are identical if their values are the same.
- UML has «primitive» dataTypes (e.g., Integer, String, Boolean, Real).
    - The «primitive» dataTypes do not any specified length, limit values, or precision/accuracy limits.
    - They can be mapped or replaced by language-specific types near implementation time.
- UML supports a user-defined discrete «enumeration» dataType. An «enumeration» has a "literals" compartment where all the possible values of the enumeration appear.
- You can precede an attribute or operation definition with a character literal representing the UML Visibility kind.
    - A " + " indicates public visibility. The attribute or operation can be seen and accessed from everywhere.
    - A " − " indicates private visibility. The attribute or operation can only be accessed within instances of the current class.
    - A "#" indicates protected visibility. Similar to private, but instances of subclasses can also access.
    - A " ~ " indicates package visibility. Similar to public, but only elements in the same package can access.
- The modeler may create additional classes and dataTypes, based on existing types.
- DataTypes, like classes, may have constraints, displayed within "{ }" to limit the values of the parts of the dataType.
    - DataTypes, like classes, may have operations, to support and enforce any abstraction the dataType represents.
    - DataTypes, including Enumerations, may participate in generalizations.
- Constraints can be added inline, in an attached note, or in a separate compartment. They normally have a Boolean value.

```
          Member
+name: FullName
-birthdate: Date
+/hasAdultPrivileges: Boolean
+isAdult(currentDate:Date):Boolean
```

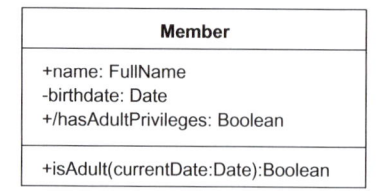

FIGURE 6.10
A class employing user-defined dataTypes.

6.3 MODIFIERS

We can tag an attribute or an operation with a modifier that changes some, usually minor, interpretation of the member. These adornments are described below.

6.3.1 Derived Properties

Now that we have useful dataTypes defined, we show that we might incorporate them. In Fig. 6.10, we depict the **Member** class that uses the `FullName` and `Date` dataTypes.

Each instance of `Member` has a `name` attribute. If I wish to refer to the `firstName` of the current member, it would be `currentMember.name.firstName`. If I wish to refer to the year that the current member was born, it would be `currentMember.birthdate.year`.

We also have another attribute on `Member`, `hasAdultPrivileges` of type `Boolean`. If you look carefully, you will see that we precede the attribute name by a slash ("/"). This has a special meaning within UML, it indicates that the attribute value is DERIVED. A derived attribute's value can be calculated as needed based on other attributes or available properties.[13]

In many libraries, the material is divided into two categories, adult vs Juvenile. If a member is underage, they are restricted from borrowing adult material. Though an adult can borrow Juvenile material, such as picture books, the Juvenile material is usually kept separate from the adult material.

We set the visibility on `name`, `hasAdultPrivileges`, and `isAdult()` to be public (+), meaning that anyone can view the values of these attributes or call the operation. We kept the `birthdate` to be private, because it is likely to be

---

[13]There are many approaches to keeping a derived attribute correct before it is used. For example, always recalculate before use, recalculate whenever any of the underlying properties change, recalculate when you're not busy, etc. As long as it correct when needed is the important thing.

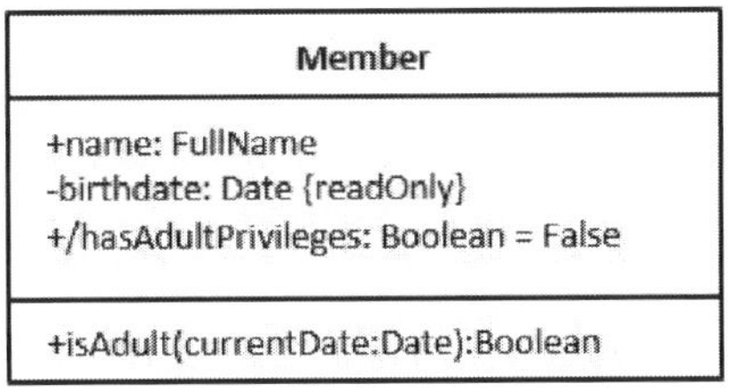

```
         ┌─────────────────────────────────────┐
         │              Member                 │
         ├─────────────────────────────────────┤
         │ +name: FullName                     │
         │ -birthdate: Date {readOnly}         │
         │ +/hasAdultPrivileges: Boolean = False│
         ├─────────────────────────────────────┤
         │ +isAdult(currentDate:Date):Boolean  │
         └─────────────────────────────────────┘
```

FIGURE 6.11
Illustrating a default value (initial value) and readOnly.

Personally Identifiable Information, that is, under US law, required to be protected from release. Even though the birthdate is private (-), it is accessible within the operation isAdult() so it can calculate the value of the hasAdultPrivileges property.

At some time, perhaps before a Member instance is about to borrow an adult book, the isAdult() operation should be called. The result would be assigned to hasAdultPrivileges. Once the member instance is declared to be an adult, the operation isAdult() does not need to be called again.[14]

It is common to name Boolean properties or operations with the form hasProperty or isInState, in order than using a True or False value is natural.

6.3.2 Default Value

6.3.2.1 Default Values for Attributes/Properties

It is also possible to assign a default value to a property. In Fig. 6.11, we modify the hasAdultPrivleges Boolean flag to have a default value of False. This means that whenever we created a new Member instance, the flag will be given an initial value of False.

This helps us because whenever the Member tries to borrow an adult book, we would check the value of the flag. If the field is False, we would then call the isAdult() operation. If the Member is an adult, then we flip the flag, so that the next time the Member tries to borrow an adult book, we will see that the **Member** already has permission.

A property without a default value will be assigned upon creation to whatever value that the programing language supports. In some case, this is zero, in other cases, it might be whatever was left in the memory from last time, and other environments use different initialization patterns. This often causes

---

[14] Because Members never get any younger. However, if the age criteria changed, we might want recalculate the hasAdultPrivileges for everyone born in the new transition year.

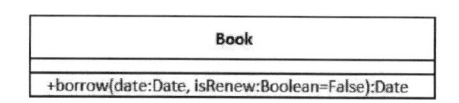

FIGURE 6.12
Example of an argument with a default value assignment.

hard to solve bugs, as every time we run the application, there may be different leftover values.

The default value is required to be of the same type as the underlying attribute.

Note that even though the *birthdate* field is marked private (-), the value is available inside to operations on **Member**. Therefore, the *isAdult()* operation can read the *birthdate* field.

6.3.2.2 Default Values for Arguments/Parameters
It is also possible to assign a default value to an operation's arguments. In Fig. 6.12, we supply a default Boolean Value, using a Boolean Literal, False, for the *isRenew* argument. We only need to change the argument for a when we are renewing the book at the same time. We cover literals in Section 6.4, Assigning Value.

6.3.3 Protecting from Change
6.3.3.1 ReadOnly
There are times that we want a property to be immune from change. We can make the property *private*, which will be a help, but that only stops changes that originate outside of the instance. If wish this to be stronger, we can add *{readOnly}* to the property. This indicates that the property should be protected from all changes once it is initialized. In Fig. 6.11, we flagged the Members birthdate to be {readOnly}. Practically, this may be too strict. It is not uncommon to need to correct fields like birthdate, perhaps, it was accidently mistyped, or the member may have been mistaken, or lying.

In most tools, readOnly is not enforced by the generated code, so it is still a good idea to make the property private.
As with many properties, the name of the property is a shorthand form for `isReadOnly = True`. The default for `isReadOnly` is `False`. Such properties are usually only displayed as an adornment if it is `True`.

6.3.3.2 Queries
A query is an operation that is not allowed to change any of the attributes values of the instance. Flagging an operation as a query, like flagging an

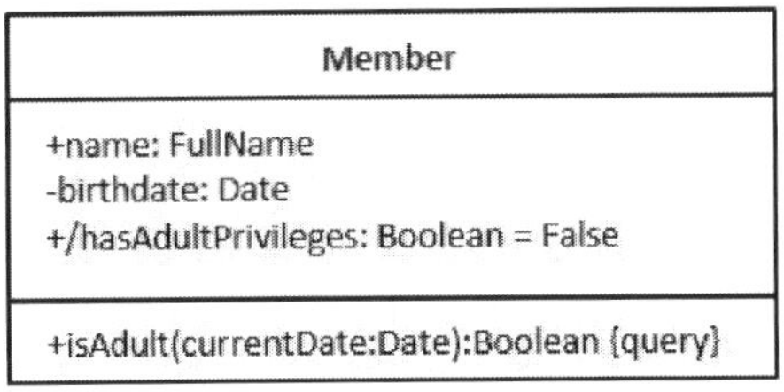

```
           Member
+name: FullName
-birthdate: Date
+/hasAdultPrivileges: Boolean = False

+isAdult(currentDate:Date):Boolean {query}
```

FIGURE 6.13
A query operation.

Table 6.2 ParameterDirectionKind

In	Passed in by the caller
Inout	Passed in by the caller and values (possibly different) are passed out by the behavior
Out	Passed out by the behavior
Return	Passed as return values back to the caller

attribute as `readOnly`, indicates your intention that the only thing that changes after the operation is the return value from the call. A query has no side effects, see Fig. 6.13.

This, like `isReadOnly`, is a modeling indication and is not always enforced by any generated code, see Fig. 6.13 for a use of {query}.

The use of query in the figure indicates that the operation *isAdult()* will not change any attribute of Member, or anything else other than returning the Boolean value. Query is an operation property, which appears as the adornment {query}.

6.3.4 Parameter Direction

The parameters for an operation can be flagged with their intended direction. There are four possible enumeration values to the Parameter Direction, as shown in Table 6.2. The default value used for the ParameterDirectionKind, when not otherwise indicated is "in." The rightmost column in the table indicates when the parameter's values be trusted, an "in" or "inout" parameter will need to have values set before they are passed into the behavior/operation. Parameters marked with "out," "inout," or "return" will have new values after the call, and any previously set value would be lost during the call.

In Fig. 6.14, the first two parameters are "in." The next parameter, Debit, represents the cost of the upcoming ride, however depending on the remaining balance on the credit card; it may only be partially fundable (requiring

```
billCC(  in CCN:String,
         in owner:NameType,
         inout debit:Currency,
         out successFlag:Boolean
      ) return ReturnType
```

FIGURE 6.14
Example operation using ParameterDirectionKind.

an additional funding source). In this case, the app leaves the remaining balance in the debit parameter, and the successFlag would be set to false. Therefore, we set their direction flags to "inout" and "out", respectively. We reserve the ReturnType for more serious failures, such as not finding the credit card, I/O, or network errors. Approaches that raise exceptions are also possible, but not covered here.

It is common practice to order the parameters by their direction (using the order of "in," "inout," "out," and "return'). As "in" is the default, it is often omitted. We also usually omit the direction kind "return" because we can normally recognize it by the location at the end of the operation call.

POINTS TO REMEMBER

- Derived attributes need to be recalculated before use because they depend on other values in the model.
  - Their definition is preceded with a "/."
- An attribute may be given a default value that are used whenever a new instance is made, if not otherwise overridden.
  - The default value appears after the attribute definition and includes a leading " = ."
- A parameter to an operation may be given a default value that are used whenever the operation is called unless a different value is supplied.
  - The default value appears after the parameter definition and includes a leading " = ."
- An attribute may be given a default value that are used whenever a new instance is made, if not otherwise overridden.
  - The default value appears after the attribute definition and includes a leading " = ."
- An attribute may be flagged as *readOnly*, indicating that it may be set only once.
- An operation may be flagged as a *query*, indicating that no attribute or state will change (no side effects).
- Each parameter on an operation may be tagged with a *parameter direction kind*. The value "in" is the default if not specified.
  - "in" indicates the operation will use the value the parameter it has when the operation was called and will not change the value of the parameter.
  - "inout" indicates the operation may both use and change the value of the parameter.
  - "out" indicates that any value set before the call is ignored, and a new value will be set on the way out
  - "return" indicates the value may be used as a return from the operation.

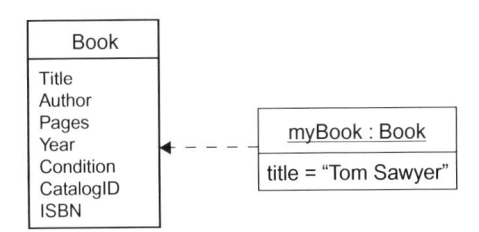

FIGURE 6.15
Class and instance.

Table 6.3 Literal Values in UML[a]

Literal Type	Representation	Default
Null	Specified as Null or an empty field. It means that no value is supplied	
String	Surrounded by double quotes. The literal does not include the quotes. The character set is unspecified[b]	
Boolean	The words true or false	False
Integer	Shown as an optional signed sequence of decimal digits	0
Natural	An unsigned integer	
Unlimited Natural	Similar to natural, but includes "*" to mean unlimited (as used in Multiplicty Ranges) "Unlimited" does not mean "infinity," it means a lack of a limit or unbounded	0
Decimal	An optionally signed Integer with or without a decimal point	
Real	A decimal literal optionally followed by "E"|"e" +/− Integer. <decimal-literal>[("e"|"E") [" + "|" − "]<natural-literal>] e.g., 3.14 E + 00, 3.14, 3	

[a]The literal definitions make an a Decimal Literal without the decimal point also an Integer Literal. An Integer Literal with no sign is also a Natural Literal. And a Real Literal without a point and without the exponent part is also an Integer Literal.
[b]Letting the character set be unspecified allows UML to supporting naming UML elements and providing opaque literals and expressions, which in turn, allows use of Unicode and other international character sets. Certain string, such as keywords, are reserved.

6.4 ASSIGNING VALUE

6.4.1 Literals

When we assign a default (initial) value to an attribute of a class or the value to the slot in an instance, we can use a Literal value. We've used many of these before. For example, in Fig. 6.16, we've used Integer Literals to set the value for date fields. In Fig. 6.15, we used a String Literal to assign the value to the title field (Table 6.3).

6.4.2 Instance Specifications

We have already introduced the reader to the concepts and notation of Instance Specifications in Chapter 4, The Organization of UML, where we emphasized that objects are on a lower level of abstraction than classes. Now, we'll emphasize the notation, capability, and features of an object/instance specification.

Let us first distinguish between objects, instances, and instances specifications. An "object" is either an element of the real world (M1) or an element of the code/implementation (M0). An "instance" is the same thing, with an emphasis on the fact that there is a class or a type (a classifier) involved, i.e., an "instance" of a class.

In Fig. 6.15, we see an Instance Specification named myBook that represents an instance of the class **Book**, that is currently named myBook, which has a title slot containing "Tom Sawyer." An instance specification is a model element (usually with corresponding diagram elements) that normally designates an instance, but can designate one of a set of instances. For example, if there are many books with the title of "Tom Saywer", the Instance Specification can refer to any one of the compatible instances.

You may think that an Instance Specification is similar to a class. A class designates a set of instances, while an Instance Specification identifies one of a potentially smaller set. In UML 2.5, an Instance Specification is a rectangular box with a name compartment and an optional slot compartment. The name compartment includes an underline name, in the above case, it is myBook, followed by a ":" and then by name of the class that the instances is an instance of, in this case, Book.

All the fields, except for the ":" are optional. If you don't indicate a class, the instance specification is indicating that the class isn't important — and an instance of any class will do. If you don't indicate the name, then the name of the instance isn't important. The name compartment can also display any relevant stereotypes.

Underneath the name compartment are the slots. These represent attributes from the class with optional literal values that are the values for these attributes at the current time. The literal value must be compatible with the types of the attributes. Often the attribute types are repeated after the slot name, as shown below.

```
title: String = "Tom Sawyer"
```

An additional constraints compartment can be added to capture any constraints on this instance. There are no operations or signals compartments. The elements that would be in these compartments would be captured in the

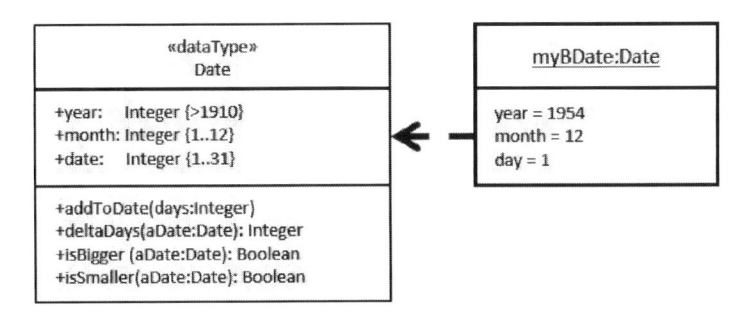

FIGURE 6.16
A dataType and instance.

class definition and do not need to be repeated. Similarly, in the slots compartment, don't repeat slots unless you really care about their values in this circumstance.

You should distinguish between the instance name and the value of any particular attribute. For example, we could have changed the class definition to have a `name:String attribute` and correspondingly change the title slot to be a name slot. In such a case, the name of the instance would still be "myBook" and the name attribute of the instance would be "Tom Sawyer."

In the example below, Fig. 6.16, we show myBDate as an instance of the dataType date. As with instances of classes, we don't show any operations compartment as with just duplicate the definitions on the type. The dashed arrow we use to connect the two elements, in Figs. 6.15 and 6.16 is an optional dependency arrow indicating that the instances depend on their class or type definitions.

6.4.3 Expressions

You can use a literal or an indirect literal via an instance specification to assign a value to a property or slot as we have seen, but you can also use an OPAQUE EXPRESSION. An opaque expression is an expression in a language that is opaque to UML. In this usage, "opaque" means "hidden" and that it is unparsable directly in UML.

Of course, if an opaque expression is also opaque to the people writing or reading the model, it won't be useful. Modelers usually write expressions in their target program language, use available system calls, or in OCL, or some other widely known syntax, such as high school mathematics.

If necessary, you can specify the target language by preceding the opaque expression string with the language name displayed in braces ({}). For example,

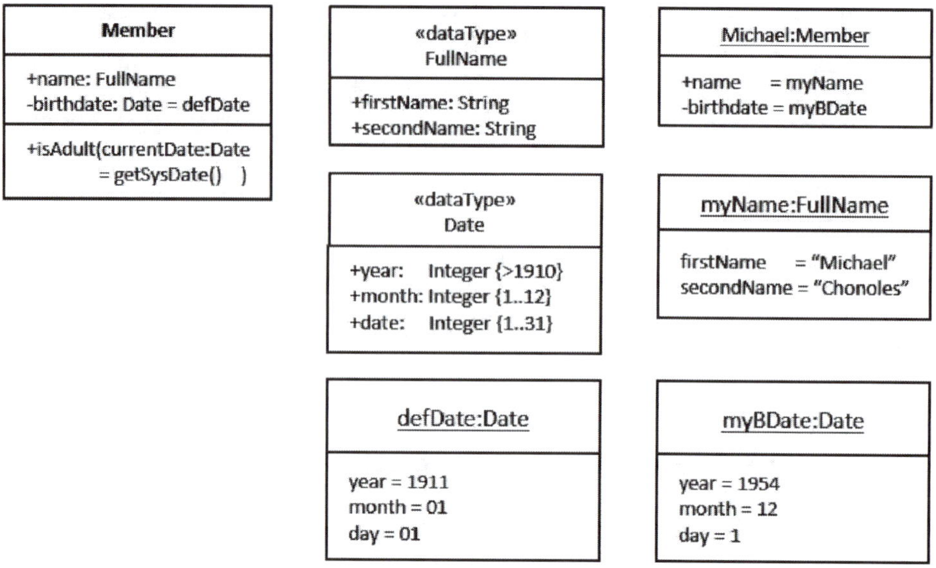

CHAPTER 6: Objects and Classes

Member
+name: FullName -birthdate: Date = defDate
+isAdult(currentDate:Date   = getSysDate())

«dataType» FullName
+firstName: String +secondName: String

«dataType» Date
+year: Integer {>1910} +month: Integer {1..12} +date: Integer {1..31}

Michael:Member
+name   = myName -birthdate = myBDate

myName:FullName
firstName   = "Michael" secondName = "Chonoles"

defDate:Date
year = 1911 month = 01 day = 01

myBDate:Date
year = 1954 month = 12 day = 1

FIGURE 6.17
Value assignments.

```
Xor                              getSysTime()
{C++} j++                        getUserID()
{OCL} i > j and self.size > i    {Ms Excel} 1.0 + sin(60)
height > length                  Else
```

In UML, most expressions, constraints, guard conditions, descriptions of behavior, and pseudocode are written as opaque expressions. As opaque expressions are not automatically parsed, constraints in UML are not always strictly in Boolean form as shown in Fig. 6.7.

In Fig. 6.17, we show how we can build up class and instances using types, instance specifications, primitive values, and opaque expressions. The class **Member** (on the left of the figure) uses two user-defined types, FullName and Date (both displayed in the center column). The class **Member** also uses a default value of defDate for the birthdate. The default defDate is defined in an instance specification shown at the bottom of the second column. It also uses an opaque expression that is a system call the value of the *currentDate* parameter. On the right of the figure, we have an instance that represents my **Member** record. This *Michael:Member* used the instance *myName* and *mybdate* to initialize the slots.

We also used Integer Literals in defining *defDate* and *myBdate*. We also incorporated opaque expressions (built from Integer Literals) in defining the constraints on *Date*.

POINTS TO REMEMBER

- UML has Literals that can be used to assign values to the Primitive types «primitive» (e.g., String, Boolean, Integer, Real).
  - You can define your own literals for your user-defined enumeration types.
- User-defined types «dataTypes» can be built out of primitive or other user-defined types.
- Additional «dataTypes» and classes can be used to build more classes and «dataTypes»
  - As types for attributes and parameters
- Instance specifications can have slots whose current values are specified using literals, opaque expressions, or built out of other instance specifications.
  - They can be used as default values for attributes and parameters
- An opaque expression is any expression that is not directly understandable by UML.
  - If it helps, you can precede the expression with the language, e.g., {OCL}.
  - They are used to assign default values, to write constraints, etc.

CHAPTER 7

Questions for Chapter 6

1. How can you mark an attribute so that it will never change after it is first set?
   A. + attrName
   B. − attrName
   C. attrName {readOnly}
   D. attrName {query}
   E. attrName {noChange}
   F. attrName
2. How can you mark an attribute so that it has Class scope?
   A. + attrName
   B. − attrName
   C. attrName {readOnly}
   D. attrName {query}
   E. attrName {noChange}
   F. attrName
3. Which sort of ship would make a good Class?
   A. Friendship
   B. Leadership
   C. Battleship
   D. Transship
   E. Ownership
4. Which sort of features can Instances have?
   A. Slots
   B. Parameters
   C. Attributes
   D. Faces
   E. Operations

115

OCUP 2 Certification Guide. DOI: http://dx.doi.org/10.1016/B978-0-12-809640-6.00008-8
© 2018 Elsevier Inc. All rights reserved.

5. What letter labels an item that the query can change?

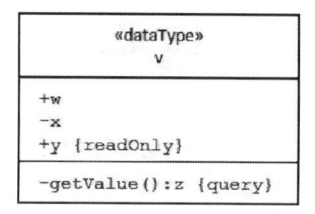

```
«dataType»
    v
---------------
+w
-x
+y {readOnly}
---------------
-getValue():z {query}
```

  A. w
  B. x
  C. y
  D. z

6. How does a DataType differ from a Class?
   A. Only a DataType can have operations.
   B. Only Class instances have identity even if all the attribute values are the same.
   C. Only a Class can have slots.
   D. Only a Class can participate in generalizations.
   E. Only a DataType can use literals.

7. On what kind of UML Diagram(s) can Instances and Classes appear?
   A. They can appear on any behavioral Diagram.
   B. Instances can only appear on Object Diagrams.
   C. Both Classes and Instances can appear on Object and Class Diagrams.
   D. Classes can only appear on Class Diagrams.

8. What is the correct and complete UML 2.5 shape for an Instance Specification?
   A.

   semiHexagon:Shape

   B.

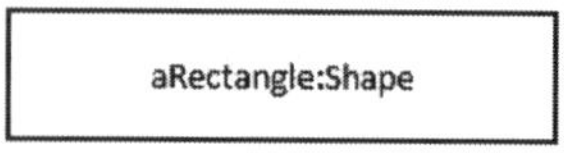

   aRectangle:Shape

   C.

   aHexagon:Shape

D.

```
underlinedRectangle:Shape
```

9. Which is a correct use of a typed Boolean Literal?
   A. isSeniorCitizen = True
   B. isSeniorCitizen = True or False
   C. isSeniorCitizen = "False"
   D. isSeniorCitizen = {myAge > 65}
   E. isSeniorCitizen = 1
10. Examine the Class below. Which choice indicates an Instance that is named Michael?

```
Person
name: String
```

A.

```
Michael : Person
name: String
```

B.

```
Person :
name: String = "Michael"
```

C.

```
Person : Michael
name : String
```

D.

```
: Person
name : String = "Michael"
```

E.

```
Person
name: String = "Michael"
```

11. In the following Class fragment, how many Types are named?

R
s:t=u
v(in w:x=y): z

   A. 0
   B. 1
   C. 2
   D. 3
   E. 4
   F. 5
12. Which choice correctly assigns the price parameter to a matching default value? Do not define additional Types or utilize Opaque Expressions.
   A. hailCar (price: Integer = 2.0,
   B. hailCar (price: Integer = "2",
   C. hailCar (price: Real = 2,
   D. hailCar (price: Float = 2.0,
   E. hailCar (price: Real = 2.0 D + 00
13. If you wish to prevent the userID parameter in the hailCar operation from being changed, what would be the safest approach?
   A. hailCar(userID, ...
   B. hailCar(−userID, ...
   C. hailCar(inout userID, ...
   D. hailCar(userID {readOnly}, ...
14. The registerMyCar operation with the Ride Hailing app allows drivers to register, either Black or Yellow-colored cars. How would this best work to register a Black Car?
   A. registerMyCar (isBlack: Boolean = True, isYellow: Boolean = False,
   B. Assign Black to 0, and Yellow to 1, then registerMyCar (scheme: Integer = 0,
   C. Create a ColorSchemeKind enumeration type, with literals "Black" and "Yellow", then registerMyCar (scheme: ColorSchemeKind = "Black",
   D. Create a ColorSchemeKind enumeration type, with literals Black and Yellow, then registerMyCar (scheme: ColorSchemeKind = Black,
15. After you create a Driver instance, what would happen if you tried to create a second Driver with the same values for the attributes?

```
                    Driver
        ───────────────────────────
        name: NameType
        age: Integer {age > 13}
        license: String
```

   A. They would be the same driver as they have the same properties
   B. You would have two drivers with the same properties
   C. An exception would be raised.
   D. The create operation would fail.
16. How should you indicate that an attribute is derived?
   A. Place an {isDerived} before the attribute definition.
   B. Place a "~" before the attribute definition.
   C. Place a "/" before the attribute definition.
   D. Place an "out" before the attribute definition.
17. How do you specify to pass an operation parameter (x) by reference?
   A. operation(byReference x:Type)
   B. operation(x:Type {isByReference})
   C. operation(x:Type (isByValue = False))
   D. operation(#x:Type)
   E. It is not possible in UML to specify this.
   F. operation (in x:Type)
18. What does the underline of anAttribute indicate?

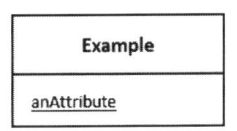

```
              Example
        ──────────────────
          anAttribute
```

   A. The value of anAttribute cannot change, i.e., it is static.
   B. All of the instances of **Example** see the same value for anAttribute.
   C. None of the instances of **Example** requires an independent initialization of anAttribute.
   D. The attribute is part of the state value.

ANSWERS FOR CHAPTER 6

1. How can you mark an attribute so that it will never change after it is first set?
   A. + attrName
   B. − attrName
   C. **attrName {readOnly}**

D. attrName {query}
E. attrName {noChange}
F. attrName

Discussion:
A—No, the "+" makes the attribute public, subject to change by anyone.
B—No, the "−" makes the attribute private, which protects from change from the outside, but operations within the class can still change them
D—No, {query} may be used on operations, to prevent the operation from changing attributes
E—No, the underline makes the attribute statically scoped. This is not related to changeability.
C—Yes, {readOnly} allows the adorned attribute to be set when the object is created, but only then.

2. How can you mark an attribute so that it has Class scope?
    A. + attrName
    B. − attrName
    C. attrName {readOnly}
    D. attrName {query}
    E. attrName {noChange}
    F. **attrName**

    Discussion:
    A and E—No, these are all variations on instance-scoped attributes
    F—Yes, the underline makes the attribute Class scoped.

3. Which sort of ship would make a good Class?
    A. Friendship
    B. Leadership
    C. **Battleship**
    D. Transship
    E. Ownership

    Discussion:
    A, B, and E—No, though these are nouns, they are abstract nouns and are unlikely to represent a Class.
    However, they might make good associations or properties. We could treat them as Classes, if we wished to reify them by looking at persistent records, for example, a sales receipt might be considered as an Ownership (record)
    D—This is a verb, it means to ship to an intermediate point, and then ship to the final destination. Transship would make an acceptable operation.
    C—Yes, a Battleship is a concrete physical Class It is a large armored warship with a battery of heavy guns and has instances. By the way,

no battleships remain in service or in reserve with any navy worldwide[1].
4. Which sort of features can Instances have?
   A. **Slots**
   B. Parameters
   C. Attributes
   D. Faces
   E. Operations

   Discussion:
   E and B—No, Operations do not appear on instances. Parameters are arguments to operations, and they do not appear on instances.
   C—No, Attributes on a Class would appear as Slots on the instance.
   D—No, Faces might appear on Actor cartoons, but not on instances.
   A—Yes, a slot is the location than an instance holds the value of an attribute.

5. What letter labels an item that the query can change?

   ```
   «dataType»
       v
   +w
   -x
   +y {readOnly}
   -getValue():z {query}
   ```

   A. w
   B. x
   C. y
   D. **z**

   Discussion:
   A and C—No, a query cannot change a value or state within the Class/type.
   D—Yes, a query can return a value.

6. How does a DataType differ from a Class?
   A. Only a DataType can have operations.
   B. **Only Class instances have identity even if all the attribute values are the same.**
   C. Only a Class can have slots.
   D. Only a Class can participate in generalizations.
   E. Only a DataType can use literals.

---

[1] Wikipedia, "Battleship" 2016.

Discussion:
A—No, both Classes and DataTypes can have operations.
C—No, neither Classes nor DataTypes have slots, though their Instances may have slots.
D—No, both Classes and DataTypes can participate in generalizations
E—No, both Classes and DataTypes can use literals.
B—Yes, if the attributes are the same for a DataType, they have the same value. Class instances have intrinsic identity, which DataType instances do not have.

7. On what kind of UML Diagram(s) can Instances and Classes appear?
   A. They can appear on any behavioral Diagram.
   B. Instances can only appear on Object Diagrams.
   C. **Both Classes and Instances can appear on Object and Class Diagrams**.
   D. Classes can only appear on Class Diagrams.

   Discussion:
   A—No, Instances and Classes are part of the static model and generally, cannot appear on behavioral diagrams.
   B—No, while Instances can appear on Object Diagrams, they also can appear on Class Diagrams.
   D—No, while Classes can appear on Class Diagrams, they can also appear on Object Diagrams.
   C—Yes, both Instances and Classes can appear on Object and Class Diagrams. They also can appear on Package Diagrams.

8. What is the correct and complete UML 2.5 shape for an Instance Specification?
   A.

   semiHexagon:Shape

   B.

   aRectangle:Shape

C.

```
    aHexagon:Shape
```

D.

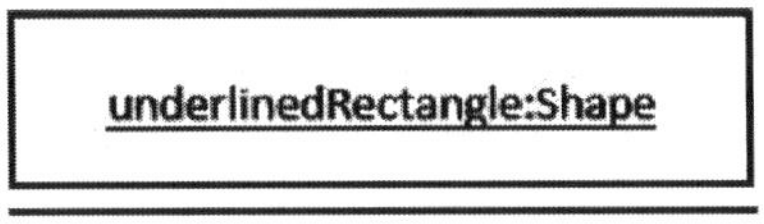

```
underlinedRectangle:Shape
```

Discussion:
A—No, this was the notation in the OML language for an Instance. OML was a competitor to UML. This shape is sometimes called a house. It is not part of UML.
B—No, this option omits the underline for the name and type.
C—No, though it is underlined, the shape is not correct.
D—Yes, this is correct. In UML, an instance takes the shape of the Classifier, in this case a Class. The title in the Title compartment is underlined.

9. Which is a correct use of a typed Boolean Literal?
   A. **isSeniorCitizen = True**
   B. isSeniorCitizen = True or False
   C. isSeniorCitizen = "False"
   D. isSeniorCitizen = {myAge > 65}
   E. isSeniorCitizen = 1

   Discussion:
   A—Yes, the Boolean Literals are either True or False.
   B—No. While the Boolean Literals are True or False; you can only assign an attribute or slot to one of these values.
   C—No, this is a Literal String assignment.
   D—No. While this might work, it is an assignment to an opaque expression in the form of a constraint.
   E—No, this is an Integer Literal assignment.

10. Examine the Class below. Which choice indicates an Instance that is named Michael?

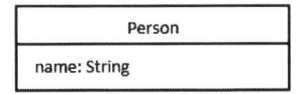

Person
name: String

A.

Michael : Person
name: String

B.

Person :
name: String = "Michael"

C.

Person : Michael
name : String

D.

: Person
name : String = "Michael"

E.

Person
name: String = "Michael"

Discussion:

This question revolves around the distinction between the contents of a variable and the name of the variable[2], and it also requires knowledge of the correct UML format for Instances.

A—Yes, this is an Instance of the Class Person. The name of the Instance is Michael. The name slot that this Instance has is unassigned.

B—No, because the Person field comes first followed by a blank Class field, this is an Instance called Person of an unspecified Class. The instance has a name slot assigned the value of "Michael."

C—No, this is the Person Instance of the Michael Class. The Class name comes second in the title of an Instance Specification.

---

[2] It is reminiscent of the situation in Lewis Carroll's "Through the Looking Glass," where the White Knight tries to explain to Alice the difference between the song's name ("The Aged Aged Man") and what the song's name is called ("Haddock's Eyes"), and what the song is called ("Ways and Means").

D—No, this is an anonymous instance of the Class Person. The name in the slot is "Michael."
E—No, this is a Class named Person. It has "Michael" assigned to an attribute.

11. In the following Class fragment, how many Types are named?

R
s:t=u
v(in w:x=y): z

A. 0
B. 1
C. 2
D. 3
E. 4
F. 5

Discussion:
E—Yes (4). The attribute (s) is typed (t), the parameter (w) is typed (x), the operation has a return type (z). In addition, the Class R is also a type, because all classes are also types.

12. Which choice correctly assigns the price parameter to a matching default value? Do not define additional Types or utilize Opaque Expressions.
A. hailCar (price: Integer = 2.0,
B. hailCar (price: Integer = "2",
C. **hailCar (price: Real = 2,**
D. hailCar (price: Float = 2.0,
E. hailCar (price: Real = 2.0 D + 00

Discussion:
A—No, 2.0 is a Real or Decimal literal.
B—No, "2" is a String literal.
D—No, Float is not a UML type.
E—No, though, UML allows exponent forms, UML only accepts "E" as the pre-exponent character (e.g., 2.0 E + 00). Using the "D" here would make this an opaque expression. In several programming language (e.g., Fortran), using the D indicates a Double precision real number.
C—Yes, in UML a literal that looks like an Integer is compatible with the Real type.

13. If you wish to prevent the userID parameter in the hailCar operation from being changed, what would be the safest approach?

A. **hailCar(userID, ...**
B. hailCar(−userID, ...
C. hailCar(inout userID, ...
D. hailCar(userID {readOnly}, ...

Discussion:
B—No, the " − " indicates an attribute is private, and not accomplish anything on an argument.
C—No, a ParameterDirectionKind of "inout" indicates that the userID parameter can be changed because it includes the "out" direction.
D—No, {readOnly} only applies to attributes.
A—Yes, in UML the ParameterDirectionKind has a default of "in" if no direction is specified.

14. The registerMyCar operation with the Ride Hailing app allows drivers to register, either Black or Yellow-colored cars. How would this best work to register a Black Car?
    A. registerMyCar (isBlack: Boolean = True, isYellow: Boolean = False,
    B. Assign Black to 0, and Yellow to 1, then registerMyCar (scheme: Integer = 0,
    C. Create a ColorSchemeKind enumeration type, with literals "Black" and "Yellow", then registerMyCar (scheme: ColorSchemeKind = "Black",
    D. **Create a ColorSchemeKind enumeration type, with literals Black and Yellow, then registerMyCar (scheme: ColorSchemeKind = Black,**

    Discussion:
    A—No, although this might work, it would be difficult if there were many possible color schemes, requiring many additional flags.
    B—No, although this might work, it produces difficult to maintain code. The designer or programmers for registerMyCar would have to remember the color scheme numbering.
    C—No, these are string literals because of they are enclosed in " ".
    D—Yes, this is a correct and appropriate use of Enumeration type. It is elegant, efficient, and easily maintainable.

15. After you create a Driver instance, what would happen if you tried to create a second Driver with the exact same values for the attributes?

Driver
name: NameType age: Integer {age > 18} license: String

A. They would be the same driver as they have the same properties
B. **You would have two drivers with the same properties**
C. An exception would be raised.
D. The create operation would fail.

Discussion:
A—No, this classifier is a Class. If it were a DataType, it would be labeled «DataType». Two instances of a DataType must have some difference in properties. Two instances of a class may have identical properties.
C—No, there is no indication in the model that this would cause a problem.
D—No, there is no indication in the model that this would cause a problem.
B—Yes, it is certainly possible to have two Class instances that have the same properties. We hope that the software would recognize that two drivers with the same license is potentially a problem.

16. How should you indicate that an attribute is derived?
    A. Place an {isDerived} before the attribute definition.
    B. Place a "~" before the attribute definition.
    C. **Place a "/" before the attribute definition**.
    D. Place an "out" before the attribute definition.

    Discussion:
    A—No, though {isDerived) might work as an uncommon property modifier when placed after the attribute definition.
    B—No, the tilde "~" indicates Package Visibility; visibility to things in the same package.
    D—No, "out" is used before an argument to indicate an argument direction. When we use "out", it means whatever value the parameter has before the operation is first ignored and then replaced.
    C—Yes, the solidus or slash "/" indicates that it is derived. Note that backslash "\" is incorrect but it common to forget which direction it goes. Often, the UML tool will correct the direction.

17. How do you specify to pass an operation parameter (x) by reference?
    A. operation(byReference x:Type)
    B. operation(x:Type {isByReference})
    C. operation(x:Type (isByValue = False))
    D. operation(#x:Type)
    E. **It is not possible in UML to specify this.**
    F. operation (in x:Type)
        A and D—No, these are wrong, as it is not possible to specify by value or by reference in UML.

F—No, though it is possible that this would be the implementation, the notation does not indicate pass by reference semantics.

E—Yes, this is correct. UML cannot specify the method of passing parameters. The intent is to make UML independent of the programming language. Many programming languages do not support pass by value or pass by reference.

18. What does the underline of anAttribute indicate?

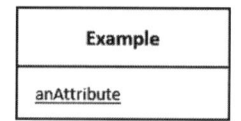

Example
anAttribute

A. The value of anAttribute cannot change, i.e., it is static.
B. **All of the instances of Example see the same value for anAttribute**.
C. None of the instances of Example requires an independent initialization of anAttribute.
D. The attribute is part of the state value.

Discussion:
A—No, while the underline indicates the attribute is "class-scoped", commonly called "static". In this case, "static" does not mean that the value cannot change.
C—No, I made this up to sound plausible without meaning anything.
D—No, while any attribute is potentially part of the state's value, the underline does not add any significant meaning relating to state machines.
B—Yes, the underline indicates that the attribute is class scoped also called "static". This means that the attribute is really an attribute of the class, and not that of an instance. All instances would see the same value for the attribute.

Packages and Namespaces

8.1 PACKAGE NOTATION

You should now know the UML symbol for a PACKAGE. The shape is a rectangular body with a tab in the upper left. If we do not wish to show any contents, we put the name of the Package in the center, see Fig. 8.1.

8.1.1 Packages and Their Contents

If we do want to show the contents of the Package, we replace the centered name with the diagram Elements that we wish to depict, bumping the name to the tab, see Fig. 8.2. In the figure, we show the Package, MyPackage, as containing the **Book** Class and an instance of **Book** (myBook).

As a VIEW, the Package can display many other Elements from the Package, not currently shown in the figure, at the option of the modeler. We can place almost anything in a Package; the only things that the Package cannot contain are Elements with clashing names[1] because a PACKAGE is a NAMESPACE, which does not allow duplicate names.

A Class is also a Namespace. It has a set of attributes (see the class symbol, **Book**, inside the figure), each with a name. Moreover, no duplicate names are allowed for attributes nor operations (under most circumstances). The attributes and operations are MEMBERS of the Class, as the Elements within a Package are members of the Package.

---

[1]This includes Classes, Types, Use Cases, Packages, Interfaces, and Activities. The technical restriction is that it must be a PACKAGEABLE ELEMENT. Things that cannot be named are usually not packageable. If the name is optional, it is still considered namable. It is a logical peculiarity of UML that a Named Element need not have a name. Items, such as Multiplicity that can't be referred to, are not Packageable.
Most behavioral elements are only allowed to be in particular namespaces. For example, a State may only be in a StateMachine namespace. However, Use Cases are Packageable.

OCUP 2 Certification Guide. DOI: http://dx.doi.org/10.1016/B978-0-12-809640-6.00009-X
© 2018 Elsevier Inc. All rights reserved.

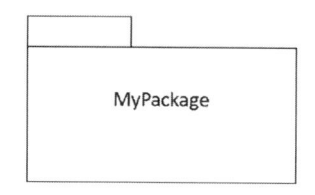

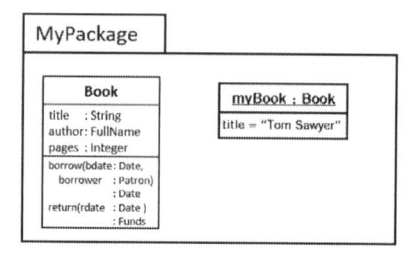

CHAPTER 8: Packages and Namespaces

FIGURE 8.1
A Package.

FIGURE 8.2
A Package depicting some contents.

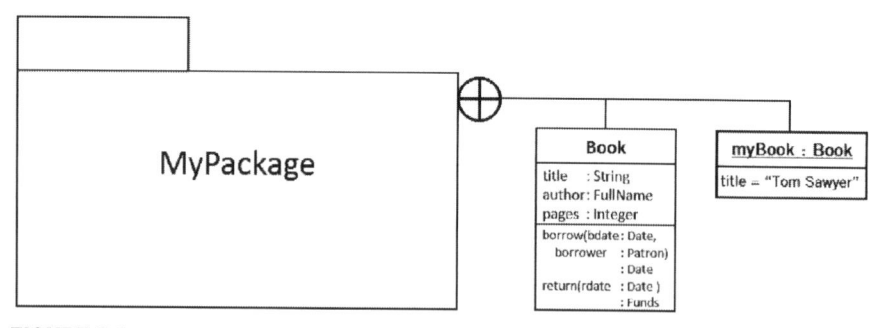

FIGURE 8.3
Using the ⊕ to show Package contents.

A third way of displaying a Package gives the modeler more flexibility in arranging the diagram. In this approach, as shown in Fig. 8.3, we use the ⊕ symbol to connect the Package symbol to the owned Elements. In UML, we use the ⊕ to indicate Package or Namespace containment, connecting the Namespace to the individual Namespace members. This approach can be presented vertically or horizontally, in a tree style (as shown below) or with individual or shared ⊕ symbols (as below).

All these Package Diagrams show the model Elements defined and owned by the Package. As an Element can only be defined once in a model, there is no

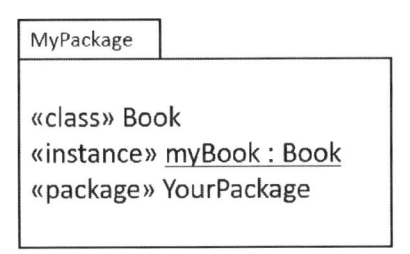

```
┌─────────────┐
│ MyPackage   │
├─────────────┴──────────────┐
│                            │
│  «class» Book              │
│  «instance» myBook : Book  │
│  «package» YourPackage     │
│                            │
└────────────────────────────┘
```

FIGURE 8.4
Package with list of members.

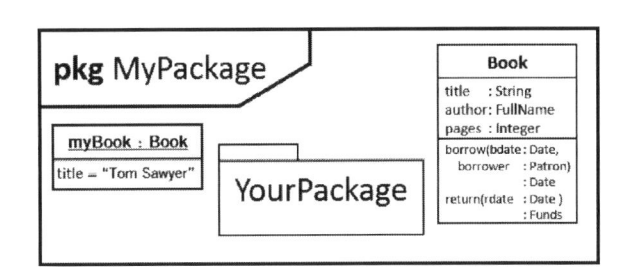

FIGURE 8.5
Package as Diagram.

multiplicity on these diagrams. The connecting line is not an association; it is just shorthand for the direct incorporation approach. The Package MyPackage contains the (one and only) definition of the Class **Book** and the instance mybook, so it is not appropriate to show any multiplicity. We can use the ⊕[2] symbol wherever Namespace and the contained Elements are indicated, though most tools will only allow this with Packages and similar Elements.

UML has one more way of representing a Package and its member Elements—Reminiscent of a Class showing its own members. We can show the Package with an internal list of members as done in Fig. 8.4. We added another Package, YourPackage, as a new member of MyPackage.

8.1.2 Diagrams of Packages

In the above examples, we have illustrated stand-alone Packages. In UML, it is also possible to draw a diagram that depicts the same situation. We show the diagram approach in Fig. 8.5.

---

[2]You can produce the ⊕ symbol in text by typing 2A01, selecting the hex string, and typing Alt-X. It is the astrological symbol for the planet Earth, with the quadrants representing the four cardinal directions (NESW).

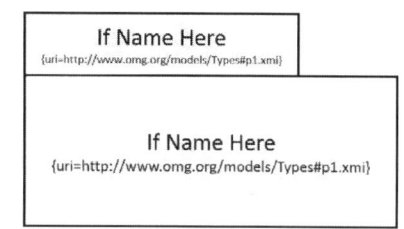

```
┌─────────────────────────────────────────┐
│           If Name Here                  │
│  {uri=http://www.omg.org/models/Types#p1.xmi}
│                                         │
│           If Name Here                  │
│  {uri=http://www.omg.org/models/Types#p1.xmi}
│                                         │
└─────────────────────────────────────────┘
```

FIGURE 8.6
URI placement.

This figure is a Package Diagram (because it shows Packages in the diagram) that shows the contents of the Package MyPackage. If we did not show the YourPackage member in the diagram, we might classify the figure as a Class Diagram[3] that depicts the content of MyPackage Package. Remember that the diagram header "**pkg** MyPackage" indicates that the diagram is a Package Namespace whose name is MyPackage. The type of diagram is mainly determined by the preponderance of Elements.

8.1.3 Uniform Resource Identifiers

A Package may have an optional URI (UNIFORM RESOURCE IDENTIFIER[4]) associated with it. This URI is any string but is intended to be a unique nonchanging string identifying the location and access protocol for the Package. In practice, the URI is used for CONFIGURATION MANAGEMENT (CM) purposes. If you are using a CM tool with your UML tool, consult the CM features to determine how this works. Often you will see something like a file descriptor pointing to an XMI[5] file, followed by a # and the name of the Package being referenced. We show sample locations and formats in Fig. 8.6.

However, the URI is optional, and even when used, it need not be dereferenceable, though it should be unique and nonchangeable. If two Packages have the same URI they should be the same Package. By using the same URI, different model databases or different UML tools can share Packages, across models or versions, if the tool vendors have implemented this feature.

---

[3]Because then it would only show a Class and an Instance.
[4]There is a standard form for a URI defined in RFC 3986 (2005) [http://www.ietf.org/rfc/rfc3986.txt]. The URI is usually a file reference or a shared file reference. I expect increasing use of formal URIs as the UML tools support enterprise-wide models.
[5]XMI, or the XML Model Interchange, is the standardized UML mechanism to exchange models or Packages across tools or locations.

POINTS TO REMEMBER

- A Namespace requires its Elements to have unique and distinguishable names.
  - A Package is a Namespace.
  - A Class's compartments are each a Namespace.
- A Namespace requires its Elements to have unique and distinguishable names.
  - A Package is a Namespace.
  - A Class's compartments are each a Namespace.
- The Package symbol looks like a folder with a tab at the upper left containing the name of the Package.
- The contents of a Package, if not elided, may be
  - Shown graphically inside the Package body
  - Listed textually inside the Package body
  - Connected to the Package with lines starting with a ⊕ at the Package side
  - Shown in a diagram with the Package name in the diagram header.
- A Package can have a URI, which should be a unique nonchangeable string used to enable CM or sharing across projects.

8.2 PACKAGES AND VISIBILITY

8.2.1 Package Member Visibility

In all the representations of Packages and their members shown above, we can precede the member name with a visibility indicator. The allowed visibility adornment is based on the visibility adornments allowed on the members of a Class, see Table 8.1. The visibility signs immediately precede the member name, usually after any stereotype. We demonstrate this in Fig. 8.7, showing how it works with the three alternative member depiction approaches (physically placed inside, member list, or ⊕ approaches).

Table 8.1 UML Visibility Notation in Packages

Symbol	Visibility Kind	Description
+	Public	A member with public visibility is visible to all elements that can access the contents of the Package (or Namespace) that owns it
−	Private	A member with private visibility is only visible inside the Package (or Namespace) that owns it
~	Package	A member with Package visibility is visible within the nearest enclosing Package (given that any intermediate owning Elements have proper visibility). Outside the nearest enclosing Package, a NamedElement marked as having Package visibility is not visible
		Not allowed on Packages or Elements directly owned by Packages
#	Protected	A member with protected visibility is visible to Elements that have a generalization relationship to the Namespace that owns it
		Not allowed on Packages or Elements directly owned by Packages. Packages do not support generalization/specializations

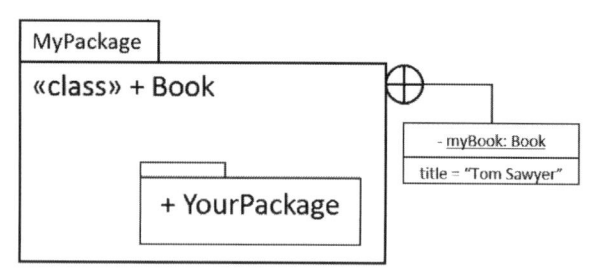

FIGURE 8.7
Visibility notation and Packages.

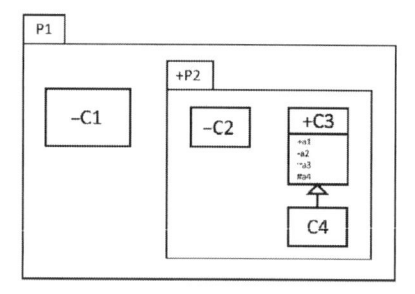

FIGURE 8.8
Visibility in Packages.

The interplay of the UML visibility notation in Packages is sometimes difficult to follow. Consider Fig. 8.8 and the associated Table 8.2.

It is easy to construct complicated visibility situations. Table 8.2 illustrates the scope of visibility for some typical examples. If you can follow the explanations given below, you will probably pass the questions on this topic on the exam. Luckily, in practical modeling, most circumstances never get complicated, as the UML tools often understand the visibility rules sufficiently to enforce correct references. Moreover, the UML tools often support a form of drag and drop to create references. As other references are usually found in Opaque Expressions, which are not automatically resolved, they will not cause any problems with the tool (though they may confuse your readers).

Packages can only be given private (−) or public (+) visibility. Elements directly within a Package (with no intervening Namespace) may also only have private or public visibility.

Table 8.2 Visibility of Package Elements

	Can these Elements See the Row Header Element?				Owning Namespace Qualified Name	Discussion
	C1	C2	C3	C4		
−C1		N	N	N	P1	Private Elements are only visible to Elements in the same Namespace (NS)
−C2	N		Y	Y	P1::P2	Private Elements are only visible to other Elements in the same Namespace (NS)
+C3	Y	Y		Y	P1::P2	Public Elements are visible to other Elements in the same NS and in containing NS
C4	N	N	N		P1::P2	The visibility of C4 is undefined
+a1	Y	Y	Y	Y	P1::P2::C3	Public Elements are visible to every element that can access the containing NS
−a2	N	N	Y	N	P1::P2::C3	Private Elements are only visible by other Elements in the same NS
~a3	N	Y	Y	Y	P1::P2::C3	Package Elements are as Public and are visible to all Elements in the same NS, but only to one level of outer NS
#a4	N	N	Y	Y	P2::P2::C3	Protected Elements are as Private, but visible to inherited NSs. Protected visibility is not allowed on Packages as they do not support inheritance

8.2.2 Inner and Outer Names

Consider Fig. 8.9. As shown in that figure, the direct Elements of P1, C1, and C2 can refer to each other by their simple name, C1 and C2. In P1, if C1 needs to refer to an Attribute `a1` in C2, it would use `C2.a1`. Likewise, if C2 needs to refer to an operation `b()` in C1, it would use `C1.b()`.

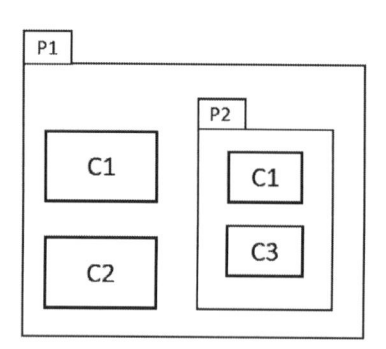

FIGURE 8.9
Hiding Elements.

Similarly, in Package P2, if C1 and C3 can use the simple name of the other member, C1 and C3. If they wish to refer to the properties of each other, they can use `C3.a1` or `C1.b()`.

The question then arises how can the Elements within P2 refer to the Elements directly in P1 or the Elements directly in P1 refer to the Elements in P2.

The problem here is that the outer names (in P1) and the inner names (in P2) have some overlap. Let us assume that everything is marked visible (+).

To refer to the inner Elements from P1, we need to use the qualified name[6]. The qualified name includes the chain of Packages from the source to the target. To refer to the inner Elements from P1, we use `P2::C1` and `P2::C3`. If we needed to refer to their features from P1, it would look like `P2::C3.a1` or `P2::C1.b()`.

The Package → Package and Package → Element uses "::" as the separator. The Element → attribute or Element → operation uses "." as the separator.
To refer to the outer Elements from P2, we can refer to C2 as C2, and we can refer to the properties of C2 as `C2.a1`. However, we cannot directly refer to C1, because the name C1 is blocked by the existence of a C1 at the P2 level. Using C1 as the reference would refer to the local C1. We have to use the qualified name to get to P1's C1, that is `P1::C1`. P2 can refer to C1's properties as `P1::C1.b()`.

Then, every Element in the diagram can refer to C2 and C3 because these name Elements are defined once, and they are visible by the rules for public (+) Elements. So the operation on C2 would still be `C2.b()` whether referred to by something in P1 or P2. Similarly, the operation on C3 would still be `C3.b()` whether referred to by something in P2 or P1.

---

[6]A fully qualified name is an unambiguous name that describes a path that of the namespaces that include the target element. In UML, Package names in the namespace list are followed by "::". Classes are followed by ".". In practice, only the namespaces up through the common ancestor of the source and target path are included.

When there is a reference to an "outer" Element, if an Element by that name exists in the local Package, then the reference will be blocked. If we wish to get the version of the blocked Element from a differ level, the reference has to use the qualified name, because the local name will "hide" the outer name. Such name blockage can be caused by a duplicate name at any level between the reference and the target.

8.2.3 Namespaces and Distinguishable Names

As mentioned in Chapter 4, The Organization of UML and later, Packages are like folders in a file drawer or directories on a computer system. A particular file or piece of paper can be only in one folder/directory at a time, though you could have distributed copies in many folders. UML Packages and computer directories are Namespaces. These require unique and DISTINGUISHABLE names for their contents.

Your computer's operating system will not allow you to have two files with identical names within the same directory/folder. A Package will not allow two Elements (of the same type) with the same name inside the Package. As in any VIEW, if an Element appears twice in a Package, each occurrence is just a representation of the same thing.

Likewise, if Elements of the same name and type appear in different Packages, they are different Elements.

UML supports other Namespaces with can contain Elements. Most people do not realize it, but the compartments of Class are also Namespaces. A particular Class cannot have nondistinguishable attributes, or nondistinguishable operations,[7] just as a Package cannot have nondistinguishable Elements.

What are the rules for nondistinguishable names?

> **Attributes:** Two attributes within a Namespace, typically the Namespace is a Class, cannot have the same name and the same or related type.
> **Operations**: Two operations within a Namespace cannot have the same signature (operation name, number, order, direction, and types of arguments).
> **Classes and other Classifiers:** Two Classes within a Namespace cannot have the same name and cannot be of the same or related type.

---

[7]All the compartments are namespaces, so that other compartments (such as signals, ports) that we have not yet discussed also require unique names within the compartment.

In this context, two types neither of which is a kind of the other are unrelated types. That is, there cannot be generalization relationships between them.

These rules allow modelers some leeway in naming, primarily for purposes such as overloading operations. Taking advantage of them too often can produce unreadable models and code despite being technically correct.

POINTS TO REMEMBER

- Packages and other Elements within a Package may be marked as public (+) or private (−). This controls whether that can be seen outside their current container (+) or not (−).
- For two Elements to have different names either their name or type must be different.
  - For behavioral Elements, the name and signature (type, order, and direction of arguments) must be different.
  - For types to be different, they must not be related to each other by generalization.
- For Elements not directly in the Package, Package visibility (~) allows the Element to seen outside its container, but only to one level.
- For Elements not directly in the Package, protected visibility (#) allows the Element to seen by specializations of its container.
  - Neither # nor ~ can be applied to Packages
  - Neither # nor ~ can be applied to Elements directly in a Package.
- An outer Element may be directly (unqualified) referenced
  - An Element with a clashing name at the same level as the referrer will hide the outer Element, forcing qualified references
  - An Element with a clashing name at an intermediate level will hide the outer Element, forcing qualified references
- A fully qualified name of an Element includes the PackageName::ElementName. The chain of PackageName:: can be as long as necessary.
  - The separator is "::" following a Package.
  - The separator is "." following a Class.

8.3 PACKAGES AND THEIR CONTENTS

Packages are the primary organizing structure for UML. Packaged Elements tend to be cohesive and only weakly coupled to Elements outside the Package. Development teams are given a set of Packages to work without much overlap.

In Fig. 8.10, we show a simple Package structure for a Car Hailing App. This approach would be suitable for an organization that has a Hailing team and a Payment team and that wanted to divide the work. If we did our division correctly, they would not often have to coordinate. Although the separate Payment Package teams will need to do some coordination with the Pricing Package team, they will not have to coordinate otherwise. This approach shown is based on separation of functionality.

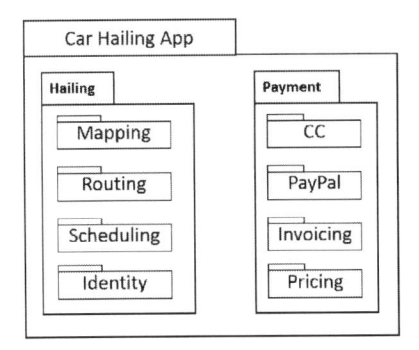

FIGURE 8.10
Possible Package structure for a Car Hailing App.

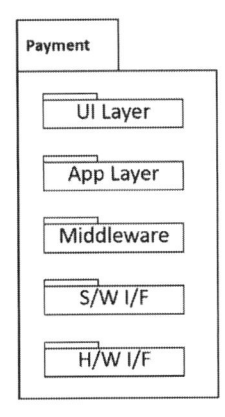

FIGURE 8.11
Layered Package architecture.

Another more recommended approach would be to produce Use Case focused Packages, see Chapter 14, Behavior: Sequence Diagrams. In that approach, you would construct a Package for each Actor: Rider, Driver, Management, and in each Package place the associated Use Cases and Classes. You would still need Packages to cover infrastructure.

A layered approach is often common, where the emphasis is on separating the project in low-level Packages containing interfaces to hardware, and the operating system; middle layer Packages containing utilities, database Packages; and higher-level Packages included the application logic. On the top-level would be User-interface Packages, see Fig. 8.11.

In most projects, you could incorporate several different organizing principles. For example, the Use Case approach might be used to divide the UI

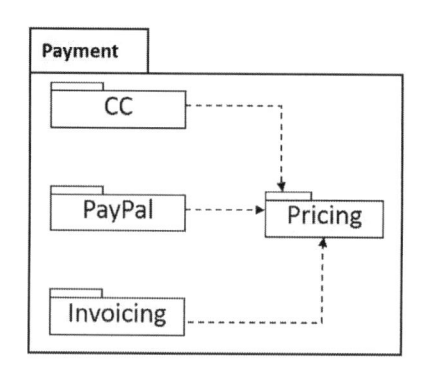

FIGURE 8.12
Package dependencies.

(User Interface) and Application Logic layers into Packages. Then the architecture and infrastructure could be distributed into separate Packages by the Layered approach.

Packages should be sized so that ongoing development and maintenance will not require too much coordination.

8.3.1 Package Dependencies

Packages can depend on other Packages. For example, the Packages within the Payment Package depend on the Pricing Package. If the Pricing Package would change, possibly the other Packages would need to change, see Fig. 8.12. It is a good Package architecture when the number of dependencies is minimized. We show the dependencies by pointing from the dependent to the independent item with a dashed arrow. In the figure, three Packages depend on the Pricing Package. However, in Fig. 8.11, how should the dependency arrows be drawn[8]?

8.3.2 Specific Elements from Other Packages

In the cases, we discussed in Section 8.2, Packages and visibility above we only need to put the `PackageName::` before the Element Name, because the Packages (P1 and P2) were directly visible to each other. Imagine two chains of Package, A1, A2, A3, ..., A10 and B1, B2, B3, ..., B10 where each Package contains the next lower-level Package. If an Element in A10 wants to refer to

---

[8]Each Package depends on the next lower level, so they would be connected with dashed arrows pointing down. It is also possible that some of the Packages would depend on multiple lower Packages, requiring additional dependencies.

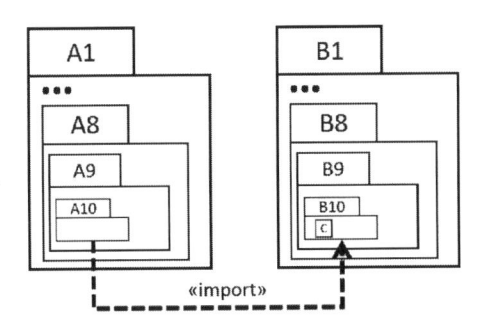

FIGURE 8.13
Package import of Package B10.

a C Element in B10, the qualified name would be long; it would be `B1::B2::B3::B4::B5::B6::B7::B8::B9::B10::C`. This is unwieldy, so UML has techniques for simplification: Import and access. The `techniques` are refinements of the dependencies discussed above that details what the dependency entails.

8.3.2.1 Package Import
Connect Package A10 with a special dependency (dashed arrow) pointing to B10 labeled with «import». Then, the whole B10 Package is treated as if it were copied inside A10. If the visibility rules and hiding rules allow, every Element in B10 is directly visible to Elements in A10, see Fig. 8.13. If a name collision occurs, the offending Element is not copied and would have to be referenced in the old-fashioned and long way using qualified names.

8.3.2.2 Element Import
If only a few Elements of B10 are required by A10, instead of importing the whole Package, you can connect the dependency arrow directly to the Elements you wish to import. This makes for simple references to the needed Elements without crowding the Namespace with Elements you do not want. You lessen the opportunity for errors by not exposing unnecessary Elements, see Fig. 8.14.

If the Element import would cause a name collision (i.e., if there were already an Element with that name in the importing Package), the import is ignored. If there were already a C in A10, but you still needed the B10::C, you can add an alias to the import. The import tag would then look like "«import» D". Then in A10 a user of B10::C would just refer to the alias D.

8.3.2.3 Comparison of Package vs Element Import
Let us look at the results from these imports. The dashed Elements on the left are a conventional way of indicating that the Elements exist as the results

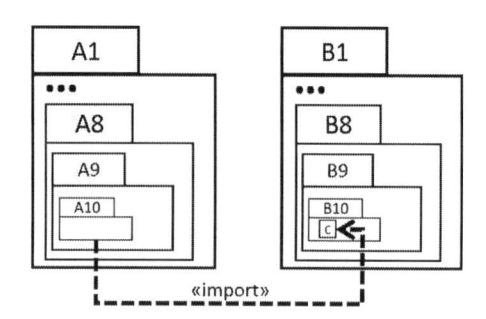

FIGURE 8.14
Element import of B10::C.

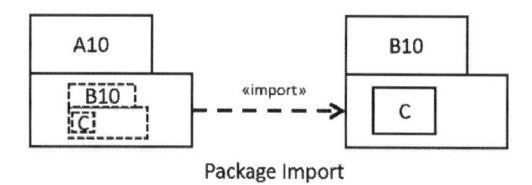

FIGURE 8.15
Results from Package import.

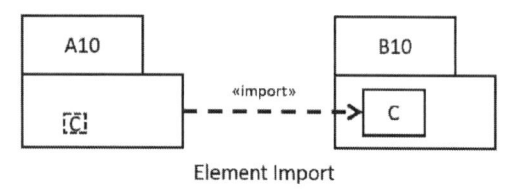

FIGURE 8.16
Results from Element import.

of importing but really reside in their original locations[9], see Figs. 8.15 and 8.16. The Element import only brings the selected Element without bringing potentially unwanted Elements, whereas the Package import brings the entire Package.

---

[9]The imported Packages and Elements are not really copied in. There are some differences between a contained Package and an imported Package, but not significant at this time.

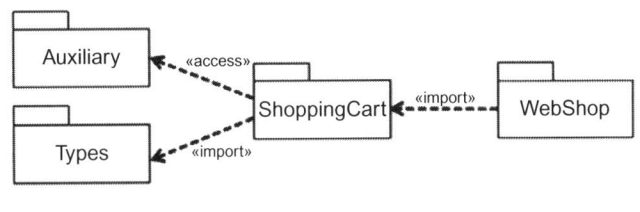

FIGURE 8.17
Access vs import. *UML 2.5 Specification Figure 7.9.*

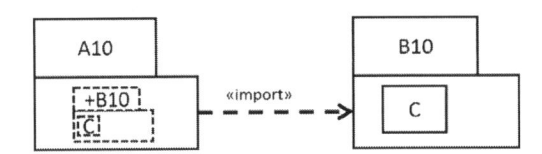

FIGURE 8.18
Import visibility.

8.3.2.4 Access
Use of the Package and Element import bring the target as a publicly visible item into the Package for use by other Elements in the importing Package. As a publicly visible item, they are further visible to anyone who imports the importing Package. Instead of «import», if you use «access» you get the same results, but the item is considered private and cannot be further imported.

In Fig. 8.17, the public members of the Types Package are imported into the ShoppingCart Package. When the WebShop Package imports the ShoppingCart Package, the public members of Types are further imported in the WebShop Package and are available for use. However, the members (private and public) of the Auxiliary Package are only privately imported into the ShoppingCart Package because «access» was used. When the WebShop Package imports the ShoppingCart Package, it does not get to see or use anything from the Auxiliary Package.

In the figures below, we show the difference between Import and access. The visibility of the imported Package is set to public (+) and the visibility of the accessed Package is set to private (−). The visibility of the C Element is not changed (Figs. 8.18 and 8.19).

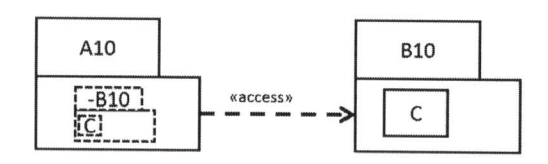

FIGURE 8.19
Access visibility.

8.3.2.5 Package Dependencies and Cycles

Many modelers make extensive diagrams showing the dependencies and other relationships between the Packages to guide them into placing Elements in their correct Package. This is good practice. It can reveal dangerous cyclic dependencies among the Packages. For example, if PA depends on PB while PB depends on PA, coordination will be very difficult. How could a decision be made on where to put something and how would the development order of the Packages be determined? If the model is forcing you to have cyclic dependencies between Packages, encapsulate the entire set of Packages involved in the chain into a higher-level Package, to hide the codependencies and assign the whole chain to one team.

8.3.2.6 Package Merge

Package Merge creates a new Package from existing ones, subject to complicated rules. Merges were used in early versions of UML 2.x, but were found to be overly difficult to use. They are not used by UML 2.5, but they are still defined in the UML specification in case there are other OMG specifications that might depend on them. Merging will probably be removed from future versions of UML.

POINTS TO REMEMBER

- A dependency between Packages is indicated by a dashed line pointing to the Independent Package (target) coming from the Dependent Package (source).
    - Avoid cyclic dependencies among your Packages.
- Besides standard dependency, a modeler may indicate that a Package needs to be copied inside the source Package
    - A publically copied Package is indicated by the «import» relationship.
    - A privately copied Package is indicated by the «access» relationship.
- An individual Element may also be imported using the «import» relationship.

8.4 PACKAGE STEREOTYPES

8.4.1 Packages and Models

Packages are the primary organizing and CM structure for UML Models. UML tools often cooperate with standard CM tools to allow check-in, check-out, change management, compare, baseline, and restore on Package boundaries.

When projects are new and subject to many changes, Packages tend to be small, because if you have to check out a Package to start editing, you do not want to lock out other modelers from doing any work. On the other hand, when maintenance work is causing changes that tend to ripple through multiple Packages, small Packages with repeated check-outs, and check-ins will cause delay to the working process. Some projects will change their Package structure as the project evolves, but it is best to pick Packages properly sized to capture closely related Elements so typical changes would only affect one Package.

Another consideration is that Packages tend to be the review structure. Just as with code, your model should be reviewed, so at the lowest level of Packages, they should be sized to be conveniently peer-reviewed models.

Every Element in UML must be owned by exactly one other higher level Element, except the top-level Packages in the model. This requirement produces a chain of ownership that must end in a Package. This is the origin of the use of Packages as the organizing Element.

One of the common stereotypes of Package allows the modeler to show that we are splitting the model by organizing principles. The stereotype is «model» which indicates that the contents of the Package are intended to be a complete version of your system based on a modeling aspect. If you remember our discussion at the end of Chapter 2, What is UML?, we talked about different types of a modeling: Such as conceptualization, requirements analysis, analysis, and design. If you have a Package whose totality of contents follows one of these aspects, you would flag the Package with the stereotype of «model».

How we use these «models» depends mostly on project methodology. Each model can offer up a complete view of the system at a particular level of abstraction. If not based on the types of modeling, the models might be based on a metamodeling level (e.g., M0, M1, ...), or modeling phase. Many projects have formal official reviews at a planned time, e.g., SRR (System Requirements Review), SDR (System Design Review), PDR (Preliminary Design Review), or CDR (Critical Design Review), or TRR (Test Readiness Review). The models produced at these times are kept in «model» Packages and baselined so that the project can go back and review them. Models, as Packages, are also Namespaces, so there is no problem having identically named Elements in each model.

Depending on the methodology, the separate «models» may be connected by a chain of dependencies. There are special types of dependencies that often are, but are not required to be used in these circumstances. An abstraction relates two NamedElements that represent the same concept at different levels of abstraction or from different viewpoints. Any of the abstractions in Table 8.3 can be associated with a string that explains how the mapping works.

Table 8.3 Types of Abstractions

Abstraction Type	Usage
«abstraction»	Relates two Elements or sets of Elements that denote the same concept but at different levels of abstraction or from different viewpoints. Adjacent to the stereotype may be a string that explains how the mapping works
«derive»	A calculable relationship between levels
«realize»	The arrowhead points to Elements that act as requirements to the Elements at the tail that realize or implement the target Elements. We often show this relationship as a dashed line with a hollow triangular arrowhead
«refine»	A relationship between two different levels of abstraction
«trace»	A generic relationship between different versions. May be bi-directional

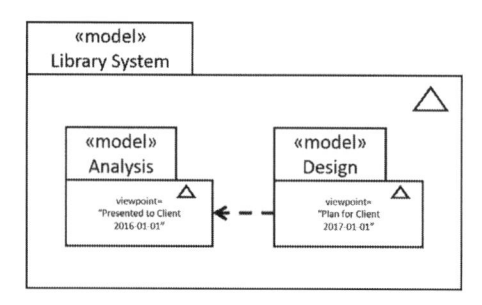

FIGURE 8.20
Example of models.

As a type of Package, models look like Package with the stereotype of «model». The optionally have a triangle adornment △ in the upper right to indicate their model status. Models may have a viewpoint field that uses a string to document the organizing principle or perspective for that model, see Fig. 8.20.

Many modelers make their top-level Packages (the ones not contained by other things) into «models». However, this is not required and would prevent models from being contained in other Packages or models (as shown in Fig. 8.20). As with most use of models, the project methodology will determine your practice.

8.4.2 Miscellaneous Stereotypes of Packages

8.4.2.1 ModelLibrary

The stereotype «MODELLIBRARY» indicates that the majority of its contents are used by other Packages or models. Typically, we use a «modelLibrary» to contain common types, units, utilities, or parts that other Packages in the system can use. The «modelLibrary» will be marked a publicly visible and potentially «imported» into the top-level Package—Ensuring visibility and accessibility by all of the system's Packages.

8.4.2.2 Framework

Similar to a «modelLibrary», a «FRAMEWORK» contains the infrastructure and architectural Elements shared my many of the other system Packages. A «framework» usually includes event and error handlers, message passing, logging, self-check, built-in-test, diagnostics, and security enforcement.

8.4.2.3 Profiles

Although PROFILES (and their associated PROFILE DIAGRAMS) are not included in the Foundational level of the OCUP-2 examinations, you need to know their purpose and use. Profiles are similar to the standard Package except for the Profile stereotype. Profiles typically contain «metaclasses» (see Chapter 4: The Organization of UML) that are tailored to aid in enforcing the project's methodology or reporting and status regime. You can use it to create or removed metaclasses or stereotypes, though typically only one person on a project is allowed. Of course, these Profiles must be available to everyone on the project, and are difficult to create, potentially introducing portability problems.

8.4.2.4 Diagrams

Diagrams of the contents of «models», «modelLibrarys», «frameworks», and «profiles» all have a <kind> field of **pkg** or **package** and the name of the Namespace in the diagram header. In many cases, the <kind> field can be omitted as it can be determined by the contents.

If the diagram primarily shows Packages and their relationships (e.g., imports, accesses, dependencies, or abstractions), the diagram would be considered a Package Diagram. If the diagram primarily shows Classes, generalization, and associations, the diagram would be considered a Class Diagram, despite the header. If the diagram primarily shows instances, it would be considered an Instance Diagram.

A Profile Diagram looks like a Package Diagram but supports a slightly different notation that allows the extension of or restriction of existing metaclasses and the definition of stereotypes. We will not cover the details in this book nor are they on the OCUP-2 Foundational exam.

POINTS TO REMEMBER

- A «model» is a type of Package that represents a model of the system for a particular aspect, which may be declared in the model.
- Separate «model» Packages are often connected by a type of «abstraction» relationship.
- Both «modelLibrarys» and «frameworks» are used to contain reusable Elements such as types, parts, units, and architectural infrastructure.
- A Profile is a type of Package and an associated diagram that allows the modeler to tailor gently the UML language for their project.

CHAPTER 9

Questions for Chapter 8

1. Which option below indicates namespace containment?

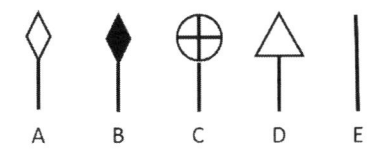

   A. A
   B. B
   C. C
   D. D
   E. E

2. Which option describes the consequence of adding a Class C1 into Package P2?

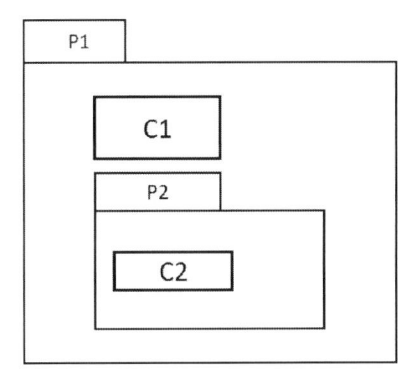

   A. The C1 in P1 cannot be accessed by anything in P2
   B. No change

C. If C2 wishes to refer to the refer to the C1 in P1, it will need to refer to it as P1.C1
D. If C2 wishes to refer to the refer to the C1 in P1, it will need to refer to it as P1::C1
E. You cannot put a C1 into P2 because it has the same name as the C1 in P1.

3. Which symbol indicates that the element is a «model»?

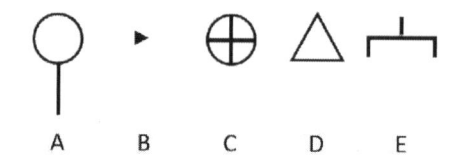

   A   B   C   D   E

   A. A
   B. B
   C. C
   D. D
   E. E

4. In the diagram fragment below, how would elements in P1 (such as X or Y) refer to W from P2?

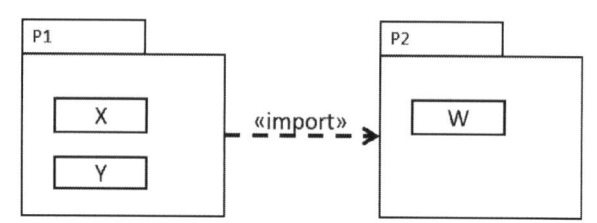

   A. W
   B. P2.W
   C. P2..W
   D. P2: W
   E. P2::W

5. How could an element import fail to accomplish anything?
   A. An element import always brings in the target element.
   B. If the target element has a name that matches an existing element in the importing Package
   C. If the target element has a name that would hide an outer element
   D. If the target element has a name that would hide an inner element
   E. If the target element is a stand-alone instance

6. Which attribute below is visible in exactly two classes?

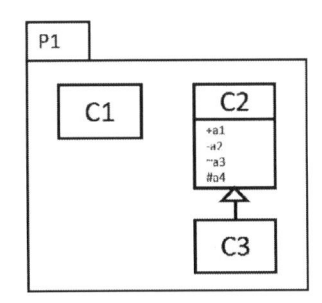

   A. No attributes are visible in exactly two classes
   B. a1
   C. a2
   D. a3
   E. a4

7. Which diagram fragment incorporates P2 into P1?
   A.

   B.

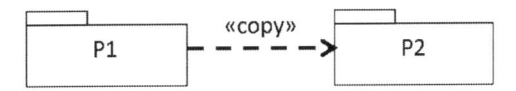

   C.

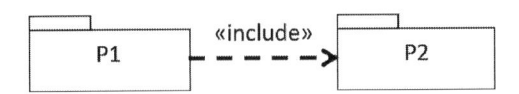

   D.

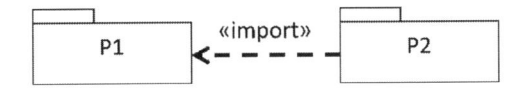

   E.

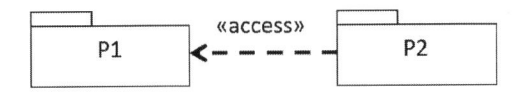

8. Which pair cannot exist in the same namespace?

   «package» system   «model» system
   «attribute» name:String   «attribute» name:NameType
   «operation» borrow(:book, :date) «operation» borrow(:date, :book)
   «instance» Tom Sawyer:Book   «instance» Tom Sawyer:Actor

   A. All pairs can coexist
   B. system
   C. name
   D. borrow
   E. Tom Sawyer
   F. No pair can coexists.

9. What change needs to be made to the following diagram to ensure that the «modelLibrary» Currency can be used in Package Invoices?

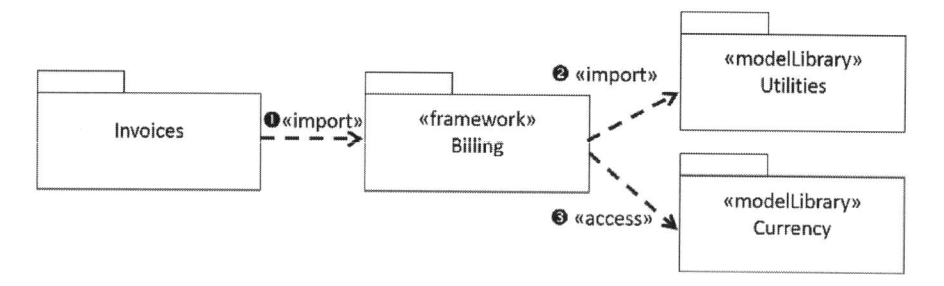

   A. Change ❶ to be an «access» relationship
   B. Change ❷ to be an «access» relationship
   C. Change ❸ to be an «import» relationship
   D. Delete the «import» string on ❶
   E. Change ❶ to be an «realize» relationship
   F. Change the Billing «framework» to be a «modelLibrary»

10. How can we denote that Package P has another Package P inside?
    A.

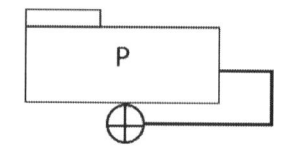

B.

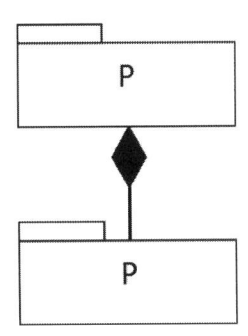

C.

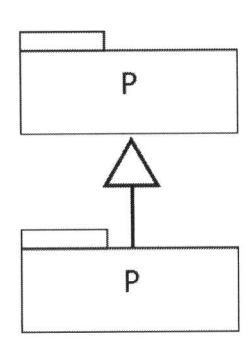

D.

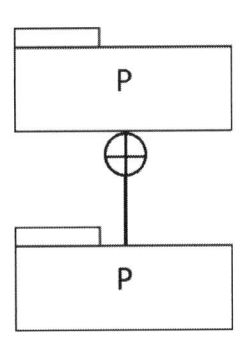

E. It is not possible to have a Package P contain another Package with the same name

11. How can we change the diagram below such that element X can see z without making it visible outside of P1?

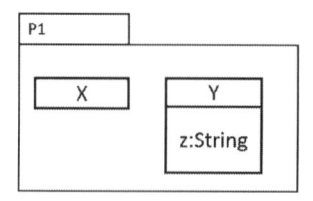

```
┌─P1──────────────────────┐
│                         │
│  ┌─────┐  ┌─────────┐   │
│  │  X  │  │    Y    │   │
│  └─────┘  ├─────────┤   │
│           │ z:String│   │
│           └─────────┘   │
└─────────────────────────┘
```

    A. It is not necessary to change anything as z is already public
    B. Add a " + " to precede Y to make Y publicly visible
    C. Add a " − " to precede z to make z privately visible
    D. Add a "#" to precede z to give z protected visibility
    E. Add a "~" to precede z to give z package visibility
    F. There is nothing that can be done to accomplish this.

12. How can we change the diagram (without changing z) below such that element X can see z without making it visible outside of P1?

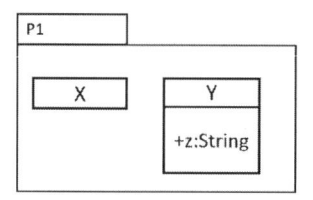

```
┌─P1──────────────────────┐
│                         │
│  ┌─────┐  ┌──────────┐  │
│  │  X  │  │    Y     │  │
│  └─────┘  ├──────────┤  │
│           │+z:String │  │
│           └──────────┘  │
└─────────────────────────┘
```

    A. It is not necessary to change anything as z is already public
    B. Add a " + " to precede Y to make Y publicly visible
    C. Add a " − " to precede Y to make z privately visible
    D. Add a "#" to precede P1 to give P1 protected visibility
    E. Add a "~" to precede P1 to give P1 package visibility
    F. Add a " − " to precede P1 to make P1 privately visible

ANSWERS FOR CHAPTER 8

1. Which option below indicates namespace containment?

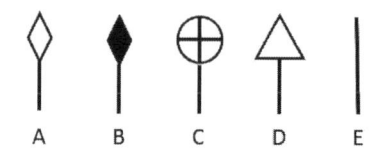

    A   B   C   D   E

A. A
B. B
C. <u>C</u>
D. D
E. E

Discussion:
A—No, this is an aggregation relationship, used between a whole and its parts.
B—No, this is a composition relationship, used between a whole and its parts.
C—Yes, the quartered circle indicates namespace containment, used between a namespace and an element definition.
D—No, this is a generalization/specialization relationship. Packages were subject to generalization or /specialization in UML 1.x, but this is not allowed in UML 2.x
E—No, a solid line indicates an association, usually between classes (classifiers)

2. Which option describes the consequence of adding a Class C1 into Package P2?

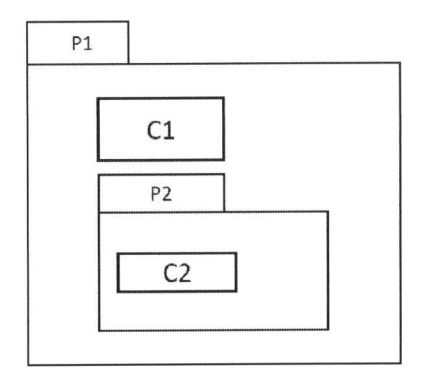

A. The C1 in P1 cannot be accessed by anything in P2
B. No change
C. If C2 wishes to refer to the refer to the C1 in P1, it will need to refer to it as P1.C1
D. **If C2 wishes to refer to the refer to the C1 in P1, it will need to refer to it as P1::C1**
E. You cannot put a C1 into P2 because it has the same name as the C1 in P1.

Discussion:
A—No, while the new C1 hides the existing C1, it does not prevent access. It makes the access require a qualified name.

B—No, the name collision prevents direct access to C1
C—No, P1.C1 is not the required form
D—Yes, the proper way to access the C1 in P1 is to use "::"
E—No, this is not true.
3. Which symbol indicates that the element is a «model»?

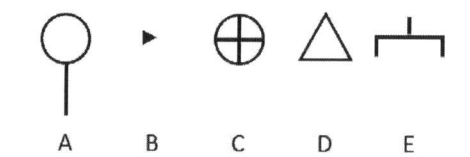

```
      ▶     ⊕   △   ┌┘
  A   B     C   D   E
```

A. A
B. B
C. C
D. **D**
E. E

Discussion:
A—No, this symbol indicates a provided interface.
B—No, this symbol indicates the direction to read an association name.
C—No, we use this symbol on a namespace containment line.
D—Yes, this symbol, when placed in the upper right of the Package, indicates that the Package symbol is actually a «model».
E—No, this symbol sometimes indicates an element is decomposable.

4. In the diagram fragment below, how would elements in P1 (such as X or Y) refer to W from P2?

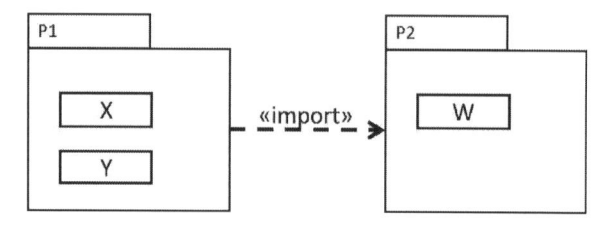

```
  P1                            P2
  ┌──────────┐                  ┌──────────┐
  │  ┌───┐   │                  │  ┌───┐   │
  │  │ X │   ├──«import»──▶    │  │ W │   │
  │  └───┘   │                  │  └───┘   │
  │  ┌───┐   │                  │          │
  │  │ Y │   │                  │          │
  │  └───┘   │                  │          │
  └──────────┘                  └──────────┘
```

A. **W**
B. P2.W
C. P2..W
D. P2: W
E. P2::W

Discussion:
A—Yes, as P2 is imported, we can omit the qualified notation.
B—No, the "." indicates a member of a Class, not an element of a Package.
C—No, two "." is not used in UML.
D—No, the ":" is used in UML to separate an attribute from its Type.
E—No, although this would work, the «import» makes the "::" unnecessary

5. How could an element import fail to accomplish anything?
   A. An element import always brings in the target element.
   B. **If the target element has a name that matches an existing element in the importing Package**
   C. If the target element has a name that would hide an outer element
   D. If the target element has a name that would hide an inner element
   E. If the target element is a stand-alone instance

   Discussion:
   B—Yes, import will work unless that importing Package has an element with a clashing name
   A, C, D, and E—An element import can fail if it causes a name clash with the importing Package.

6. Which attribute below is visible in exactly two classes?

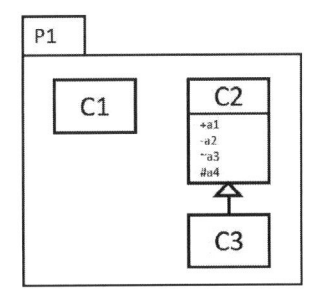

   A. No attributes are visible in exactly two classes
   B. a1
   C. a2
   D. a3
   E. **a4**

   Discussion:
   A—No
   B—No, A1 has public visibility, and is visible to all, C1, C2, and C3

C—No, A2 has private visibility, is only visible to C2, and not visible outside the defining Class.
D—No, A3 has package visibility, and is visible to C1, C2, and C3, but not outside the Package (P1)
E—Yes, A4 has protected visibility and is visible to C2 and C3, because C3 is a specialization of the defining Class (C2).

7. Which diagram fragment incorporates P2 into P1?

   A.

   P1 «import»→ P2

   B.

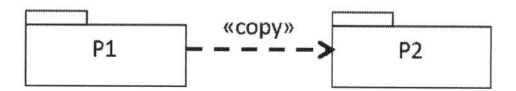

   P1 «copy»→ P2

   C.

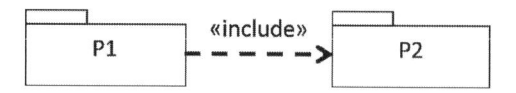

   P1 «include»→ P2

   D.

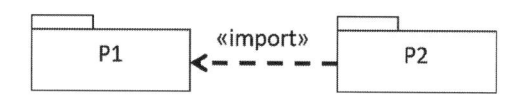

   P1 ←«import» P2

   E.

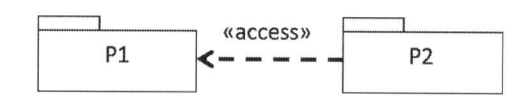

   P1 ←«access» P2

Discussion:
A—Yes, «import brings in the contents.
B—No, «copy is not used between Packages
C—No, «include» is used between Use Cases
D—No, «import» is the correct name but is in the wrong direction.
E—No, «access» would work but it is the wrong direction.

8. Which pair cannot exist in the same namespace?

   «package» system   «model» system
   «attribute» name:String   «attribute» name:NameType
   «operation» borrow(:book, :date) «operation» borrow(:date, :book)
   «instance» Tom Sawyer:Book   «instance» Tom Sawyer:Actor

   A. All pairs can coexist
   B. **system**
   C. name
   D. borrow
   E. Tom Sawyer
   F. No pair can coexists.

   Discussion:
   A—No, one pair has a name clash.
   B—Yes, because a model is a subtype of Package, an attempt to import it causes a name collision.
   C—No, the attributes are of different and unrelated types.
   D—No, the signatures of the operations are different.
   E—No, these are two different types of Tom Sawyer.

9. What change needs to be made to the following diagram to ensure that the «modelLibrary» Currency can be used in Package Invoices?

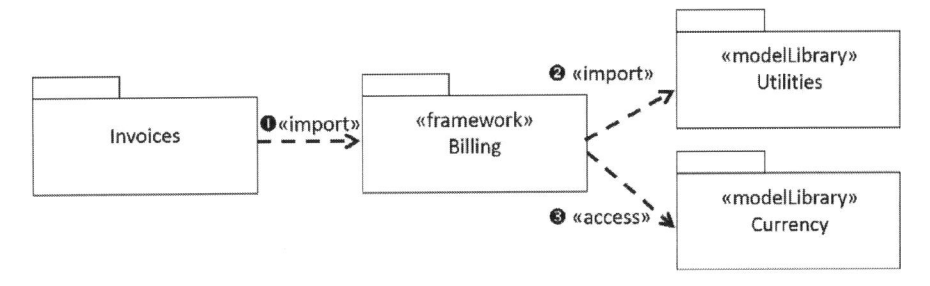

   A. Change ❶ to be an «access» relationship
   B. Change ❷ to be an «access» relationship
   C. **Change ❸ to be an «import» relationship**
   D. Delete the «import» string on ❶
   E. Change ❶ to be an «realize» relationship
      Change the Billing «framework» to be a «modelLibrary»

   Discussion:
   A—No, this change does not affect the visibility of Currency.
   B—No, this change would block Utilities from being used. Access makes the element private to further imports.

C—Yes, this would make the Currency copied into Billing publicly, and available for imports by others.

D—No, this change would make the relationship into an undifferentiated dependency. None of the Packages would be available to Invoices.

E—No, a realize relationship would require Invoice to be an implementation of Billing.

F—No, the type of Package element does not change the meaning of the relationships.

10. How can we denote that Package P has another Package P inside?

   A.

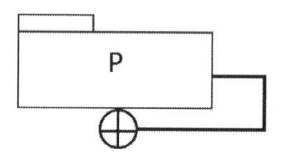

   B.

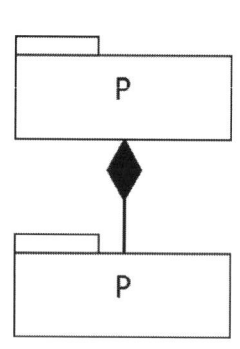

   C.

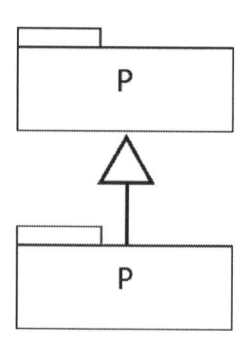

D.

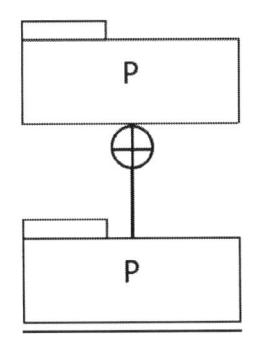

E. It is not possible to have a Package P contain another Package with the same name

Discussion:
A—No, if this worked, it would have the same Package on the inside and the outside.
B—No, this is composition and works between classes.
C—No, generalization is not allowed between Packages in UML 2.5.
D—Yes, not necessarily a smart thing though.
E—No, not true.

11. How can we change the diagram below such that element X can see z without making it visible outside of P1?

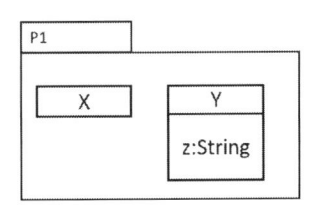

   A. It is not necessary to change anything as z is already public
   B. Add a " + " to precede Y to make Y publicly visible
   C. Add a " − " to precede z to make z privately visible
   D. Add a "#" to precede z to give z protected visibility
   E. **Add a " ~ " to precede z to give z package visibility**
   F. There is nothing that can be done to accomplish this.

   Discussion:
   A—No, the visibility of z is undefined
   B—No, the default is that Y is already visible
   C—No, making z private will prevent X from seeing it
   D—No, making z protected will only allow subclasses of Y to see it

E—Yes, making z package visible will allow only other elements in P1 to see it, but not those outside of P1

F—No, E is the answer.

12. How can we change the diagram (without changing z) below such that element X can see z without making it visible outside of P1?

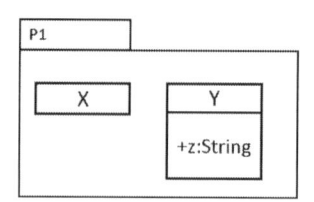

```
P1
┌─────────────────────────┐
│  ┌─────┐   ┌─────────┐  │
│  │  X  │   │    Y    │  │
│  └─────┘   ├─────────┤  │
│            │+z:String│  │
│            └─────────┘  │
└─────────────────────────┘
```

A. It is not necessary to change anything as z is already public
B. Add a " + " to precede Y to make Y publicly visible
C. Add a " − " to precede Y to make z privately visible
D. Add a "#" to precede P1 to give P1 protected visibility
E. Add a " ~ " to precede P1 to give P1 package visibility
F. **Add a " − " to precede P1 to make P1 privately visible**

Discussion:

A—No, though it is true that z is already publicly visible, it would be also be visible outside of P1.

B—No, the default is that Y is already visible.

C—No, making z private will prevent X from seeing it.

D—No, it is not legal to give a Package protected visibility. Packages do not support generalization in UML2.

E—No, it is not legal to give a Package visibility.

F—Yes, if the Package is made private, none of its contents can be seen outside.

CHAPTER 10

Finishing the Static Model

10.1 MULTIPLICITY

Though we introduced MULTIPLICITY several times earlier, we now take the opportunity to review and expand your knowledge of how UML multiplicity works.

In UML, multiplicity is the potential range of the number of items. We can apply multiplicity to attributes, operation arguments, and association ends. The UML metamodel also uses multiplicity to constrain the relationships among metamodels elements. The multiplicity ranges always include the CARDINALITY value, which is the exact number of items in the M0 domain.

We will discuss association ends in a later section, but their multiplicity ranges work the same as described here.

10.1.1 Representing the Multiplicity of Attributes

Examine Fig. 10.1. We depict the **Book** Class, showing several attributes. As we have found that many books have more than one author[1], we need to allow for several authors. In this example, we allowed an instance of **Book** to have three authors. What might be some problems with this solution?

1. *What is the limit?* Many books have more than three authors. Microsoft Word allows for up to 99 authors per document. We could follow this approach and accommodate author1 through author99, but even this would not be enough.
   In the scientific research domain, some papers have greater than 3500 authors. Allowing for 3500 + authors would certainly take up more room that the average case[2].

---

[1] By the way, authors would include corporate bodies, conferences, etc.
[2] The Anglo-American Cataloging Rules (AACR), which most English-speaking countries use to catalog library materials, only allows for up to three authors. If there are more, the first author is recorded and "*et al.*" is used.

```
            ┌─────────────────────┐
            │        Book         │
            ├─────────────────────┤
            │ title    : String   │
            │ author1: Person     │
            │ author2: Person     │
            │ author3: Person     │
            │ pages    : Integer  │
            │ ...                 │
            └─────────────────────┘
```

FIGURE 10.1
Book with specific room reserved for additional authors.

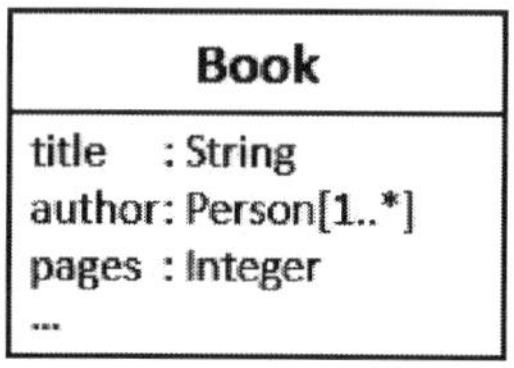

```
            ┌─────────────────────┐
            │        Book         │
            ├─────────────────────┤
            │ title  : String     │
            │ author: Person[1..*]│
            │ pages  : Integer    │
            │ ...                 │
            └─────────────────────┘
```

FIGURE 10.2
Book with a multivalued attribute.

2. *Is this stored efficiently or sparsely?* There is no rule that the author values are densely stored in the first few author slots. Perhaps, there is an author1 and an author99 and no between authors. This arrangement would certainly make manipulating the author list slow and cumbersome.
3. *How can we loop over them?* Most programming languages would make it difficult to implement a loop that cycled over author1 through author99 if the mechanism were based on the variable name.

Examine Fig. 10.2. We depict the **Book** Class, showing three attributes. The author attribute has a multiplicity assigned, solving the three problems mentioned above. We show the multiplicity as a range from the LOWER-BOUND to the UPPER-BOUND (inclusively) of the number of possible values that the field can hold. The "*" is an indicator of "UNBOUNDED." So this multiplicity indicates that there can be one or more (with no limit) authors associated with a **Book**[3].

We say that the author attribute is MULTIVALUED because the upper-bound is more than one. When we read the attribute with the multiplicity, we can say, "There are ONE OR MORE authors" or "There is at least one author."

---

[3]The "*" (unbounded) is not the same thing as "infinity," as we cannot have an infinite number of anything in the real world, even in computer systems. Unbounded indicates that we can use any value as great as we might want or need.

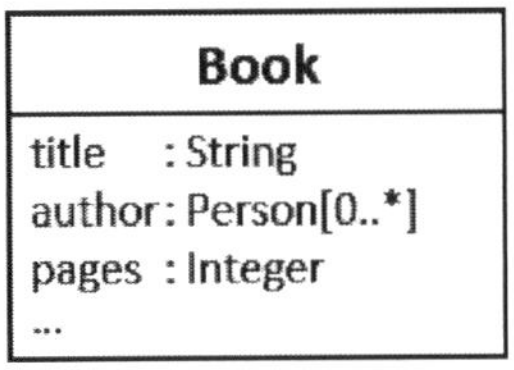

```
        ┌─────────────────────┐
        │       Book          │
        ├─────────────────────┤
        │ title  : String     │
        │ author: Person[0..*]│
        │ pages  : Integer    │
        │ ...                 │
        └─────────────────────┘
```

FIGURE 10.3
Book allowing zero authors.

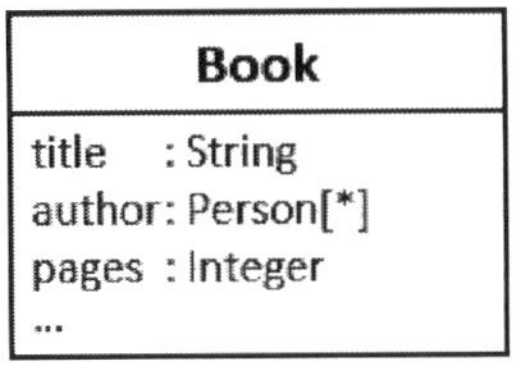

```
        ┌─────────────────────┐
        │       Book          │
        ├─────────────────────┤
        │ title  : String     │
        │ author: Person[*]   │
        │ pages  : Integer    │
        │ ...                 │
        └─────────────────────┘
```

FIGURE 10.4
Alternate form of "Many."

When there is a lower-bound and an upper-bound for a multiplicity, it is a requirement that

Lower-bound ≤ upper-bound

Examine Fig. 10.3. We again depict the **Book** Class. This time, we allow there to be zero authors. In the previous figure, we might have assumed that we would use "Anonymous" as the author of a book without authors. More likely, the display software would automatically know that an empty author name should be displayed/printed as Anonymous.

This author attribute is still multivalued because the upper-bound is more than one. When we read the attribute with this multiplicity, we can say, "There are zero or more authors" or "There are MANY authors." UML uses "many" to include zero. I prefer "The **Book** may have many authors" to emphasize both the optionality and the unbounded natures.

Now examine Fig. 10.4. This figure is equivalent to the previous Fig. 10.3. Using [*] alone in the multiplicity field is equal to using [0..*], allowing us to elide the "0" lower-bound.

Some readers may be wondering why there is no multiplicity showing on the pages attribute. Is not this also a range? Not exactly. Though the value of pages has a range, there is only one value of the number of pages associated with a **Book**. The author field has many values, so it gets a multiplicity. If we wanted to show the range for the value of pages, we would use a constraint (as done in Fig. 10.7).

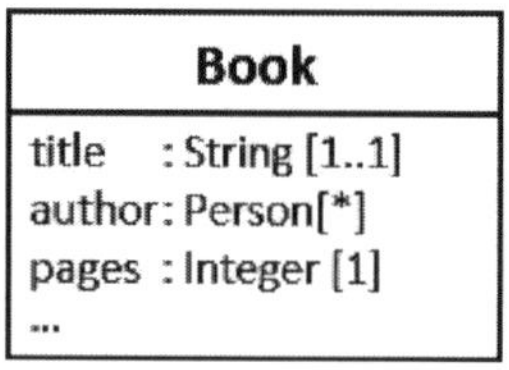

```
        Book
title  : String [1..1]
author: Person[*]
pages  : Integer [1]
...
```

FIGURE 10.5
Exactly one.

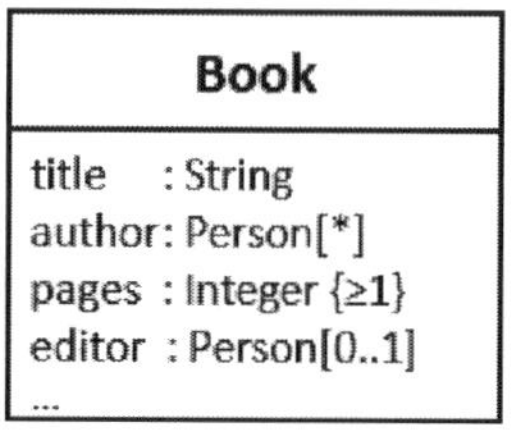

```
        Book
title  : String
author: Person[*]
pages  : Integer {≥1}
editor : Person[0..1]
...
```

FIGURE 10.6
Constraint and optional.

Now examine Fig. 10.5. We can show a multiplicity for the title and pages attributes. In this case, as the fields are mandatory but cannot exist more than once per book, we use a multiplicity of one. The title attribute shows both a lower-bound and an upper-bound of one [1..1]. We can say, "There is EXACTLY ONE title."

The pages' attribute uses just a 1 in the multiplicity field. If just one value is shown in the multiplicity, it is used as both the lower- and upper-bounds, so [1] and [1..1] are equivalent.

The default multiplicity when unspecified is [1], so Figs. 10.4 and 10.5 mean the same thing. In Fig. 10.6, we restored the default format of Fig. 10.5. We also added the constraint on the number of pages as discussed above. In Chapter 6, Objects and Classes, we showed several alternative forms for indicating the constraint. Another approach would be

   pages :Integer {in 1..*}

Remember that constraints are surrounded by {} while multiplicity is surrounded by []. In this constraint, we also use the ".." that indicates a UML range.

We also added another attribute, editor. This attribute also has the type of Person. The multiplicity is shown as [0..1], indicating that the field is either

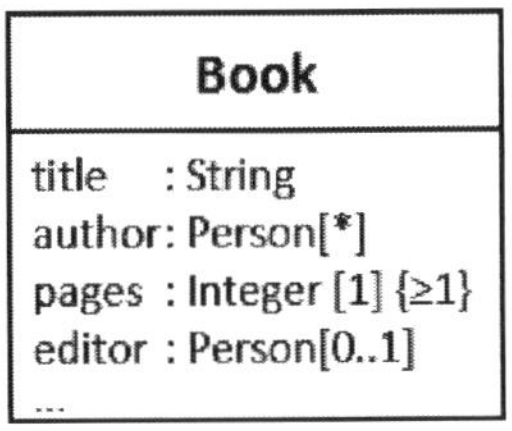

```
         ┌─────────────────────────────┐
         │           Book              │
         ├─────────────────────────────┤
         │ title  : String             │
         │ author: Person[*]           │
         │ pages  : Integer [1] {≥1}   │
         │ editor : Person[0..1]       │
         │ ...                         │
         └─────────────────────────────┘
```

FIGURE 10.7
Multiplicity and constraint.

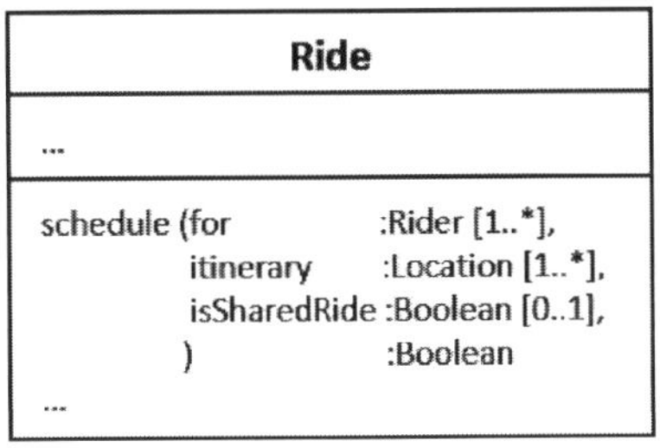

```
         ┌─────────────────────────────────────────────┐
         │                   Ride                      │
         ├─────────────────────────────────────────────┤
         │ ...                                         │
         ├─────────────────────────────────────────────┤
         │ schedule (for            :Rider [1..*],     │
         │           itinerary      :Location [1..*],  │
         │           isSharedRide   :Boolean [0..1],   │
         │           )              :Boolean           │
         │ ...                                         │
         └─────────────────────────────────────────────┘
```

FIGURE 10.8
Operation parameters showing multiplicity.

there or not. Some books do not have an editor. We can say, "The editor attribute is optional" or "The **Book** MAY have an editor." "May" is used to indicate that the lower bound is 0.

We revisit the situation of two attributes of the same type in Fig. 10.20.

In Fig. 10.7, we show an attribute with both a constraint and a multiplicity (pages). In these situations, we show the multiplicity first. The default multiplicity when unspecified is [1], so Figs. 10.6 and 10.7 mean the same thing. However, in Fig. 10.7, we show both the constraint and multiplicity for pages.

10.1.2 Representing Argument Multiplicity

We can use multiplicity on operation arguments. These work the same as the multiplicity on attributes. The default multiplicity when not shown explicitly is [1]. Using an argument with a multiplicity of [0..1] indicates that the argument is optional. In Fig. 10.8, we show the schedule operation for a Ride. There must be one or more Riders and one or more Locations. We also show an optional Boolean flag indicating that the Ride may be shared.

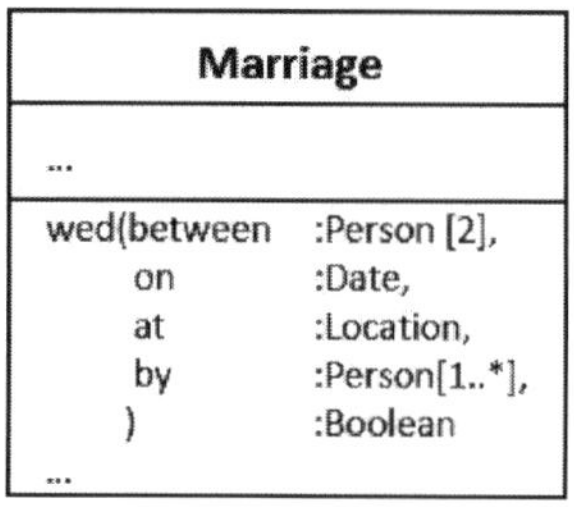

Marriage	
...	

wed(between
    on
    at
    by
)
	:Person [2],
	:Date,
	:Location,
	:Person[1..*],
	:Boolean

...	

FIGURE 10.9
Marriage showing exact multiplicity.

In Fig. 10.9, we show another operation[4], this time with an argument that must have exactly two participants.

We use multiplicity in the argument lists of operations, but we may also use multiplicity with signals, receptions, and other behavioral elements.

10.1.3 Multiplicity Properties and Collection Types

Whenever we have a multivalued item (i.e., whose upper-bound of the multiplicity is greater than one), we have some questions that we may wish to ask.

- Does the sequence of values matter?
- May any of the values be duplicates?

10.1.3.1 Set

In UML, a multivalued property is a set. A set in UML, and traditionally, disallows duplicates and has no defined order. In the above examples, the multivalued properties, without further markup, are sets. No person should be an author on a specific book more than once. No person can be a rider on a specific trip more one than once. A person cannot marry themselves. A person cannot be a celebrant[5] at a particular marriage more than once.

10.1.3.2 Ordered Set

In a set, there is no first or last or nth position. Though the implementation may be done with an array, technically, you cannot guarantee that any apparent order is repeatable. If you want a stable order, or if sets are not the best

---

[4]The naming convention for operation arguments employed here allows the operation and arguments to sound more like natural English; though coding the operation may be slightly more difficult. Use whatever approach with which you are most comfortable.

[5]The celebrants would be the Persons being passed into the `Marriage.wed()` operation via the "by" parameter.

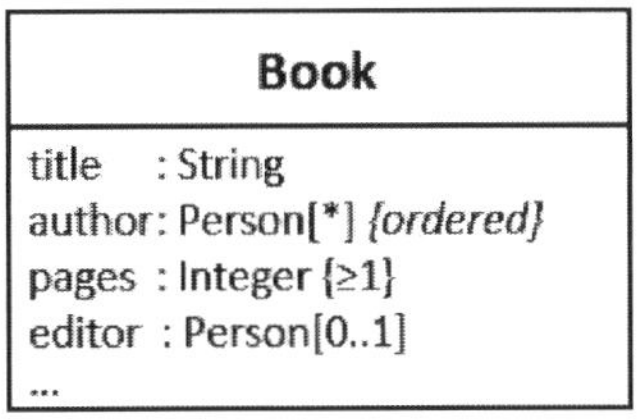

```
        ┌─────────────────────────────┐
        │          Book               │
        ├─────────────────────────────┤
        │ title   : String            │
        │ author: Person[*] {ordered} │
        │ pages  : Integer {≥1}       │
        │ editor : Person[0..1]       │
        │ ...                         │
        └─────────────────────────────┘
```

FIGURE 10.10
Book with an ordered and unique multivalued attribute.

solution for the multivalued property, you must flag the collection as being {ORDERED} or {ISORDERED = TRUE}.

For example, as an author, I certainly recognize that the order of the listed authors conveys prestige, with the first author being considered more important. To see how this looks, examine Fig. 10.10. We added the {ordered} property to the author attribute. This property indicates that the group of authors forms an ORDERED SET, and the order needs to be preserved unless explicitly changed.

10.1.3.3 Unique
The ordered set collection still does not allow for duplicates. This restriction is acceptable for the author attribute because the same person cannot appear as an author more than once for a book. The default is {UNIQUE} or {ISUNIQUE = TRUE}.

10.1.3.4 Bag
A bag is the type of collection that applies when a property can appear more than once (nonUnique), but there is no inherent order. Consider the items bought on a supermarket-shopping trip. A person may buy the same item more than once, and the order is not important. We call this collection type a bag[6].

10.1.3.5 Sequence
In the operation `Ride.Schedule()` as shown in Fig. 10.8, we have a multivalued argument itinerary. The itinerary is a set of locations that the ride must visit. These have a natural order, the first stop, the second stop, … the last stop. However, there is no reason why the ride cannot visit some of the same stops more than once (Fig. 10.11).

Ordered and nonUnique collections are common. For example, consider sampling the barometric pressure at a location every day at the same time.

---

[6]This is correct name and is not just a pun.

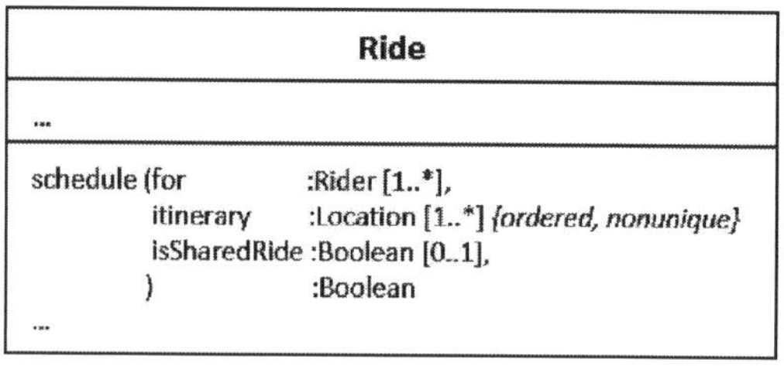

```
                    ┌─────────────────────────────────────────────────┐
                    │                      Ride                       │
                    ├─────────────────────────────────────────────────┤
                    │ ...                                             │
                    ├─────────────────────────────────────────────────┤
                    │ schedule (for        :Rider [1..*],             │
                    │          itinerary   :Location [1..*] {ordered, nonunique} │
                    │          isSharedRide:Boolean [0..1],           │
                    │          )           :Boolean                   │
                    │ ...                                             │
                    └─────────────────────────────────────────────────┘
```

FIGURE 10.11
Ride showing an ordered and NonUnique parameter.

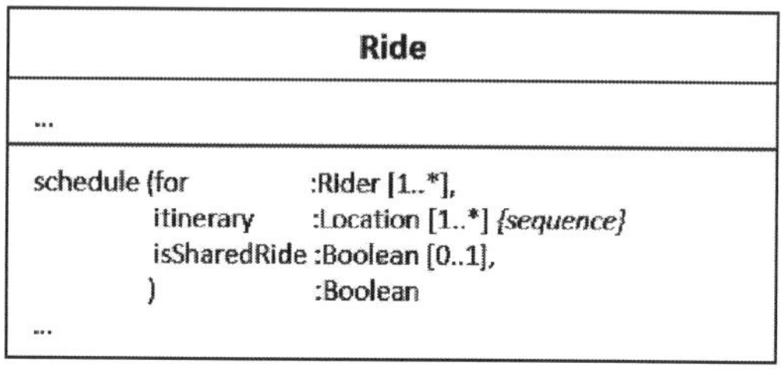

```
                    ┌─────────────────────────────────────────────────┐
                    │                      Ride                       │
                    ├─────────────────────────────────────────────────┤
                    │ ...                                             │
                    ├─────────────────────────────────────────────────┤
                    │ schedule (for        :Rider [1..*],             │
                    │          itinerary   :Location [1..*] {sequence} │
                    │          isSharedRide:Boolean [0..1],           │
                    │          )           :Boolean                   │
                    │ ...                                             │
                    └─────────────────────────────────────────────────┘
```

FIGURE 10.12
Use of sequence.

The results are ordered, but we allow duplicate measurements values. Similarly, consider the closing values of the stock market over time.

As they are common, it is convenient to refer to them by their collection name of SEQUENCE or SEQ. You can use {seq} or {sequence} instead of {ordered, nonUnique}[7], see Fig. 10.12.

Occasionally, one may see the term {stream} used instead of {sequence}. Though streams may be sequences, the term stream primarily describes how the elements arrive over time.

You can see the various combinations of the multiplicity properties in Table 10.1.

10.1.4 Discontinuity

In UML 1.x, there was the ability to specify a multiplicity range that was discontinuous with possible values separated by commas. For example, for commercial automobiles, it was possible to specify some properties as:

    door   : DoorType [2, 4]
    cylinder: CylinderType [4, 6, 8]

---

[7]These multiplicity properties do not have a required order. So {ordered, nonUnique} and {nonUnique, ordered} are equivalent in effect.

Table 10.1 Multiplicity Properties (Modified from UML 2.5 specification Table 7.1)

isOrdered =	isUnique =	Collection Type	Comments
False	True	Set	These values are the default for multiplicity properties, equivalent to {unordered, unique}
True	True	Ordered set	{ordered}. Equivalent to {ordered, unique}
False	False	BAG[a]	{nonUnique} or {bag} Equivalent to {unordered, nonUnique}
False	False	Sequence or ORDERED BAG	{unordered, nonUnique} or {seq} or {sequence}

[a] The term "bag" is a common name for collections that allow duplicate entries and is the term used within UML. In mathematics, they are also called multisets.

This notation is no longer supported[8]. At present, only allows the low.. high or single value approaches. If you wish to forbid particular values, you must now use constraints.

For example,
  door   : DoorType [2..4] {*Three doors is not valid*}
  cylinder: CylinderType [4..8] {*Only even values are allowed*}

POINTS TO REMEMBER

- An attribute or argument may have more than one value. The range on the number of values is the multiplicity.
  - [Lower-Bound..Higher-Bound]
  - If only one value appears in the range, it acts as both the lower and higher bounds.
- Use an "*" to indicate an unlimited value (not infinite)
  - [0..*] or [*] both indicate "0 or more" or "many."
  - [1..*] indicates "one or more."
- If the upper-bound is larger that 1, the attribute/argument is "multivalued."
- If the lower bound is 0, the attribute/argument is "optional" or "may."
- If the multiplicity is multivalued,
  - *Sets* are unordered and do not allow duplicates {unordered, unique}. Sets are the default
  - *Bags* are unsorted but allow duplicates {unordered, nonUnique}
  - *Ordered Sets* are ordered and do not permit duplicates {ordered, unique}
  - *Sequences* (seq) are ordered and allow duplicates {ordered, nonUnique}

---

[8] They were not used that much. In addition, in the run-time environment, it is difficult to go from 2 to 4 without first going through 3.

FIGURE 10.13
Association line formats.

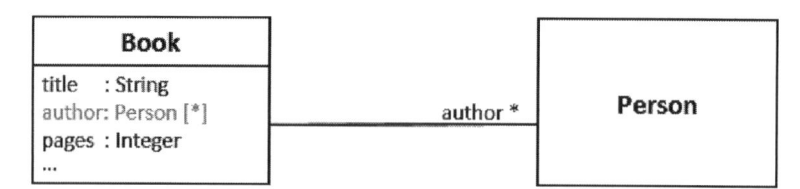

FIGURE 10.14
Book-person association.

10.2 ASSOCIATIONS

Associations represent a family of relationships between two classes. UML represents associations as lines connecting the classes. The lines are single, solid lines of any format. In Fig. 10.13, we show the standard ways of connecting an association, from most preferred to least preferred. Straight lines are usually preferred, followed by rectilinear lines, then oblique lines, and then followed by curves. All are acceptable, and you should use what conveys your intent best.

Consider an association as an alternative form of showing attributes.

In Fig. 10.14, we show an association between Book and Person by connecting them with a line. At the end of the association line show the multiplicity [*] and the association end name (often called the ROLE name). We can read this as

> A **Book** has many **Persons** in the role of author
> or
> A **Book** has a set of many authors who are **Persons**

10.2.1 Attribute and Role Adornments

On the left in Fig. 10.14, we show in grayed text the author attribute that means the same thing. Normally, we do not use both formats for the same property because it can get confusing (and redundant).

In Fig. 10.15, we added the properties of {ordered} and {readOnly} to the role name.

> A **Book** has a read-only, ordered set of many authors who are **Persons**
> or
> A **Book** has an ordered set of many **Persons** in the role of authors

Most everything that we can place on an attribute, we can place on an association end. In Table 10.2, we show almost all the possible adornments for an Attribute. We try to give an example of the notation, and the multiplicity, i.e., the number of times that notation can appear. So a 0..1 is an optional field, 0 is a field that cannot appear, 0..* indicates the notation can appear as often as you need. The order shown is the approximate order that they can appear. Of course, these tables are not complete; there are special cases in UML that we do not need to cover for this exam.

We have covered each of these properties except for the inherited flag (^), so consider this an opportunity to review.

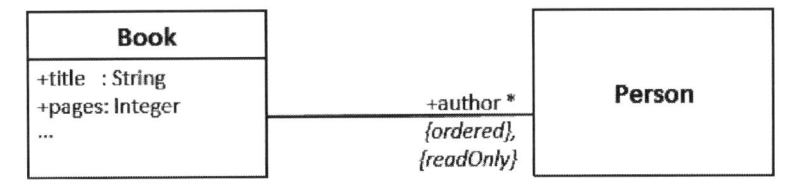

FIGURE 10.15
Association and other adornments.

Table 10.2 Properties for Attributes

Name	Notation	Multiplicity on an Attribute	Comment
Visibility	+, −, #, or ~	0..1	
Inherited flag	^	0..1	Covered later in this chapter
Derived	/	0..1	
Stereotype	« »	0..*	
Property name	String	0..1	Very rare to be empty for an attribute
Static scope	Underline	0..1	The default is class scope (no underline)
Property type	:TypeName or :ClassName	0..1	Rare to be empty for an attribute
Multiplicity range	[L..H]	0..1	The default = [1]
Multiplicity properties	e.g., {set}	0..*	If the multiplicity is multivalued, then the default is {set}
Default value	= value	0..*	One value allowed per multiplicity
Constraints and other properties	{ }	0..*	

CHAPTER 10: Finishing the Static Model

Compare Table 10.2 with Table 10.3. In Table 10.3, we show the properties that we can assign to an association end. Most of the properties are the same for both attributes and associations, except for the following:

- AggregationKind (normally shown only on an association), which we cover later
- Qualifiers (normally shown only on an association), but are not on the first exam
- Multiplicity brackets (used on attributes but not on an association)
- Default value (normally only on an attribute)

Why would modelers use the association format over the attribute format?

Associations have the advantage of the ability to characterize both directions of a relationship between a class and its property. Using the association form

Table 10.3 Properties on Role Ends

Name	Notation	Multiplicity on a Role	Location	Comment
Aggregation kind	None, shared, composite	0..1	On source side (the whole side)	Covered later in this chapter
Qualifier	Enumeration Type	0..*	On source side	Not on first exam
Ownership	●	0..1	On target side (the owned side)	Not on first exam, though examples may appear, it should not be relevant to the answers
Visibility	+ . − . #, or ~	0..1	On target side, before association end name	
Inherited flag	^	0..1	On target side, before association end name	Covered later in this chapter
Stereotype	« »	0..*	On target side	
Derived	/	0..1	On target side	
Static scope	Underline	0..1	On target side	
Property name	String	0..1	0..1	
Property type	:TypeName or :ClassName	0..1	Normally, the type/class of the connected element is the type/class	
Multiplicity range	L..H	0..1	No brackets are used on association end multiplicity	
Multiplicity properties	e.g., {set}	0..*	If the multiplicity is multivalued, then the default is {set}	
Default value	= value	0	Does not appear to be used on association ends	
Constraints and other Properties	{ }	0..*	On the target side	

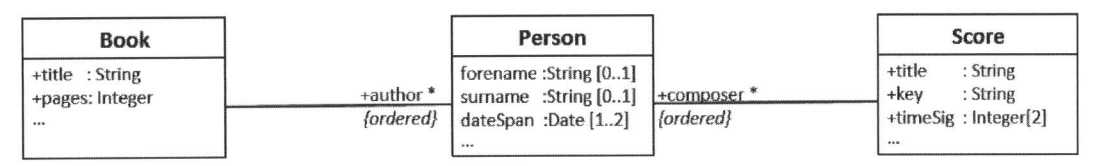

FIGURE 10.16
Book-person-score.

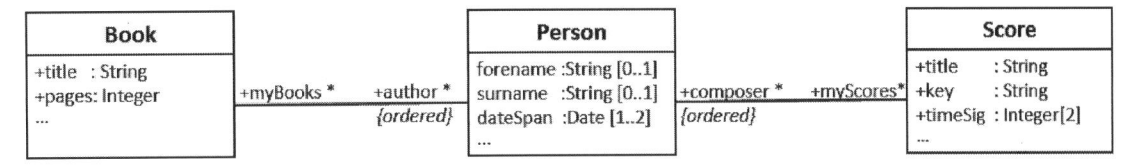

FIGURE 10.17
Bidirectional associations.

is most common when the property is a class (rather than a datatype). The individual classes (or dataTypes) now can be further connected to classes, and the diagrams indicate a fuller picture of their relationships.

You can also add attributes, operations, and receptions to both sides. For example, the **Person** Class can have a forename, a surname, and a date span[9]. Moreover, a **Person** Class can have relationships of their own. See Fig. 10.16. In this example, a **Person** can also be both a composer of a **Score** and an author of a **Book**.

10.2.2 Reading Associations

However, if we can go from **Book** to **Person** and from **Score** to **Person**, we can also go from **Person** to **Book** and **Person** to **Score**. We should consider supplying association end adornments on the other sides.

In Fig. 10.17, we added the information to help read the associations in both directions.

---

[9] The field names are based on the Anglo-American Cataloging Rules (AACR), also incorporated into the Machine Readable Cataloging (MARC) version 21 maintained by the Library of Congress (LOC). The Person record is part of the LOC Name Authority File (NAF) database. It is what guarantees that all library material uses the same spelling of an author's name. It allows for variants, but it has one official name record so that once can find all material by an author even if you use a variant.

```
          Book                                                      Person
+title  : String              is authored by            forename :String [0..1]
+pages: Integer  +myBooks *              +author *      surname  :String [0..1]
...                                      {ordered}      dateSpan :Date [1..2]
                                                        ...
```

FIGURE 10.18
A named association.

Book → Person	A **Book** may have an ordered set of many **Persons** in the role of author
Person → Book	A **Person** may have **Books** in the role of myBooks
Person → Score	A **Person** may have an ordered set of many **Scores** in the role of myScores
Score → Person	A **Score** may have many **Persons** in the role of composer

When you read an association, you start with one side but only read the adornments on the other side, the *target* side. The far side is the *target* side; the near side is the *source* side.

Associations can have names, independent of the names at the ends or the names of classes/types at the ends. These names are usually a verb form such as found in Fig. 10.18. The name used is "is authored by." When you supply a name, it is best to write one that reads from left to right or top down.

When you read an association, always start with "one," "a," "an," or "each" or something similar. The multiplicity is only read on the target side. We ignore the multiplicity and adornments on the source side.

In Fig. 10.18, we are modeling the relationship from A **Book** to Many **Persons** and A **Person** to many **Books**. This reading is a consequence of the equivalence of an association to an attribute. As an attribute is only the property of an instance, the association end on the target side is also only a property of an instance.

Book → Person: A **Book** *is authored by* an ordered set of many **Persons** in the role of author

When you read in the other direction, you generally will need to change the verb form from active to passive or vice versa.

Person → Book: A **Person** *authors* a set of many **Books** in the roles of myBooks

In Fig. 10.19, we named the association "authors," the third person active form of the present of "to author." When we read in the other direction, we

FIGURE 10.19
Association with reading direction.

Table 10.4 Properties for an Association

Name	Notation	Multiplicity on an Association	Location	Comment
Navigability	→	0..1	Inline and adjacent to the target classifier	Not on first exam, though examples may appear, it should not be relevant to the answers
Stereotype	« »	*	Above the association name	
Association name	String	0..1	Adjacent to the association line and centered	Helps in reading and understanding the association
Reading direction	▶ or ◀	0..1	Next to where the association name is	It shows the direction that the association name should be read

FIGURE 10.20
More than one associations between classes.

used "is authored by," the passive form. We also added another bit of notation, the reading direction indicator ▶ or ◀. This triangle points in the direction that the association name is intended to be read. This indicator is useful in making the diagram more understandable. However, it makes editing the diagram (such as changing the orientation of the association) more difficult as it may require a manual maintaining of the triangle direction.

See Table 10.4, for other properties allowed for an association.

It is certainly possible to have more than one association between two classes, as shown in Fig. 10.20. We read each association independently. However, starting at one class, the role names at the target classes must be

FIGURE 10.21
Association to a datatype.

unique. The role names map to the attribute names when they are in the attribute format subject to the restriction that within a class's namespace we cannot have two attributes with the same name[10]. It is ok to have blank role names, as the tools will generate some opaque string behind the scenes. In the figure, the role names myBooks and myEdits must be different (which they are). Similarly, author and editor must be different (which they are).

10.2.3 Associations and Datatypes

As we discussed, we can show an attribute as an Association. In the examples above, we showed attributes, whose type is a class, (e.g., **Book**, **Person**, or **Score**), and how they work. When the attribute's type is a datatype, everything works about the same, except usually the only direction modeled is from the source class to the target datatype. The association name is also typically not used, see Fig. 10.21.

POINTS TO REMEMBER

- An attribute can be presented as an association and vice versa, with little loss of information.
  - Multiplicity on an association does not use brackets.
  - Default values are typically not displayed on associations.
- The role name (association end name) is effectively the name of an attribute of the source Class.
- Attributes of a Class type or a Datatype are both allowed.
  - When the association connects to a Datatype, a simpler display is typically used.
- Starting at a particular Class, all its target role names should be unique.
- An association can have a name, which is usually a verb. The direction to read the name is indicated by ▶ or ◀.
  - When reading the association name in the opposite direction convert the association name from active to passive or vice versa.
  - ("rents" ←→ "is rented by," "rides" ←→ "is ridden by")
  - When there is no association name, the reader usually supplies "has."

---

[10]This is overly strict, but a good idea. The namespace rules are a bit more complicated.

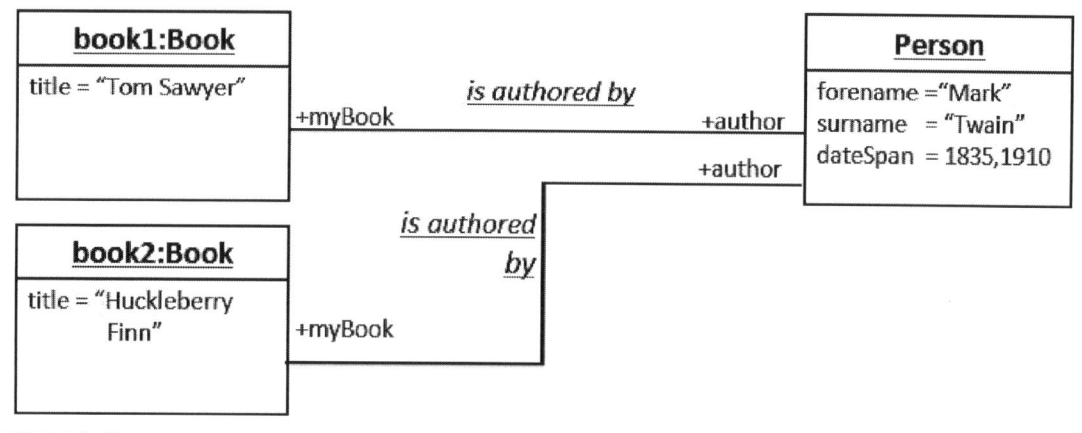

```
                                                                    10.2 Associations    179
```

book1:Book
title = "Tom Sawyer"

is authored by
+myBook   +author

Person
forename ="Mark"
surname   = "Twain"
dateSpan = 1835,1910

+author

is authored by

book2:Book
title = "Huckleberry Finn"
+myBook

FIGURE 10.22
Links and instances.

10.2.4 Links and Instances

The above material discusses how we show associations on Class Diagrams. When we are working with an Object Diagram, we use Instances instead of Classes, and Links instead of Associations, see Fig. 10.22. The UML specification allows us to omit the underline for the Association name, but it is not a good habit.

POINTS TO REMEMBER

- A Link is to an Association as an Instance (Object) is to a Class.
  - Association names, when shown on a link, are often underlined.
  - Blank link names may also be underlined (_).
  - No multiplicity appears on a link as it is always one instance on each side.

10.2.5 Composition and Aggregation

So far, except for the example with the datatype, we have modeled all the associations and links in this chapter as having symmetric strength. That is, the two ends of the relationship, the roles, each an equivalently strong relationship to the other side. We can consider the author:**Person** as an attribute of **Book**, just as we can consider the myBook:**Book** as an attribute of **Person**.

If we wish to indicate an asymmetric binding, we can model the relationship as a composition or an aggregation. UML shows both relationships with a

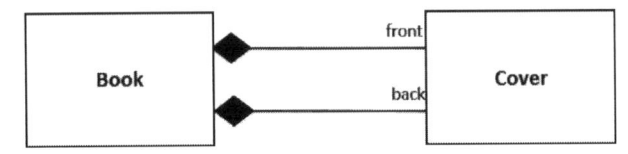

FIGURE 10.23
Composition.

FIGURE 10.24
Two compositions with roles.

diamond[11] (a solid diamond ◆ for COMPOSITION and a hollow diamond ◊ for AGGREGATION), which is placed in-line with the association and adjacent to the dominant side.

10.2.5.1 Composition

We use composition to indicate a WHOLE-PART relationship, placing the diamond on the whole side, as shown in Fig. 10.23. Note that the missing multiplicity on the diamond side defaults to 1.

When we use composition, the whole is responsible for the life of the part. If we delete (or burn up) the **Book**, the **Cover** is also deleted. The multiplicity at the whole side must be either [1] or [0..1]. For example, a **Cover** cannot be covering more than one **Book**. If it not possible to remove a Cover, the multiplicity at the diamond must be [1]. If it is possible to remove a **Cover**, then the multiplicity must be [0..1].

The multiplicity at the part end can be any legal value. We allow for two **Covers** because one would be the Front and other the Back, as we show in Fig. 10.24. We also use separate composition relationships instead of the more common tree-like structure as we show in Fig. 10.25.

As a composition is a kind of an association, any of the role or association adornments can appear. However, it is common not to name these compositions, but allow the reader to say:

---

[11] A diamond is a quadrilateral with four equal-length sides and opposite angles equal. It is a rhombus or lozenge. As used in UML, the longer dimension is usually placed in line with the association line shown in Fig. 10.23.

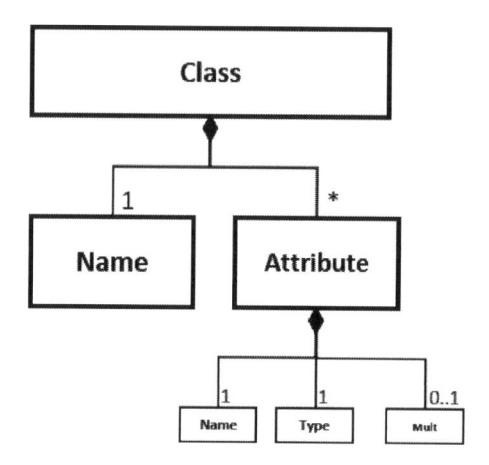

FIGURE 10.25
Partial metamodel of UML class using composition.

A **Book** is composed of two **Covers**
or
A **Book** has two parts that are **Covers**
or
A **Cover** is a part of a **Book**

In these relationships, we technically can say that the AggregationKind = Composite. In a regular association, the AggregationKind = None. AggregationKind is a property of association as shown in Table 10.3.

Composition is asymmetric: a Book can have Covers as parts, but the Covers cannot have the same Book as a part. Composition is also transitive, see Fig. 10.24[12]. Transitive means that since the **Mult** (the class in the lower right) is part of an **Attribute** and an **Attribute** is part of the **Class**, then, the **Mult** can also be considered part of the **Class**. If we delete a **Class**, we wind up deleting all the instances that are part of it, including the **Mult**.

This sort of tree is very common for composition or aggregation relationships. We can use them, for example, for Bill-of-Materials, depicting metamodels, or process decomposition.

10.2.5.2 Aggregation

An aggregation is a weak form of Composition or perhaps a strong form of Association. The AggregationKind = Shared. We call it "shared" because the

---

[12]Technically, both the attribute name and attribute type are optional, but just at least one of them must be there. This is a more advanced topic than the Foundational Exam.

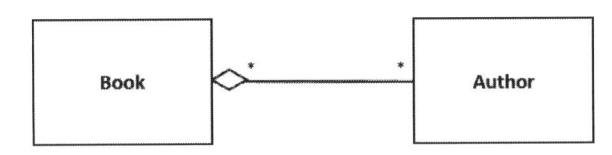

FIGURE 10.26
Aggregation—Shared.

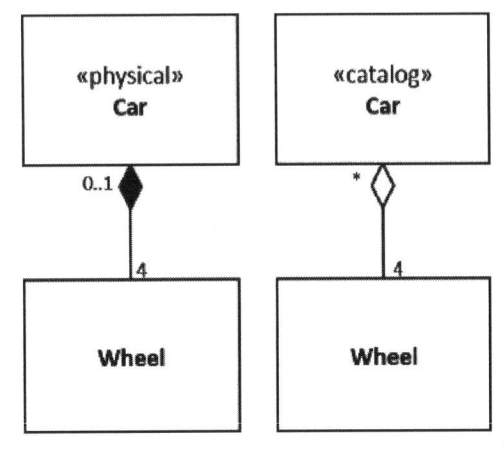

FIGURE 10.27
Physical vs catalog composition.

target end can be associated with of more than Book. When you read an aggregation, you usually should just use "has." We show an example of an aggregation/shared in Fig. 10.26.

> A **Book** has many **Authors**
> or
> An **Author** is a shared part of many **Books**

Unfortunately, as you might realize, the semantics of an aggregation is nearly identical to that of a regular association. Anytime we use an aggregation, we could probably replace it with a plain association. You should only use an aggregation if you want to emphasize a part-like relationship, but one that is not as strong as a composition.

10.2.5.3 Physical vs Catalog Composition

One possible way of looking at the differences between composition and aggregation is to compare physical parts *vs* catalog parts, check Fig. 10.27. On the left, we are modeling a physical **Car**. A **Wheel** is clearly part of a physical **Car**[13]. A **Wheel** cannot be part of more than one **Car** at a time, and the **Car** controls, in a way, the existences of the wheels. If you crush the **Car**, you also destroy the **Wheels**.

On the right side of the figure, we placed a Car in a catalog. A catalog is a logical structure and not a physical structure. In a catalog, a particular wheel model may be shared across many car models. Therefore, the wheels are shared aggregation on the right, but a composition on the left.

POINTS TO REMEMBER

- Composition and Aggregation are stronger forms of Association.
  - Parts of a Composition may only be part of 0..1 whole. They cannot be shared.
  - Parts of an Aggregation may be parts of many wholes. They can be shared.
  - Both use diamonds on the whole side of the relationship.
    - Composition uses a solid diamond
    - Aggregation uses a hollow diamond
  - The other adornments of an Association can be used on either Composition or Aggregation; subject to the restriction, that the Composite End cannot have a multiplicity of more than 1—It cannot be multivalued at that end.
- Aggregations are similar to plain associations.
  - If you downgrade an aggregation to an association, there is little loss of power.
  - The value of AggregationKind = shared.
  - The parts of an Aggregation often map to catalog parts.
- The whole end of a Composition is responsible for the life of the part end.
  - If you delete the whole, any parts still connected are destroyed.
  - The value of AggregationKind = Composite.
  - The parts of a Composition often map to physical parts.

10.3 GENERALIZATION, SPECIALIZATION, AND INHERITANCE

We showed a large generalization earlier which is presented in Fig. 10.28. The hollow arrowhead points from a specific to a more general type. Hence, GENERALIZATION is the name for moving up and SPECIALIZATION for moving down. Generalization/Specialization can be used between Classes and also between Use Cases.

We might read the top relationships of this diagram as:

> A Structure Diagram IS A Diagram
> or
> A Structure Diagram is a KIND OF (or SORT OF) Diagram

---

[13] It is true a **Car** could have 0..4 **Wheels**, but I'm trying to simplify here.

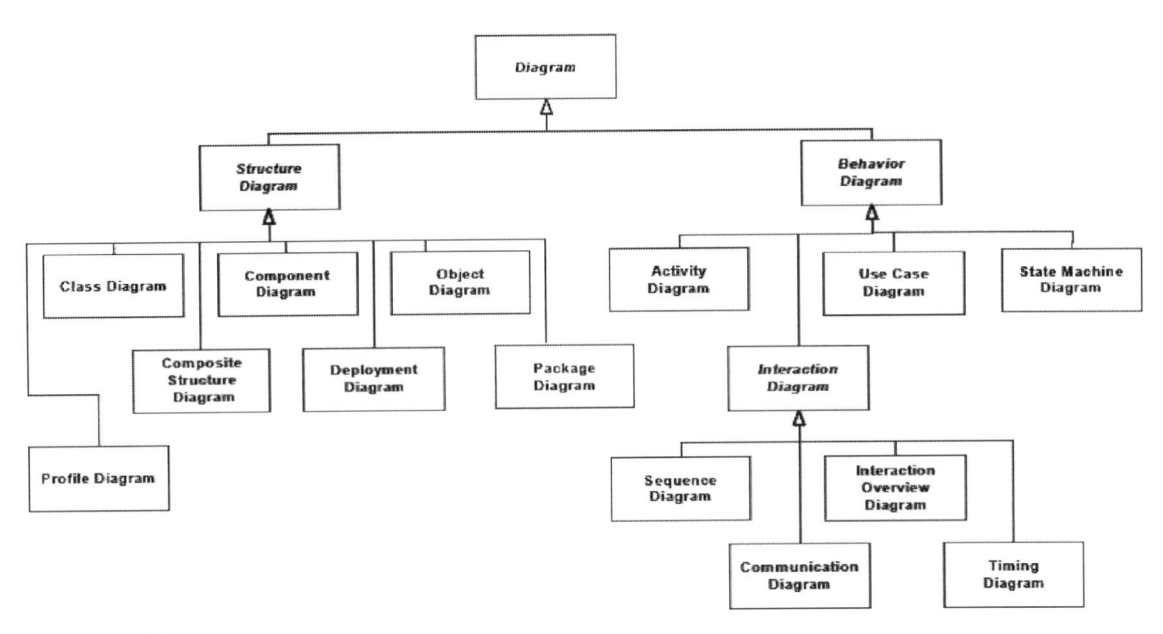

FIGURE 10.28
Generalization diagram of UML diagrams.

or

A Structure Diagram is a specialization of a Diagram

or

A Diagram is a generalization of Structure Diagram and Behavior Diagram

or

Structure Diagrams and Behavior Diagrams are CHILDREN of Diagram

or

A Diagram is a PARENT of Structure Diagram and Behavior Diagram

The specialization relationship allows a SUBCLASS (the bottom end) to SUBSTITUTE for the SUPERCLASS (the end with the arrowhead). For substitution to work, all the features of the superclass (e.g., attributes, operations, constraints, signals, receptions, and association) that are available on the superclass must also be available on the subclass.

We normally draw the generalization triangle pointing up and have all the subclasses sharing the same triangle in a tree-like shape. However, you can have each subclass use its own triangle, and the direction can be in any orientation, subject to considerations on readability.

In Fig. 10.29, we show an example of how inheritance works. The features of the superclass *Borrowable Material* (`title`, `callNo`, and `borrow()`) are

10.3 Generalization, Specialization, and Inheritance

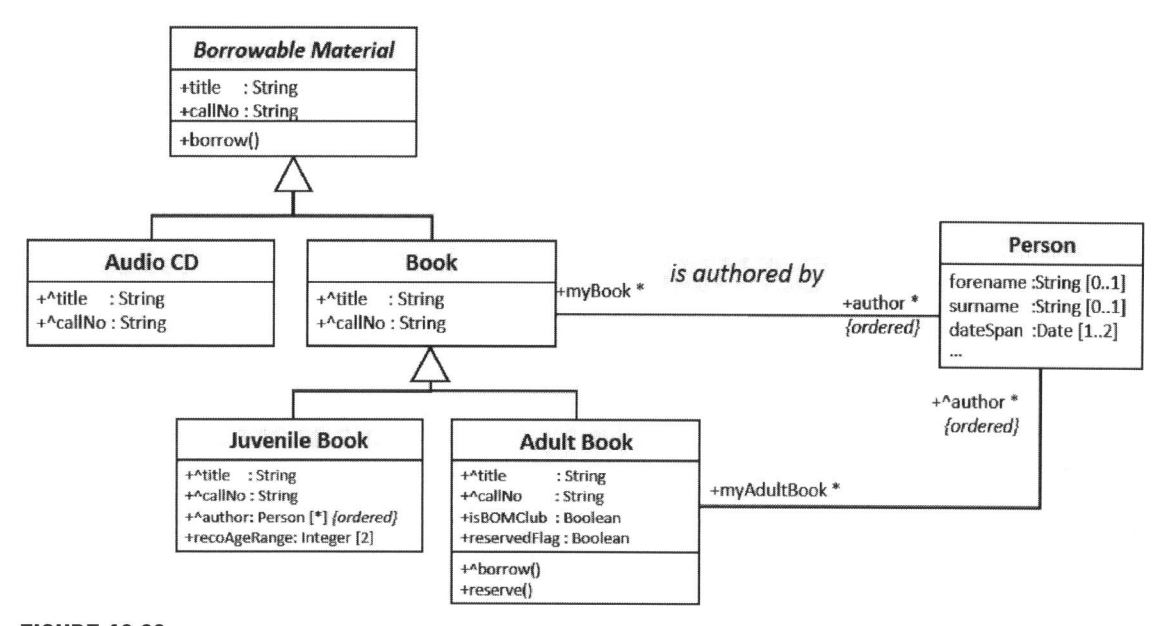

FIGURE 10.29
Inheritance example.

available on all the subclasses. In Audio CD and Book, the two attributes (`title` and `callNo`) are repeated. UML recommends using the caret (^) to precede inherited features to distinguish them from features that are native to the class. We do not have to show an inherited feature at all. For example, we did not repeat `borrow()` on **Audio Cd** or **Book**, but it is there.

In earlier versions of UML, there was no (^) notation to indicate inherited features. Modelers often grayed out the feature name to indicate that it was inherited. However, this is not now standard.

On **Book**, we also added another property, that of `author:`**Person**. We show that this feature is also inherited in **Juvenile Book** by showing `^author:` **Person**. We show that this feature is inherited in **Adult Book** by showing `^author:`**Person** on the end of the association. As previously discussed, we did not have to show these as the association would be inherited naturally. We also added new attribute and operations on the **Book** subclasses. Also, note that the role name at the **Book** end and the **Adult Book** end is not inherited. These are properties of **Person**.

When a feature is requested on a subclass, the definition of the feature is retrieved. If it cannot be found in the current subclass, the chain of super-classes above the subclass is examined to find the closest definition. When the closest definition is the found, it is retrieved and used. The UML

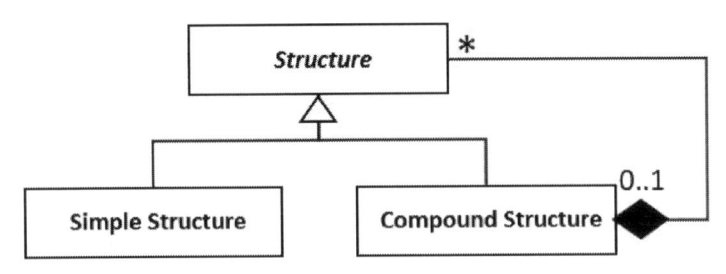

FIGURE 10.30
Reflexive parsing structure.

specification does not explain what happens if the definition is never found as that is an implementation/language concern.

We consider the **classes** with italic names as abstract. Equivalently, we can use an {*abstract*} flag before or after the **class** name. We consider the nonitalic named **classes** as concrete. A concrete **class** can have instances (objects) created of the **Class**, but abstract classes cannot have direct instances.[14]

We can also flag an operation as abstract, using the same techniques as we used for flagging abstract classes (the italic name for the operation or {*abstract*} after the operation name). An abstract operation is an operation with a defined argument list, but no implementation defined, that is, the mechanism for performing the operation's work is not available. If a class has an abstract operation, then the class must also be abstract.

If there are abstract classes, they must be superclasses. As an abstract class cannot have instances, the subclasses must be able to have instances to be useful. If there are abstract operations, the subclasses must eventually resolve the missing methods.

At the very bottom of an inheritance hierarchy, all the classes must be concrete. They must be able to have instances, and all their operations must have a method supplied.

10.3.1 Reflexive Structures Using Generalization

One common modeling idiom that also illustrates the power of combing composition with generalization allows for parsing of structures, see Fig. 10.30. In that figure, we show two types of **Structures**, **Simple**, or **Compound**. A **Compound Structure** has many **Structures** as parts, which can be either **Simple** or **Compound**. If we make the Structure represent a

---

[14]A child concrete class can have instances. These instances are indirect instances of the parent abstract class.

Mathematical Expressions, we can depict how expressions are built from sub-expressions. This pattern could also represent clauses in English Sentences, or Parts in a Mechanical Assembly.

We made the *Structure* class an abstract class (in italics) because all structures must be either a **Simple Structure** or **Compound Structure**. No structure can exist that is not resolved to be one of the subclasses. In such circumstances, the Generalization/Specialization is considered "complete" or "covering." It is common in such circumstances to make the superclass abstract.

10.3.2 The Process

10.3.2.1 The Generalization Process

When you have several classes with similar attributes and similar behaviors, you can look for common features. Consider that a jurisdiction may have licensing procedures for dogs, cats, tigers, snakes, and alligators. Instead of treating them all separately, if you abstract the common features from each class and create a new superclass to house these common features, you could define many of the features only once. You could create a **Pet** class— Allowing a loop through all the pets during renewal season without making separate loops for each subclass.

If the details of getting or renewing a license were different for each subclass, you would define an abstract operation on the **Pet** class called `renewLicense()`. Each subclass would have to have the specific implementation for the operation. However, the users of the **Pet** class would not have to deal with the details and would not need to know what type of **Pet** is currently being handled.

10.3.2.2 The Specialization Process

The specialization process works about the same but from the other direction. Imagine you had a simple pet license that would handle dogs and cats. If somehow the political powers force you to allow Tiger[15] licenses, you can create a **Tiger** as a subclass of **Cat**, and then you could handle the **Tiger** license. You will probably need a separate method on the **Tiger** to enforce whatever safety rules a **Tiger** license requires. However, other than the new method on **Tiger**, you would probably not have to change **Cat**, **Dog**, or any other class.

10.3.3 Polymorphism

An operation on a superclass will be inherited by its subclasses. Not only will the argument list be inherited, but if any method is supplied (the

---

[15] It is a very bad idea to have a Tiger as a Pet.

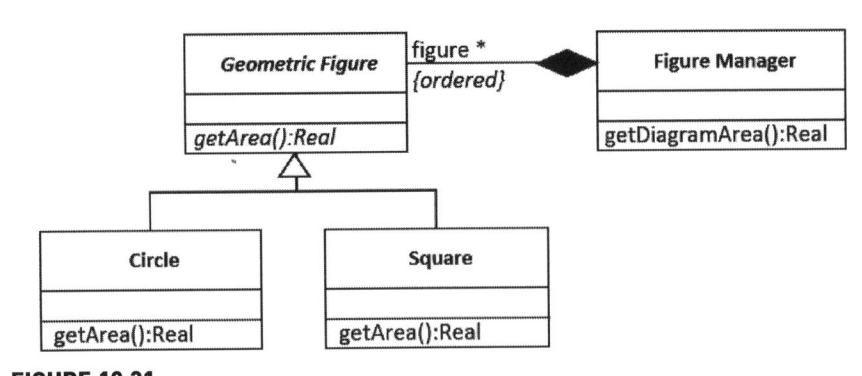

FIGURE 10.31
Polymorphism example.

method is the implementation of the operation), it will also be inherited. If the superclass's method is missing, the operation is abstract, and methods will need to be supplied for the subclasses to make them concrete. Even if the method is available on the superclass, it can be overridden on the subclasses by simply supplying a method anywhere the default method is not sufficient. When we supply different methods for logically the same operation on different subclasses, we call that POLYMORPHISM.

Examine Fig. 10.31. In the figure, the **Figure Manager** class is managing an ordered set of **Geometric Figures**. One of the operations that the **Figure Manager** can perform is to sum the areas of all the Figures on a diagram (`getDiagramArea()`). To accomplish this task, it will loop through all the **Geometric Figures** in the figure ordered set. Each time it gets a new **Geometric Figure** from the set, it will call the `getArea()` operation. The **Figure Manager** will not need to know that a **Circle**'s area uses π and that a **Square**'s does not. Each class knows how to perform its own operations. The **Figure Manager** could just process in a tight loop, all the figures without looking at them or determining their type. If we added a new subtype of **Geometric Figure**, for example, a **Rhombus**, neither **Geometric Figure** nor **Figure Manager** would have any changes.

If we looked at the code of FigureManager.getDiagramArea(), we would see something like:

```
totalArea = 0
loop over GeometricFigures in ordered set of Figure:GeometricFigures

  get next GeometricFigure
  totalArea = totalArea = GeometricFigure.getArea()
  endLoop

return totalArea
```

Polymorphism is a big advantage for object-oriented development, as changes do not propagate, and testing the type of an object is often not needed. It incorporates information hiding, i.e., the details of the `getArea()` operation are not exposed outside of the **Circle** or **Square**.

POINTS TO REMEMBER

- In Generalization, we have a superclass (or parent class) that holds some features common to the subclasses (or child classes).
- In Specialization, we have subclasses that inherit any attribute, association, operation, method, constraint, and reception that are defined on the superclass.
  - Generalization and Specialization are two aspects of the same relationship seen from different perspectives.
  - Features (including association ends/roles) at the lower level that are inherited from a higher level can be elided or preceded with a ^ to show explicitly that the feature is inherited.
- When you ask a subclass to perform an operation, it searches up the inheritance tree for the closest supplied method for that operation.
- We can declare Classes as abstract, possibly because we defined some features incompletely.
  - An abstract operation on a class automatically makes the class abstract.
  - Abstract classes cannot be instantiated directly because such an instance would be incomplete.
  - A concrete subclass can substitute for the superclass as all its features are defined.
  - Abstract classes support encapsulation and information hiding. A user of the abstract class need not know what actual subclass is being substituted.
- Polymorphism describes having the same operation appear on different subclasses with different methods.
  - Using Polymorphism also for dynamic determination of the correct method based on the subclass, eliminating the maintenance effort when new subclasses are created.
  - Objects know how to perform their class's methods.

CHAPTER 11

Questions for Chapter 10

1. Which multiplicity below is multivalued?
   A. [0]
   B. [1]
   C. [0..1]
   D. [2]
   E. [1..1]
2. Which multiplicity below allows for an infinite number of values?
   A. [?]
   B. [∞]
   C. [*]
   D. [0..*]
   E. It is not possible to have a multiplicity that includes infinity
3. The Presidents of the United States (and most countries) form what type of Collection?
   A. Bag
   B. Ordered Set
   C. Ring
   D. Sequence
   E. Set
4. The results of a car race would be best kept in what type of collection?
   A. Bag
   B. Ordered Set
   C. Ring
   D. Sequence
   E. Set

5. Which multiplicity expression is valid?
   A. [−2..3]
   B. [2,3]
   C. [2..3]
   D. [3..2]
   E. [2 3]
   F. [2...3]
   G. None of the above expressions are valid
6. Which of the relationships below allow substitution of instances of one class for another?
   A. aggregation
   B. dependency
   C. conjugation
   D. specialization
   E. twinning
7. Which of the relationships below indicate a "whole-part" relationship?

   A   B   C   D   E

   A. A
   B. B
   C. C
   D. D
   E. E
8. Which relationship would be most useful between a **Subcompact** car and a **Limousine**?
   A. Generalization/Specialization
   B. Containment
   C. Dependency
   D. Implementation
   E. None

9. How many of the classes shown on following diagram fragment have a relationship to **Person**?

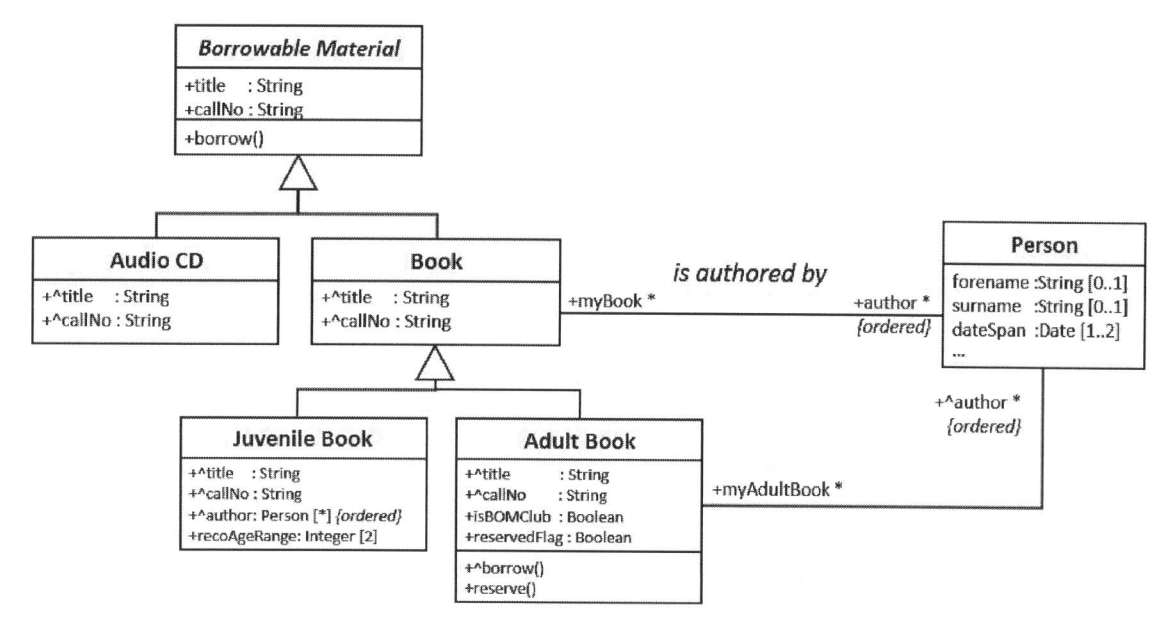

- A. 1
- B. 2
- C. 3
- D. 4
- E. 5
- F. 6

10. You have the two classes below: **Whole** and **Part**. You need to connect them to indicate that the **Whole** contains many **Parts** in a whole-part composition relationship. What connection should you use?

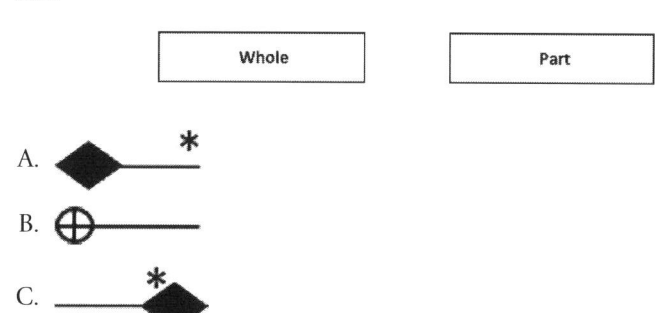

D. ◆—*
E. ◇—*
F. ◇—*

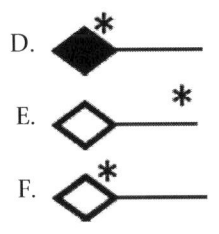

11. The operation sortPair() takes two integers and returns them in sorted order. No duplicates are allowed. What is the argument list for the sortPair() operation?
    A. sortPair(pair: Integer [2])
    B. sortPair(inout pair: Integer)
    C. sortPair(inout pair: Integer [0..2])
    D. sortPair(inout pair: Integer [*] {ordered}, {unique})
    E. sortPair(inout pair: Integer [2] {ordered})
    F. sortPair(inout pair: Integer [2] {ordered}, {no dups})
    G. sortPair(inout pair: Integer [2] {ordered}, {unique})

12. Examine the following class diagram fragment. What is the range of the number of objects (instances) of all the classes that can compatibly exist assuming that there is only one **Class-1** instance?

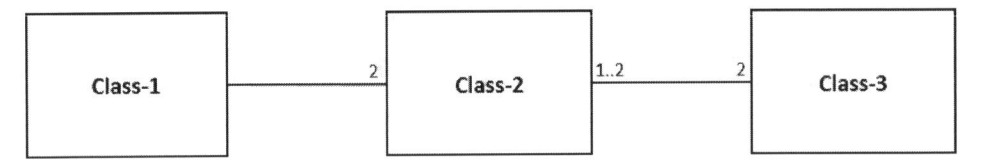

Class-1 —2— Class-2 —1..2 2— Class-3

   A. [1..3]
   B. [1..5]
   C. [5]
   D. [1..7]
   E. [7]
   F. [5..7]

13. Examine the diagram below. Assuming that there is a least one instance of any of the classes, which statement is true?

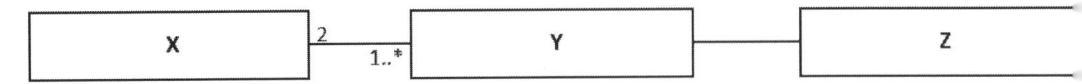

X —2 / 1..*— Y —— Z

   A. There are only two Xs.
   B. There is only one Z.
   C. There can be an infinite number of Ys.

D. For every **Y** instance, there are three times as many other instances.
E. For every **Y** instance, there are no more than three other instances.

14. Examine the diagram below. In Class **W**, which attribute is not valid?

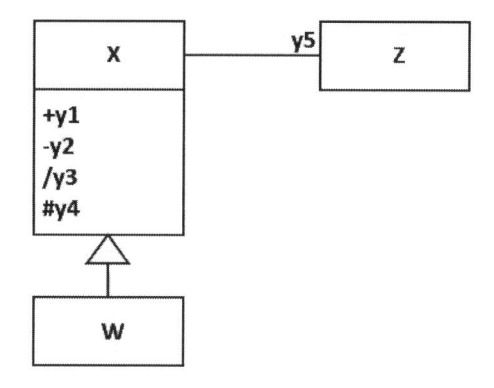

```
┌─────────┐         y5   ┌─────┐
│    X    │──────────────│  Z  │
├─────────┤              └─────┘
│ +y1     │
│ -y2     │
│ /y3     │
│ #y4     │
└─────────┘
     △
     │
┌─────────┐
│    W    │
└─────────┘
```

   A. ^y1
   B. ^y2
   C. ^y3
   D. ^y4
   E. ^y5

15. Before the advent of modern surgical techniques and ignoring conjoined twins, what would be the relationship between a person and their heart?
   A. Composition
   B. Containment
   C. Aggregation
   D. Inheritance
   E. Polymorphism

16. Consider the relationship from a book to its authors. Which relationship of the choices below would best describe it?
   A. Composition
   B. Containment
   C. Aggregation
   D. Inheritance
   E. Polymorphism

17. Consider the multiplicity adornments (e.g., {ordered}, {unique}). What type of collection do they make?
   A. Sequence
   B. Stream
   C. Ordered Set

D. Bag
E. List
F. Set

18. Which one of the following depicts a legal UML relationship?

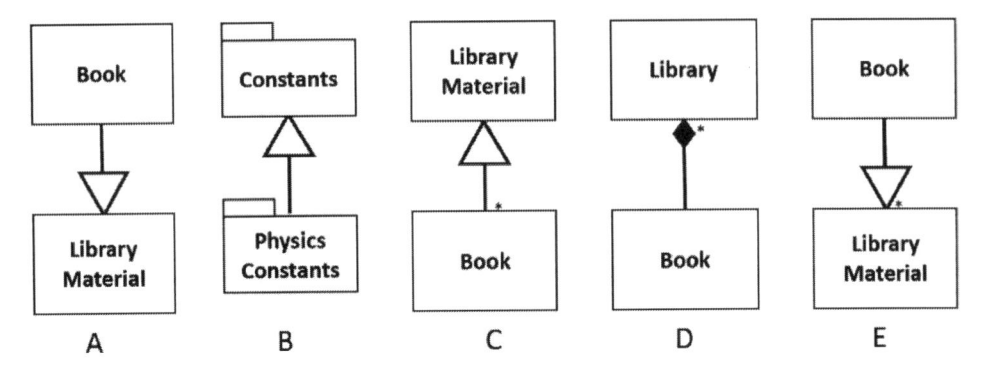

Book → Library Material	Constants △ Physics Constants	Library Material △ Book	Library ♦—* Book	Book ▽—* Library Material
A	B	C	D	E

A. A
B. B
C. C
D. D
E. E

ANSWERS FOR CHAPTER 10

1. Which multiplicity below is multivalued?
   A. [0]
   B. [1]
   C. [0..1]
   D. **[2]**
   E. [1..1]

   Discussion:
   A multivalued multiplicity indicates that the item can have more than one value.
   A—No, this multiplicity indicates that no values are allowed.
   B—No, this allows only one value.
   C—No, this allows no more than one value.
   D—Yes, this allows two values, which is more than one.
   E—No, this only allows one value.

2. Which multiplicity below allows for an infinite number of values?
   A. [?]
   B. [∞]

C. [*]
D. [0..*]
E. **It is not possible to have a multiplicity that includes infinity**

Discussion:
A—No, the ? is not a legal value for multiplicity.
B—No, the ∞ is not a legal value for multiplicity.
C,D—No, the * indicates unlimited natural, i.e., as large as you want. This is not the same as infinity.
E—Yes, this is correct. Any computer system cannot have an infinite number of anything.

3. The Presidents of the United States (and most countries) form what type of Collection?
   A. Bag
   B. Ordered Set
   C. Ring
   D. **Sequence**
   E. Set

   Discussion:
   The collection of Presidents is ordered, but allows duplicates. That is, the same person may be President more than once. Not only can they be elected more than once in a row (two or more consecutive terms), but other Presidents can appear in between. For example, Grover Cleveland was elected as the 22nd President (in 1885) and the 24th President (in 1893). He is the only person to serve two nonconsecutive terms.
   A—No, Presidents are considered ordered (though not necessarily orderly).
   B—No, duplicates have occurred.
   C—No, while a Ring is a type of collection, it is a collection type of UML.
   D—Yes, ordered and allowing duplicates.
   E—No, a set does not have an order and does not allow duplicates.

4. The results of a car race would be best kept in what type of collection?
   A. Bag
   B. **Ordered Set**
   C. Ring
   D. Sequence
   E. Set

   Discussion:
   A, C, D, E—No.
   B—Yes, race results are ordered and no driver can cross the finish line more than once.

5. Which multiplicity expression is valid?
   A. [−2..3]
   B. [2,3]
   C. **[2..3]**
   D. [3..2]
   E. [2 3]
   F. [2...3]
   G. None of the above expressions are valid

   Discussion:
   A—No, you cannot have a negative number of items.
   B—No, a comma is not a legal multiplicity separator in UML 2.5. It was possible in UML 1.x.
   C—Yes, the correct format is [Lower Bound .. Upper Bound].
   D—No, it must go low→high.
   E, F—No, the separator is "..".
   G—No.

6. Which of the relationships below allow substitution of instances of one class for another?
   A. aggregation
   B. dependency
   C. conjugation
   D. **specialization**
   E. twinning

   Discussion:
   A—No, aggregation is a weak whole-part relationship.
   B—No, while there may be a dependency-like relationship involved, it is not sufficient.
   C—No, conjugation is not a UML relationship.
   D—Yes, if **X** is a specialization of **Y**, **X** can substitute for **Y**.
   E—No, twinning is not a UML relationship.

7. Which of the relationships below indicate a "whole-part" relationship?

   A. A
   B. **B**
   C. C
   D. D
   E. E

Discussion:
A—No, this indicates that a feature is inherited.
B—Yes, this is a composition relationship, indicating a whole-part relationship.
C—No, this indicates namespace containment.
D—No, this indicates generalization/specialization.
E—No, this indicates an association.

8. Which relationship would be most useful between a **Subcompact** car and a **Limousine**?
   A. Generalization/Specialization
   B. Containment
   C. Dependency
   D. Implementation
   E. **None**

Discussion:
A—No, neither vehicle is a "kind of" the other.
B—No, while a **Subcompact** might fit into a stretch **Limousine**, neither is a part of the other.
C—No, neither depends on the other.
D—No, neither is an implementation of the other. Some stretch **Limousines** may be made by cutting a regular **Limousine** in half and inserting a chassis extension. They would never start with a **Subcompact**.
E—Yes, there is no useful relationship. However, we could generalize both the **Subcompact** and the **Limousine** and create a superclass called **Vehicle**.

9. How many of the classes shown on following diagram fragment have a relationship to Person?

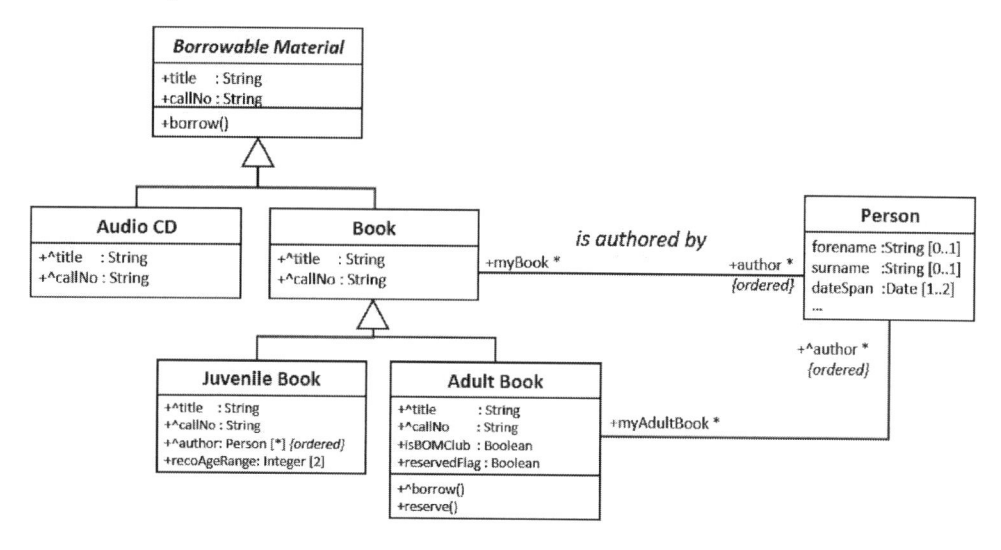

A. 1
B. 2
C. <u>3</u>
D. 4
E. 5
F. 6

Discussion:
Both **Book** and **Adult Book** show an explicit association relationship to **Person**. **Juvenile Book** has an explicit inherited relationship to **Person** via an attribute. Therefore, the answer is three, C.

10. You have the two classes below: **Whole** and **Part**. You need to connect them to indicate that the **Whole** contains many **Parts** in a whole-part relationship. What connection should you use?

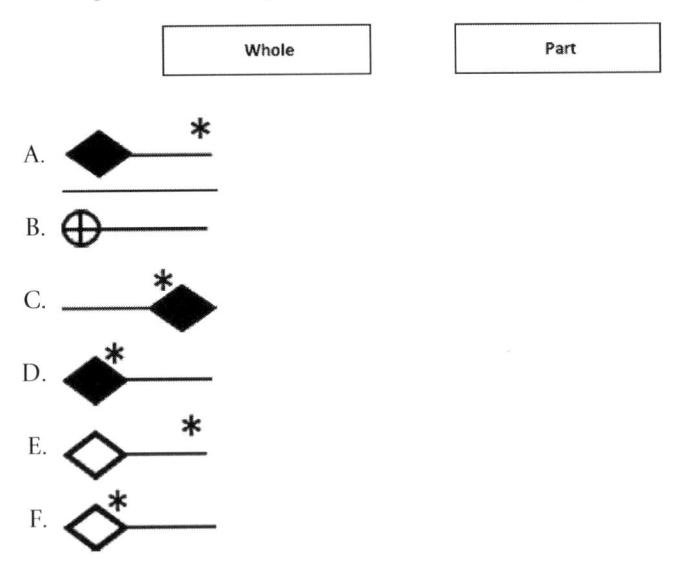

| Whole | | Part |

A. ◆———————*
B. ⊕———
C. ———*◆
D. ◆*———
E. ◇———*
F. ◇*———

Discussion:
A—Yes, the solid diamond indicates an exclusive whole-part relationship.
B—No, this indicates a namespace containment relationship.
C—This is pointing in the wrong direction. It also has a * next to the solid diamond which is not valid.
D—A whole-part relationship may not have a * next to the solid diamond. It indicates that a part can be part of several wholes, which is not possible.
E—This is a shared or catalog containment.
F—This indicates that there is one part that is part of many wholes.

11. The operation sortPair() takes two integers and returns them in sorted order. No duplicates are allowed. What is the argument list for the sortPair() operation?
   A. sortPair(pair: Integer [2])
   B. sortPair(inout pair: Integer)
   C. sortPair(inout pair: Integer [0..2])
   D. sortPair(inout pair: Integer [*] {ordered}, {unique})
   E. sortPair(inout pair: Integer [2] {ordered})
   F. sortPair(inout pair: Integer [2] {ordered}, {no dups})
   G. **sortPair(inout pair: Integer [2] {ordered}, {unique})**

   Discussion:
   The problem statement requires

both input and output	inout
exactly two fields	[2]
the order is important	{ordered}
no duplicates are allowed	{unique}

   G—is the answer

12. Examine the following class diagram fragment. What is the range of the number of objects (instances) that can compatibly exist assuming that there is only one **Class-1** instance?

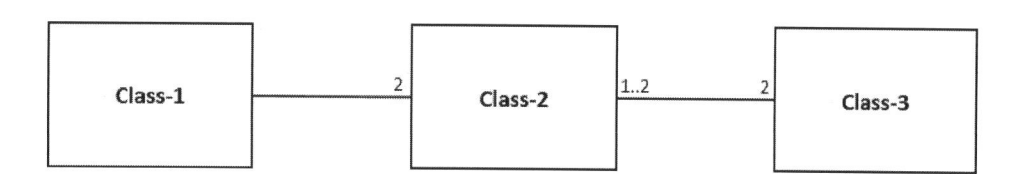

   Class-1 —2— Class-2 —1..2   2— Class-3

   A. [1..3]
   B. [1..5]
   C. [5]
   D. [1..7]
   E. [7]
   F. **[5..7]**

   Discussion:
   You might need a little scratch pad to follow this.
   If there is one **Class-1**, then there are two **Class-2s**.
   If there are two **Class 2s**, then, as each **Class-2** can have two **Class-3s**, that is, there can be four **Class-3s**. Given one **Class-1**, two **Class-2s**, and four **Class-3s** we can have seven instances in total.

However, each **Class-3** can be connected to two **Class 2s**. Each of these associations would count twice. Eliminating the duplicates gives us five total instances. So the range is [5..7].

To see how the five instances appear diagrammatically, look at the figure below.

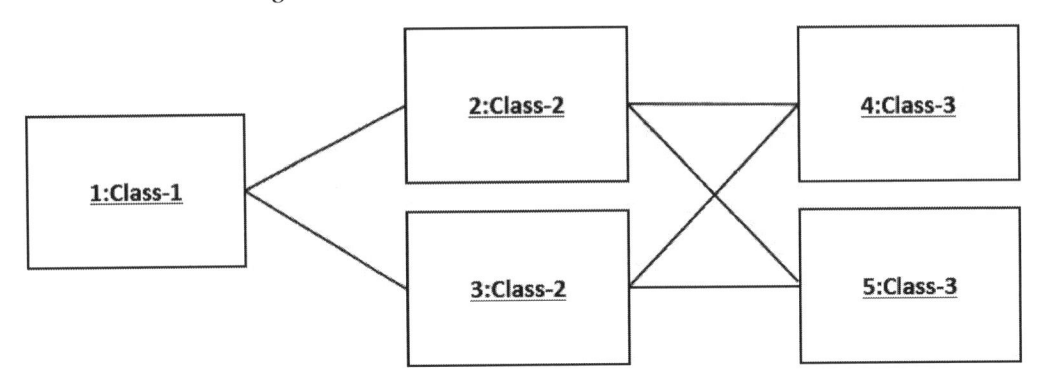

Each **Class-2** has two **Class-3s** and each **Class-3** has two **Class-2s**, which meets the requirements.

13. Examine the diagram below. Assuming that there is a least one instance of any of the classes, which statement is true?

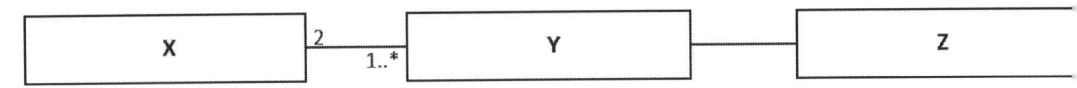

   A. There are only two **Xs**.
   B. There is only one **Z**.
   C. There can be an infinite **number** of **Ys**.
   D. For every **Y** instance, there are three times as many other instances.
   E. **For every Y instance, there are no more than three other instances.**

   Discussion:
   A—No, if there is more than one **Y**, there can be more than two **Xs**.
   B—No, if there is more than one **Y**, there can be more than one **Zs**.
   C—No, the "*" allows for as many **Ys** as you want, but not infinity.
   D—No, there will be one **Z** for each **Y**, but because an **X** can point to more than one **Y**, there need not be two **Xs** for each **Y**.
   E—Yes, based on the discussion on answer D, there can be less than three other instances, but no more than three.

14. Examine the diagram below. In Class **W**, which attribute is not valid?

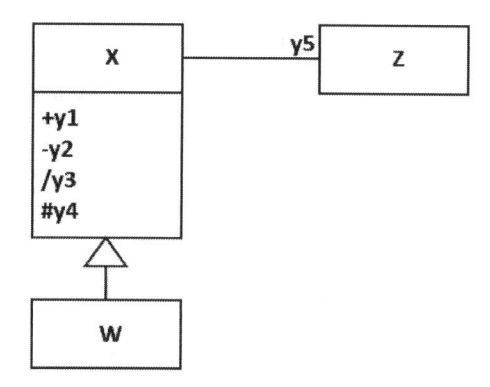

```
        X         ──y5── Z
   +y1
   -y2
   /y3
   #y4
    △
    │
    W
```

   A. ^y1
   B. **^y2**
   C. ^y3
   D. ^y4
   E. ^y5

   Discussion:
   B—A private (−) attribute is not visible to subclasses.

15. Before the advent of modern surgical techniques and ignoring conjoined twins, what would be the relationship between a person and their heart?
   A. **Composition**
   B. Containment
   C. Aggregation
   D. Inheritance
   E. Polymorphism

   Discussion:
   A—Yes, a person must have a heart. It cannot be part of more than one person. If a person dies, his/her heart also dies.
   B—No, a person is not a storage location for a heart definition.
   C—No, aggregation would only be correct if two or more people could share a heart.
   D—No, a heart is not a type of person.
   E—No, polymorphism is not relevant here.

16. Consider the relationship from a book to its authors. Which relationship of the choices below would best describe it?
   A. Composition
   B. Containment

C. **Aggregation**
D. Inheritance
E. Polymorphism

Discussion:
Many modelers would use association here, as we did in the previous chapter. The question, however, asked about the choices given.
A—No, more than one book can share an author
B—No, a book is not storage location for an author definition.
C—Yes, aggregation is correct as two more books can have the same author.
D—No, an author is not a type of book.
E—No, polymorphism is not relevant here.

17. Consider the multiplicity adornments (e.g., {*ordered*}, {*unique*}). What type of collection do they make?
A. Sequence
B. Stream
C. Ordered Set
D. Bag
E. List
F. **Set**

Discussion:
The multiplicity adornments can be placed in any order, though duplicates are not allowed.
A—No, a Sequence may have duplicates
B—No, a Stream is sort of a Sequence but emphasizes their arrival times
C—No, the adornments may be in any order
D—No, a Bag allows duplicates
E—No, a List is not a UML term, but it normally would be equivalent to an Ordered Set
F—Yes, no order, and no duplicates.

18. Which one of the following depicts a legal UML relationship?

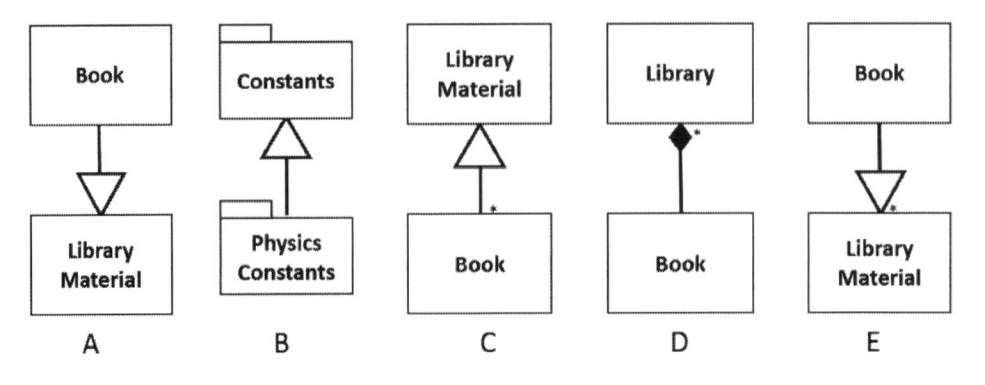

A. **A**
B. B
C. C
D. D
E. E

Discussion:

A—Yes, the relationship does not depend on the diagrammatic direction.

B—No, Packages do not support generalizations in UML 2.5.

C—No, Generalization does not support multiplicity. Each side may always have many instances, so do not use multiplicity.

D—No, a Composition (solid diamond) may not have many owners.

E—No, Generalization does not support multiplicity. Each side may always have many instances, so do not use multiplicity.

CHAPTER 12

Use Cases

12.1 FINDING USE CASES

Use Cases are the simplest UML diagram, but probably one of the most useful. Even though packages are the organizational element that captures the decomposition into work packages, team assignments, or tasks, it is the Use Case diagrams that help you decide what these tasks are and how they should be grouped and the scope of the work.

Each Use Case represents a purpose or goal that some user wants the system to help achieve. In a ride-hailing app[1], the potential passenger uses the app to hire a car at a specified location. The potential passenger may also have other goals, such as obtaining the estimated cost, time to pick up, time to arrive, Establish a Payment Method, among other things. The driver may also have goals, such as to identify potential riders, starting location and time, and ending location.

To be useful, the system must return value to the users, but in Use Case terminology, we do not call them users; we call them Actors. This covers the gamut of users, including clients, customers, maintenance staff, managers, and workers. Anyone who wants to use (or is forced to use) the system would be an Actor.

In the Library system, the Actors would include Patrons, Browsers, Librarians, Circulation Desk Staff, Shelving Staff, Catalogers, and people involved in Accessioning and Deaccessioning material. In a ride-sharing example, the Actors would include Potential Passengers (Riders), Drivers, and Managers. In both systems, there may be others, such as Auditors and Human Resource Professionals.

We may also include as Actors: other systems, devices, sensors, or databases that interact with our system.

---

[1]Such as Uber, Lyft, Curb, Hailo (UK), Gett (Israel), Jugnoo (India), Travly (Pakistan), Ola (India), Didi Chuxing (China). They are everywhere!

Each Use Case must return some value to the Actor. Many programmers get a bit confused about "returning some value to the Actor." Returning value indicates that some desirable outcome occurs. This is very different from a return value from a function call or subprogram. Use Cases tend to be on a much higher level that these software returns and may not be so simple. In the ride-hailing app example, canceling a ride might be a goal that the Actor has. The value would be that the ride was successfully canceled to the benefit of the Actor[2].

Use Cases are part of the behavioral model of the system. We often consider the system's Use Cases as operations on the system. We then list the Use Cases in the operations compartment of the system element. Each Use Case also indicates a family of scenarios, bound by sharing similar goals. We can detail these scenarios using structured text, storyboards, sequence diagrams, state machine diagrams, or communication diagrams.

12.1.1 Naming Use Cases

We show Use Cases as ellipses with the name of the Use Case inside the ellipses. Tool vendors are allowed to put the name underneath the ellipses to simplifying their diagraming effort. See Fig. 12.1. The name of the Use Case indicates the goal that the Actor has. Usually, the names are verb phrases in an ongoing present tense.

The naming conventions for Use Cases recommend avoiding both noun or participle forms for behavior. So, therefore, do not use "Hailing a Ride," "Borrowing a Book," "Ride-Hailing," or "Book Borrowing." Likewise, you should avoid completed behaviors, such as "Hailed a Ride" or "Borrowed a Book." Use Cases should be completable, but not already completed. Use Cases that only deliver a trivial value should also be avoided, e.g., "Push a Button"[3].

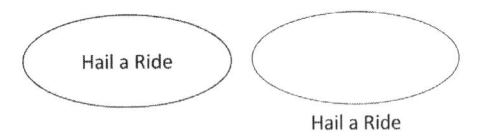

FIGURE 12.1
Basic Use Case notation.

---

[2] Do not talk about the "Happy Day Scenario". The Use Case should be a goal the Actor desires. This is not the same as something that is desirable. Consider "Execute Prisoner" or "Start War". Use the correct descriptive name, but it is not appropriate to make value judgements in your model.
[3] "Push a Button" is probably always too small to be a good Use Case, unless the System involved is an exoskeleton that aids handicapped users. However, you will see when we discuss the «include» relationship that it is sometime useful to extract small reusable sub-goals / behaviors. See § Include below.

Some good names include

"Hail a Ride," "Establish a Payment Method," "Find a Passenger," "Cancel my Ride."

Because Use Case diagrams are simple, they are usually codeveloped with representatives of the Actors and given to the Actor community to review. This is valuable because the Actors can easily see if all their own goals are included and may be able to see if there are any irrelevant goals. We, therefore, name the Use Cases using the terminology of the Actors, avoiding jargon or implementation concepts. We try to use simple, unambiguous terms that everyone can understand. Early informed feedback is critical to most projects.

System developers tend to organize their projects around the Use Cases because it makes the project more understandable by all parties. If your project is producing requirements or design documents (most will), consider organizing them by Actor and then by Use Case. Also, consider building your package structure by making packages of related Use Cases, following the Use Case inspired outline (see Fig. 12.2).

When working on a project, if you find that you are focusing your effort without addressing the delivery to the Actors the goals of a Use Case, you are probably just working on a technology "whiz-bang" or "gilding the lily." Such efforts are often descoped. If you are not producing value, you may not be valued.

One trick to help in the proper naming of a Use Case is to precede the goal with the words: "*O System, please help me to* ..." or a similar variant.

- *O System, please help me to* Hail a Ride
- *O System, please help* Hail a Ride *for me.*
- *O System, please help me to* Establish a Payment Method
- *O System, please help to* Establish a Payment Method *for me.*

```
Actor 1
    Use Case 1.1
    Use Case 1.2
    ...
Actor 2
    Use Case 2.1
    Use Case 2.2
    ...
Actor n
```

FIGURE 12.2
Use Case inspired outline.

If you follow these forms, your Use Case names will generally work out correctly and will be easy to understand. However, there are some types of Use Cases where this naming approach does not always work. For example, if the System or Actor is autonomous, such as a robot or a clock. These Use Cases (e.g., Stand Up or Keep Time) do not have traditional Actors with traditional goals.

12.1.2 Actors

Finding the Actors is not particularly difficult. Look at your system (or subsystem or component) that you are working on and identify all the external entities that deal with it. These would be all the sources or sinks for data, information, or events. This would include all the people, external systems, databases, or sensors that interact with your system.

You can discount pass-through Actors. A pass-through Actor is usually a device that just passes along input and outputs from other Actors. For example, consider a computer keyboard and the monitor; they act as intermediaries between the end user and the computer system. Unless you are designing the hardware, these devices are transparent, and they do not need to be Actors. Instead, consider the end user as the Actor and consider the pass-through Actors as internal devices (or design elements) of the system under consideration.

We depict Actors as stick figures, such as in Fig. 12.3. We can arrange Actors into hierarchical generalization structures and organize them with packages. Though uncommon, we can give Actors properties and give them associations to other model elements.

FIGURE 12.3
Actor symbol.

```
┌─────────────┐
│             │
│  «Actor»    │
│   name      │
│             │
└─────────────┘
```

FIGURE 12.4
Alternative Actor symbol.

We show an alternative format for the Actor symbol in Fig. 12.4. This format is a Class box with the «Actor» stereotype. The box and the stick figure notation are otherwise equivalent diagram elements. Most modelers use the stick figure predominately.

However, the box approach is useful if you wish to emphasize that the Actor is not a person—perhaps it is an external system or database. It is also useful if we wish to show the Actor's properties. As a Class box, it can be divided into compartments, showing attributes, operations, signals, and constraints.

On a Use Case diagram, we connect the Actor to the Use Cases that they participate in using an association line. If we connect more than one Actor to a Use Case, then all the Actors are required for the Use Case to run.

Because Use Case diagrams are usually notional and aimed at a relatively nontechnical audience, we tend not to indicate the typical adornments that an association can have. However, we can use multiplicity and arrowheads if they are necessary to clarify the situation. For a summary of what these adornments mean see Table 12.1. For example, the arrowheads indicate which Actor contacts the system to start the Use Cases or if the Use Case contacts an Actor to start the behavior. Note that once the Use Case is initiated, data and messages can flow in both directions irrespective of the direction of the arrow.

A Use Case often has a primary Actor that initiates or triggers the Use Case. We consider the other Actors as secondary Actors. The Use Case name and goals are usually from the perspective of the primary Actor.

When there is no multiplicity shown on the side of Use Case, we normally assume a 0...1 value. If we had assumed exactly 1, it would require every instance of the Actor to be participating in an instance of the Use Case, which is overwhelmingly false. As this is probably not legitimate, it would be preferable to show the multiplicity explicitly. For example, in Fig. 12.5, two Chess Players are required to Play Chess Match, but not every Chess Player is currently participating in a match.

Table 12.1 Adornments on Actor–Use Case Associations

Actor	Use Case	Description	Examples
	→	Actor initiates the Use Case	Patron Borrows Book
			Rider Hails a Ride
			In Fig. 12.9, the Borrower is the initiating Actor
	←	This Use Case contacts the Actor to start the behavior	System Notifies Patron Book is overdue
			System Notifies Rider Car is available
			In Fig. 12.9, the External Library System is a secondary Actor
	Multiplicity >1	The Actor can start more than one of these Use Cases. Interpretation as sequential or overlapping operation is a variation point	Patron Borrows Book
			Rider schedules a future car
			Rider Hails several Rides for large party
Multiplicity > 1		This Use Case requires the availability of more than one of these Actors	Two officers together scuttle the enterprise
			Two tennis players are necessary to start a tennis match. See Fig. 12.5
Multiplicity includes 0 in range		This Use Case does not always require this Actor to participate	Withdrawing cash from a bank does not always require a teller (e.g., by using an ATM)

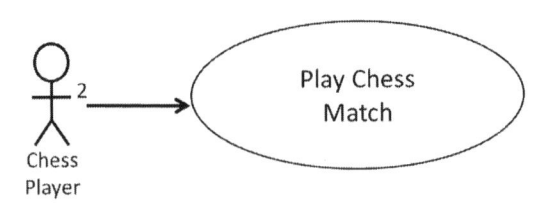

FIGURE 12.5
More than one required Actor.

It is, of course possible to use separate Actor symbols if the participants are different. In Fig. 12.6, we show both the Driver and Rider as participants in the Hail Car Use Case, though neither is required to always be participating. We put all of them in the Hailing App package. This does not mean that the physical people are in the package, but that our model information on them is kept in this package.

12.1.2.1 Human Actors

Do not identify people by their name but use the roles they play when dealing with the system. Each unique role makes for a unique Actor. Many individuals can act in the same role. Moreover, an individual may play different roles at different times. We depict this situation in the metamodel diagram in Fig. 12.7.

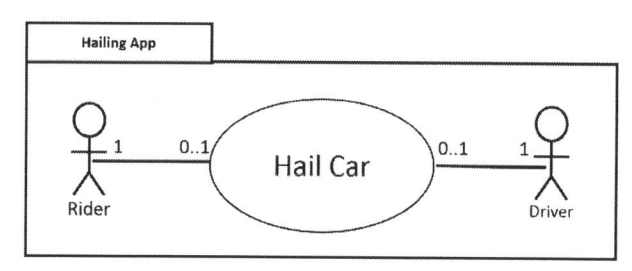

FIGURE 12.6
Multiple Actors for a single Use Case in a package.

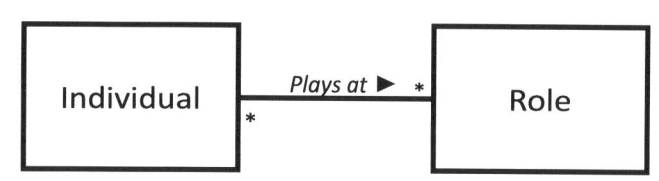

FIGURE 12.7
Relationship between individuals and roles.

For example, in the United States, the President signs bills into laws. You would not use the President's birth name as the name of the Actor, because as time goes on, we get new individuals in that role.

In this following example, people may change their roles: Many companies reimburse their workers for travel expenses, after the manager has approved the expenses. However, when the manager travels, the manager needs a higher level manager to approve. Instead of picking as potential Actors, the job titles of "Worker" and "Manager." chose the more descriptive role names of "Traveler" and "Expense Approver." A particular Manager can sometimes act in the role of Expense Approver and sometimes act in the role of Traveler. Similarly, the same person, who drives a car for a ride-hailing app, may also be a rider at a different time.

Job titles are not usually good names for Actors because they are too political and not sufficiently descriptive.

When naming an Actor in English consider using names with agent suffixes. Such terms often end with a suffix of *-er, -or, -ee, -yer, -ster, -eur, -ar, -ist, -ian,* or *-ier*[4] (e.g., *traveler, senator, employee, lawyer, barrister, restaurateur, liar, scientist, librarian,* or *cashier*).

---

[4] Avoid the suffixes indicating diminutive or feminine roles, such as *—ess* (e.g., *actress*) or *—trix* (e.g., *aviatrix*). Also, avoid names based on diseases (e.g., *diabetic*). These have negative social connotations.

12.1.2.2 External System Actors

An external system that interacts with our system during the execution of our Use Case is also an Actor. Though such systems don't have explicit goals or wishes, they do have a perspective. Their goals can be determined by investigating the purposes of the external systems and why it might be designed to interact with your system. Often, there is a representative of the external system that can answer questions to determine its goals as an Actor. We show an example of an External System Actor in Fig. 12.9.

12.1.2.3 Database Actors

Even though we do not generally consider that database Actors have goals, they can be modeled as Actors because they are the sources and sinks of data. If there is no goal, they cannot initiate a Use Case, but they can participate. If the Database is under full design control of the development team, the database is usually considered part of the target system, that is, it is an internal design item and is not shown in the diagram. However, if the database preexists, then it might be useful to put it on the diagram. See Fig. 12.8.

12.1.3 Subject

One alternative way of looking at Use Case is that they are the services that are offered to the Actors. The Subject of a Use Case is just the system or system component that offers up these services. When you first attack a problem, the Subject would be the entire system. If your project is large and uses a divide-and-conquer approach, such as decomposition, each subsystem would become a Subject when the work is at the subsystem level. From the perspective of each subsystem, however, any other communicating subsystem would be an Actor (an external source or sink of information, events, or data).

Therefore, in one model, a model element may be a Subject, but in a different model, the same element may be an Actor, depending on what you are concentrating on for your System of Interest[5].

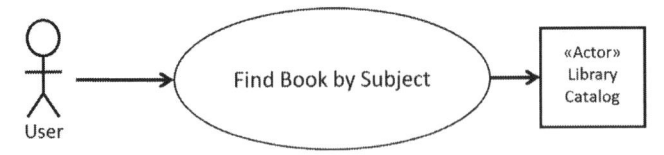

FIGURE 12.8
Database Actor.

---

[5]Many UML tools will not let you have a model element that is both an actor and not an actor at the same time. You can display them differently, such as using the stick figure form or the box form. Alternatively, you can duplicate the elements and name them differently.

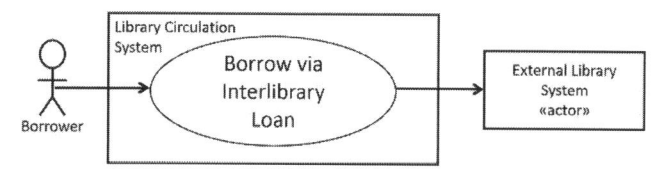

FIGURE 12.9
Interlibrary Loan Use Case.

FIGURE 12.10
Relationship between Use Cases and Subjects.

In Fig. 12.9, the *Library Circulation System* is the `Subject`. It represents the system that is offering the Use Case, Borrow via an Interlibrary Loan, to the primary (initiating) Actor, the Borrower.

The arrowhead from the Borrower to the Use Case indicates that the Borrower contacts the Use Case. A secondary Actor, the External Library System, is contacted by the Use Case. Because the External System is not a person, we use the option to employ a stereotyped Class box.

A Subject must be a classifier, able to exhibit behavior. In a Use Case diagram, the Subject is a diagram element that is a box with the name in the upper-left corner. An optional stereotype in «» may be placed above the Subject name.

Sometimes, we call the Subject the `system boundary`. As more than one system can offer up the same Use Case, a Use Case can appear within multiple System Boundaries. In Fig. 12.10, we show a metamodel diagram indicating the relationship between Subjects and Use Cases. Though it is possible to have a Use Case without a Subject, there is usually at least one Subject for a Use Case. In Fig. 12.11, we show an example of the Hail Car Use Case being offered by two Subjects.

12.1.4 Other Use Cases

There are Use Cases that are triggered by the system itself, usually by timers or by sensors. We have several ways of modeling these situations. For example,

1. Model the Clock or Sensor as an Actor. For example, "The Clock (as Actor) wants the Alarm to Ring."

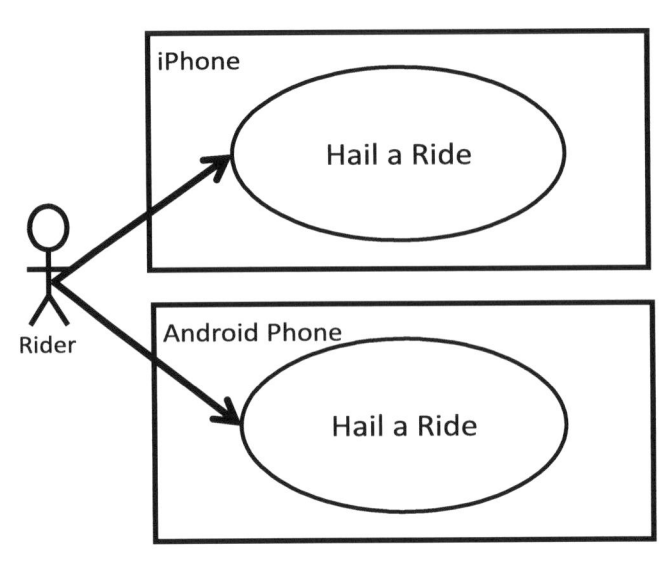

CHAPTER 12: Use Cases

FIGURE 12.11
Two Subjects can offer the same Use Case.

2. Treat the one who sets the alarm or sensor threshold as the Actor. For example, "The Sleeper (as Actor) wants the Alarm to Ring."
3. Treat the ringing as the separate part of a two-part Use Case. "The Sleeper (as Actor) Sets the Alarm to Ring and it later Rings."

The best way of modeling such situations is project dependent, though most modelers appear to use option 1. For example, in a smartphone, a Use Case may be, for example, "The Wi-Fi sensor wants to Connect."

POINTS TO REMEMBER

- Consider a Use Case as a service that the System of Interest offers to some external Actor.
  - You may also consider a Use Case as
  - A way that an Actor uses the system to return some value to the Actor,
  - A family of related scenarios bound by a common goal,
  - An operation of the system,
  - A Use Case is normally shown as a named Oval.
- An Actor is an external entity that wants to use the system to obtain some value or to achieve some goal.
  - We may also treat as an Actor any external source or sink of messages, events, or data.
  - Do not treat as an Actor any pass-through devices that just pass on communications from the outside (e.g., keyboards, terminals).
  - You may also avoid Actors that are completely under the control of the design team (e.g., databases, even internal workers).
  - You may need to consider timers and sensors as types of Actors depending on your methodology.

- A Subject is the classifier that offers up the Use Cases to the Actors. It is usually the System or a Subsystem of Interest.
  - A Use Case can have many Subjects
- Name Use Cases from the perspective of the Actors in present tense verb phrases, capable of completion, but not yet completed.
- Actors should be a role, not a person's name or business title.
- Show an Actor as a stick-figure human, though a stereotyped box can be used.
- A Subject's name is usually a noun that names a system or part of a system.
- A Subject is shown as a box with the name and optional stereotype in upper left.

12.2 SIMPLIFYING USE CASES

Often, you will find that the Use Case is complex. Usually, the behavior that is invoked by the Use Case is documented using other UML diagrams (e.g., sequence, communication, activity, or state machine diagrams) or other forms of documentation (text, storyboards, flowcharts, or tables). If the Use Case is complex, then the other documentation will also be complex. If you have complicated Use Cases, you will want to use some of the standard decomposition techniques to simplify and to reuse.

12.2.1 Generalization

Both Actors and Use Cases can be generalized/specialized. When an Actor is specialized, all the specialized Actors can participate in the same Use Cases that the general Use Case can. They also, as expected, inherit any properties that are declared on the general Use Case. See Fig. 12.12 for an example of Actor generalization/specialization.

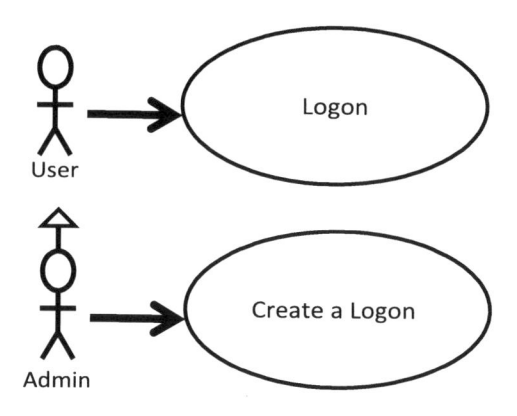

FIGURE 12.12
Actor inheritance.

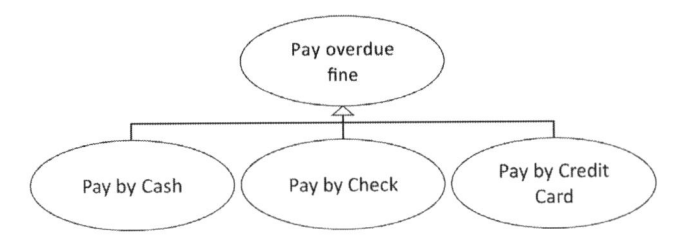

FIGURE 12.13
Use Case generalization.

In this example, a User Actor can Logon and an Admin Actor can Create a Logon. However, because an Admin is a type of User, an Admin can also Logon. Consider how we would interpret the diagram if we dropped the generalization and instead connected the Admin directly to the Logon Use Case. In such a situation, both a User Actor and an Admin Actor would be needed to Logon. In the standard situation, if more than one Actor connects to Use Case, they all must be available for the Use Case to proceed. The Actor generalization certainly makes the diagram clearer.

Use Case generalizations are useful when there are several approaches to achieve the same Use Case goals. See the example in Fig. 12.13. In our Library System, we occasionally have Patrons who need to pay overdue fines. We would then connect the Patron Actor to the Pay Overdue Fine Use Case. Our Patron has three ways of Paying—Paying by Cash, Paying by Check, or Paying by Credit Card. Whatever requirements, diagrams, or goals we attach to the general Use Case are also applied to the specific Use Cases, though we can add more detail in the specialized versions. This approach also allows us to add simply new specialized Use Cases, such as Pay by PayPal or Pay by Apple Pay[6], if the requirements change.

It is possible to combine both types of generalization as shown in Fig. 12.14. In this case, the Actor generalization indicates that a Vision-Impaired Patron is a type of Patron and can do everything a Patron can do, including Borrowing Material. However, a Vision-Impaired Patron is allowed to Borrow Large Print Material, while a general Patron is not permitted to do so. The logic of Borrowing Large Print Material is a specialization of the more general Borrow Material. The diagram indicates that the Vision-Impaired Patron is allowed to Borrow Material, even if it is not large print (e.g., a CD or videotape).

---

[6]Or Samsung Pay, Android Pay, or CurrentC.

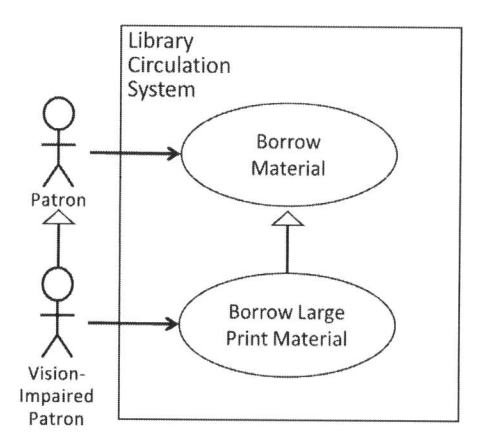

FIGURE 12.14
Generalization of Actor and Use Case.

12.2.2 Include

With large Use Cases, you may often find that several Use Cases share common subgoals or common subbehaviors. To share without duplication, UML has the «include» mechanism to help you accomplish this. The «include» mechanism is also useful to split apart large Use Cases into smaller ones that are easier to handle.

We use the include to pull out behavior that must be executed if the Use Case behavior completes. Because the behavior is part of the Base Use Case, the Base Use Case is not complete without the Included Use Case, and the goals of the Base cannot be completely met without the inclusion.

The following list identifies the steps to pull out common behavior to create an «include» Use Case:

1. Identify a behavior with a goal that is common to several Use Cases and create a Use Case to hold it.
2. Extract any requirements or descriptions from the original Use Case (now called the Base Use Case).
3. Place the extracted material in the new Use Case, if not there already.
4. Connect the Base Use Case with the new Use Case (now called the Included Use Case) with a dashed arrow from the Base Use Case to the Included Use Case.
5. Stereotype this line with «include».
6. Do not connect any Actors to the Included Use Case, unless only the Included Use Case needs the Actor. If an Actor participates with both the Base and Included Use Cases, it should only be connected to the Base.
7. Repeat the process from step 2 for other Use Cases that should also include the new Use Case.

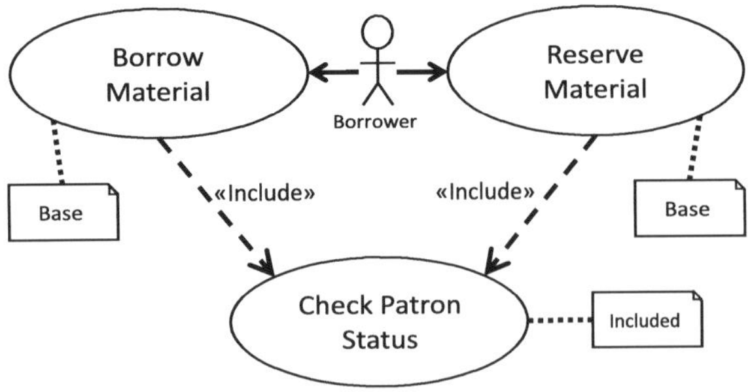

FIGURE 12.15
Included Use Case example.

In Fig. 12.15, we show an example of an Included Use Case, "Check Patron Status." It is included within both "Borrow Material" and "Reserve Material" to see if the Borrower has the correct Patron Status to allow Borrowing or Reserving. Remember that the boxes with folded corners are notes that add commentary to a diagram. The Borrower is the primary/triggering Actor for both Base Use Cases. The Borrower is also an Actor to the "Check Patron Status" Use Case.

The Included Use Case's contents insert inside the Base Use Case. It is not like a subroutine call as there are no parameters nor return values. It is more like a copy and paste, or an in-line macro expansion.

There are no limits on the number of Included Use Cases connected to a Base, as long as each Included Use Case is necessary to meet the Base's goals and complete the required functionality. An Included Use Case can also include additional Use Cases so that the same Use Case can act as both a Base and an inclusion at the same time. An Included Use can have new Actors if the included behavior requires other participating Actors that the Base does not independently need.

In previous versions of UML, we used to call the «include» relationship «includes» or «uses». These have been replaced by «include».

12.2.3 Extend

UML supplies an ability to add-on new functionality to a Base Use Case. As usual with such add-ons[7], the Base Use Case offers complete functionality, but the add-on provides a way to extend the functionality of the Base. We call this new behavior an extension Use Case.

---

[7]Also called "add-ins", "addins", "plug-in", or "plugins".

12.2.3.1 Using an Extension

The Base Use Case goal can be met without also meeting the extension goal. An extreme example is when the extension purpose is not related to the core goal. Consider the behavior "Fill Out Survey" when attached to the "Borrow Book" Use Case. The "Fill Out Survey" is not necessary to complete the "Borrow Book" goal, even though we might attach them together, with the "Fill Out Survey" as an extension.

It is also common to use an extension when there is a second delivery/release situation supporting new functionality. Instead of modifying the Base Use Case to add the new capabilities, we model the second delivery functionality as an extension. As the initial delivery was sufficient to meet the Base's goals or functionality, it was already complete, and the new capabilities are potential extensions. This is logically equivalent to have the second release behavior treated as an add-in.

Consider the Use Case "Hail a Ride." It may be a later version that allows the car to be reserved for a future time, "Reserve a Car." This "Reserve a Car" would be an extension of the normal path of "Hail a Ride."

Another common use of extensions is to capture behavior that is optional at run-time. I do not believe that this is indeed legitimate if the extension is still required occasionally to meet the Base, however, you will see this in the UML literature.

Consider the Use Case, "Return Book": occasionally it will also be necessary to "Pay Fine." Many modelers would make "Pay Fine" an extension, though I would make it an Included Use Case because I believe it is needed to meet the goal of "Return Book." If you feel that Pay Fine is not required to implement Return Book, then make it an extension. This distinction is tricky and it is probably not worth the time spent in arguing about this on a project. It often winds up being a big source of contention that is not that significant[8].

When you model an extension Use Case, you have the ability to specify the conditions (if any) that the extension behavior is run under.

12.2.3.2 The «Extend» Notation

An extension Use Case is drawn as a Use Case oval, with a dashed arrow line from the extension to the Base. On the dashed line, place the «extend». See Fig. 12.16. This is the opposite direction from that of the «include».

---

[8] I've been a consultant on many projects, specializing in UML. Arguing about whether a Use Case should be extension or an inclusion usually requires more time than it is worth. If it not obvious use an «include». If Use Case modeling is being done precisely because this project intends to use the Use Case model to help in scheduling development tasks, there could be value to getting this correct, but this is an advanced technique that is unfortunately rarely used.

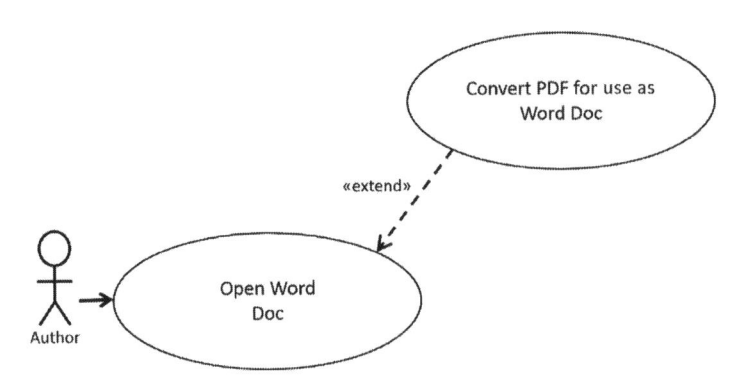

FIGURE 12.16
An example of an add-in as an extension.

The author is also an Actor to the "Convert PDF" Use Case. The extension Use Case's contents insert inside the Base Use Case. Just as with «include», an «extend» is not like a subroutine call as there are no parameters nor return values. It is more like a copy and paste, or an in-line macro expansion.

There are no limits on the number of extension Use Cases connected to an extended Use Case. An extension Use Case can «include» other Use Cases and can have «extends» of its own. The same extending Use Case can extend more than one Use Case. Furthermore, an extending Use Case may itself be extended[9].

In previous versions of UML, the «extend» was called «extends».

12.2.3.3 Extension Points

As extensions are optional from the perspective of the Base Use Case, there exists additional notation that helps in identifying when and where to insert the extension. We can attach a constraint to the «extend» arrow, indicating the condition that must be true for the extension to be applied. We use the standard constraint notation, a note symbol, with the label "condition."

We can also place inside the extended Use Case a list of locations, called extension points. These are locations where the extension can be inserted if the condition is true. UML doesn't have a standard way of identifying these locations, though commonly they are the name of a state in a state machine for the Base Use Case.

Both the extension points and condition are optional. You can use neither, either, or both. The condition can refer to an extension point to indicate where the condition will be tested. In Fig. 12.19, the Base

---

[9]UML 2.5 Specification (OMG 2013) p 671.

```
                        ┌─────────────────────────────────────┐
                        │ condition: {customer selected HELP}  │
                        │ extension point: selection           │
                        └─────────────────────────────────────┘
                                        ╱
                                       ╱
      ╭─────────────╮                 ╱
     ╱  Extension    ╲◄─ ─ ─ ─ ─ ─ ─ ╱        ╭─────────────╮
    │    points       │   «extend»            │              │
     ╲  selection    ╱                         ╲            ╱
      ╰─────────────╯                           ╰──────────╯
      Perform ATM transaction                    On-line help
```

FIGURE 12.17
Using extension points and conditions from UML 2.5 specification Fig. 18.3.

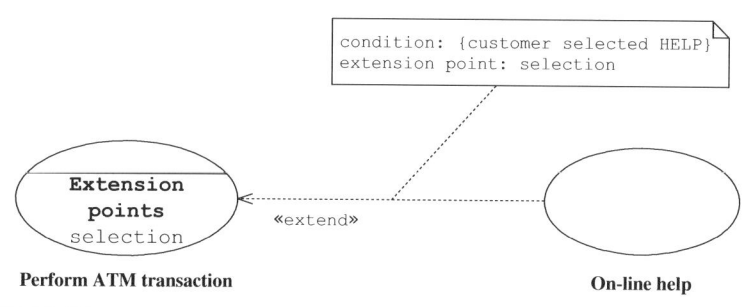

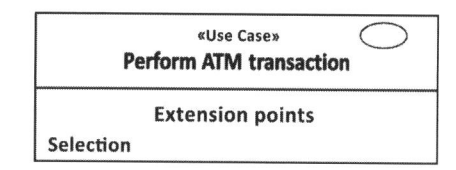

```
┌─────────────────────────────────┐
│         «Use Case»         ◯    │
│      Perform ATM transaction    │
├─────────────────────────────────┤
│        Extension points         │
│  Selection                      │
└─────────────────────────────────┘
```

FIGURE 12.18
Alternative format showing Use Case as a classifier.

Use Case is "Perform ATM Transaction." This Use Case has an extension point "selection." The extension Use Case, "On-line Help" will be inserted into Perform ATM Transaction at the "selection" extension point, when the condition "customer selected HELP" is true (Fig. 12.17).

There is an alternative format for the Use Case and extension points that uses a classifier rectangle. This format, shown in Fig. 12.18, is sometimes more useful when there are many extension points or inheritance is involved. The Use Case oval in the upper right gives a visual indication that the classifier represents a Use Case. The compartment name is "extension points."

12.2.4 Owners

Every element in UML must be owned by exactly one other element[10]; this also applies to the Use Case-related elements. We can show that a Use Case, Actor, or Subject is owned by a package by placing the diagram element in a package. Packages are the usual way of organizing these elements[11].

---

[10]You should remember the exception to this "everything is owned rule". Some packages may be unowned, to prevent infinite recursion.
[11]If a Subject is owned by a Package, unless the Use Cases offered by the Subject are explicitly owned by some other element, or if the Use Case appears within other Subjects that are owned by other Packages, we usually assume that the Package is the owner of the offered Use Cases. This is unclear in the UML specification and will not be tested.

If the ownership of a Use Case is not clear, we precede the name of the Use Case with the ownership path, e.g., **OwningPackage: Use Case Name**. Individual UML tools have several optional variations allowed to show the path name.

If you place a Use Case in a Class box, we assume that the Class is the Subject. However, if we need to indicate that the Class is the owner, we put the Use Case in a separate compartment. We show an example of both a **SubjectClass** and an **OwningClass** in Fig. 12.19. In the Subject (on the left), the name of the Subject is in the upper left-hand corner, though in the Class (on the right), the Class name is centered and has a compartment separator.

12.2.5 Use Case Diagrams

A Use Case diagram generally depicts several Use Cases along with their Actors. We consider Use Case diagrams to be behavioral diagrams, despite the notation being similar to structural diagrams. When the UML tool allows for direct execution of the model, or for execution of the generated code within the tool, it is possible for the tool to highlight automatically the currently executing Use Case.

The diagram header <kind> is usually **pkg**, though other namespace containers are possible, e.g., class and component. We show an example of a package containing the Use Case diagram in Fig. 12.20. This diagram is equivalent to Fig. 12.6.

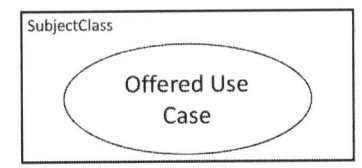

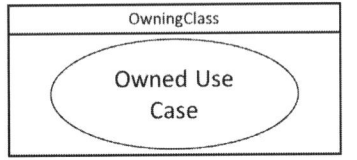

FIGURE 12.19
The difference between a Class as Subject and a Class as owner.

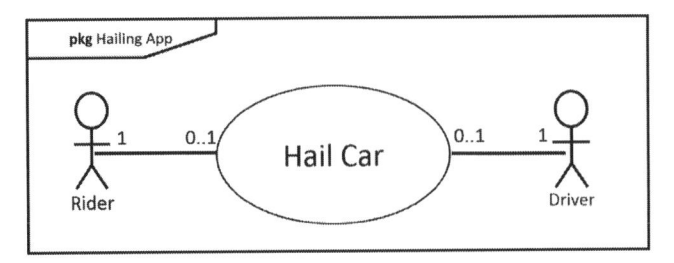

FIGURE 12.20
Use Case diagram within a package.

The Subject or system boundary is usually a class representing the entire system or a UML component representing a subsystem. More than one Subject can be shown on the same diagram. Use Cases offered by more than one Subject are repeated in each Subject as necessary.

If a complicated Actor hierarchy is involved, especially if you are displaying properties for the Actors, a separate diagram in the same package is often created.

If **pkg** is used, and no Subject or system boundary is shown, we usually assume that the system as a whole is the Subject. If a class or component is the <kind> of diagram, and no Subject is depicted, we usually assume that the diagram element is the Subject (e.g., if the Use Case diagram is shown in a Class, we typically assume that the Subject is the Class), though it is not required to be so.

POINTS TO REMEMBER

- Both Use Cases and Actors can participate in generalizations, encouraging reuse.
  - Specialized Actors can participate in any Use Case the more general Actor can participate in.
  - Specialized Use Cases allow Use Cases to share goals, but allowing varying approaches to reaching the goals.
- Pull out common behaviors or subgoals from a Base Use Case to allow several Base Use Cases to share via «include».
  - The notation for an include is a dashed arrow line from the Base to the inclusion, labeled with «include».
  - An «include» is a mandatory part of the Base and is needed for the goal to be reached.
  - A Base may include many other Use Cases. An Included Use Case can be used by many Bases.
  - Use «include» to encourage reuse or to limit the size of a Use Case to encourage modularity.
- An extension is some behavior that is added to a Use Case to act as an add-in, subsequent delivery capability, or optional path.
  - The notation for an extension is a dashed arrow line from the extension to the Base, labeled with «extend».
  - An «extend» is an optional part of the Base that is not needed for the goal of the Base to be reached.
  - A Base may be extended by many other Use Cases. An extension Use Case can extend many Bases.
- An extension can optionally have a condition that identifies under what condition the extension will be used.
- An extended Use Case can have an "extension points" compartment indicated where the extensions will be inserted.
- Every Use Case must have an owner, usually a package, but components and classes can also own Use Cases.
- When an owner is a classifier, the Use Cases are shown in a separated compartment, with the name of the classifier centered.
- Generally, Use Cases, their Actors, and Subjects are depicted in a package diagram.

CHAPTER 13

Questions for Chapter 12

1. Which of the following choices would make a Use Case name under most likely scenarios?
   A. Go to Sleep
   B. Bought Food
   C. Shopping On-line
   D. Discombobulate Absquatulators
   E. Register New Logon
2. Of what model are Use Cases considered part?
   A. Structure Model
   B. Behavior Model
   C. Activity Model
   D. Runway Model
   E. Design Model
3. Which of the following line styles will one find commonly on a Use Case diagram?

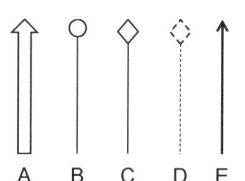

   A   B   C   D   E

   A. A
   B. B
   C. C
   D. D
   E. E
4. Consider as your system boundary a major consumer-oriented bank at the system level. What choice below has only legitimate Actors yet is most complete?
   A. Depositor
   B. Depositor, Borrower

227

OCUP 2 Certification Guide. DOI: http://dx.doi.org/10.1016/B978-0-12-809640-6.00001-5
© 2018 Elsevier Inc. All rights reserved.

C. Depositor, Borrower, Teller
D. Depositor, Borrower, Teller, Manager
5. Which of the Use Cases below is specified as a complete behavior, capable of standing alone?

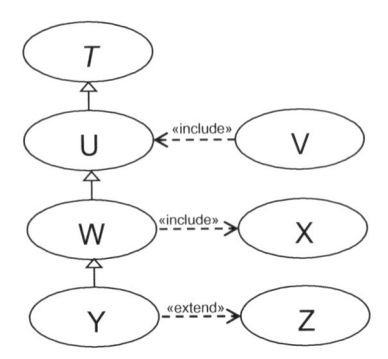

A. T
B. U
C. V
D. W
E. X
F. Y
G. Z

6. During chess tournaments, often a single Chess grandmaster plays multiple exhibition matches simultaneous each against a player. Which diagram fragment below best describes the situation?

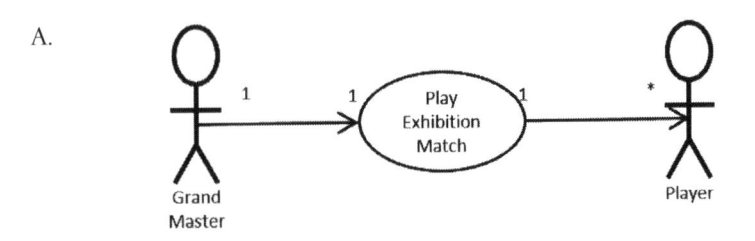

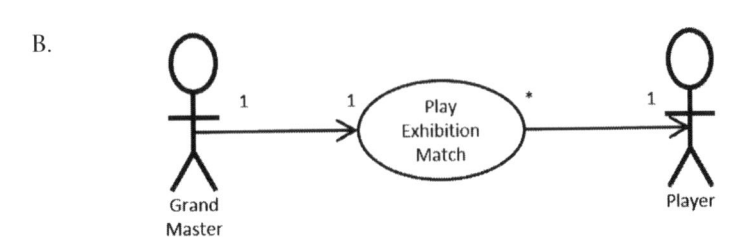

A.

B.

Questions for Chapter 12 229

C.

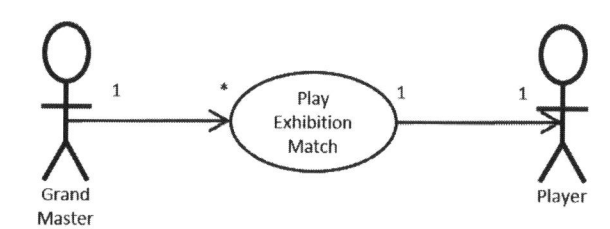

Grand Master —1—*→ (Play Exhibition Match) —1—1→ Player

D.

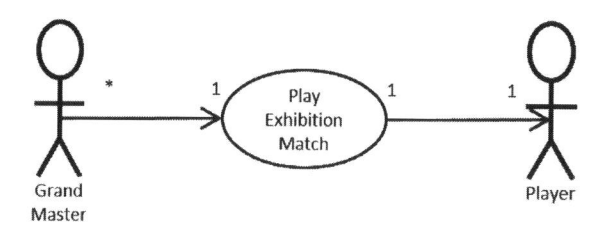

Grand Master —*—1→ (Play Exhibition Match) —1—1→ Player

E.

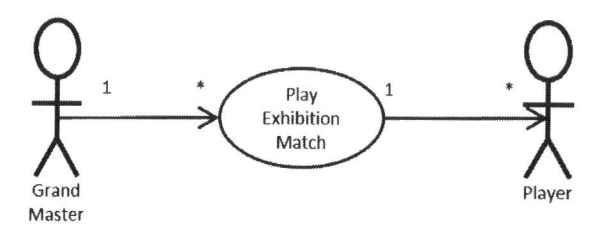

Grand Master —1—*→ (Play Exhibition Match) —1—*→ Player

F.

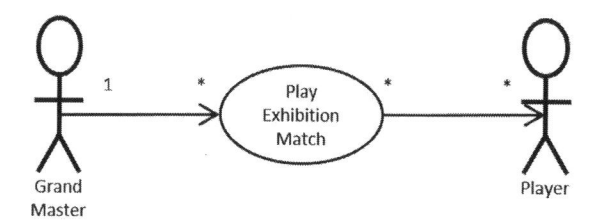

Grand Master —1—*→ (Play Exhibition Match) —*—*→ Player

G.

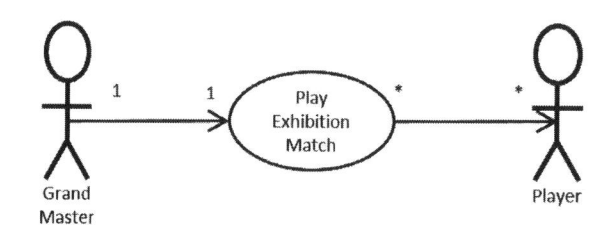

Grand Master —1—1→ (Play Exhibition Match) —*—*→ Player

7. The Patron can borrow or return books at the Library. Which diagram fragment below captures these facts?

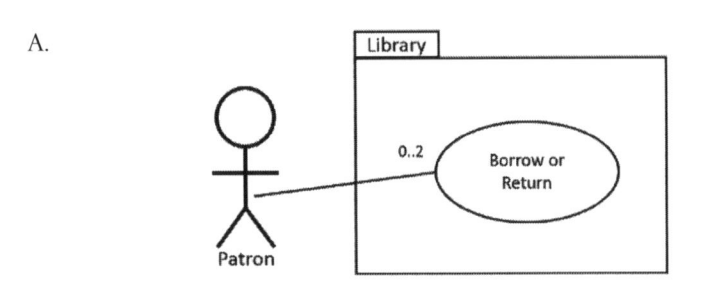

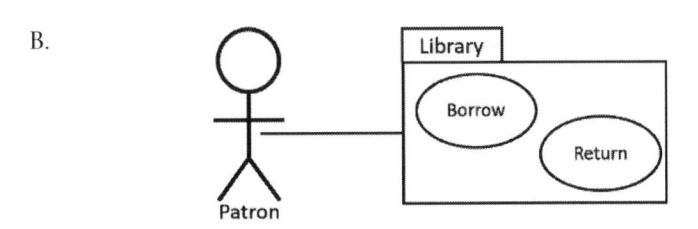

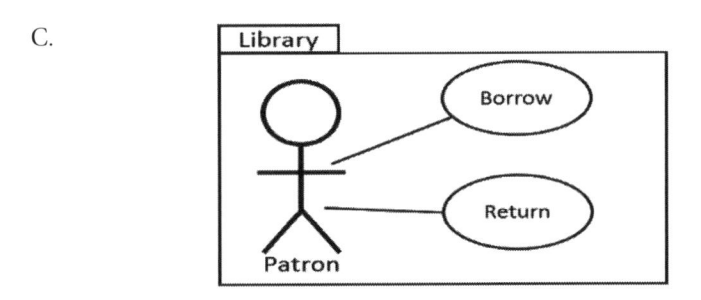

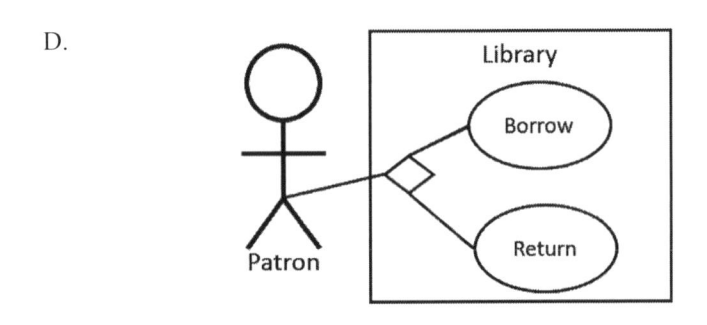

A.

B.

C.

D.

E.

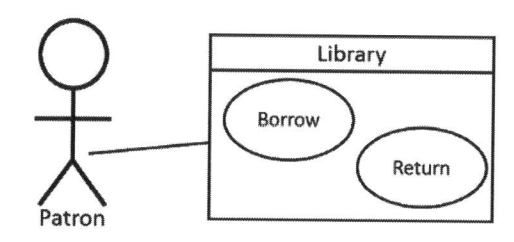

8. In which diagram fragment is X the Subject?

A.

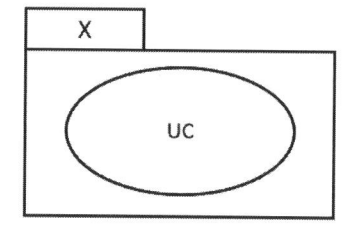

B.

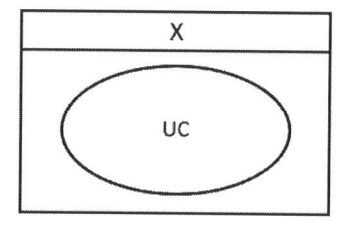

C.

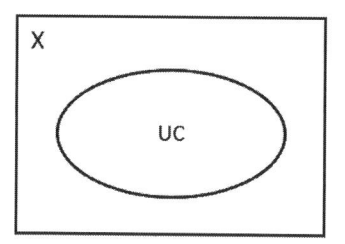

D.

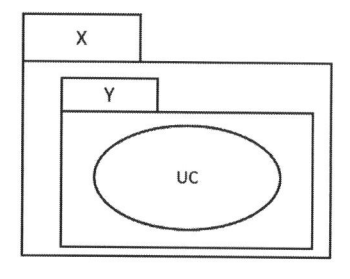

9. The Ride Hailing App supports both Hailing a Car and Hailing a Rickshaw as the only choices. Which diagram fragment best depicts this situation?

A.

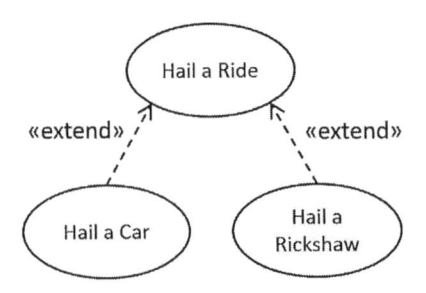

```
            Hail a Ride
      ↗                ↖
  «extend»          «extend»
      ⋮                ⋮
  Hail a Car      Hail a Rickshaw
```

B.

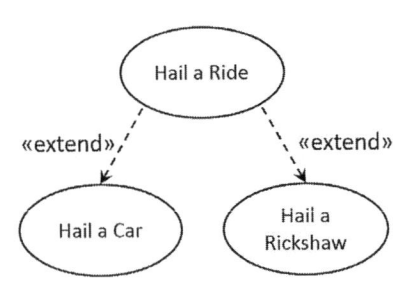

```
            Hail a Ride
      ⋮                ⋮
  «extend»          «extend»
      ↓                ↓
  Hail a Car      Hail a Rickshaw
```

C.

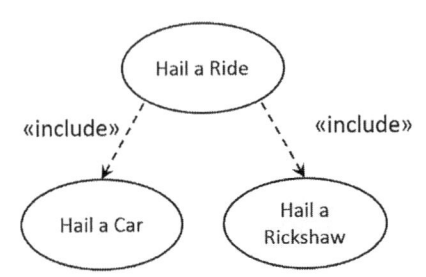

```
            Hail a Ride
      ⋮                ⋮
  «include»        «include»
      ↓                ↓
  Hail a Car      Hail a Rickshaw
```

D.

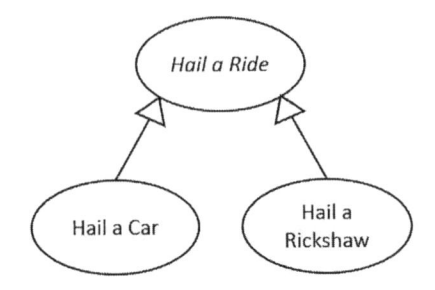

```
            Hail a Ride
         △         △
         │         │
     Hail a Car   Hail a Rickshaw
```

10. Of the following, which indicates a good reason to use a generalization among Use Cases?
    A. When there is more than one way of meeting the same Actor's goal.
    B. When one Use Case needs the services of another Use Case to meet the Actor's goals.
    C. When two or more Use Cases need to communicate each other along with the Actor.
    D. When one Use Case can be inserted into another.
    E. When two or more Use Cases share the same Subject.

ANSWERS FOR CHAPTER 12

1. Which of the following choices would make a Use Case name under most likely scenarios?
    A. Go to Sleep
    B. Bought Food
    C. Shopping On-line
    D. Discombobulate Absquatulators
    E. **Register New Logon**

    Discussion:
    A—No, not normally a Use Case, unless the Subject is a Robot or an exoskeleton.
    B—No, A past, completed behavior.
    C—No, participles or gerunds are not normally acceptable, they do not fall into the name pattern of "O System, please help me to …."
    D—No, this means to Confuse Thieves or Kidnappers. Not normally a good Use Case because it is hard to imagine the correct Subject, and certainly it is not using the end users language or terminology.
    E—Yes, this is something an Actor might want the System to help with.
2. Of what model are Use Cases considered part?
    A. Structure Model
    B. **Behavior Model**
    C. Activity Model
    D. Runway Model
    E. Design Model

    Discussion:
    A—No, though the notation (associations, generalizations) is more similar to a class diagram, we consider Use Cases as part of the Behavior Model.
    B—Yes, because it shows potential behaviors of the system.

C—No, you can use Activities to model the behavior within a Use Case, but there is no relevant Activity Model.
D—No, Not part of the UML domain.
E—No, though Use Cases can be used during design, they are more of an Analysis or Conceptual modeling activity.

3. Which of the following line styles will one find commonly on a Use Case diagram?

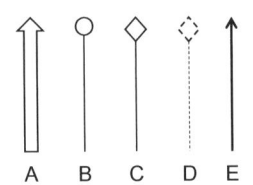

A. A
B. B
C. C
D. D
E. **E**

   Discussion:
   A—No, this is not a UML line type.
   B—No, used to show a provided interface.
   C—No, this shows aggregation.
   D—No, this is not a UML line type.
   E—Yes, this connects an Actor to a Use Case indicating if the Actor contacts/triggers the Use Case (when the arrowhead touches the Use Case), or if the Use Case contacts the Actor (if the arrowhead is touches the Actor).

4. Consider as your system boundary a major consumer-oriented bank at the system level. What choice below has only legitimate Actors yet is most complete?
   A. Depositor
   B. **Depositor, Borrower**
   C. Depositor, Borrower, Teller
   D. Depositor, Borrower, Teller, Manager

   Discussion:
   A—No, though Depositor is good, but there is a more complete answer.
   B—Yes, both Depositor and Borrower are served by the bank.
   C—No, the Teller is really part of the system. This job could be automated, consider an ATM. Perhaps, the purpose of this system is to propose an Internet bank.

D—No, both Teller and Manager are part of the system and are inside the system boundary.

5. Which of the Use Cases below is specified as a complete behavior, capable of standing alone?

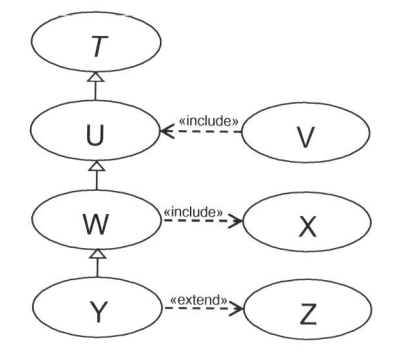

A. T
B. U
C. V
D. W
E. X
F. Y
G. **Z**

Discussion:
We can discount U, W, and Y. As they are specialized versions of T, they inherit the behaviors and goals of T and are not complete descriptions of behaviors in themselves.
A—No, T is an abstract Use Case (examine the italics of the name). By definition, an abstract Use Case cannot stand-alone.
B—No, U is an inclusion inside of V, that is the behavior of U is inserted inside of V. Though it is possible to be also a stand-alone Use Case, it is not common.
C—No, Base Use Case V requires the mandatory insertion of U and cannot be a stand-alone Use Case.
D—No, Base Use Case W requires the mandatory insertion of X and cannot be a stand-alone Use Case.
E—No, X is an inclusion inside of W, that is the behavior of X is inserted into W. Though it is possible to be also a stand-alone Use Case, it is not common.
F—No, Y is an extension of Z and is intended to live inside of Z (or similar). Though it is possible to also be a stand-alone Use Case, it is not common.

G—Yes, because Z does have an optional extension (Y), it should be capable running by itself as Y should not be necessary to reach Z's goals.

6. During chess tournaments, often a single Chess grandmaster plays multiple exhibition matches simultaneous each against a player. Which diagram fragment below best describes the situation?

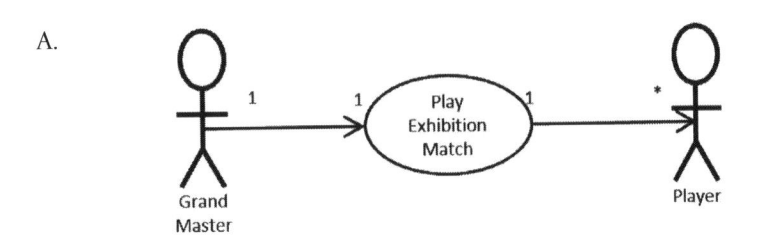

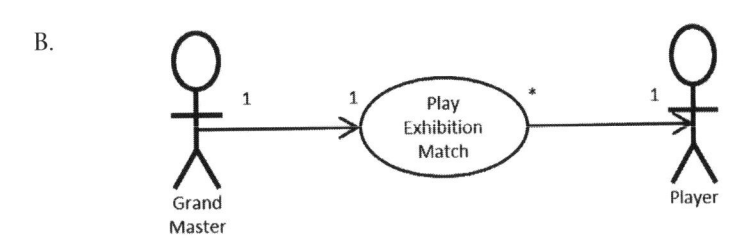

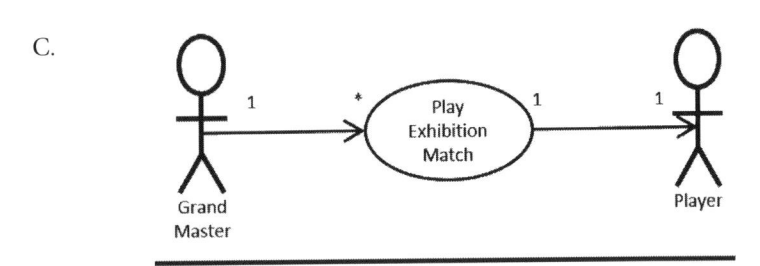

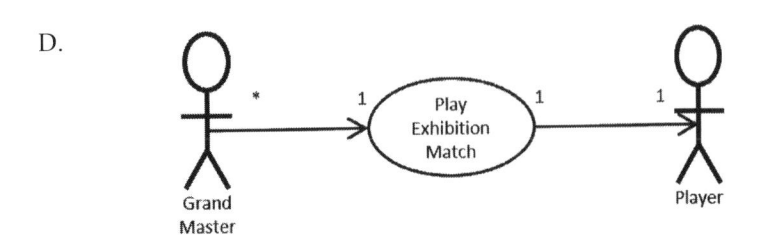

A.

Grand Master 1 — 1 Play Exhibition Match 1 — * Player

B.

Grand Master 1 — 1 Play Exhibition Match * — 1 Player

C.

Grand Master 1 — * Play Exhibition Match 1 — 1 Player

D.

Grand Master * — 1 Play Exhibition Match 1 — 1 Player

E.

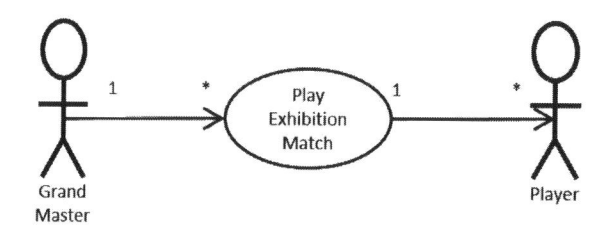

[Use case diagram: Grand Master (1) → * Play Exhibition Match * ← 1 Player]

F.

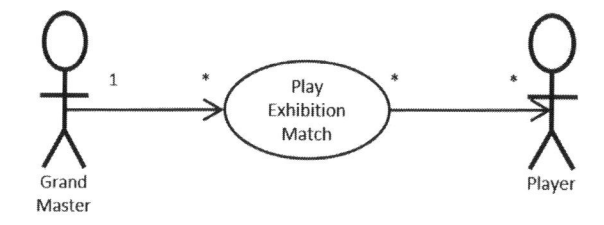

[Use case diagram: Grand Master (1) → * Play Exhibition Match * ← * Player]

G.

[Use case diagram: Grand Master (1) → 1 Play Exhibition Match * ← * Player]

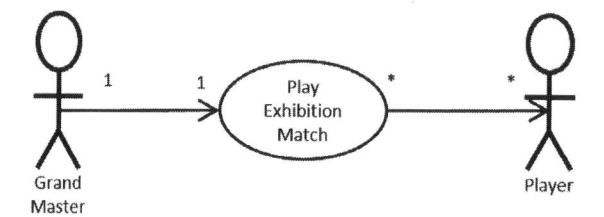

Discussion:
   The first thing is to consider is how many matches may be playing at a time. One grandmaster is playing many games. This leaves us only C, E, and F as possible answers. Then, how many Players per Match? Only one. This indicates that C is the answer. To check, ask yourself how many matches is each Player playing, Only one. This confirms that C is correct.

7. The Patron can borrow or return books at the Library. Which diagram fragment below captures these facts?

A.

Patron — 0..2 — (Borrow or Return) [Library]

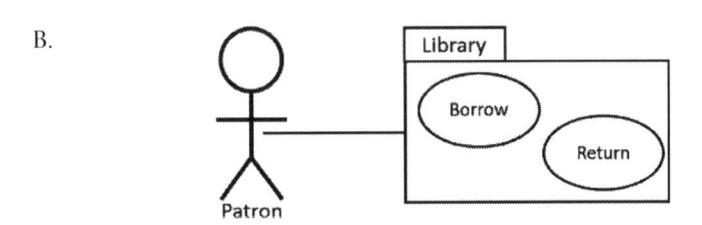

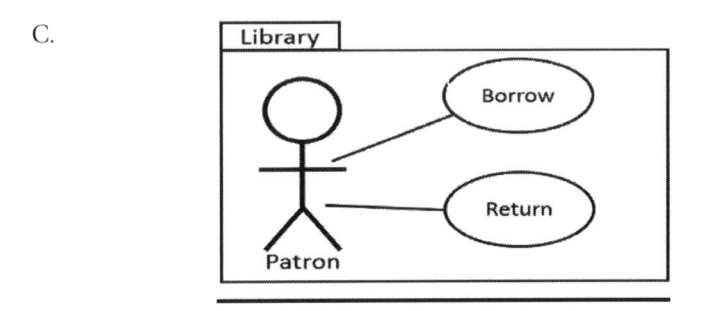

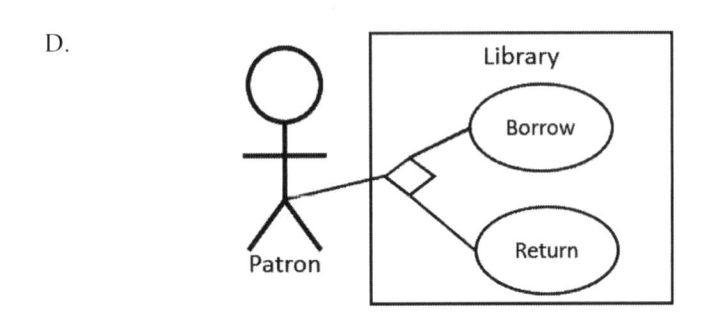

B.

Patron — [Library: (Borrow), (Return)]

C.

[Library: Patron — (Borrow), Patron — (Return)]

D.

Patron — ◇ — (Borrow), (Return) [Library]

E.

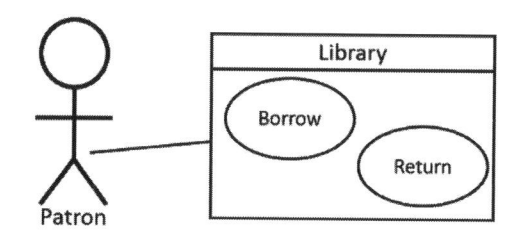

Discussion:
A—No, Using an "or" to reference two Use Cases is not supported.
B—No, the Patron has a relationship to the Library package, but not to the Use Cases.
C—Yes, the two Use Cases are owned by the Library and the Patron is properly connected to them. A better answer might have the Use Cases offered by a Library subject, but this is not necessary
D—No, the use of a diamond is not supported here.
E—No, the two use cases are owned by the Library classifier, but the Patron is not properly connected to them.

8. In which diagram fragment is X the Subject?

A.

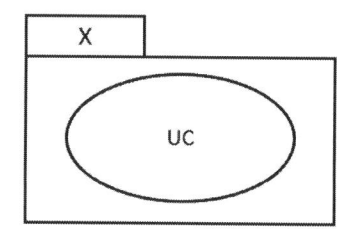

B.

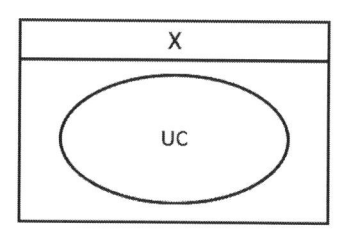

C.

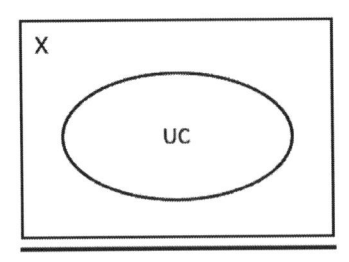

D.

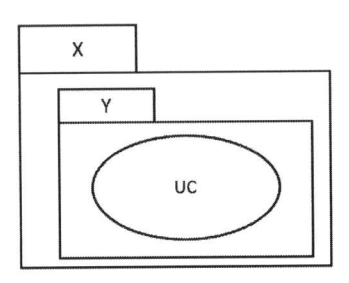

Discussion:
A. and D. are eliminated because a Subject must be a classifier able to offer up the Use Case. A package is only a container.
B—No, though B is a classifier, it is shown here as the owner of the Use Case.
C—Yes, X is both a classifier and the Subject. Note that there is no compartment line and the classifier name is left justified.

9. The Ride Hailing App supports both Hailing a Car and Hailing a Rickshaw as the only choices. Which diagram fragment best depicts this situation?

A.

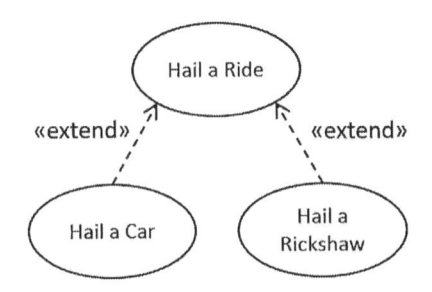

B.

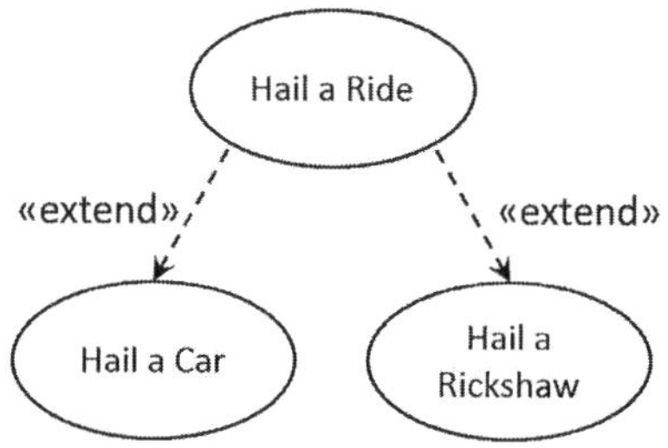

C.

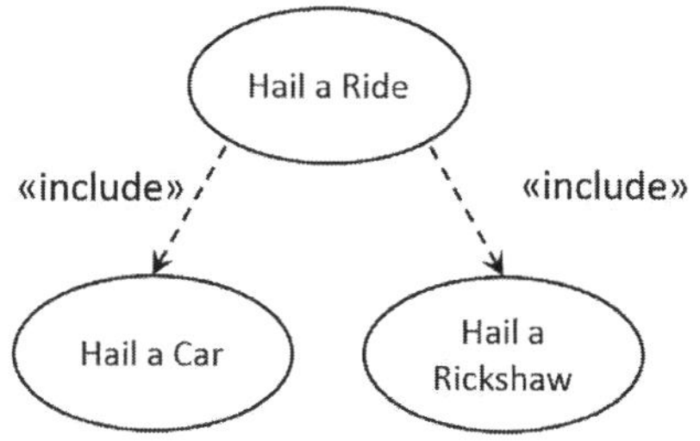

D.

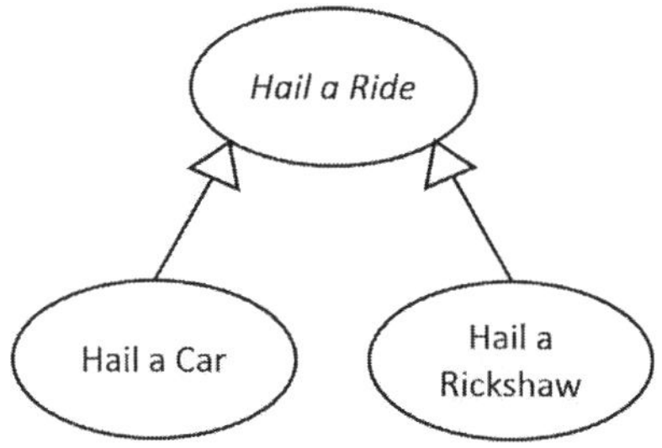

Discussion:
A—No, as Hail a Car and Hail a Rickshaw are the only options, Hail a Ride cannot be stand-alone Use Case.
B—No, this option would make Hail a Ride as an optional add-on to Hailing a Ride and Hailing a Rickshaw.
C—No, both includes are mandatory, though only once could be used at a time.

D—Yes, this allows Hail a Car and Hail a Rickshaw to share the goals and behaviors of Hail a Ride. As Hail a Ride is abstract (based on it having an italic name), it is not a standalone Use Case.

10. Of the following, which indicates a good reason to use a generalization among Use Cases?
    A. **When there is more than one way of meeting the same Actor's goal.**
    B. When one Use Case needs the services of another Use Case to meet the Actor's goals.
    C. When two or more Use Cases need to communicate each other along with the Actor.
    D. When one Use Case can be inserted into another.
    E. When two or more Use Cases share the same Subject.

Discussion:
A—Yes, generalization of Use Cases allows for variation of implementation or goals
B—No, the common needs of the Use Cases should be extracted and placed in an ≪included≫ Use Case.
C—No, Use Cases don't communicate in this way
D—No, inserted a Use Case into another Use Case sounds like an ≪extend≫ relationship
E—No, not relevant

CHAPTER 14

Behavior: Sequence Diagrams

14.1 SEQUENCE DIAGRAM HISTORY

SEQUENCE DIAGRAMS are one of the oldest diagrams in the UML toolkit. We can trace the diagram's origins to Message Sequence Charts (MSC) standardized in 1993[1]. The notations of Sequence Diagrams and MSC have continued to fluctuate but despite some differences in notation and emphasis, the two diagram types remain close in look and feel.

14.2 LIFELINES

Sequence diagrams show the exchanges and interplay of messages among ELEMENTS in some useful BEHAVIOR, called an INTERACTION. An Interaction is a unit of behavior. The elements must be CONNECTABLE ELEMENTS, but for our purposes, we will often call the connectable elements PARTICIPANTS in the Interaction. These participants are not classes or objects; they are closer to typed ROLES in a collaboration or parts of a structured classifier (practically the parts of composition relationship). They are named in the format of roleName: TypeName, where either part of the name may be empty, but not both. As they are not objects, we do not underline the participant names, though UML allowed this in earlier versions. The TypeName is typically the name of a Class or a DataType. When we omit the roleName, any participant of that type may be substituted. When we omit the TypeName, any participant in the specified role, no matter what class, should be sufficient.

After the roleName, you may see a [selector] in square brackets. It is not part of the name of the participant, but the selector indicates which element of a multivalued role we intend to use.

---

[1] It is still part of the Specification and Description Language (SDL) standardized by the International Telecommunication Union-Standardization (ITU-T).

CHAPTER 14: Behavior: Sequence Diagrams

FIGURE 14.1
Sample sequence diagram participants.

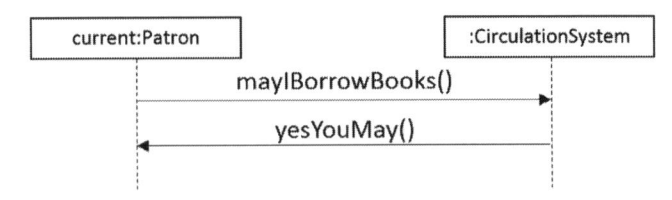

FIGURE 14.2
Sequence diagram lifelines.

```
roleName [selector]: TypeName
    or
connectableElementName [selector]: ConnectableElementType
```

In practice, the selector is usually an integer-valued index to an array of elements of the given type.

In Fig. 14.1, we see two participants (connectable elements): Patron in the current role and a Circulation System, otherwise unnamed. In a Sequence Diagram these connectable elements "head" a LIFELINE, depicted as a straight downward dashed line (see Fig. 14.2). Each lifeline represents a time-ordered sequence of EVENTS (called OCCURRENCES), from top to bottom[2], that are SENT from or RECEIVED on the lifeline. The figure shows the PATRON sending a MESSAGE mayIBorrowBooks to the CirculationSystem. Followed by the CirculationSystem sending the yesYouMay() message back.

From the perspective of the each timeline, moving from the top of the diagram to the bottom represents the order of time. Therefore, at the Patron, the yesYouMay message is received after the Patron sends the mayIBorrowBooks. At the CirculationSystem, the mayIBorrowBooks message is received before it sends the yesYouMay message.

Commonly, we find the messages ending with parentheses, for example, yesYouMay(). At the NOTIONAL level, use of parentheses is rare, but otherwise, it is a place for argument values[3]. The notional level indicates an attempt to give the model reader a notion of what is going on, without attempting to be formally correct or to specify a detailed implementation.

---

[2]UML 2.5 allows Sequence Diagrams to have their timelines oriented horizontally, but I have not ever seen it done, and I do not know of any tool support. However, it is possible. Other interaction diagrams, such as Timing Diagrams, regularly use horizontal timelines.

[3]It also serves as a reminder that the messages are operations and signals.

The HEAD of the lifeline is usually a rectangle; however, other shapes can be used to indicate the type of the participating connectable element, depending on the stereotypes used in your methodology (e.g., Active Class, Entity Class, and Control Class).

The heads of the lifelines that participate in a Sequence Diagram usually all align at the top of the diagram. However, lifelines can be created during an Interaction, in which case the heads are located at the point of creation. Row 6 of Table 14.1 show how this done.

You will probably find many examples in the literature of lifelines headed by Actors. Unfortunately, Actors cannot be connectable elements and cannot be parts. On the other hand, all the UML tools will support the use of Actors as lifelines. This approach is usually explained as reasonable because of changing system perspective. For example, if you focus on one subsystem, all the other subsystems will be as an Actor to the subsystem of interest, but all the subsystems are ultimately only parts of the system-as-a-whole.

If you want to use an Actor as a Sequence Diagram participant, my recommendation, as a methodologist, would be to go ahead if it makes sense in your circumstances and the tool support is available.

14.3 MESSAGES

A message is a communication from one lifeline to another. They are normally horizontal arrows leaving the sending lifeline and arriving at the receiving lifeline[4]. In Table 14.1, rows 1 through 4 show messages being sent and received.

Argument values can be passed in all these messages. Be careful that the argument values match up with the formal parameter types where the message is defined.

14.3.1 Synchronous Messages

A message with a solid arrowhead indicates a SYNCHRONOUS MESSAGE. A sending lifeline sends a synchronous message to the receiving lifeline. The sender waits for a return. Typically, we implement this by an operation call. In Fig. 14.2, we have an exchange of synchronous messages.

---

[4] A lifeline can send a message to itself at a later point on the same lifeline. In this case, the sending lifeline and receiving lifelines are the same. We call these messages SELF-MESSAGES. An example of this technique is shown in row 8 of Table 14.1.

Table 14.1 Lifeline Occurrences

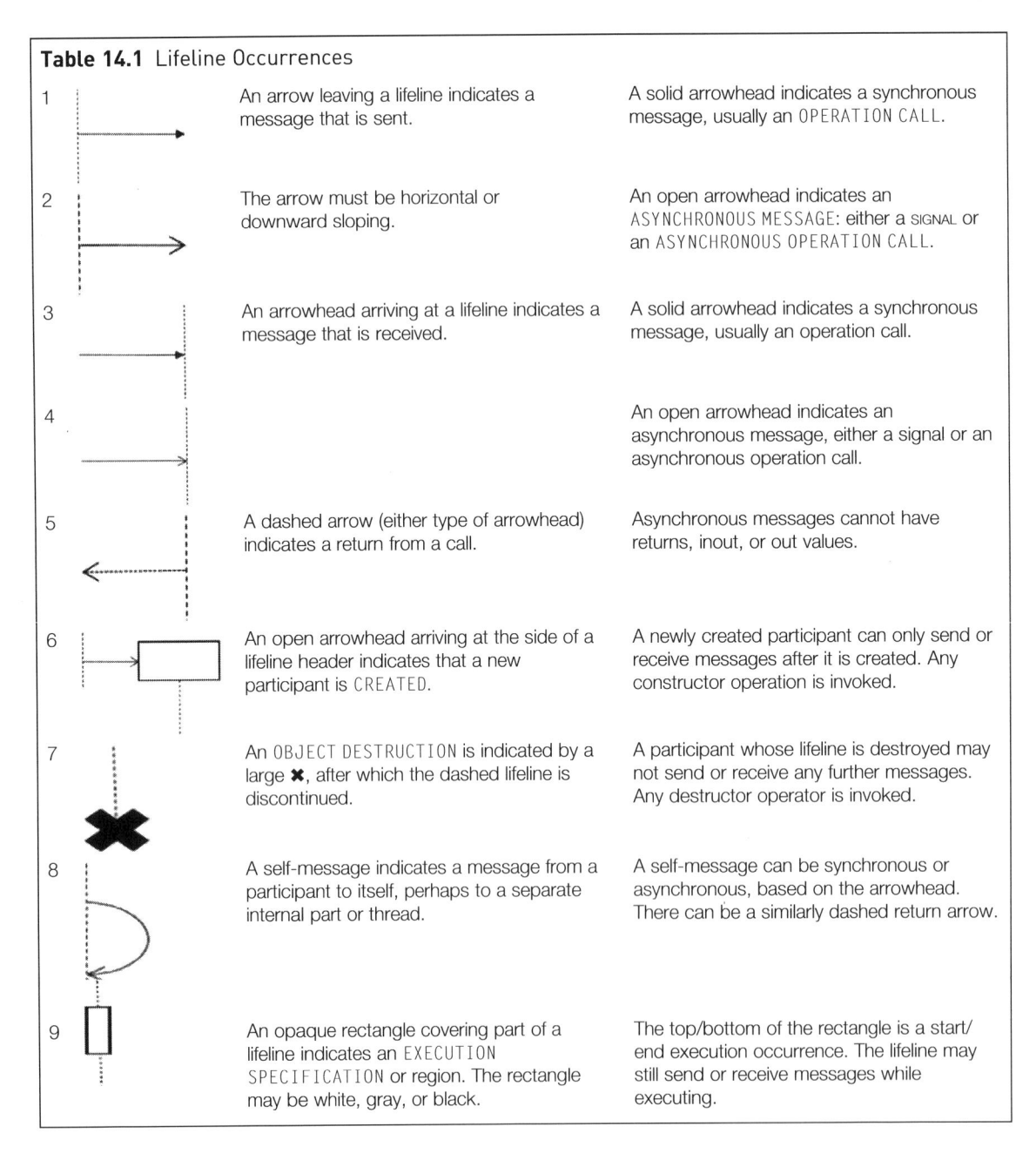

1	→→	An arrow leaving a lifeline indicates a message that is sent.	A solid arrowhead indicates a synchronous message, usually an OPERATION CALL.
2	→→	The arrow must be horizontal or downward sloping.	An open arrowhead indicates an ASYNCHRONOUS MESSAGE: either a SIGNAL or an ASYNCHRONOUS OPERATION CALL.
3	→→	An arrowhead arriving at a lifeline indicates a message that is received.	A solid arrowhead indicates a synchronous message, usually an operation call.
4	→→		An open arrowhead indicates an asynchronous message, either a signal or an asynchronous operation call.
5	←--	A dashed arrow (either type of arrowhead) indicates a return from a call.	Asynchronous messages cannot have returns, inout, or out values.
6	→□	An open arrowhead arriving at the side of a lifeline header indicates that a new participant is CREATED.	A newly created participant can only send or receive messages after it is created. Any constructor operation is invoked.
7	✖	An OBJECT DESTRUCTION is indicated by a large ✖, after which the dashed lifeline is discontinued.	A participant whose lifeline is destroyed may not send or receive any further messages. Any destructor operator is invoked.
8	↺	A self-message indicates a message from a participant to itself, perhaps to a separate internal part or thread.	A self-message can be synchronous or asynchronous, based on the arrowhead. There can be a similarly dashed return arrow.
9	▯	An opaque rectangle covering part of a lifeline indicates an EXECUTION SPECIFICATION or region. The rectangle may be white, gray, or black.	The top/bottom of the rectangle is a start/end execution occurrence. The lifeline may still send or receive messages while executing.

A synchronous message can be associated with a REPLY, that can have RETURN values, with a returnType or out or inout PARAMETERS. A reply uses a particular form of the message arrow as shown in row 5 of Table 14.1.

While the sender waits until getting the return, it does not mean the sender is necessarily blocked from sending or receiving other messages. Nonblocking yet synchronous behavior is allowed in order to account for the possibility that the sender may have multiple parts or threads, and the waiting may block only one.

As operations, they appear in the operations COMPARTMENT of the receiving lifeline on a Class Diagram (or similar).

14.3.2 Asynchronous Messages

A message with a V-shaped arrowhead indicates an ASYNCHRONOUS MESSAGE. An asynchronous message is sent without causing the sender to wait for a reply. The recipient must be an active class, with the asynchronous message being a hardware or software interrupt. Most of the web-based interactions are asynchronous messages from the browser to the server followed by another asynchronous message going the other way.

Although an operation may be called asynchronously, most asynchronous messages are sent using SIGNALS. Because no reply is possible, an asynchronous message cannot have a return or output parameters. In Fig. 14.3, we show the **Wakeup** Signal on the left. A Signal can only have input parameters, which we list in the Signal's compartment. In this case, a parameter to the **Wakeup** Signal is message:String. Signals can also be shown on State and Activity Diagrams.

On the right in Fig. 14.3, we show the **System** Class. It is an active Class (optionally indicated by the doubled sides). In its RECEPTIONS compartment, we show the signals that the Class can receive. In this case, we show the Signal **Wakeup**. In the receptions compartment, we show the receptions in an operation-like format.

14.4 TIME & OCCURRENCES

While time passes as you move down the lifelines, the time scale is not uniformly spaced on a lifeline, and time may move at different speeds on each lifeline.

«signal» **Wakeup**	«device» **System**
message:String	receptions «signal» Wakeup(message:String)

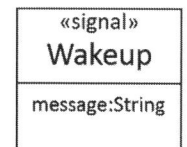

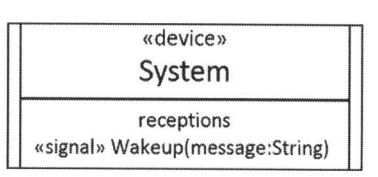

FIGURE 14.3
Signal and reception.

```
      :Left                          :Right
       m1!                            m2!
          \                          /
           \                        /
            \                      /
             \                    /
              \                  /
       m2?     \                /   m1?
        <------                  ------>
```

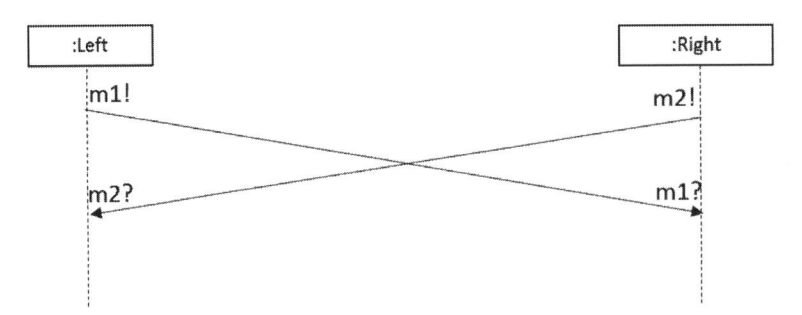

FIGURE 14.4
Crossing messages with multiple traces.

Messages may be downward sloping. You can use the slope to indicate time is involved in the transfer of the message from one lifeline to another. Consider that the lifelines may represent widely dispersed participants, e.g., satellites, networked computers, or hailed cars.

Because each lifeline is independent, it is often difficult to determine the order that things occur where they are on different lifelines. The things (usually arrows) that impinge upon each lifeline represent an ordered set of OCCURRENCES from top-to-bottom being earlier-to-later.

The ordering rules are:

1. A message end must occur after the message start. This rule is basic CAUSALITY.
2. Occurrences on a single lifeline are time-ordered from top-to-bottom. This rule is the definition of the lifeline. This rule enforces a strict ordering of occurrences on the lifeline.
3. The return, if any, from a message, can only occur after the original message is received. This rule is a consequence of rule 1 and rule 2.

These rules allow for multiple paths through a sequence diagram. On the diagram taken as a whole, the occurrences form a PARTIAL ORDERING. We call each valid order of occurrences a TRACE. When messages cross each other, it causes an opportunity for multiple traces; see Fig. 14.4. Traces are often displayed in angle brackets 〈 〉.

In Fig. 14.4, we follow the common convention to label the sending of a message with an "!" and the receiving of a message with a "?"[5]. There are two messages: m1 and m2.

---

[5]No convention is official. Pay attention to what convention is in use for each question on the exam; as they may not all use the same convention. Other common conventions instead of 〈!, ? 〉 are 〈!, *〉 and 〈→,←〉.

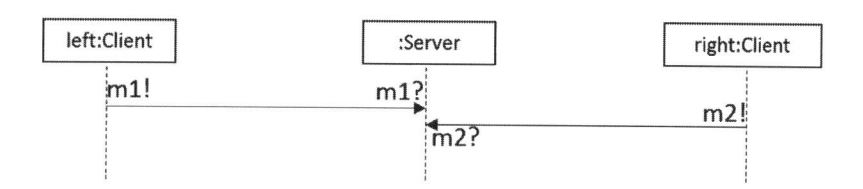

14.4 Time & Occurrences

```
left:Client            :Server           right:Client
   |                      |                    |
   |------- m1! -------->m1?                   |
   |                      |<------- m2! -------|
   |                     m2?                   |
```

FIGURE 14.5
Multiple traces from three lifelines.

Following the rule 1, we know that m1! must occur before m1? and m2! must occur before m2?. In addition, m1! must occur before m2? and m2! must occur before m1? based on rule 2.

However, there are no rules ordering m1! and m2!. So there are two possible orders ⟨m1!,m2!⟩ or ⟨m2!,m1!⟩. Similarly, there are no rules governing the order of m2? and m1?. So there are two possible orders ⟨m2?,m1?⟩ and ⟨m1?,m2?⟩. Together we now have four possible traces for this sequence diagram.

⟨m1!, m2!, m2?, m1?⟩   ⟨m1!, m2!, m1?, m2?⟩
⟨m2!, m1!, m2?, m1?⟩   ⟨m2!, m1!, m1?, m2?⟩

Without message crossing, there is only one possible trace when there are only two lifelines. However, when there are more than two lifelines, you can also get multiple traces.
Though UML does allow CROSSED MESSAGES, it does not allow crossing or bending lifelines.

In Fig. 14.5, we have three lifelines and multiple traces. Consider that there are no rules governing the order of m1! and m2!. How many traces can you find in the figure?[6]

There are many types of occurrences, but only a limited number can appear on the OCUP 2 Foundation exam. See Table 14.1.

1. The solid arrow with a filled-in (solid) arrowhead is the sending of a synchronous message. If this is a notional[7] sequence diagram, then it just means that the sender is ensured that the recipient gets the

---

[6]As the rules cover all the other possible orderings except for the order of m1! and m2!, there are only two traces.
⟨m1!,m1?,m2!,m2?⟩   ⟨m2!,m1,!m1?,m2?⟩
Notice that we have not determined how long it takes the messages to reach from the clients to the server. This is the fundamental source of the uncertainty in the traces.
[7]As a reminder, we construct a *notional* diagram when we intended to convey a notion (an idea) of the general picture of the situation and behavior. It is intended to be *notationally* accurate, but it will often eliminate optional indicators of implementation detail.

message. Otherwise, it means that the sender is invoking an operation on the recipient and that the sender will wait for a response. Diagraming the response is optional, but if it appears, it will look like the example in row 5. The message name is placed above the arrow and follows the syntax of an operation as defined earlier. The called operation must be a member of the recipient's OPERATIONS or inherited from a superclass of the recipient. The parameters of the operation may be given values appropriate to the scenario.

2. The solid arrow with a V-shaped arrowhead is the sending of an asynchronous message. If this is a notional sequence diagram, then it just means that the sender is not waiting for a response. The recipient class must be an active class, though that fact is not always modeled in any way.

   These asynchronous messages are usually SIGNALS, and they must be a member of the recipient's RECEPTIONS or inherited from a superclass of the recipient. Signals have the same syntax as operations, but have no RETURN value or OUT or INOUT parameters, as these require a response from the recipient.

   These asynchronous messages can also be operations that are called asynchronously.

3. Receiving a solid arrowhead means that an operation has been called on the recipient. If an operation by that name is not defined on the recipient, the superclasses are searched for a definition. If no definition if found then, the behavior is undefined.

4. Receiving a V-shaped arrowhead indicate a signal has been asynchronously received by the recipient participant. If a reception by that name is not defined on the participant, the superclasses are searched up the inheritance chain for a definition. If no definition if found, then the behavior is undefined.

   The recipient must be of an ACTIVE type and may not issue a return.

5. A dashed arrow indicates a return from an operation call. In informal modeling, this can be a notional return, but when formal modeling, it must match the return type of the operation call. It may also use a more complicated format that indicates the operation call, though this format will not be on the OCUP2 Level 1 exam.

   In Fig. 14.6, we show examples of Table 14.1 rows 1..5, i.e., the sending and receiving of synchronous and asynchronous messages and a return message from an operation call.

6. An arrow with an open V-shaped arrowhead arriving at the header box indicates the participant is created, as depicted in Fig. 14.7. This name of the message may be the name of the constructor with parameters filled in, or it can just be notional. If it is not an explicit call to the

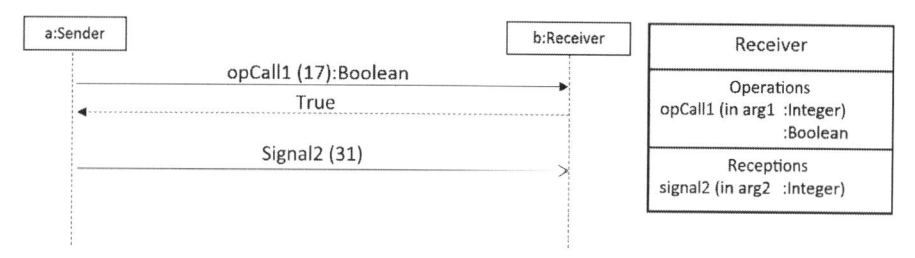

FIGURE 14.6
Sample sequence diagram and recipient class.

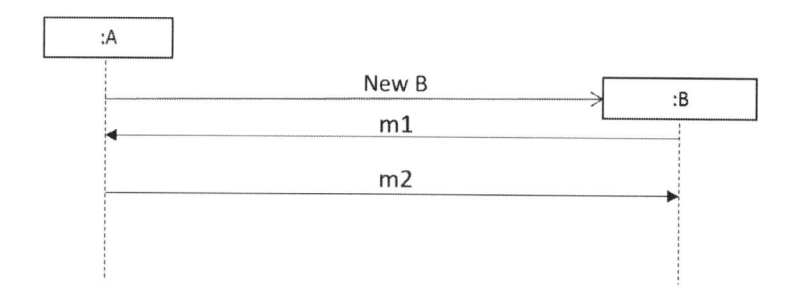

FIGURE 14.7
Lifeline creation.

constructor, the constructor is called. After OBJECT CREATION, the participant can now participate equally with the preexistent lifelines. All lifelines that are not at the very top of the diagram must be created before they can participate.

In the example figure, Lifeline A creates the B lifeline. After B is created, it synchronously sends the M1 message to A (or calls the M1 operation on A). Then A synchronously sends the M2 message to B (or calls the M2 operation on B).

7. A large ✖ at the bottom of a lifeline indicates that the lifeline is destroyed and cannot continue to participate in more behavior. The lifeline should not extend lower than the ✖. A lifeline can be killed in response to an incoming message, or it can decide to self-destruct. In Fig. 14.8, we depict the DESTRUCTION of lifeline A that looks like it is triggered by m1.

Any lifeline that starts at the top of the Sequence Diagram must be preexisting before the Interaction[8]. Any lifeline that does not reach the bottom of the Sequence Diagram does not exist after the Interaction.

---

[8] An interaction is the unit of behavior represented by the Sequence Diagram. See 15.2 Lifelines and 15.6 Sequence Diagrams.

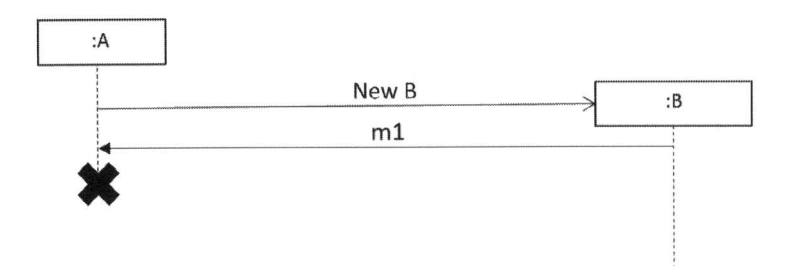

FIGURE 14.8
Creating and destroying a lifeline.

In the figure, lifeline A preexists but is destroyed by the end of the Interaction, while lifeline B is created and remains available after the Interaction is complete.

8. This notation indicates a self-message. It follows all of the same rules governing messages, but it is from one time on a lifeline to another time (a later time) on the same lifeline.
9. An opaque box placed over a lifeline indicates an `EXECUTION SPECIFICATION`, that is, the lifeline is executing some behavior or waiting for a lower-level behavior to finish. As a lifeline can contain multiple threads of execution, a lifeline can still send or receive additional messages while being covered by an execution specification. In addition, there can be multiple overlapping execution specifications. An execution specification is often called an `ACTIVATION`.

POINTS TO REMEMBER

- A Sequence Diagram shows how participating elements exchange messages over time in an Interaction.
    - A participating element must be a connectable element.
    - No objects (instances) are allowed by the UML 2.5 Specification.
    - Actors are not allowed (though are commonly used in practice).
- The participating elements are shown as lifelines.
    - A lifeline is shown as a vertical dashed line under a header.
    - Often a header is a rectangular box, though it might have a different shape if there is a stereotype involved.
    - The name in the header is of the format `roleName : TypeName`
- There are two main types of messages: Synchronous and Asynchronous.
    - Synchronous messages are operation calls and may return a result to the caller.
    - Synchronous messages are shown with a solid arrowhead.
    - Operations may be displayed in the operations compartment of the destination participant.
    - Asynchronous messages allow no return, out, or inout arguments

- Asynchronous messages are shown with a V-shaped arrowhead
- An asynchronous message may be an asynchronous operation call and shown with the other operations in the operations compartment of the destination participant.
- An asynchronous message may be a signal. A signal may be shown in the receptions compartment of the destination participant.
* Lifelines can be created or destroyed.
  - A created lifeline shows a V-shaped arrow connected to the side of the header.
  - A destroyed lifeline ends with a large ✖.
* Messages go from sender to receiver and may be horizontal or downward sloping.
* A self-message can go from a lifeline to itself, as long it goes to a later (lower) point.
* A self-return can also go from the lifeline to itself after the arrival of the self-message.
* An occurrence is any point on a lifeline, including:
  - A message being sent
  - A message being received
  - A return being sent
  - A return being received
  - An execution specification starting
  - An execution specification ending
  - Sending a creation command (new) to make a new lifeline
  - The new lifeline being created

14.5 EXECUTION SPECIFICATION

An Execution Specification is a vertical rectangle that is opaque and overlays over a part of a lifeline to indicate that the lifeline is busy executing some behavior. Execution Specifications are optional and typically used in complex diagrams where the execution stack is useful to see or where the end of some behavior is of interest. However, if you use it on any lifeline in a Sequence Diagram, you should use it on all the lifelines in the diagram.

You may name Execution Specifications. In order not to clutter the diagram, names are usually reserved for those circumstances where the name of the executing behavior does not match the name of the message.

In Fig. 14.9, the Right lifeline starts being busy; then it sends the m1 message synchronously to the Left timeline, which becomes busy executing in response to the message. Meanwhile, the Right timeline suspends until the execution is finished and the Left lifeline returns to the Right. Then, the Right timeline resumes its previous execution.

As in all Sequence Diagrams, explicitly drawing the return is optional, especially if it only conveys the transfer of control back to the caller. In the above figure, if we elided the return, you would still be able to determine when it occurs.

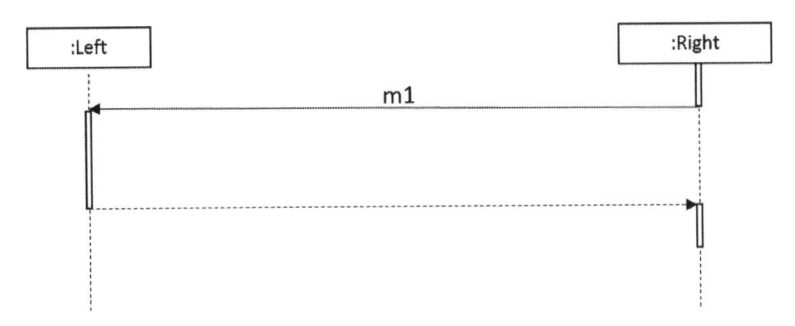

FIGURE 14.9
Execution specification.

How many occurrences do you see on this diagram? Before you count, consider that two occurrences that are at the same location on a lifeline are still separate occurrences.[9]

There are several approaches to using Execution Specifications. In Fig. 14.9, we show that the Right lifeline is not busy by omitting the rectangle while the Left is busy on the Right's behalf. However, you may see models that show both lifelines as being busy during this time, as the Right is busy, that is, busy waiting. We show an example of this approach below.

In Fig. 14.10, Lifeline C is busy even while waiting for Lifeline A to return. During A's execution, it invokes a callback on C, explaining the overlapping execution specification on C. When the callback returns to A, that execution ends.

Then A's execution concludes with a return to Lifeline C.

POINTS TO REMEMBER

- An execution specification indicates that some behavior is executing in the lifeline.
  - It is an opaque rectangle obscuring a part of the lifeline, whose starting point indicates the behavior start.
  - The ending point indicates the end of the behavior.
  - Waiting for another lifeline to finish may be shown as a gap in the rectangle.
  - A lifeline can have overlapping execution specifications if the lifeline gets another call while executing.

---

[9](1) Start of Right's first Execution, (2) End of Right's first Execution, (3) Sending of message m1, (4) Receiving of Message m1, (5) Start of Left's Execution, (6) End of Left's Execution, (7) Sending of the Return message, (8) Receiving of the Return, (9) Start of Right's second Execution, and (10) End of Right's second Execution. Therefore, there are 10 occurrences in Fig. 14.9.

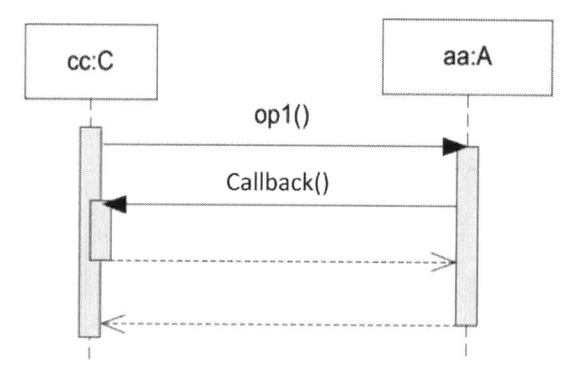

FIGURE 14.10
Overlapping execution specifications. UML 2.5 Specification Fig. 17.2.

14.6 SEQUENCE DIAGRAMS

Sequence diagrams show the exchanges and interplay of messages among participants in some useful behavior. We call this content an INTERACTION. Interaction is a unit of BEHAVIOR that focuses on the exchange of information between CONNECTABLE ELEMENTS. As a Behavior, an Interaction is a type of Class and is, therefore, a type of NAMESPACE.

A Sequence Diagram has the same sort of frame and header all the UML 2 diagrams have, a pentagonal header with the diagram namespace type in bold (**sd**) followed by the namespace name. In Sequence Diagrams, the namespace name is the name of the Interaction See Fig. 14.11.

For historical reasons, though the namespace type is an Interaction in the diagram header the type is **sd**. This **sd** is also the type used for Timing Diagrams, Communication Diagrams, and Interaction Overview Diagrams. These diagrams are also considered Interaction Diagrams, but they will not be on the Foundation exam.

Within a model, if two Interaction Diagrams have the same name, they are views into the same Interaction namespace. Some of the UML tools will properly enforce this and allow the diagrams to share elements. Other tools will just treat the identically named diagrams as independent. Others will prevent the duplication.

The diagram boundary box is potentially important as it has meaning when messages come from or go to the boundary. In the first exam, we will not cover these features.

CHAPTER 14: Behavior: Sequence Diagrams

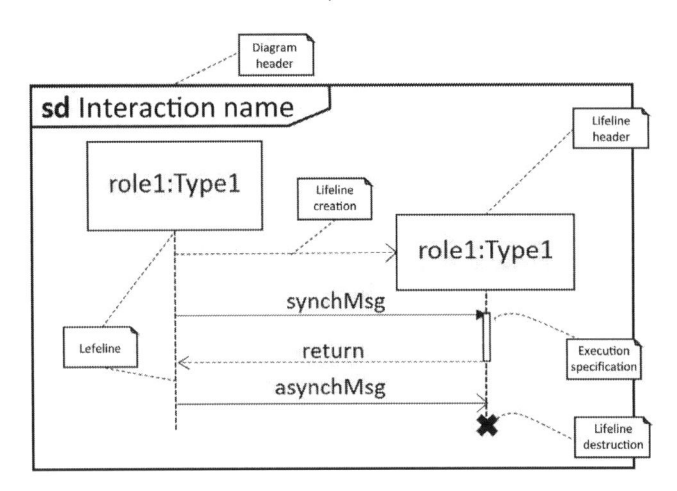

FIGURE 14.11
Principal parts of a sequence diagram.

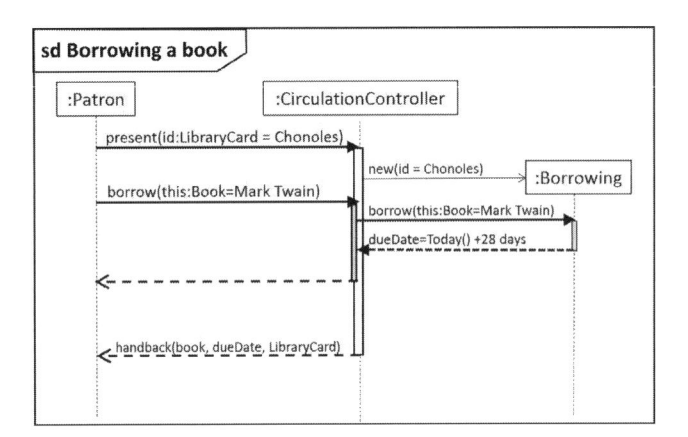

FIGURE 14.12
Borrowing a book scenario.

14.7 PRACTICAL SEQUENCE DIAGRAMS

In this chapter, we have covered the features of Sequence Diagrams that are covered by the first OCUP 2 exam. Using these features, we can draw simple single-pass paths without looping. While multiple traces are possible as described in this chapter, we still find that all the modeling messages must be sent and received without fail.

The complete Sequence Diagram specification is much more powerful. It includes a robust set of control structures: the equivalent to optionality, if-then-else, alt, loop, if, break, parallel spawn, critical regions, and support for behavior and structural composition.

Even without the additional control constructs, the Sequence Diagram can illustrate how a behavioral scenario works with specific argument values supplied for the formal parameters.

In Fig. 14.12, we see a simplified version of the Borrowing a Book scenario. For some of the formal parameters, we supplied specific argument values for the scenario. Here we see the Patron Chonoles showing his LibraryCard and then borrowing the Mark Twain Book. A dueDate is calculated, and a borrowing record is created. Then the LibraryCard, the Book, and the dueDate are all handed back to the Patron.

In this chapter, we have covered the basics of the very powerful UML 2.5 Sequence Diagrams. You should now be able to pass the questions in the next chapter and do well on the Interactions section on the OCUP 2 exam.

CHAPTER 15

Questions for Chapter 14

1. Which diagram type is not a UML 2.5 behavioral diagram?
   A. Use Case Diagram
   B. Sequence Diagram
   C. Interaction Diagram
   D. Collaboration Diagram
   E. Timing Diagram
2. Which one of the following potential lifelines needs to be changed?

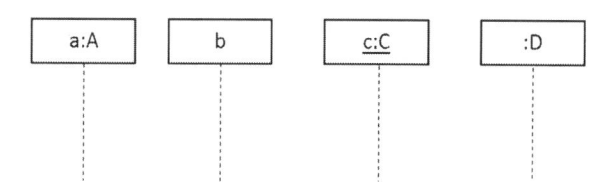

   | a:A | b | c:C | :D |

   A. A
   B. B
   C. C
   D. D
3. Which of the following messages is incorrectly drawn?

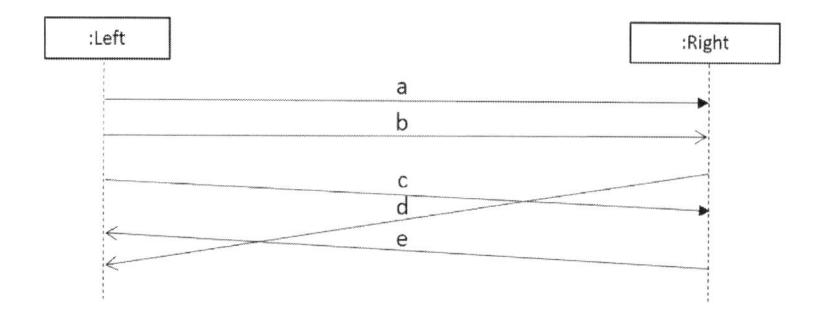

   :Left   :Right
   a
   b
   c
   d
   e

259

OCUP 2 Certification Guide. DOI: http://dx.doi.org/10.1016/B978-0-12-809640-6.00016-7
© 2018 Elsevier Inc. All rights reserved.

A. a
B. b
C. c
D. d
E. e

4. Which one of the following potential lifelines needs to be changed?

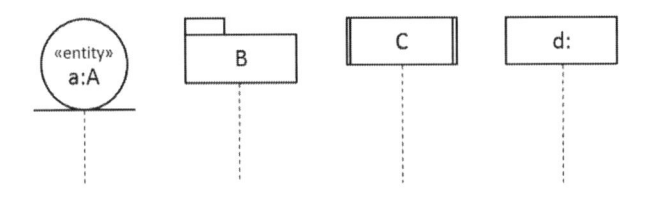

A. A
B. B
C. C
D. D

5. Which of the messages in the below diagram is not compatible with the definitions shown in the class **Player**?

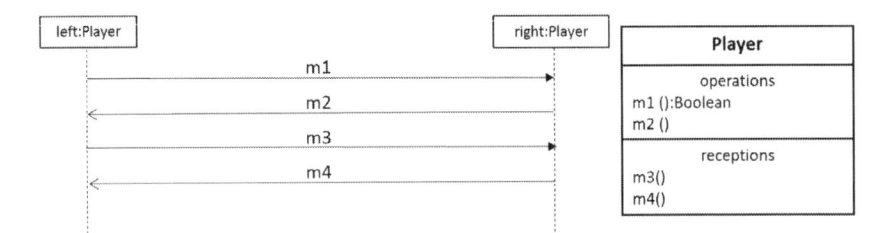

A. m1
B. m2
C. m3
D. m4

6. In the Sequence Diagram fragment below, there are three messages and six occurrences. How many different traces are there in this diagram?

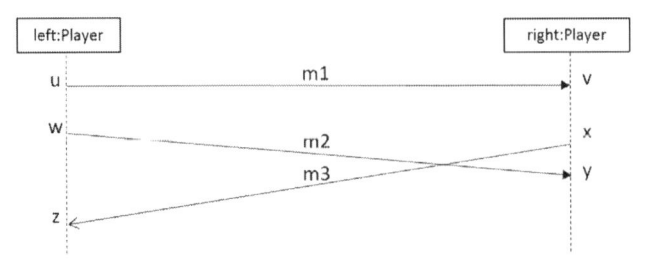

A. 1
B. 2
C. 3
D. 4
E. 5
F. 6
G. 7

7. A large X is used to accomplish what purpose in a Sequence Diagram?
   A. X is the graphical end of the lifeline.
   B. X indicates the destruction of the lifeline.
   C. X marks the spot.
   D. X marks where to dig.
   E. X marks the start of a balking message.
   F. X marks the start of a timed message.
8. Which lifeline needs to be replaced?

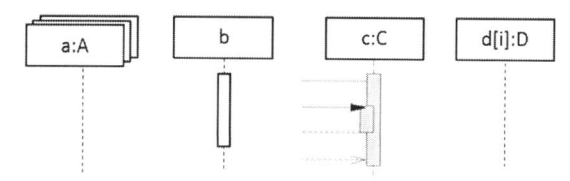

   A. a
   B. b
   C. c
   D. d
9. What is an Interaction?
   A. An Operation call
   B. A use of an Interface
   C. A unit of Behavior
   D. A Reception
   E. An instance of a Use Case
10. What is wrong with the following Sequence Diagram?

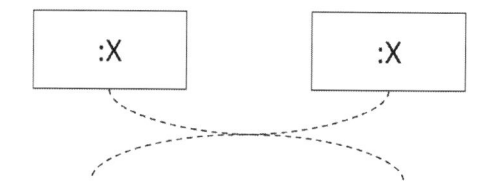

    A. Nothing.
    B. It is not allowed to have two lifelines with the same name.
    C. There are no messages shown.
    D. Lifelines must be straight and may not cross.

11. What needs to be changed in the following Sequence Diagram?

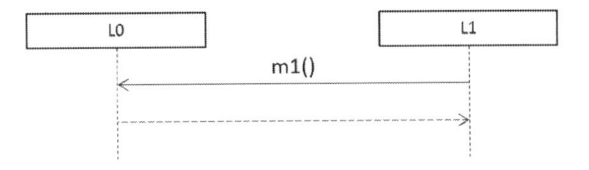

   A. The empty () needs to be removed or filled in.
   B. The first message should move from right to left.
   C. The arrowhead on the dashed line should be made into a solid arrowhead.
   D. The m1 is a signal and cannot have a return. Instead, change m1 into a synchronous operation call by making it have a solid arrowhead.

12. How many occurrences are there in the following Sequence Diagram?

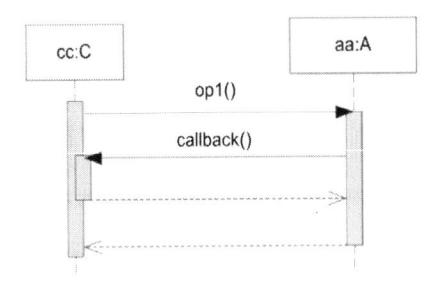

   UML 2.5 Specification Figure 17.2
   A. 7
   B. 8
   C. 10
   D. 12
   E. 14
   F. 16

13. Which arrow format below indicates an asynchronous message?

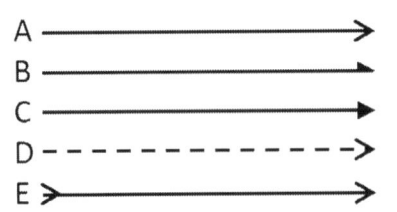

A. A
B. B
C. C
D. D
E. E

ANSWERS FOR CHAPTER 14

1. Which diagram type is not a UML 2.5 behavioral diagram?
   A. Use Case Diagram
   B. Sequence Diagram
   C. Interaction Diagram
   D. **<u>Collaboration Diagram</u>**
   E. Timing Diagram

   Discussion:
   A—No, Use Case diagrams are formally part of the UML 2.5 behavioral diagram, though they feel a bit different.
   B—No, a Sequence diagram is a kind of an Interaction diagram and is one of UML 2.5 behavioral diagrams.
   C—No, Interaction diagrams show the interaction of participants when they exchange messages.
   D—Yes, this was a UML 1.4 behavioral diagram but is not one in UML 2.5. The descendant of the 1.4 Collaboration diagram we now call a Communication diagram in UML 2.5.
   E—No, Timing Diagram is a rarely used UML behavioral diagram.

2. Which one of the following potential lifelines needs to be changed?

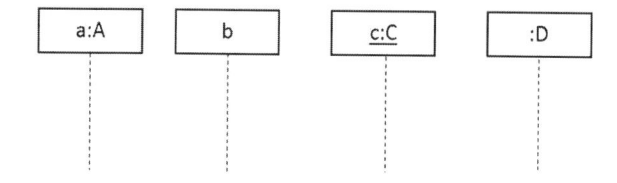

   | a:A | b | c:C | :D |

   A. A
   B. B
   C. <u>C</u>
   D. D

   Discussion:
   A—No, this is the normal lifeline.
   B—No, the type or class name, the part of the name that follows the role name and is preceded by the ":" is an optional field.

C—Yes, instances are not connectable elements. You can see that it is an instance by the underline.
D—No, the role name, the part of the name that precedes the ":", is not a required field.

3. Which of the following messages is incorrectly drawn?

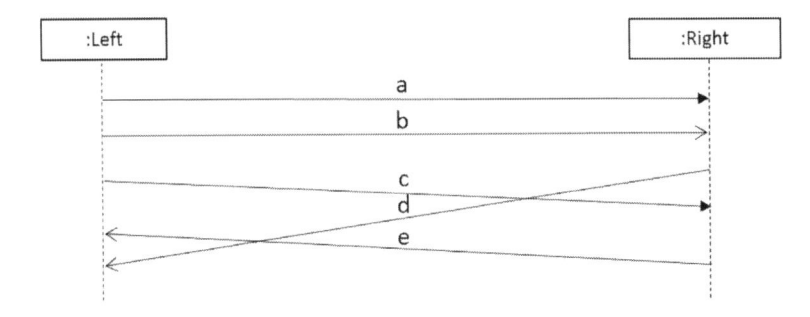

A. a
B. b
C. c
D. d
E. e

Discussion:
A—No, this is not incorrect, this is normal synchronous message.
B—No, this is not incorrect, this is a normal asynchronous message.
C—No, this is not incorrect, a download sloping synchronous message is allowed. It shows that the message takes time to arrive.
D—No, this is not incorrect, a download sloping asynchronous message is allowed. It shows that the message takes time to arrive.
E—Yes, this message is an illegal upward sloping asynchronous message. It is not allowed to have an upward sloping message.

4. Which one of the following potential lifelines needs to be changed?

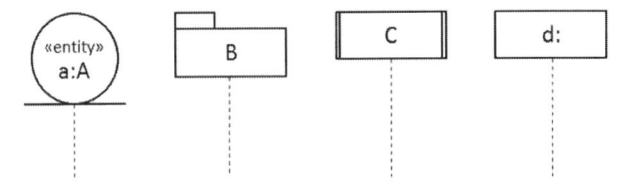

A. A
B. **B**
C. C
D. D

Discussion:
A—No, this symbol indicates an «entity», part of the Rational Unified Process (RUP) methodology, similar to flagging it as a domain element. If you are not familiar with that methodology you may be excused for choosing this element, but there another choice that is definitely wrong.
B—Yes, a Package is not a connectable element. It cannot be a part. Consider that a Package is essentially a folder.
C—No, this symbol indicates an active class, which means that it has its own thread. This means the element can initiate messages on its own without it being a response
D—No, this is a normal lifeline for an anonymously typed part.

5. Which of the messages in the below diagram is not compatible with the definitions shown in the class **Player**?

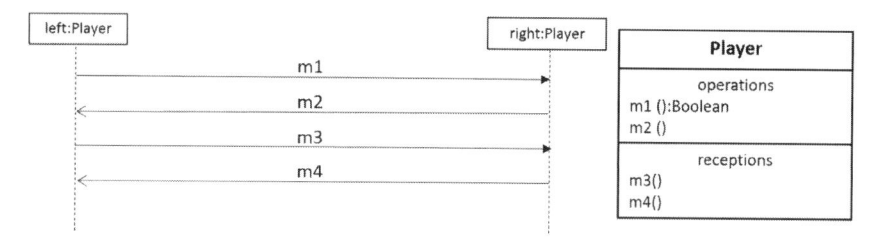

A. m1
B. m2
C. **m3**
D. m4

Discussion:
Messages m2 and m4 are asynchronous messages because of their v-shaped arrowhead. They may be signals (shown in the receptions compartment) or asynchronous operation calls.
A—No, m1 is compatible with the m1 operation on the Player. It must be a synchronous call because it has a return type.
B—No, m2 is an asynchronous message because it has a v-shaped arrowhead. In this case, it has a compatible match in the operations compartment. This is an example of an asynchronous operations call.
C—Yes, m3 is not compatible. The only match in Player is a reception. However, a reception must be an asynchronous signal. However, the arrowhead indicates that it is a synchronous message.
D—No, m4 is compatible with the reception in Player.

6. In the Sequence Diagram fragment below, there are three messages and six occurrences. How many different traces are there in this diagram?

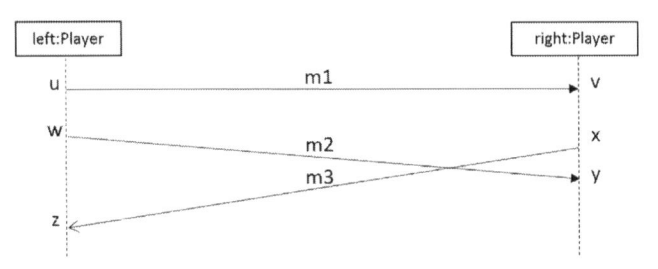

```
left:Player                              right:Player
    |            m1                          |
    u─────────────────────────────────────▶ v
    |                                        |
    w◀───────────────┐                       x
    |                 \      m2             /|
    |                  \                   / |
    |                   \    m3           /  |
    |                    \               /   y
    |                     \             /
    z◀─────────────────────\───────────/
    |                                        |
```

A. 1
B. 2
C. 3
D. 4
E. 5
F. <u>6</u>
G. 7

Discussion:

Remember that the ordering rules require that a message cannot be received before it is sent, based on causality. In addition, the occurrences are ordered top→down on each timeline, but otherwise different timelines are independent.

Examine messages m2 and m3. Of these two messages, there are two independent possible initial occurrences, w and x. There are also two possible final occurrences, y and z. Two × Two = 4

⟨w, x, y, z⟩ ⟨w, x, z, y⟩ ⟨x, w, y, z⟩ ⟨x, w, z, y⟩

Thus, there are four traces through these two messages.

Now consider m1. Occurrence u must be first and occurrence v must be after u. In addition, v must be before x (they are on the same timeline). However, v can occur before or after w.

Consider the four traces above; v can be inserted after w in the first two traces. This gives us two more traces to consider.

⟨u, v, w, x, y, z⟩ ⟨u, v, w, x, z, y⟩ ⟨u, v, x, w, y, z⟩
⟨u, v, x, w, z, y⟩ ⟨u, w, v, x, y, z⟩ ⟨u, w, x, z, y⟩

This means that F (6) is correct.

7. A large X is used to accomplish what purpose in a Sequence Diagram?
   A. X is the graphical end of the lifeline.
   B. <u>X indicates the destruction of the lifeline.</u>

C. X marks the spot.
D. X marks where to dig.
E. X marks the start of a balking message.
F. X marks the start of a timed message.

Discussion:
A—No, though the X is at the graphical end of the lifeline, it is not the purposes of the X.
B—Yes, the X indicates the destruction of the lifeline.
C—No.
D—No.
E and F—No, neither balking nor timed messages are used in UML 2. These message types were used in the Booch Method's Notation.

8. Which lifeline needs to be replaced?

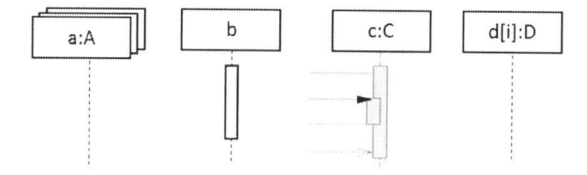

A. a
B. b
C. c
D. d

Discussion:
A—Yes, this is the UML 1.x symbol for a multi-object, representing, for example, the elements in a set or sequence. However, UML 2 removed this feature. The capability was replaced with an alternative approach, which we show in option D.
B—No, this is fine. It shows a lifeline with an execution specification.
C—No, this is also fine. It shows a lifeline with an execution specification, that while executing, gets a call to do some other behavior, usually in another thread.
D—No, this is fine. It shows the selector part of the header field. This indicates that the *i*th element of d:D is participating.

9. What is an Interaction?
   A. An Operation call
   B. A use of an Interface
   C. **A unit of Behavior**
   D. A Reception
   E. An instance of a Use Case

Discussion:
A—No, though an Operation call may be part of an Interaction. It is not an Interaction itself.
B—No, not related.
C—Yes, an Interaction should be a useful unit of behavior.
D—No, not related. However, a Lifeline with a matching reception may receive an asynchronous message that is a signal.
E—No, not related. However, we may often diagram the behavior of a Use Case as an Interaction.

10. What is wrong with the following Sequence Diagram?

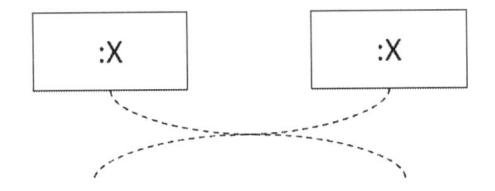

A. Nothing.
B. It is not allowed to have two lifelines with the same name.
C. There are no messages shown.
D. **Lifelines must be straight and may not cross.**

Discussion:
A—No, not correct.
B—No. It is allowed to have two lifelines with the same name, though rare. As Sequence Diagrams are namespaces, these two lifelines represent the same element, but it is legal. It is useful to repeat a lifeline when the number of lifelines is large and you wish to minimize message-lifeline crossing.
C—No. It is allowed have no messages on a lifeline.
D—Yes, this diagram is very silly and illegal.

11. What needs to be changed in the following Sequence Diagram?

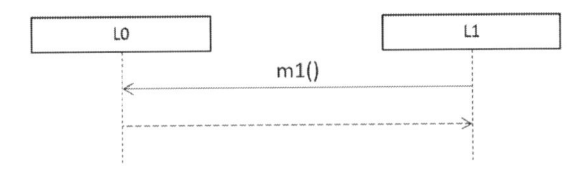

A. The empty () needs to be removed or filled in.
B. The first message should move from right to left.
C. The arrowhead on the dashed line should be made into a solid arrowhead.

D. **The m1 is a signal and cannot have a return. Instead, change m1 into a synchronous operation call by making it have a solid arrowhead.**

Discussion:
A—No, While messages usually have () after the name this is not needed and the () need not be filled in.
B—No, the direction is acceptable.
C—No, that doesn't accomplish anything.
D—Yes, a signal (asynchronous) can't have a return, so if you change the signal to an operation (synchronous) it would be correct.

12. How many occurrences are there in the following Sequence Diagram?

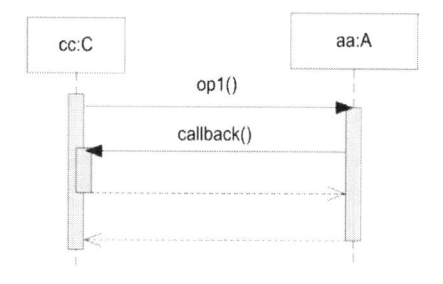

UML 2.5 Specification Figure 17.2
A. 7
B. 8
C. 10
D. 12
E. **14**
F. 16

Discussion:
   Each completely drawn message or return has two occurrences: the send and the return.
   Each completely drawn execution specifications have two occurrences: the start and the end, counting there are three execution specifications and four messages. $(3 + 4) \times 2 = 14$

13. Which arrow format below indicates an asynchronous message?

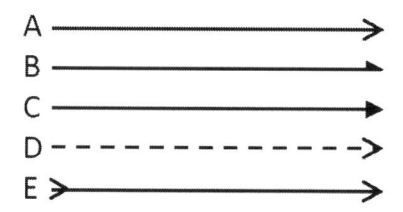

A. **A**
B. B
C. C
D. D
E. E

Discussion:
A—Yes, this is correct.
B—No, this was the format for asynchronous messages in UML 1.x.
C—No, this is the format for synchronous messages.
D—No, this is the format for return messages.
E—No, UML does not have tails on its arrows.

CHAPTER 16

Behavior: Activity Diagrams

16.1 WHAT IS AN ACTIVITY DIAGRAM?

16.1.1 Activity Diagram History

UML 1 introduced ACTIVITY DIAGRAMS as a sort of multiple-object State Machine diagram. As state machines are limited to modeling the states of only one object at a time, the Activity Diagram was extended to allow the modeler to show how multiple objects could work together. As such, the UML 1 notation was based on the state machine notation. It looked like a traditional flow chart diagram with regions, called SWIMLANES, each assigned to an object to be responsible for the behaviors in that swimlane.

Because Activity Diagrams duplicated most of the State Machine notation, the tool vendors did not concentrate on implementing it, and modelers tended to avoid it. Everyone realized that having two behavior diagram types with similar, but not identical semantics, was not a good situation.

Instead of eliminating Activity Diagrams, when UML 1.x transmuted to UML 2, Activity diagrams changed their foundation. Instead of being based on events and transitions, Activity Diagrams became based on PETRI NETS with TOKEN passing. Surprisingly, this did not invalidate all[1] of the existing UML 1.x Activity Diagrams nor change their general look. It did add more expressive power and flexibility.

One consequence of changing the foundation of Activity Diagrams is that the terminology has become more confusing. For example, what we call EDGES we can also be called FLOWS, depending on whether we are considering their ability to connect graphically or their carrying capacity. This alternative terminology can be a little puzzling, but we will try to explain (and use) the

---

[1]Unfortunately, UML 1.x diagrams that had multiple edges (flows) entering an action node will work differently if at all in UML 2.x diagrams. However, some UML 1.x diagrams that had multiple edges leaving an action will still generally continue to work the same in UML 2.x diagrams. Luckily, you are not required to know how the diagrams used to work, only how they work now.

OCUP 2 Certification Guide. DOI: http://dx.doi.org/10.1016/B978-0-12-809640-6.00017-9
© 2018 Elsevier Inc. All rights reserved.

Table 16.1 Activity Diagram Basics

	GeneralType	Symbol	Name(s)	Description
1	Control node	●	Initial Node, Starting Ball	This indicates the start of the activity diagram. It only allows outgoing edges/flows
2		◉	Final Node, Activity Final, Bullseye	If an activity flow ever reaches a Final Node, the activity execution ends, even if other behavior is still going on. It only allows incoming edges/flows. There can be more than one incoming edge, but no outgoing edge
3		◇ [No]/[Yes]	Decision Node	Flow leaves the decision diamond in the direction where the guard evaluates to true. A guard is a Boolean expression in square brackets "[]". If no guard is true, the behavior is undetermined. If more than one guard is true, one of the true branches will be taken, chosen in an undetermined and unpredictable manner. A branch labeled with [ELSE] is taken, (if available) if none of the other branches' guards evaluates to true
4		◇	Merge Node	Flows can enter from multiple edges but only come out the main edge. Like a merge in traffic, only one flow (car) can traverse the merge node at a time
5	Executable node	Action	Action Roundangle	When all the input edges are sufficiently populated, the action starts. When the action finishes, all the output edges are populated
6	Edge	→	Control Flow	A control flow can traverse the v-headed arrow when it connects to a node

common variations in this chapter to help you become familiar with the use by modeling practitioners.

An ACTIVITY is a Behavior depicted as a sequence of subordinate behaviors, either atomic ACTIONS or further decomposable lower level ACTIVITIES, connected by CONTROL FLOWS and OBJECT FLOWS. These subordinate behaviors may be initiated because predecessor behaviors in the model finish their execution or because the input objects and data become available to the subordinate behavior or because of triggering events from outside.

The flow of execution is modeled as Activity Nodes connected by Activity Edges. An Activity Node can be an EXECUTABLE NODE (see Table 16.1), indicating the execution of a subordinate behavior, such as an arithmetic computation, a call to an operation, or a manipulation of object contents. Both ACTIONS and lower level ACTIVITIES are considered Executable Nodes. An Activity Node can also be a CONTROL NODE that controls features such as synchronization, decision, and concurrency. The ACTIVITY EDGES indicate the flow of TOKENS, carrying control or object (data)[2].

---

[2] These tokens can convey permission to execute. For more detail, see Section 16.1.2.

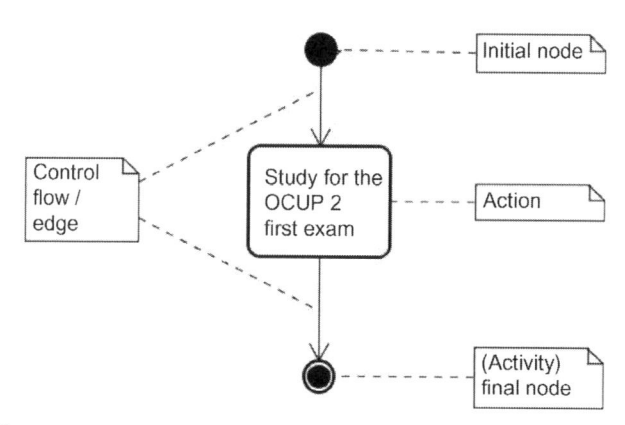

FIGURE 16.1
Basic activity diagram.

Essentially, the Activity nodes start to execute when all their immediate predecessors finish executing. In UML 2.5, a control edge/flow carries a control token, just a permission to start executing[3].

In the examples below, we use control tokens and control flows for illustrative purposes. Though object tokens and flows look a little different and work slightly differently from their control cousins, they have similar essential effects. In Fig. 16.1, we show a very simple Activity Diagram that illustrates an Action (STUDY FOR OCUP 2 FIRST EXAM), an INITIAL NODE (sometimes called a START NODE), and a FINAL NODE. The edges between them are control flow edges, as control information flows on these edges. Once the Activity starts (at the Initial Node), the control edge flows to the Action, the Action takes some time to complete, and once the Action is complete, the lower control edge flows to the Final Node and then, the processing of this diagram stops. If there were a second action after the STUDY for action (between the action and the final node), also connected by an arrow, this action would be executed after the first action finished, and so on until the final node was reached.

This is the general way of processing works in Activity Diagrams. Remember that the tagged icon (the one with the folded down corner) can appear on any diagram and indicate a note or comment. These comments are attached by dashed lines to elements that need to be annotated. As always, make sure your annotations are correct and clear. Placing incorrect, misleading, or outdated comments will quickly make your diagrams difficult to fix.
The Action on the diagram, "Study for the OCUP 2 First Exam," is an OPAQUE ACTION. An opaque action or behavior is one that is not written in native

---

[3]In SysML, a control token may also have an inhibitory effect.

UML. It is not expected that UML environment would be able to enforce the rules and execute. The diagram has four comments, one action, one initial node, and one final node.

Of course, being limited to a linear, step-by-step flow of behaviors would not be very expressive or impressive. In Fig. 16.2, we introduce a `DECISION` node (the diamond on the left) and a `MERGE` node (the diamond on the right). We recognize the decision node diamond because it has one edge going in and more than one labeled flow going out. The labels, called `GUARDS`, when they evaluate to true, enable the flow in that direction. Any number of alternative flows can come out of the diamond, assuming that you can have room to draw them. Depending on the guard, the flow moves to the action *Hail a Car* or the action *Hail a Shared Car*. In each case, when the action finishes, the flow moves to and through the merge diamond into the final node (the bullseye). We can recognize that this second diamond is a merge node because it has multiple ways in and only one nonlabeled exit.

This pattern of Decision node followed by alternative behaviors followed by a Merge node typifies an `IF-THEN` or a `CASE/SWITCH` pattern in code when only one condition can be true.

It is also possible to get `LOOPS` in Activity Diagrams. To produce a loop, you usually need to reverse the order of the decision and merge nodes (see Fig. 16.3).

In this Activity diagram, the flow also starts at the solid ball, which indicates the initial node. The flow goes through the merge node (the leftmost diamond) and into the Borrow action. After finishing the Borrow action, the flow moves into the decision node (the rightmost diamond). We recognize that this is a decision node because it has one edge going in and more than

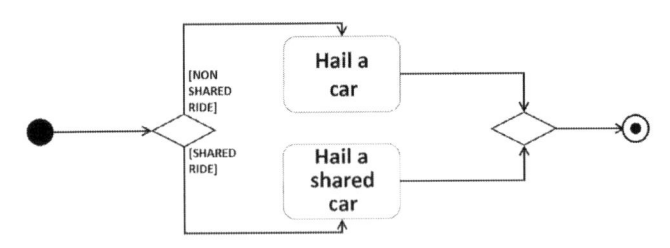

FIGURE 16.2
Activity diagram with alternate flows.

FIGURE 16.3
Activity with merge and decision nodes indicating a do until loop.

one labeled flow going out. If we have [NO MORE] books, we flow through to the final node (the bullseye). If we have [MORE BOOKS TO BORROW], we go up and back to the Merge node. We can detect that this first diamond is a merge node because it has multiple ways in and only one nonlabeled exit. When we reach the final node, the behavior is over. This produces the DO-UNTIL pattern. In DO-UNTIL, the loop is always executed at least once.

In some tools and methodologies, ◇ the wide diamond is a merge and the ◇, the vertical diamond, a decision (i.e., when turned 90° on its side). In other approaches, it is the exact opposite. Others place a "D" in the decision diamond and an "M" in the merge diamond. Generally, for the most common cases leading to the OCUP exam, it will be easy to determine the intention of a particular diamond symbol, by counting the input edges and output edges. If there is only one input edge, it is a decision. If there is only one output edge, it is a merge[4].

You might wonder why I didn't draw the diagram similar to the one in the figure (see Fig. 16.4).

The rule is:

For an action to begin executing, all of the mandatory input edges *must* be populated.

Because of this rule, the diagram will never execute. *Borrow this Book* can only start when it has both input flows available at the same time: The one from the Initial Node (from the left) and the one from the decision diamond (from the top). This can never happen. Therefore, the execution would stall. It is not an illegal diagram so your tool may not complain, so be wary.

There is a similar rule for an action finishing, though it does not cause as many problems.

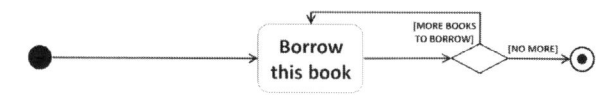

FIGURE 16.4
Loop antipattern??[5] (This does not work).

---

[4]It is possible to have combination decision-merge nodes that have multiple input and multiple output edges. It is also possible to have an additional input flow marked «decisionInputFlow». These are rarely used and are certainly not on the Foundation level exam.
[5]The use of "??" is common in annotating moves in chess games to indicate that the move is a blunder. Not an illegal move, but one that was certainly wrong. In UML, the use of this antipattern is certainly a blunder.

When an action finishes, all the output edges *will* be populated.

In Fig. 16.5, we depict a slightly more complicated flow. In this figure, we have added an additional three-way decision on the right (see how that works, though the exit edges may come from any point on the surface of the diamond) and have added an ELSE guard that is taken if none of the other guards are true. We probably should have added another action to cancel the ride at this point, but I wanted to show how a pass-through decision would look.

We also do not technically need the merge diamond in this case. All the edges could directly connect to the final node. However, it is good methodological practice to have the merge and decision nodes come in pairs as it helps the reader or modeler to recognize the pattern of the structure and to detect subtle modeling errors.

In Fig. 16.6, we show the structure of another type of loop, that of DO-WHILE. In this loop pattern, the decision comes first, and the merge node is last. This loop can be completely skipped if the guard does not hold when it is first entered. This contrasts to the DO UNTIL loop shown in Fig. 16.3, which always executes at least once. Please be sure that you can follow the difference.

Another common pattern to recognize is the IF THEN ELSE IF THEN ENDIF. As shown in Fig. 16.7, we have two If-Else pairs, though there could be many.

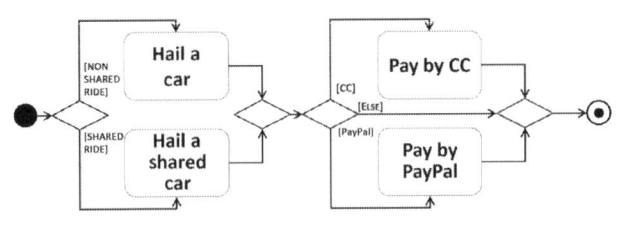

FIGURE 16.5
Activity with concatenated ifs.

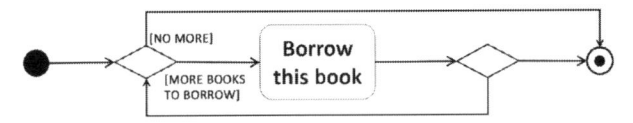

FIGURE 16.6
Activity with a Do While loop.

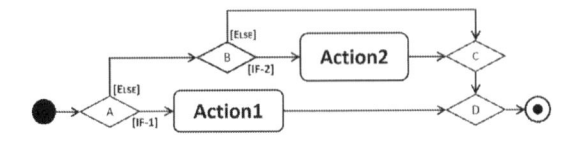

FIGURE 16.7
Activity with If Then ElseIF EndIF.

As shown in the diagrams below, the final merge could be omitted if you have all the flows directly end on the Flow Final node.

This pattern differs from one with a three-way test on a decision node because this directs the order that the conditions are evaluated. If [IF-1] is true, the [IF-2] guard is never evaluated and may be true or false. In a three-way test, if they are both true, it is unpredictable how the diagram will behave, and either branch may be taken. Ordering the tests will give you better control of the behavior and may be more efficient.

In Fig. 16.7, you should be able to identify which diamonds represent *decisions* and which diamonds represent *merges*. You should also be able to detect which decision goes with which merge[6].

POINTS TO REMEMBER

- An UML activity diagram contains a set of behavioral nodes connected by predecessor antecedent relationships.
- An activity diagram supports both control and object (data) flow edges.
- A control edge is a simple arrow leaving the source node of the control edge to the target node of the edge. It carries permission to start executing. This permission is carried in a control token emitted by the source node.
- If several control edges target the same behavioral node, they are all required to be populated with tokens before the target can start.
- One type of control node is the decision node. It looks like a diamond with one input edge and two or more output edges.
  - Associated with the decision diamond is a condition being tested.
  - Each outgoing edge should be identified with a separate value for the condition.
  - The token on the input edge will then follow an output edge with a value of True.

16.1.2 Single Token Diagrams

In each of the above figures, there is only one locus of execution in each diagram fragment at any time. One way of looking at this is to imagine that there is a token that travels through the diagram conveying permission to execute.

A token is an abstract indicator that, on a control edge, indicates that the previous step has finished execution and gives permission for the next step to execute. Consider a token as something like a baton in an Olympic relay race. No token, no baton, and the next competitor cannot start running (or executing).

When the edge represents an object or data flow, the token can convey the object or data along with permission to start to execute. Consider this as a

---

[6]Diamonds A and B are the decisions. Diamond C and D are the merges. A and D go together. B and C go together.

baton-carrying relay race with the baton holding a document inside the baton. If there is more than one entering edge, all must carry their own baton.

In the examples below, we use control tokens and control flows for illustrative purposes. Though object tokens and flows look a little different and work slightly differently from their control cousins, their essential effects are similar.

Again, consider Fig. 16.7. The Activity creates a Token at each Initial Node when the diagram starts. From there, a copy of the token is emitted along every edge leaving each Initial Node (remember edges can only leave, not enter, an Initial Node). In the example figure, there is only one token at a time, and it is a control token. The token moves through the diagram, obeying the true-valued guard conditions at each Decision Node.

When there is only one input edge to an action, all the action needs to start is a single token on that edge. As both Action1 and Action2 have only one incoming edge each, the arrival of a token starts the Action executing. When an Action finishes, tokens populate all its outgoing edges. In our diagram, the Actions have only one outgoing edge each. You can identify the outgoing edges by the direction of the attached arrows.

Whenever a token arrives at a merge node, it just passes through to the next node.

When a token arrives at the Activity Final Node, processing is halted throughout the diagram, and the token is destroyed.

16.1.3 Concurrent (Multi-Token) Diagrams

16.1.3.1 Explicit Token Creation

Single-threaded activities are very limiting; in most real applications, many things can be going on at once. UML supports several ways of creating additional tokens that can independently traverse an activity diagram at the same time.

An explicit way of creating additional tokens is to use the Fork Control node (see Table 16.2 Line 3). When a token comes in at the input edge, it is duplicated as needed to populate the output edges. Downstream this produces CONCURRENT behavior in the paths of the tokens. "Concurrency" is used in UML to mean that the relative order of the behaviors or events is not defined and may overlap.

In Fig. 16.8, we depict an example of explicit token creation using the Fork control node. An identical token is then sent to each of the A1.a and A1.b behaviors. We have no idea which behavior starts first. We say that the two behaviors start *concurrently*. Also, we have no idea which behavior

16.1 What is an Activity Diagram?

Table 16.2 Activity Diagram Basics: Actions and Control Nodes

	General Type	Symbol	Name(s)	Description
1	Executable node			All these Executable Nodes below (the actions) start when all input edges are sufficiently populated
2	Executable node	Action	Action Roundangle	When the action finishes, all the output edges are populated
3	Control node		Fork	The input flow and its token are copied and emitted on each of the outgoing edges
				This copies the tokens and increases the number of tokens in the diagram, enabling concurrent processing
4	Control node		Join	When all the input flows (along with their tokens) arrive at the Join, an output flow is emitted (with its token) on the output edge
				This eliminates all but one of the tokens arriving
				If not all of the edges have tokens, processing cannot continue and hangs at the Join
5	Control node	⊗	Flow Final	Any token reaching the Flow Final is destroyed (i.e., consumed); however, if there are more active tokens in the diagram, execution is continued until they are also consumed

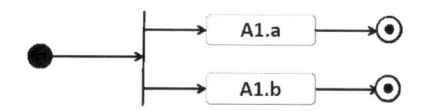

FIGURE 16.8
Explicit token creation via fork node inducing concurrency.

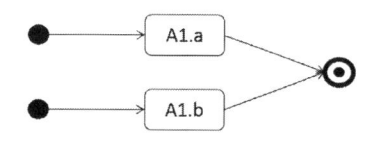

FIGURE 16.9
Explicit token creation via initial nodes inducing concurrency.

ends first. All behaviors stop when the first token reaches an Activity Final Node.

In Fig. 16.9, we see a diagram that is equivalent to Fig. 16.8. Every Initial Node in an activity diagram causes new tokens to be emitted on its outgoing edges when the diagram starts. All these tokens are created concurrently. When the behaviors finish, control is passed to the Activity Final Node.

The diagram is finished as soon as a first token reaches the Activity Final Node.

16.1.3.2 Implicit Token Creation: Forking a New Path

Control Tokens can be created whenever a fork occurs, not just the explicit ones caused by UML fork node or caused by additional initial nodes. Any activity diagram executable node that has more than one control flow leaving it, when it finishes, will place concurrent control tokens on the output edges (see Fig. 16.10). In this case, Action A has two control flow outputs and thus, both B1.a and B1.b start concurrently when A finishes. The diagram ends whenever either B1.a or B1.b finishes, causing a token to reach the Activity Final Node, which ends the diagram.

16.1.3.3 Multiple Forks

Though all of the above examples show a token forking into two tasks, UML allows for more flexible forking. In Fig. 16.11, we see a fork that produces from 3 to 5 possible tasks. The first two possible tasks are guarded and will only be created if the governing guards are true.

16.1.3.4 Forking vs Spawning

You may read that the UML Fork node *spawns* a new task or something like that. We typically do not use the "spawn" terminology, as it usually implies

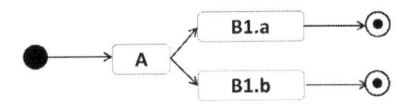

FIGURE 16.10
Forking without the fork node.

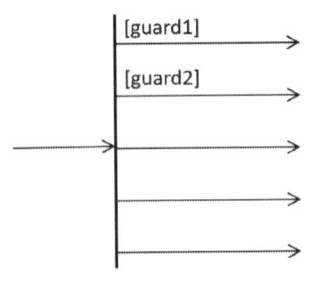

FIGURE 16.11
Multiple forks with some guarded.

a hierarchical relationship between the associated tasks[7]. "Forking" is more appropriate as each token/task is independent. When a fork occurs, it is not that a new subordinate token is created. A fork is a clone of a task, while spawn could be considered as a child. Generally, this distinction is not important, though it may help in understanding what is going on.

16.1.4 Consuming Tokens
16.1.4.1 Multiple Forks

Just as we can produce new tokens, we can consume tokens. The notation is a matching fork, with more inputs and only one output as shown in Fig. 16.12. This is now a JOIN NODE (see Table 16.2 Row 4). In this figure, we depict two edges becoming one edge. This is two tokens becoming one token.

This follows the same criteria that we use with decision and merge nodes: The notation is essentially the same, the major difference is the number of entering edges and leaving edges[8] (Table 16.3).

When a token approaches a Join node, it waits until all the other edges that connect to the Join have their tokens populated. This is a wait to allow for a synchronization. The number of Joined edges needs not match the number of Forked edges, and the joined edges may come from different Forks.

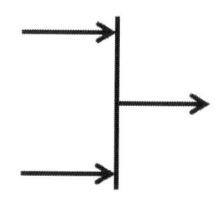

FIGURE 16.12
Join node with two tokens/edges.

Table 16.3 Number of Edges Entering or Leaving Per Type of Control Node

Node Type	Number of Edges Entering	Number of Edges Leaving
Fork or Decision	1	*
Join or Merge	*	1

---

[7] For example, spawn are the usually large number of eggs produced by an aquatic animal.
[8] This simple rule of thumb does not always work for the more advanced UML 2.5 material found on later exams.

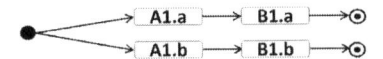

FIGURE 16.13
Free running and asynchronous ending.

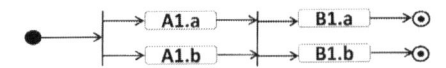

FIGURE 16.14
Synchronous starting but asynchronous ending.

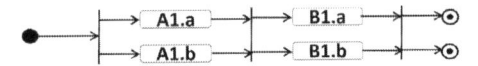

FIGURE 16.15
Fully lockstep.

Without the synchronization bar, the tokens flow freely. Consider the Fig. 16.13. In this figure, the A1 steps (A1.a and A1.b) start at the same time, but the B1 steps each start when their respective A1 steps finish. It is possible that B1.a starts before A1.b finishes, as there is no evidence of synchronization. In fact, it is possible that the B1.a finishes before A1.b finishes. The first token that reaches an Activity Final Node (the bullseye) will stop the whole diagram. It is a race to the finish.

An alternative approach is shown below. Consider the Fig. 16.14.

In this above figure, both the A steps start at the same time, as in Fig. 16.13. Adding the Fork bar between the start node and the actions is an additional forced synchronization, but it does not change anything. However, adding the Fork bar between the As and Bs means that neither B step can start until both As finish. This can be repeated before every new step forcing the steps to execute in lock step.

Still, in this diagram, the first B that finishes ends the diagram as a whole. However, B1.a cannot start until A1.b finishes, and B1.b cannot start until a1.a finishes.

In Fig. 16.15, the As and Bs both start and end together. This is a full lockstep approach. It is often used in fault-tolerant systems as the results from the top line of execution can be compared with the results from the bottom-line of execution after each step, to detect if there are unexpected differences. If there are three identical lockstep paths, a voting-style error checking can be

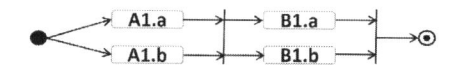

FIGURE 16.16
Another approach.

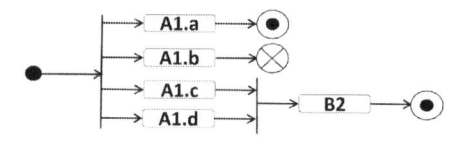

FIGURE 16.17
Use of flow final and activity final.

used to detect any process that produces an inconsistent result or a result that is delayed.

Examine Fig. 16.16. This diagram looks different, but it acts the same as one of the diagrams above. Can you detect which one?[9]

16.1.4.2 Flow Final
There is a special control node used to terminate a token without ending the entire diagram (see Table 16.2 Row 5). This control node is called a FLOW FINAL NODE. Examine Fig. 16.17. This diagram will end whenever A1.a or B2 finishes, whichever finishes first. When that occurs, if any of the other actions are still running, they are abandoned. However, if A1.b ends before this, just that thread ends. Both A1.c and A1.d have to finish before B2 can even start.

16.1.5 Joining at an Action
If an action has more than one input edge, normally the action requires *all* the edges to be populated with tokens before the action starts. This is nearly equivalent to having a logical *join* right before the action. Thus, when more than one edge ends on an executable node, the number of live tokens is decreased to one. During the execution of the node, only one token is active. After the execution is finished, the number of active tokens grows to match the number of edges leaving the executable node (see Fig. 16.18) for the Joining and Forking at the node boundary and Fig. 16.19 for the use of join/fork bars.

---

[9]Figure 16.16 is effectively the same as Figure 16.15. The two A steps start concurrently whether they are started from an explicit Fork node or an implicit one starting at the Start node. At the end of the diagram, a direct edge from the Join node acts the same as two edges from the Join node.

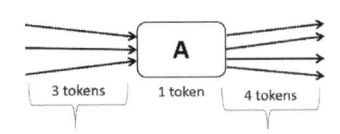

FIGURE 16.18
Joining and forking at a node boundary.

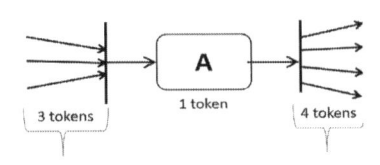

FIGURE 16.19
Equivalent joining and merging using join and fork nodes.

POINTS TO REMEMBER

- A token is a conceptual focus of execution that moves over edges and enables executable nodes to fire.
    - A token moves from predecessor to successor when a behavior finishes.
    - In a Decision node, a token will move through and exit through a path with a true-valued guard.
        - A Merge Node is a convenient way of structuring your execution paths.
    - In a Fork node, the incoming token will be duplicated. Every outgoing path will get a copy of the token.
        - This will cause edges capable of concurrent execution.
        - Concurrency in UML means that the order of the execution is not known and will not be synchronized.
        - Forks will also occur if an action has more than one exiting edge.
    - A Join Node combines tokens and reduces the number of tokens.
        - A Join will also occur if an action has more than one entering edge.
    - An Activity Final Node will kill all tokens in the diagram.
    - A Flow Final Node will kill only the entering token.

16.2 TIMERS AND TIMING EVENTS

UML supports the ability to set timers/alarms to cause behaviors to kick off when the correct time arrives. The Wait for Time Event looks like a pair of triangles in the shape of an old-fashioned hourglass (see Table 16.4 Line 1). This is an executable node, an action. It is triggered when an edge and its token arrive at the node (usually from the left). Underneath the node is an indication when the timer should expire. It could be a specific time, though

16.2 Timers and Timing Events

Table 16.4 Activity Diagram Basics: Actions and Control Nodes

	General Type	Symbol	Name(s)	Description
1	Executable node	Time Trigger	Timer	The Timer starts waiting for the Time Trigger event when all its input edges are populated. If there are no input edges, it starts waiting when the enclosing region is entered
			Wait for Time	When the time event occurs, e.g., when the Time Trigger is reached, the Timer emits control flows on all its output edges
			Accept Time Event	The time trigger can be a particular time, e.g., New Year's Eve (Jan 1, 2018, 00:00:00.000). More commonly, it is a repeating time, e.g., end of the month, or a delta time, e.g., every 10 s
2	Executable node	Request for ride	Send Event	This action starts when all its input edges are populated. If there are no input edges, it starts when the enclosing region is entered
			Send Message	When the action starts, it emits a signal by the specified name that may be accepted by a similarly named reception elsewhere (See row 3 of this table). Usually used for cross-task communication
				If there is an output edge, a control token is output so that it can be considered finished
3	Executable node	Response from driver	Wait for Event	This wait action starts when all its input edges are populated, or if there are no input edges, it starts when the enclosing region is entered
			Wait for Message	When the action starts, it waits for a signal (message) by the specified name. The entity holding this node must be an active classifier with the signal listed in its reception compartment
			Receive Event	
			Receive Message	When the proper signal arrives, the contents of the signal (if any) are emitted along with a token on the output edge

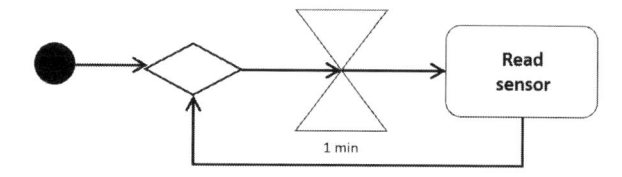

FIGURE 16.20

Restart 1 minute after the last sample finished.

usually it is a time relative to the cycle of the ongoing activity. It could also be a repeating time, e.g., every 2 minutes. In Figs. 16.20 and 16.21, we see examples of a sensor that is read every 1 minute the difference between them are whether we are looking at the inter-start time or -end time.

If you follow the flow of the diagram, the timer is reset after the ReadSensor action if finished. Even if the ReadSensor action takes a different amount of

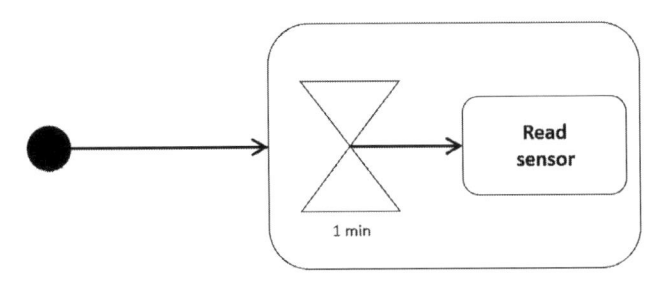

FIGURE 16.21
Restart every 1 minute even if the last sample not yet finished.

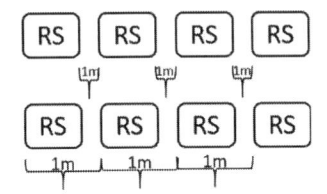

FIGURE 16.22
Inter execution times.

time every time it runs, the ReadSensor action will have a constant delta time between its ending and the next start. You may see this in the top part of Fig. 16.22.

Another way of starting a Wait for Time Event is not to have any explicit starting edge. In such cases, as soon as the containing region is entered, the wait starts executing. As long as the region is active, the Wait for Time Event will restart. This produces a timing pattern with a constant time between successive starts of ReadSensor as shown in the bottom part of Fig. 16.22[10].

POINTS TO REMEMBER

- A Wait for Time event allows the Activity diagram to wait for a particular time or to use the time to determine what action to do.
  - The wait can be initiated by an entering edge, or if there are no entering edges, by being within an entered region.

---

[10]If the duration of ReadSensor is longer than the inter execution time, more than one copy of ReadSensor may start to execute. Other possibilities may occur if the ReadSensor is reentrant. Do not worry how a potential overlap is handled as it is advanced material.

16.3 OBJECT FLOWS/EDGES

Though our examples have been concentrating on control flows, we need to explain how to model object flows to have the complete capability to describe or design software intensive systems. Normally, control tokens on edge can determine when a behavior can be allowed to start, but most software-oriented behavior requires data to be passed to the behaviors.

Consistent with the rest of UML, Objects are represented by rectangular shapes. An object node is depicted by a rectangle. In Fig. 16.23, you can see two alternative approaches to showing object edges/flows, all utilizing a form of a rectangle. The state information is optional and is generally used only when the same object type is both an input and output. For example, perhaps a Book is input into an action, Borrow, and is also an output from the same action. What changes is the state—first, it is *notBorrowed*, and afterward, it is in the state of *Borrowed*. The ability to specify the state changes should be coordinated consistently with your material that you may have on a state diagram so that the changes to the states can be coordinated. In the below diagrams, the states would all be the same as it cannot change just because an edge is transversed.

In the upper half of Fig. 16.23, we use the OBJECT NODE format. This approach is used when it might be necessary to specify, whether the tokens should be removed in a First In, First Out (FIFO) or Last In, First Out (LIFO) manner, or whether other queueing methods might be needed. In the lower half of Fig. 16.23, we use the OBJECT PIN format. This is also a type of object node best used to indicate the form and multiplicity for a PARAMETER.

One of the differences between control flows and object flows is that UML has the ability to specify on object flows, delays, multicast/copying of tokens, ordering (e.g., FIFO, LIFO), selection of tokens by data value/conditions, and transformations. In the current exam, these capabilities are not used but are referred to in the exam.

In Fig. 16.24, we depict an action, Borrow Book, with four pins. The arrow shows the direction of the pin (input or output), and we can show the name of the pin, the type of the pin, and the state of elements on that pin. This is

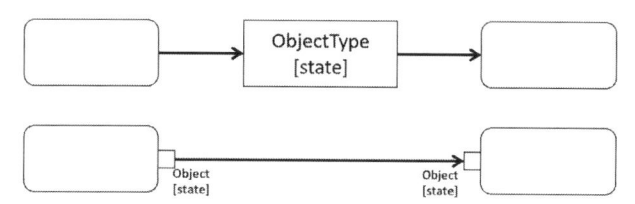

FIGURE 16.23
Alternative object edges/flows.

the same as the arguments on an operation. Note that we cannot really show an input/output pin. If we need a bidirectional pin, we show the pin twice, once in each direction.

In the Fig. 16.25, we show the same situation as above but use a slightly different notation. We can place the arrow within the pin. We can also specify the multiplicities on all of these formats. If the lower bound on the multiplicity of a pin is 0, it is optional to populate the pin with tokens (Fig. 16.25, Table 16.5).

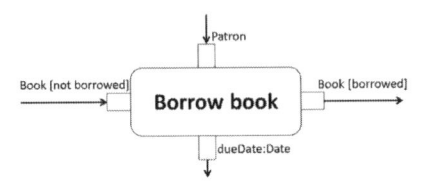

FIGURE 16.24
Action with pins.

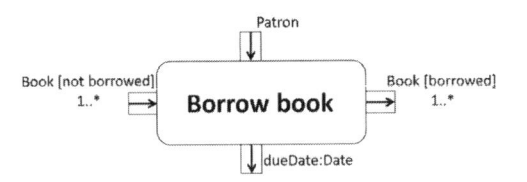

FIGURE 16.25
Action with alternative format pins.

Table 16.5 Activity Diagram Basics: Actions and Control Nodes

	General Type	Symbol	Name(s)	Description
1	Object node	Name	Object Node, Object Store	May hold object tokens of the Name type
2	Control node		Fork	The input flow and its token are copied and emitted on each of the output edges
				This copies the tokens and increases the number of active tokens in the diagram, enabling concurrent processing
3	Control node		Join	When all the input flows (along with their tokens) arrive at the Join, an output flow is emitted (with its token) on the output edge
				This eliminates all but one of the tokens arriving
				If not all of the edges have tokens, processing cannot continue and hangs at the Join
4	Control node		Flow Final	Any token reaching the Flow Final is destroyed (i.e., consumed); however, if there are more active tokens in the diagram, execution is continued until they are also consumed

POINTS TO REMEMBER

- An object flow is similar to a control flow, but it can convey
  - Object Instances
  - Data Values
  - Physical Items
- An object flow can be represented by a pin on actions and by object parameters on activities.
- An object store (rectangle) is an alternative to using pins on both sides of an object flow.
- Object flows provide additional support for multicast, selection, transformation, and ordering of tokens.

16.4 ADVANCED TOPICS

16.4.1 Weights

Typically, an edge conveys only one token (either control or object) at a time. However, in some circumstances, an edge may be declared to require more than one token in order to allow any tokens to pass. In UML 2.5, we flag such edges with a WEIGHT, e.g., weight = nnn where nnn is the number of required tokens or weight = some variable name. The edge holds on to the tokens until the required number of tokens arrive—then, they are delivered to the target node. If the required number of tokens never arrives, the held tokens are lost.

The weight feature is typically used after some token source that may generate multiple tokens on its own, such as after a Wait for Time Event or Wait for Message Event. This is an advanced feature and will be more thoroughly covered in the Advanced Exam.

16.4.2 Stream

When we examine the input parameters of an action or activity, we commonly understand that the input parameters must all be available before the behavior starts. This matches the typical conventions to a subroutine or subprogram. When you call the subprogram, the arguments must first be available. However, there are situations when additional argument values can be supplied even after the behavior starts. This is typical for physical behaviors. A Morse code operator continues to decode incoming encrypted cipher text (the patterns of dots and dashes) and produces clear text (natural language, such as English). In a similar manner, the Morse code operator can continue to decode clear text.

Such inputs or outputs are flagged as {isStreaming} or {streaming}. This is an Intermediary feature and will be more thoroughly covered in the

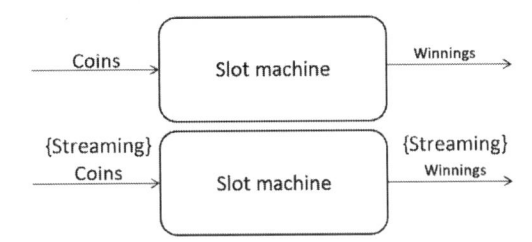

FIGURE 16.26
Streaming.

Intermediary Exam. Inputs or outputs flagged as Streaming can continue to appear even though the behaviors have already started. In the example below (Fig. 16.26), two different slot machine behaviors are illustrated. The top example shows a slot machine that takes coins and produces winnings (if any). The bottom example shows a slot machine that allows for the continual addition of new coins and can produce winnings without ending the session.

The streaming tags can be added to pins or parameters.

16.4.3 Send/Receive Messages/Events

Similar to the Wait for Time Event actions, we can have a Wait for Message Event action. It looks like a pentagon with two adjacent sides indented, as shown in Table 16.4, row 3 and Fig. 16.27.

In the symbol is placed the name of the message or event that you want the model to wait for. As with other actions, this can be kicked off when the token arrives at the left. Also as with the Wait for Time Event, if there is no explicit starting token edge, as long as the enclosing region is active, new matching messages will continue to be received here.

If the message arrival is what is interesting in that it kicks off some other behavior, the outgoing edge should be a control edge. However, if the content of the message is of interest, the outgoing edge should be an object flow containing the message.

The matching Send Message action looks like a pointy pentangle. It usually has an object flow edge (containing the message/object) to kick it off. If it has an outgoing edge, it is usually a control edge (Fig. 16.28).

Using paired send/receive messages is one way that Activity diagram can communicate with each other and with other diagrams, such as State Machine or Sequence diagrams.

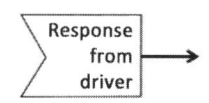

FIGURE 16.27
Wait For message/signal.

FIGURE 16.28
Send message/signal.

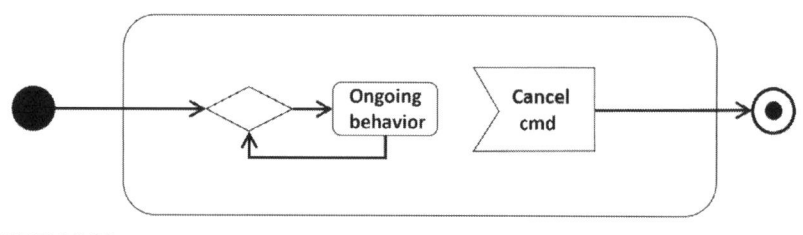

FIGURE 16.29
Cancel command.

Usually, classes that can receive messages will have a reception compartment with the message stereotyped as «signals».

In Fig. 16.29, we see a Wait for Message (Cancel Cmd) that when received interrupts the continuous loop of Ongoing Behavior. A similar effect could have been achieved with the Wait for Message replaced by a Wait for Time Event if the Cancel was set for a particular time. These are common usage patterns in Activity diagrams.

16.4.4 Local Pre/Postconditions

UML allows the modeler to specify pre- and postconditions for actions. We show this by placing the pre- or postconditions in standard note icons and attach them to the action, as shown in Fig. 16.30. These are considered local conditions because they only apply to the Dispense Drink action and not to the larger diagram (not shown).

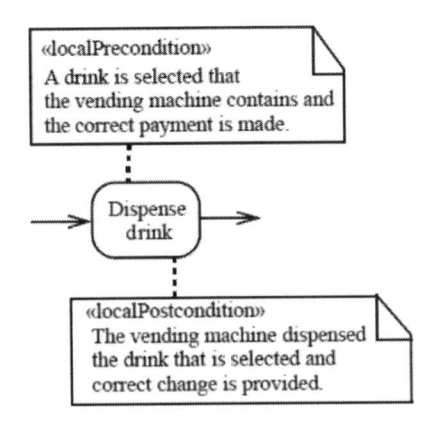

FIGURE 16.30
Local pre- and postconditions. *UML 2.5 Specification Fig. 16.9.*

Unfortunately, UML does not specify an enforcement mechanism for the conditions, nor what happens if they are violated. Therefore, the pre/postconditions are mostly used to document the intention of the modeler.

POINTS TO REMEMBER

- UML normally enables the transport of a token as soon as it enters an edge. By specifying a weight requires a higher minimum number of tokens before transport.
- A streaming pin or parameter allows for additional tokens to arrive after the behavior starts or additional tokens to exit before the behavior ends.
- UML has actions to send and to receive messages. Both the send and receive can be activated by arriving tokens as other actions do.
    - The receive (Wait for Message) can also be activated by being within an active region.
- The modeler can declare local pre/postconditions that apply to an action.

16.5 ACTIVITY DIAGRAMS

All the material discussed earlier in this chapter describes potential contents of an Activity Diagram. An activity diagram also has a frame. In Fig. 16.31, we depict the standard Activity Diagram shape. The shape looks like an action.

An Activity Diagram optionally can also have pre- and postconditions. Compared to the «local conditions» we covered earlier, which only apply to a single action, these are global conditions and apply to the entire diagram. As with the «local» conditions, UML does not specify an enforcement

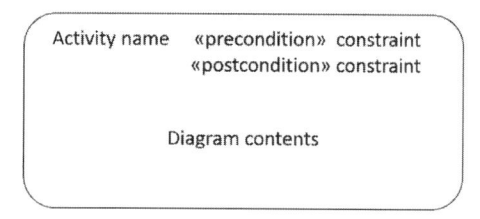

FIGURE 16.31
Standard activity diagram shape.

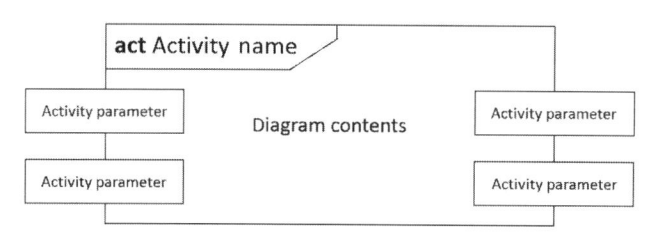

FIGURE 16.32
Activity diagram in standard UML form.

mechanism for the conditions, nor the consequences if they are violated. They are generally used to document the intention of the modeler.

Activity Diagrams can also be represented in the standard UML diagram form with a header. In this form, the diagram kind is **act**. Activity Parameter Nodes impinge on the sides. These are also a type of object nodes. They represent input and output parameters to the Activity. You can distinguish between input and output parameters by looking at the direction any connected edges (object flows) take from the Parameter node, though usually parameters on the left and top are input parameters and parameters on the right and bottom are output nodes (Fig. 16.32).

16.5.1 Activities

Occasionally, we find it convenient to display an activity in a compact form, for example, without showing the inside diagram. We can do it by using the Activity shape with the impinging parameters though we leave the diagram part empty. Instead, we used the standard symbol (that looks like a trident) indicating that decomposition is possible. These "compact" activity forms can be connected in a manner similar to actions (see Fig. 16.33). Unfortunately, the trident is not required notation. Use the trident or activity parameter notation to distinguish activities from actions.

16.5.2 Invoking an Activity

More common than the "compact" activity in Fig. 16.33, whenever we want to invoke an existing activity from within another activity diagram, we create an action that does the job for us (Fig. 16.34).

This is an Action, as indicated by the use of an Action's pins, but we can see that it refers to an activity by the trident. Generally, in a tool clicking on this figure will open the activity diagram that defines the activity being invoked.

While an Activity Diagram is a namespace, duplicate named elements are allowed as they are considered instances.

16.5.3 Calling an Operation

Similar to invoking an Activity is calling an operation. The following action (see Fig. 16.35) calls an operation by the name of Call Me. The information in parentheses is optional if the location of the operation can be determined without it. The ability to call an operation or an activity allows the activity model to use features defined on class diagrams or other activity diagrams.

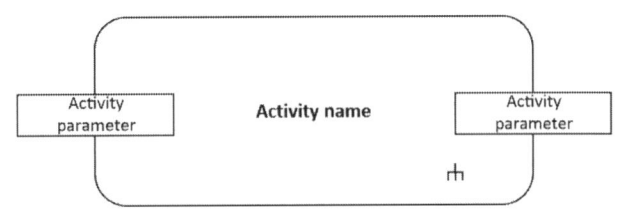

FIGURE 16.33
Compressed form of Activity.

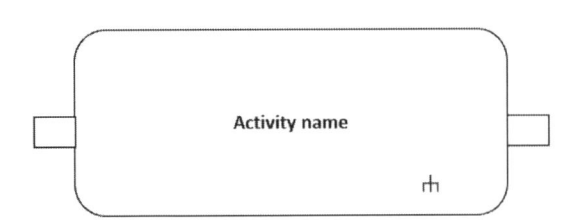

FIGURE 16.34
An action invoking an activity.

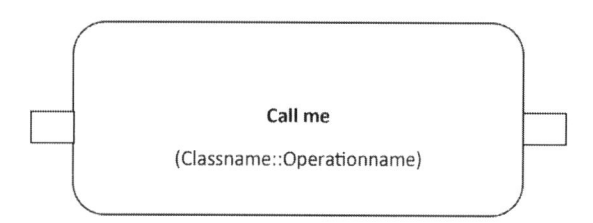

FIGURE 16.35
An action calling an operation.

POINTS TO REMEMBER

- An Activity diagram looks similar to an action but has activity parameter nodes (a form of object node) instead of pins.
- An Activity can be displayed in a stand-alone manner or connected to other activities.
- An Activity diagram supports global pre- and postconditions.
- An Action can be constructed to invoke an existing Activity or call an existing operation.

CHAPTER 17

Questions for Chapter 16

1. Which symbol is used to start a UML 2.5 Activity Diagram?

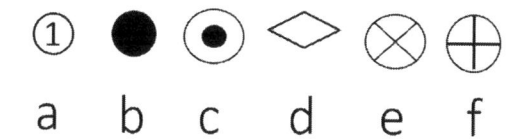

    a b c d e f

    A. a
    B. b
    C. c
    D. d
    E. e
    F. f

2. Which action is guaranteed to be the last one to finish executing?

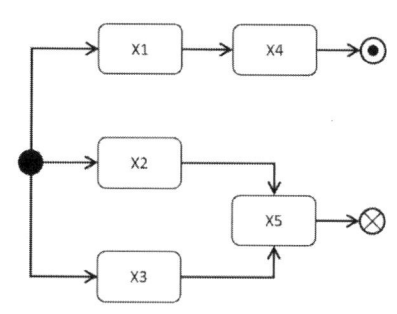

    A. X1
    B. X2
    C. X3
    D. X4
    E. X5
    F. There is no guaranteed "last" step to execute as the order is unpredictable

OCUP 2 Certification Guide. DOI: http://dx.doi.org/10.1016/B978-0-12-809640-6.00018-0
© 2018 Elsevier Inc. All rights reserved.

3. Which actions will never start?

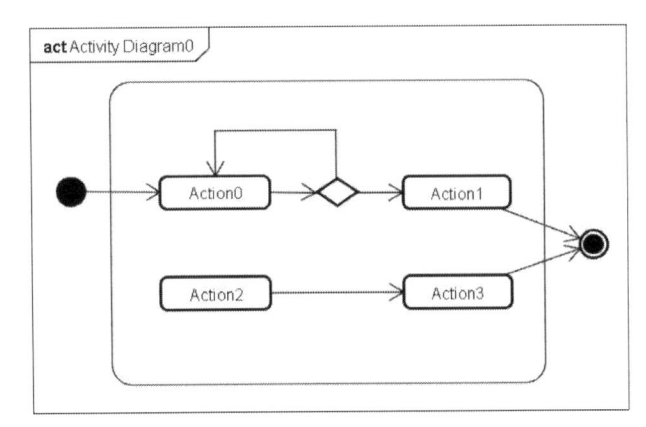

   A. None of the actions will start
   B. Action1, Action2, and Action3
   C. Action2 and Action3
   D. Action0 and Action1
   E. Action1
   F. All actions start
4. Many of the Activity Diagram nodes or actions have matching inverses; e.g., we can match an Initial Node with an Activity Final Node. Which choice below does not have such an inverse?
   A. Fork Node
   B. Decision Node
   C. Join Node
   D. Send Signal Action
   E. Wait Time Action
5. Which of the symbols below indicates a type of action?

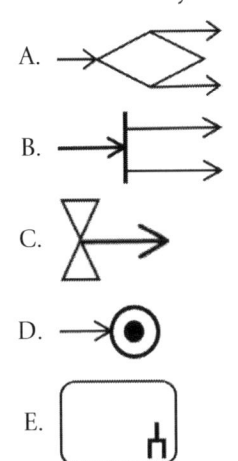

   A.

   B.

   C.

   D.

   E.

6. An Activity has an Activity Final Node, with more than one incoming edge. When does the Activity finish?
   A. The Activity finishes when all the incoming edges have supplied at least one token.
   B. The Activity finishes when at least one incoming edge has supplied one token.
   C. The Activity finishes when the majority of incoming edges have supplied at least one token.
   D. The Activity finishes when at least one incoming edge has supplied one token and no token is moving in other parts of the diagram.
   E. The Activity finishes when at least one incoming edge reaches a Flow Final Node, not an Activity Final Node.
7. Which of following Nodes may not be part of an Activity Diagram?
   A. Activity Parameter Node
   B. Control Node
   C. Executable Node
   D. Object Node
   E. Sentinel Node
8. Examine the Activity Diagram fragment below. What sequence of behavior completions is not legal?

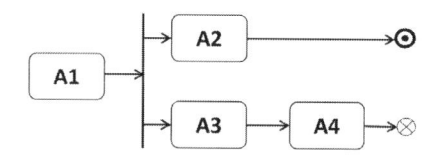

   A. A1, A2
   B. A1, A3, A2
   C. A1, A3, A4, A2
   D. A1, A2, A3, A4
   E. The diagram is missing a join node and cannot finish.
9. Which action might never start?

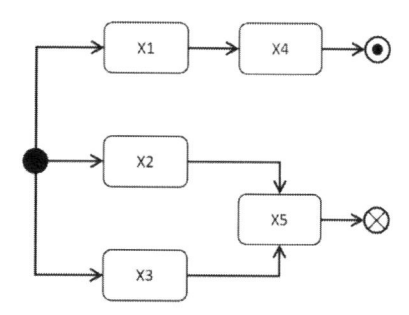

A. X1
B. X2
C. X3
D. X4
E. X5

10. Which symbol, if reached, always indicates the end of execution of an Activity Diagram?

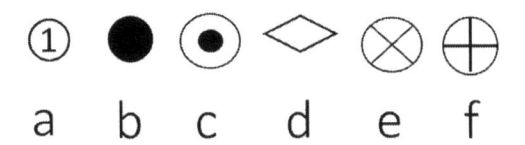

   ① ● ◉ ◇ ⊗ ⊕
   a   b c d e f

A. a
B. b
C. c
D. d
E. e
F. f

11. What statement is true about the diagram Exercise1 below?

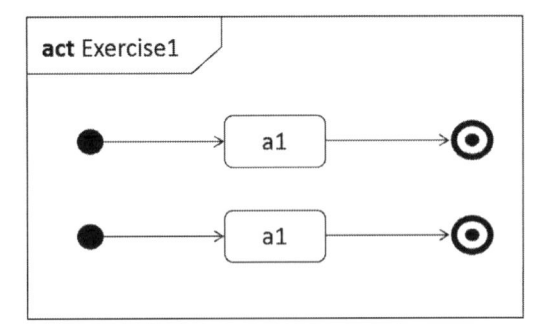

act Exercise1

● → a1 → ◉

● → a1 → ◉

A. It is an invalid diagram as it has multiple Initial Nodes.
B. It is an invalid diagram as it has multiple Activity Final Nodes.
C. It is an invalid diagram as it has two Actions with the same name.
D. It is a valid diagram.

12. The Chess game starts when two Players and the Referee shows up. Which diagram reflects that situation?

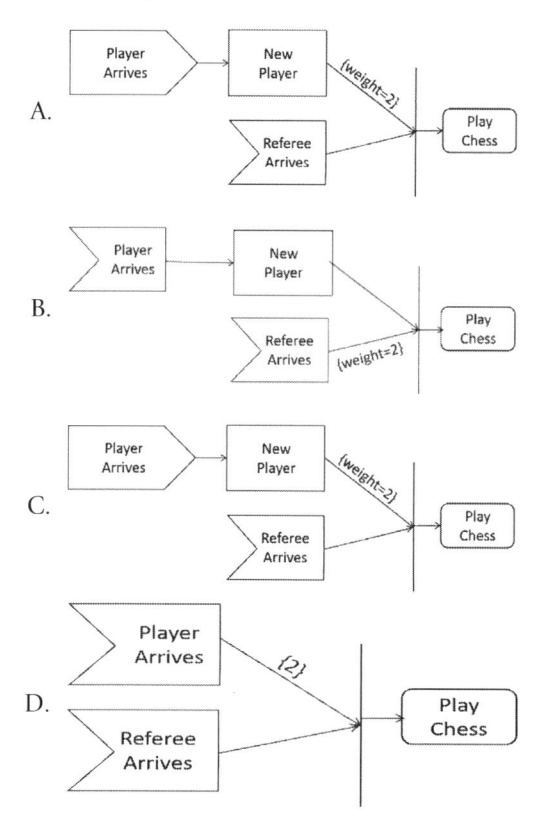

A.

B.

C.

D.

13. On an Activity Diagram, a diamond-shaped symbol appears. It has one edge going in and three edges leaving. What can we say about this symbol?
    A. It is a decision node with a three-way decision.
    B. It is a decision node with a four-way decision.
    C. It is a merge node with a three-way decision.
    D. It is a merge node, which merges three paths.
    E. It is a fork node, which forks to three paths.
14. When discussing an Activity Diagram, what is a token?
    A. A token is used to get you on a subway in some ●→ cities.
    B. A token is a small symbol that looks like a ball with an arrowhead.
    C. A token represents an object or focus of control that traverses Activity Diagram edges or resides at a node.
    D. A token represents a guard condition on an Activity Diagram.

15. Which diagram fragment conveys the modeler's intent correctly?

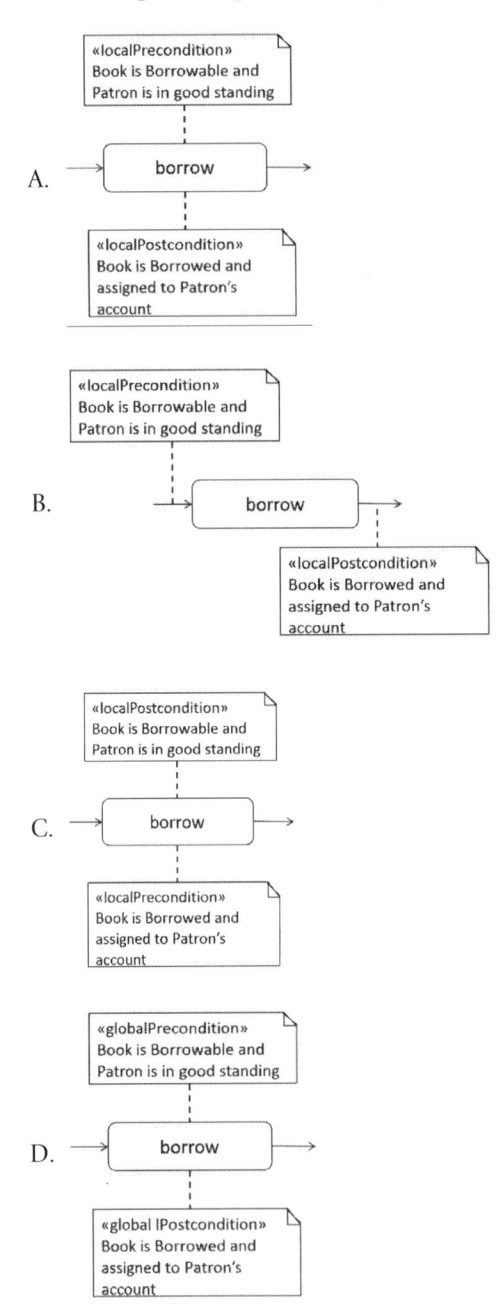

A.

«localPrecondition»
Book is Borrowable and
Patron is in good standing

borrow

«localPostcondition»
Book is Borrowed and
assigned to Patron's
account

B.

«localPrecondition»
Book is Borrowable and
Patron is in good standing

borrow

«localPostcondition»
Book is Borrowed and
assigned to Patron's
account

C.

«localPostcondition»
Book is Borrowable and
Patron is in good standing

borrow

«localPrecondition»
Book is Borrowed and
assigned to Patron's
account

D.

«globalPrecondition»
Book is Borrowable and
Patron is in good standing

borrow

«global lPostcondition»
Book is Borrowed and
assigned to Patron's
account

16. Which of the following potential Activity Diagram model elements do not belong?
   A. Activity Parameter
   B. Object Node
   C. Pin
   D. Stored Query

ANSWERS FOR CHAPTER 16

1. Which symbol is used to start a UML 2.5 Activity Diagram?

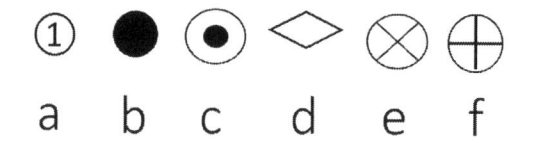

   A. a
   B. **b**
   C. c
   D. d
   E. e
   F. f

   Discussion:
   A—No. While it often used to indicate the start of thing, e.g., a path on a map, it has no use in UML.
   B—Yes. The solid ball is used in both Activity Diagrams and State Machines Diagrams to indicate the start of execution, the start node. It is also called the InitialNode in an Activity Diagram.
   C—No. This symbol indicates an Activity Final node. It ends all execution on the diagram.
   D—No. This symbol indicates either a decision node or a merge mode. It is a decision node if there is only one input edge and several guarded output edges. It is a merge node if there are several input edges and only one output edge.
   E—No. This symbol indicates a Flow Final Node. The Activity diagram kills all input tokens, but the rest of diagram may continue.
   F—No. This symbol is not used in Activity Diagrams. In static diagrams, it would indicate namespace containment.

2. Which action is guaranteed to be the last one to finish executing?

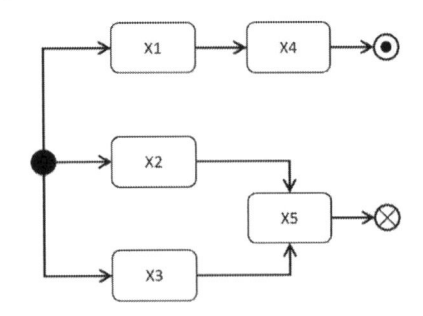

A. X1
B. X2
C. X3
D. **X4**
E. X5
F. There is no guaranteed "last" step to execute as the order is unpredictable

Discussion:
D—This Activity Diagram has only one way to end, i.e., via the Activity Final node, ⊙. When the Activity Final node is reached, the diagram stops. The immediately preceding step, X4, must therefore be the last step to finish executing.

3. Which actions will never start?

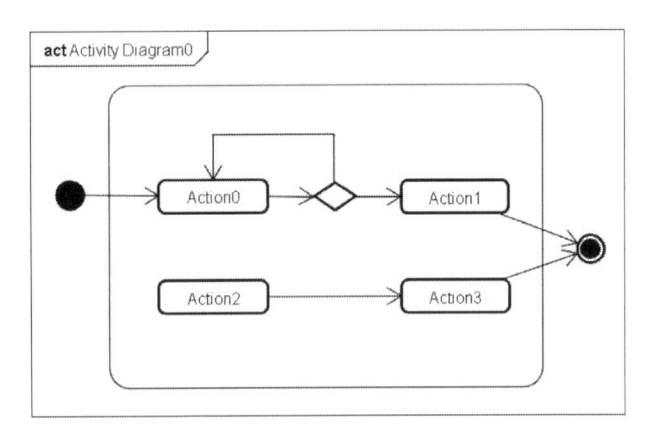

A. **None of the actions will start**
B. Action1, Action2, and Action3
C. Action2 and Action3

D. Action0 and Action1
   E. Action1
   F. All actions start

Discussion:
A—Yes.
Action 0 would normally start after the control token from the Activity Start Node (the ball) reaches it. However, there is another token that is required. This token should arrive on the flow entering Action0 from the top. Unfortunately, this flow can only be populated with a token after Action0 finishes. This will never happen. It is a legal situation, but a logical impossibility, so Action0 cannot start. Action1 only follows after Action0 finishes, so Action1 cannot start either.
Action 2 and Action3 cannot start because there is no entering edge to Action2.

4. Many of the Activity Diagram nodes or actions have matching inverses, e.g., we can match an Initial Node with an Activity Final Node. Which choice below does not have such an inverse?
   A. Fork Node
   B. Decision Node
   C. Join Node
   D. Send Signal Action
   E. **Wait Time Action**

Discussion:
A—No. A Fork Node matches up with the Join Node. They both use a solid bar (vertical or horizontal) as the notation.
B—No. A Decision Node matches up with a Merge Node. They both use a diamond as their notation.
C—No. A Join Node matches up with a Fork Node They both use a solid bar (vertical or horizontal) as the notation.
D—No. A Send Signal Action uses an outward-pointing (convex) pentagon. It matches with the Wait for Event Action, which uses an inward-pointing (concave) pentagon.
E—Yes. There is no match for a Wait Time Action. The notation for a Wait Time Action is two triangles oriented as an hourglass.

5. Which of the symbols below indicates a type of action?

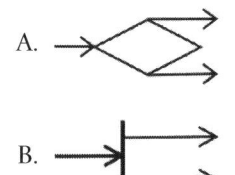

   A.

   B.

C. ⋈→

D. →◉

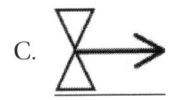

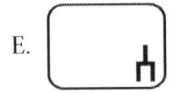

E. [activity node symbol]

Discussion:
A—No. This is a Decision Node, a type of control Node
B—No. This is a Fork Node, a type of control Node
C—Yes. This is a Wait for Time Event Node. It is a type of action
D—No. This is a Activity Final Node, a type of control Node
E—No. This is an Activity Node, a type of executable Node

6. An Activity has an Activity Final Node, with more than one incoming edge. When does the Activity finish?
    A. The Activity finishes when all the incoming edges have supplied at least one token.
    B. **The Activity finishes when at least one incoming edge has supplied one token.**
    C. The Activity finishes when the majority of incoming edges have supplied at least one token.
    D. The Activity finishes when at least one incoming edge has supplied one token and no token is moving in other parts of the diagram.
    E. The Activity finishes when at least one incoming edge reaches a Flow Final Node, not an Activity Final Node.

Discussion:
B—Yes, the first token that reaches an Activity Final Node terminates the diagram. This is different from most other Nodes in Activity Diagrams, which requires all incoming edges to supply tokens.
A, C and D—No, only one token from one edge is sufficient.
E—No, a Flow Final Node can terminate a diagram if there are no other active tokens in the diagram. Only an Activity Final Node will always terminate a diagram when a token arrives.

7. Which of following Nodes may not be part of an Activity Diagram?
    A. Activity Parameter Node
    B. Control Node
    C. Executable Node
    D. Object Node
    E. **Sentinel Node**

Discussion:
A—No. These are nodes where objects can enter the diagram.
B—No. Control Nodes include decision, fork, join, and merge Nodes.
C—No. Executable Nodes include Action and Activity Nodes.
D—No. Object Nodes hold data or objects as they pass through the diagram.
E—Yes. Sentinel Nodes are not part of UML. They are type of Lymph node that would be the first Lymph node to contain cancer cells and would therefore detect the cancer first.

8. Examine the Activity Diagram fragment below. What sequence of behavior completions is not legal?

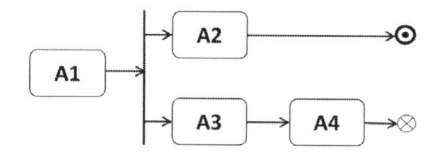

A. A1, A2
B. A1, A3, A2
C. A1, A3, A4, A2
D. **A1, A2, A3, A4**
E. The diagram is missing a join node and cannot finish

Discussion:
The Activity Diagram will end with the activity final node is reached, which occurs after A2 finishes. All legal orders must end with A2. If A2 is fast, it is possible it would finish before A4 or A3 would finish.

9. Which action might never start?

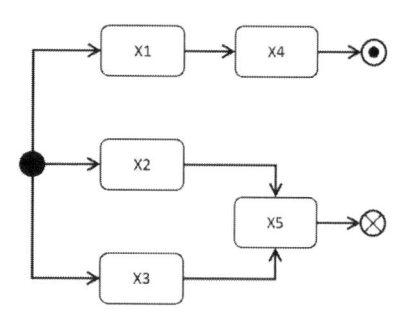

A. X1
B. X2
C. X3
D. X4
E. **X5**

Discussion:
X1, X2, and X3 all start as soon as the Activity Diagram starts. As the Activity Diagram ends when X4 finishes, if X1 and X4 are quick or either X2 or X3 are slow, it's possible that the Diagram will finish before X5 gets to start. Also, consider that the diagram formatting may mislead you to think that the columns finish concurrently.

10. Which symbol, if reached, always indicates the end of execution of an Activity Diagram?

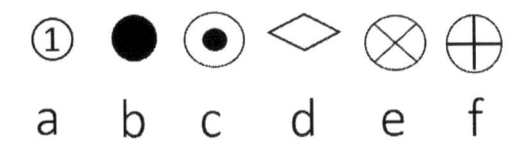

    ① ● ⊙ ◇ ⊗ ⊕
    a   b   c   d   e   f

A. a
B. b
C. c
D. d
E. e
F. f

Discussion:
A—No. While it often used to indicate the start of thing, e.g., a path on a map, it has no use in UML.
B—No. The solid ball is used in both Activity Diagrams and State Machines Diagrams to indicate the start of execution, the start node. It is called the Initial Node in an Activity Diagram.
C—Yes. This symbol indicates an Activity Final node. It ends all execution on the diagram.
D—No. This symbol indicates either a decision node or a merge mode. It is a decision node if there is only one input edge and several guarded output edges. It is a merge node if there are several input edges and only one output edge.
E—No. This symbol indicates a Flow Final Node. The node kills all input tokens, but the rest of diagram may continue.
F—No. This symbol is not used in Activity diagrams. In static diagrams, it would indicate namespace containment.

11. What statement is true about the diagram Exercise1 below?

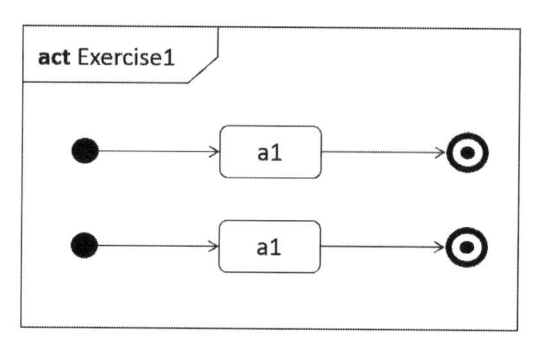

    act Exercise1

    [diagram: two parallel flows, each from an initial node → a1 → activity final node]

    A. It is an invalid diagram as it has multiple Initial Nodes.
    B. It is an invalid diagram as it has multiple Activity Final Nodes.
    C. It is an invalid diagram as it has two Actions with the same name.
    D. **It is a valid diagram.**

    Discussion:
    A—Legal. Each Initial Node starts concurrently.
    B—Legal. Whichever Activity Final Node is first reached ends the diagram.
    C—Legal. Even though an Activity Diagram is a namespace, two actions with the same name are considered separate instances of the same action.
    D—Correct. The diagram is legal.

12. The Chess game starts when two Players and the Referee show up. Which diagram reflects that situation?

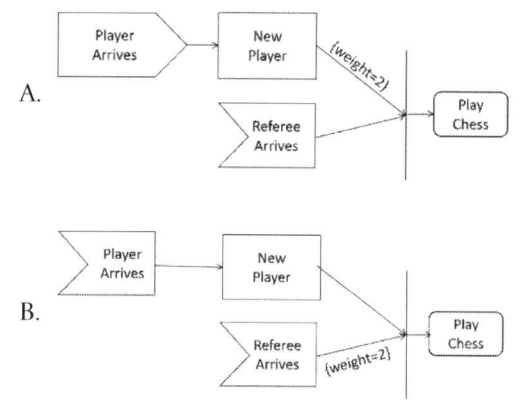

    A. [diagram: Player Arrives → New Player, with {weight=2}; Referee Arrives; join → Play Chess]

    B. [diagram: Player Arrives → New Player; Referee Arrives {weight=2}; join → Play Chess]

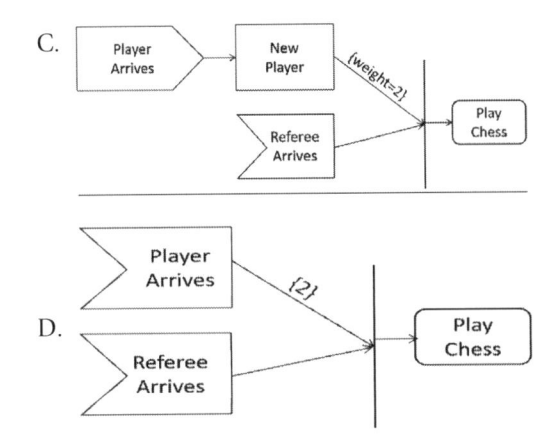

C.

[Diagram: Player Arrives → New Player; Referee Arrives; both join to Play Chess with {weight=2}]

D.

[Diagram: Player Arrives; Referee Arrives; both join with {2} to Play Chess]

On an Activity Diagram, a diamond-shaped symbol appears. It has one edge going in and three edges leaving. What can we say about this symbol?

Discussion:
A—No. The top line on this diagram starts with a Send Message, not a receive
B—No. This requires two Referees and one player
C—Yes. This requires two Players and one Referee
D—No. This uses the incorrect syntax for weight

13. On an Activity Diagram, a diamond-shaped symbol appears. It has one edge going in and three edges leaving. What can we say about this symbol?
    A. **It is a decision node with a three-way decision.**
    B. It is a decision node with a four-way decision.
    C. It is a merge node with a three-way decision.
    D. It is a merge node, which merges three paths.
    E. It is a fork node, which forks to three paths.

Discussion:
A—Yes. A diamond on an Activity Diagram either is a decision or merge node. A decision node has one input edge and multiple output edges. If there are three outgoing edges, then there is a three-way possible decision to make. It is a decision node with a three-way decision.

14. When discussing an Activity Diagram, what is a token?
    A. A token is used to get you on a subway in some cities.
    B. A token is a small symbol that looks like a ball with an arrowhead.
    C. **A token represents an object or focus of control that traverses Activity Diagram edges or resides at a node.**
    D. A token represents a guard condition on an Activity Diagram.

Discussion:
C—Yes, A token conveys the control or the data being passed. It does not have a graphical representation.

15. Which diagram fragment conveys the modeler's intent correctly?

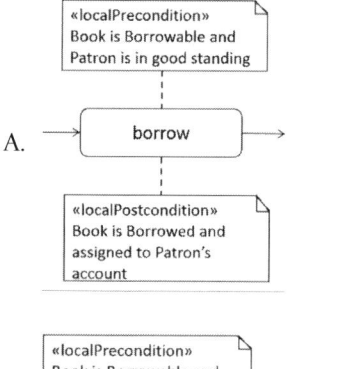

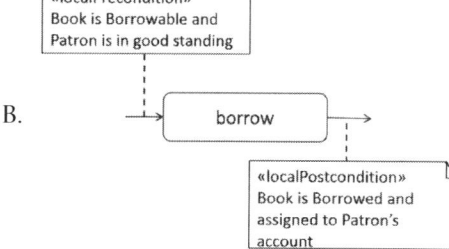

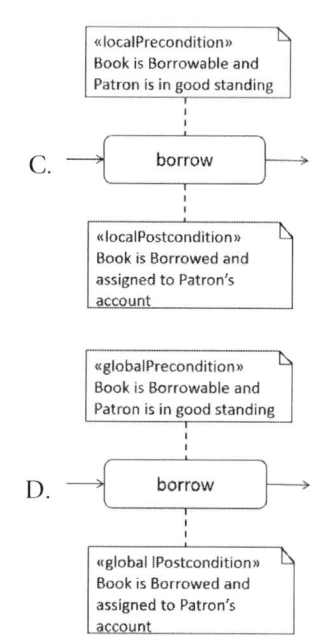

A.
«localPrecondition»
Book is Borrowable and Patron is in good standing

borrow

«localPostcondition»
Book is Borrowed and assigned to Patron's account

B.
«localPrecondition»
Book is Borrowable and Patron is in good standing

borrow

«localPostcondition»
Book is Borrowed and assigned to Patron's account

C.
«localPrecondition»
Book is Borrowable and Patron is in good standing

borrow

«localPostcondition»
Book is Borrowed and assigned to Patron's account

D.
«globalPrecondition»
Book is Borrowable and Patron is in good standing

borrow

«global lPostcondition»
Book is Borrowed and assigned to Patron's account

Discussion:
A—Yes. These match the standard library borrowing and use the correct notation.
B—No. The constraints apply to the action, not to the edges.
C—No. The constraints are in the wrong order.
D—No. These are local conditions.

16. Which of the following potential Activity Diagram model elements do not belong?
    A. Activity Parameter
    B. Object Node
    C. Pin
    D. **Stored Query**

Discussion:
All but Stored Query are types of Object Nodes.
A—An Activity Parameter is an Object Node on the border of an Activity Diagram mapping to an input or output to the Activity.
B—An Object Node is the generic category.
C—A pin is a connection to an Object Edge, indicating an input or output to an action.
D—Yes. While a Stored Query may be a useful thing, it does not directly have any UML presence.

CHAPTER 18

Behavior: State Machine Diagrams

18.1 WHAT IS A STATE AND STATE MACHINE

A state is a condition that an object or behavior (such as a Use Case) can be in for more than a moment. Some property (or properties) is invariant over time, and these properties are relevant to how the object behaves. Properties would include attribute (slot) values, parts and their values, and properties of associated (linked) objects and may include ongoing behavior. The time can be of long or short duration.

A State Machine shows the possible path of states that the object can traverse. There is only one state machine for a class. All instances of a class share the same state machine, though each instance may be in its own state, generally independent of the other instances. As a new instance is made, it becomes subject to the rules of the state machine and starts the state machine at the same Initial State. As an instance is destroyed, it also ends its pass through the state machine at a Final State.[1]

Similarly, every run-time execution of a behavior shares the behavior's state machine and follows the legal paths as defined in the machine. Throughout the life of the instance or the life of the behavior execution, the path through the state machine is defined by the rules of the state machine and the interactions with incoming Events. If the state machine is sufficiently complex, it is possible that no two instances share the same state path location at the same time.

Usually, an object remains in its state until some incoming event causes the object to transition into another state. To see how states look diagrammatically, examine the "roundtangles" in Fig. 18.1. A state is also a namespace (i.e., a container enforcing unique naming) and is usually named. The name may appear in the body of the state (left in Fig. 18.1) used when the body of the roundtangle is otherwise empty. Normally, the name is placed in a name compartment (center in Fig. 18.1). The name may also be put in an attached

---

[1] There can be many ways for an instance to be destroyed, so there can be many final states. There can only be one initial state per state machine.

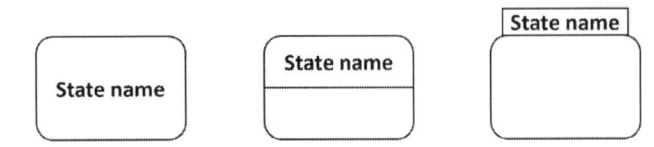

FIGURE 18.1
State examples.

tab (right in Fig. 18.1). We usually reserve the tab form for situations where diagrams appear in the roundtangle body.

Because a state machine diagram is also a namespace, if two roundtangles appear with the same name on the same diagram, they represent two views of the same state (and are confusing). However, unnamed states are considered as each representing a unique state.

Many states can be formalized[2] by specifying a logical constraint on the object's values (slots). For example, a Person is in the state of being a Teenager if the Person's age obeys a specific constraint:

{13 ≤ Person.age ≤ 19}

In this case, an incoming event of the Person's 20th birthday changes the state. Can you come up with another event that changes the state?[3]

We can also base a state on the properties of an associated object. A **Person** can be in the state of Widowed if his/her spouse is no longer living.

{Person.spouse.isLiving = False}

A subsequent marriage event can change this **Person**'s state.

In Fig. 18.2, we show a Class Diagram for **Person** that supports the Widowed state definition. It is considered a good practice to ensure that any defined states are made possible (by defining the necessary attributes and links) in the remainder of the model. Otherwise, the model may be inconsistent or incomplete.

Sometimes, a state may be based on an ongoing activity[4] or behavior. Consider that a **Car** in a hailing service can be Busy, Cruising, or Idle.

---

[2] It is not always easy or necessary to formalize the state definition. A good simple state name may be sufficient if it can unambiguously differentiate between being in the state and not.

[3] The event of death may be considered as changing the state. By the way, the state of being Dead is considered a Final State. A final state is an absorbing state with no possibility of moving on and no ongoing activity.

[4] In formal models, you may choose these activities from the Activity Diagrams.

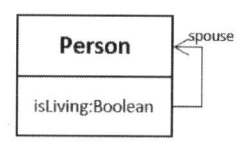

FIGURE 18.2
Class diagram supporting the widowed state.

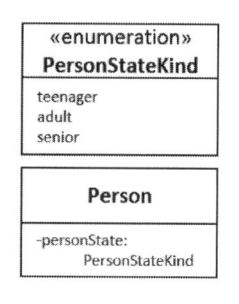

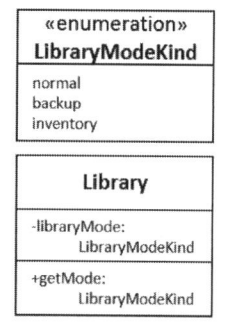

FIGURE 18.3
State and mode enumerations.

18.1.1 States and Modes

The words STATE and MODE are often used interchangeably, though MODE is not a term from UML. While "state" is the more general term, some modelers use "mode" to refer to a system-level state that changes how individual objects behave when the system is in that state.
A system might be in a Normal Operating Mode (e.g., Running, Idle, or Stopped), an Intensified Mode (e.g., Alert or Emergency), a Degraded Mode (e.g., Error or Recovery), or a Support Mode (e.g., Test or Maintenance).
In a **Library** system, there probably would be modes for Backup and Inventory. In the **Hailed Car** system, we would expect a Surge Pricing Mode.

Because an object's behavior is dependent on its state, it is often convenient to have a private enumerated attribute in the object containing the name of the possible state so that it can be easily tested. A system may also have a similar private attribute, though you should consider creating a public accessing operation so that the parts of the system can retrieve the current mode.

Modes are modeled exactly like states of a **System** object. We show the enumerations needed to support some of these states and modes. See Fig. 18.3.

18.1.2 Differences Between States

The usefulness of a state can be judged by examining how an object acts differently in that state as compared to other states. If an object accepts the same set of queries, signals, and operation calls in two different states, and responds identically to these behavior requests, the two states are essentially the same. If there is no discernable difference, collapse the two states into one state.

18.1.3 Qualitatively Different States

When any attribute is different, it is possible to define a new state. Unfortunately, this is not always useful. Consider a **Clock**. There is a state where the **Clock** is 1:00 am, and one where it reads 1:01 am, and one where it reads 1:02 am, and so on. This approach would make an enormous, not very useful, state machine, with at least 720 states. If we went to seconds and modeled a 24-hour **Clock**, we would have 86,400 states,[5] all of them nearly the same. For a **Clock**, instead, we might want to have the possible states of Running, Stopped, BeingSet, AlarmSetOn, 24HourModeOn, and Ringing. Can you think of any missing states?[6]

To be a useful state, something observable must be different, and there must be a qualitatively different and relevant behavior of the object. When the **Clock**.whatTimeIsIt() query is performed in any one of the 86,400 states, the behavior works the same, even though the time returned is different. If the only difference between the results of operations in two states is a quantitative difference, perhaps the states are the same.

If the only difference is a quantitative difference, we also usually treat them as one state. Consider the GPS device in a hailed car or the car's cell phone. As the car moves, the GPS returns different location values to a query. Even though the results are different, we would consider them the same state. However, a typical GPS device might have, at a minimum, such useful states as, Off, Searching for Sufficient Satellites, and Tracking Location.

This sort of state list is common for sensors, e.g., Off, Getting Ready/Initializing, and Sensing/Recording. Occasionally, where there may be a target or threshold value, you will also have states relating to whether the

---

[5] 86,400 secStates/day = 24 hour/day × 60 minute/hour × 60 secStates/minute.

[6] For binary states, if there is a state an object can be in, there is automatically a state of not being in it. Such as 24HourModeOn→24HourModeOff. Some modelers use Venn-like diagrams to check that they have all the possible states. You also might consider a state of being Accurate, Fast, or Slow. Before you include these states, consider how the **Clock** would act differently in those states, and how the **Clock** would know which state it finds itself in. You may have the choice between modeling the state, or it's complement, or both.

target has been reached if or the threshold value has been passed: `At Its Destination, Alarming`.

When choosing states, choose states where the object's behavior is significantly different from its behavior in other states, and the differences are relevant to understanding the object and contributing to understanding the system.

18.1.4 Naming States

Because states are relatively persistent, they are usually named using nouns or adjectival phrases that could be applied to the underlying class name. The state of a **Person** between the ages of 12 and 20 years would be best named either `Teenager` or `Teenaged Person`. Often, the name of the underlying class is elided so you might see a state called `Teenaged [Person]`.[7]

Unless there is a standard domain terminology, states are usually named after the criteria for defining the state. For example, `isTeenager`, `isAdult`, `isSeniorCitizen`. However, the "is" prefix is often omitted to keep the names small. Dropping the prefix is ok if it does not introduce any ambiguity. The names can also be based on the last operation handled by the object. **Person**.`isMarried`, **Book**.`isBorrowed`, **Car**.`isHailed`, **Worker**.`isRetired`. In such cases, it is also common to drop the "`is`" prefix.

A state can also be named after a long-performing activity that is running, while in the state: `Idle, Cruising, Searching,` or `Cruising`. For any ongoing operations, the state name is often a gerund (a verb phrase ending in "`ing`"), `Waiting, Cruising, Reading, Idling`. These names may be identical to a corresponding activity from the Activity Diagrams.

A very short-lasting behavior is not a good choice for a state unless the state can be detectable from outside and is meaningfully distinct from adjacent states. We often capture such short-lasting behavior as ACTIONS in the State model, as they are often thought to be parallel to the actions in the Activity model. We discuss actions in the State model later.

18.1.5 Overlapping States

In the natural world, there are many possible states from which to choose. For example, consider the state `isAdult` and `isSeniorCitizen`. Depending on how these states are defined, they may be disjoint, completely overlapping, partially overlapping, or one contained inside the other (a subset).

---

[7]With the name of the underlying class being elided.

a. If the two states are completely overlapping, where if the object is in the first state it is surely in the second state and viceversa, we have two identical states, no matter how we define the states. This situation is also not a problem, just pick one name

{Person.Teenager = 13 ≤ Person.age ≤ 19}
{Person.Adolescent = 13 ≤ Person.age ≤ 19}

b. If the two states are completely disjoint, this is the usual and preferred arrangement. This situation is not a problem

{Person.Teenager = 13 ≤ Person.age ≤ 19}
{Person.Adult = 20 ≤ Person.age}

c. If one state is completely nested inside another, we have a state and a SUBSTATE. By the given definitions, a Teenager is a substate of Juvenile

{Person.Juvenile = 6 ≤ Person.age ≤ 19}
{Person.Teenager = 13 ≤ Person.age ≤ 19}

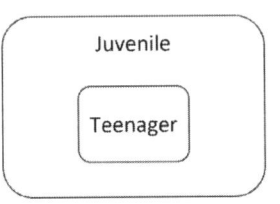

A substate is shown as a full state in its own right but contained in its SUPERSTATE. The parent state, as is any state with one or more contained REGIONS, is called a COMPOSITE STATE. See Fig. 18.4

FIGURE 18.4
(Composite) State with substate.

d. If the two states are partially overlapping yet are intrinsically related, there is a potential difficulty

PROBLEM
{Person.Teenager = 13 ≤ Person.age ≤ 19}
{Person.Juvenile = 6 ≤ Person.age ≤ 15}

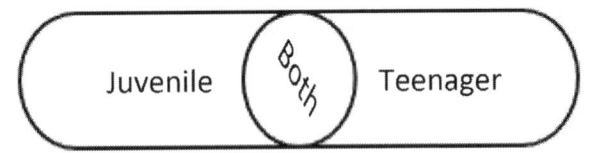

What is often done is to use a Venn diagram approach to identify the uniquely constrained separate regions. See Fig. 18.5. Then create separate states for each region. See Fig. 18.6

FIGURE 18.5
Venn diagram (not a state machine diagram).

SOLUTION
{Person.Teenager = 16 ≤ Person.age ≤ 19}
{Person.Juvenile = 6 ≤ Person.age ≤ 12}
{Person.Both = 13 ≤ Person.age ≤ 15}

FIGURE 18.6
Three state solution.

e. If the two states are partially overlapping and not intrinsically related, there are still potential solutions. One approach is to separate the states into orthogonal aspects and to create a separate State Diagram for each aspect
This situation may be supported by separating the attributes and operations into separate parts as shown in Fig. 18.8
This approach is similar to making one of these aspects into a mode as in Section 18.1.1
Imagine that Patrons who live in the Library's county have different permissions from Patrons of other counties, similar to the various age-based permissions. See Fig. 18.7

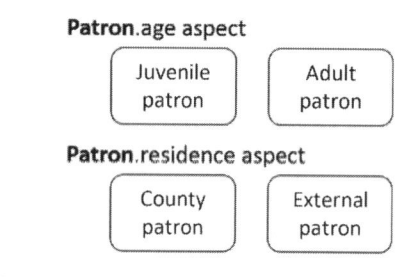

Patron.age aspect

Juvenile patron | Adult patron

Patron.residence aspect

County patron | External patron

FIGURE 18.7
Separate state aspects.

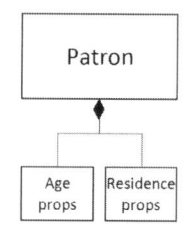

FIGURE 18.8
Separate class aspects.

In the current UML version of State Machine Modeling, it is not directly possible to model overlapping states. In this section, we discuss several ways of dealing with this difficulty.

18.1.6 Finding States

Consider a **Patron** in a library, as shown in Table 18.1. The table shows some states that an object of class **Patron** can be in by using a constraint-based expression of the attributes values of the particular **Patron**. Even without the formal definition of these states, we certainly have a notional understanding of Adult, Minor, Senior, Living, and InGoodStanding.

As you should be able to see, that while `Adult`, `Minor`, and `Senior` are mutually exclusive, the other states need not be. As defined below, they are independent of Living and `InGoodStanding`. However, because we have included `Living` as part of the definition of `InGoodStanding`, we have introduced a dependency between them.

When we find overlapping states, we can treat them as outlined in Section 18.1.5.

Table 18.1 State Criteria Based on Attributes

State	Criteria
Adult Patron	{62 yrs ≥ Patron.age ≥ 18 yrs}
Minor Patron	{17 yrs ≥ Patron.age ≥ 9 yrs}
Senior Patron	{Patron.age ≥ 63 yrs}
Living Patron	{(123 yrs ≥ Patron.age) and isNull(Patron.dateOfDeath)}[a]
Deceased Patron	{(123 yrs < Patron.age) or isNotNull(Patron.dateOfDeath)}[b]
InGoodStanding	{count(Patron.BookOverdue) = 0) and sum(Patron.OutstandingFine) ≤ $5.00) and Patron.Living}

[a] The oldest verified person on record lived to the age of 122 years, 164 days. https://en.wikipedia.org/wiki/List_of_the_verified_oldest_people_retrieved_2016-10-08.
[b] Following De Morgan's laws for the negative of an "and" expression, $\sim(a \lor b) \cong (\sim a \lor \sim b)$.

Table 18.2 State Criteria Based on Navigation Properties

State	Criteria
Married Patron	isNotNull(Patron.spouse)
Widowed Patron	isNotNull(Patron.spouse) and isNotNull(patron.spouse.dateOfDeath)

In the table, we have used object constraint language (OCL)-like expressions to produce the criteria for the states. Usually, these expressions should be easy to understand. However, you may use natural language or other techniques to define the states as long as the state definitions are not fuzzy and are capable of final evaluations. Intuitive names are always possible if formal definitions become difficult.

For the purpose of this table, we define a person's age to be the age at the last birthday.

We can also define states based on the navigability to other objects or their properties (Table 18.2).

States can also be defined by ongoing (or implied) operations. Such operations need to take some time and states are typically only useful if the operation is waiting for something. For example, consider:

```
(Patron)  Waiting for a Reserved Book to Become Available
(Rider)   Waiting for Hailed Ride
(Driver)  Cruising for a Hail
(Book)    Shelved
```

These ongoing operations can often be found in Activity Diagrams when an Action requires an external input to move to the next Action.

POINTS TO REMEMBER

- The UML state model captures discrete event-driven behavior using a finite state machine approach
- A State captures a situation during which some invariant condition holds
  - The condition may be explicitly defined, e.g., by using OCL or informally indicated by the name of the state
- A class or behavior (e.g., a Use Case or operation) may have states
- A mode is a type of state at the system or subsystem level
- An element in a state should be distinguishable from being in other states by having different behavior or responses to behavior that are relevant to the run-time system
  - Purely quantitative differences in responses do not often flag a different state
- A State is diagrammatically indicated by a roundtangle

- A state may be a simple state or a composite state completely containing some number of substates
- Overlapping states are not allowed. When overlapping states appear necessary, there are several techniques to handle the situation. For example,
  - Create a separate state for each uniquely constrained region.
  - Treat them as separate aspects of the element and treat one aspect as if it were a mode.

18.2 TRANSITIONS

Having all the states defined for an object or behavior might be a good goal to characterize a part of your application, but it is not a particularly useful contribution to understanding the dynamic behavior of your application unless you can also comprehend the whens, hows, and whys of state change. In UML, a state change is called a TRANSITION and is modeled by a directed line (an arrow) from the starting state to the ending state. Each transition involves exactly two states, though the starting and ending states may be the same (see Fig. 18.16). Any nontransition element that a transition can enter or leave may be called a VERTEX.

18.2.1 Events

We annotate the transition arrow with the name of the event(s) that trigger the change in state as shown in Fig. 18.9. Usually, the annotation is placed

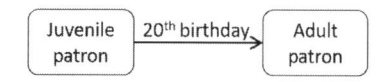

FIGURE 18.9
States with transition.

above the arrow. If more than one event may trigger the transition, the events are separated by commas.

An event in a State Machine Diagram is essentially the same as an event in an Activity Diagram. It can be a signal arriving or an operation being called, that is, a message arriving in a Sequence Diagram. It can also be a timer expiring. Advanced modeling also allows for an event arising from properties being changed or conditions being reached.

If the state machine is for a classifier, you should find any arriving signal in the classifier's RECEPTIONS compartment (or in an inherited receptions compartment). Similarly, an operation being called would be in the operations compartment (or in an inherited operations compartment). A special reserved trigger, "all," matches any received event, whether operation or signal, that the object is prepared for.

Just as it is not necessary to define the states formally, it is not necessary to define the event formally, if the meaning is clear and unambiguous. Of course, by the time you generate the code, you will need something explicit to follow.

When the arriving event conveys arguments, specific values may be shown in the argument list as done in Sequence Diagrams.

18.2.2 Simple State Machine

Let us model the state machine for one of the simplest possible examples that of a standard light switch. This switch is often called an SPST switch (Single Pole Single Throw). In US terminology, it is called a two-way switch (ON/OFF). In British terminology, this is a one-way switch (only controlling one circuit).

There are two states (ON/OFF) and two events: Switch Turned On and Switch Turned Off. Placing the events on the necessary transitions, we get Fig. 18.10.

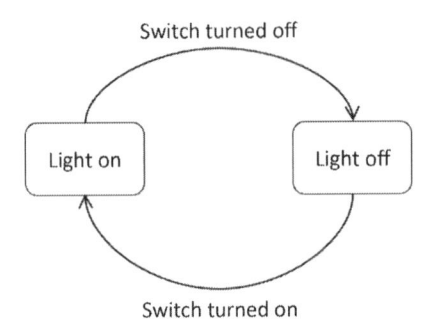

FIGURE 18.10
Simple switch.

As in most State Machine Diagrams, the destination state depends on the originating state and the triggering event.

Look at Fig. 18.11. This figure is very similar to Fig. 18.10. However, there is only one event used. In this case, the target state only depends on the source state.

These diagrams are so simple that many methodologists would say that it is not necessary to model. You should be concentrating your efforts where you hope to gain new insight or to address your biggest risks. Of course, if you hope your model will help you automatically to generate the run-time code or to be used for system simulation, you will even have to model simple switches or retrieve them from a model library.

We can look at a slightly more complicated switch, the Single Pole Double Throw in Fig. 18.12. In US terminology, it is called a three-way switch (ON/OFF/ON). In British terminology, this is a two-way switch (controlling two circuits). We added a ball with a pointer to the Both Off state. This ball and

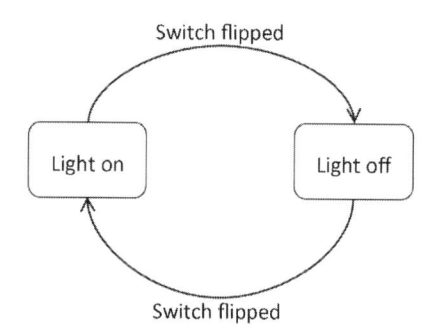

FIGURE 18.11
State-dependent transitions.

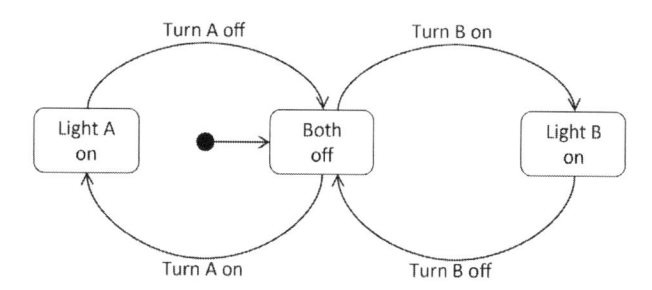

FIGURE 18.12
SPDT with initial pseudostate.

pointer is an INITIAL PSEUDOSTATE that indicates which of the states the object is in when the object is first created.

18.2.3 Guard Conditions

Similar to how conditions are used in other diagrams, it is possible to put a condition on a transition, which, when true, allows the transition to fire. This condition is called a GUARD CONDITION. It can be a Boolean expression involving properties values of the current object, parameters of the incoming event, or property values of reachable objects. It can be a Boolean variable or a Boolean query. If the evaluation of the guard condition has side effects, you may have a malformed model with unpredictable results.

When an event arrives at an object that is potentially interested in that event, the transitions of that object are examined to determine of any active state depend on the arriving event. If any are found, their guard conditions are evaluated. If a true guard condition is found, the transition fires and any ongoing behaviors in the current state are interrupted. If a guard condition that evaluates to false is found, the search continues looking for another possible candidate transition. If multiple transitions have guard conditions that evaluate to true for the same event, the transition chosen may be arbitrary. By the way, if no guard condition is given on a transition, we assume there is a [True] condition that always evaluates to true.

It is possible for a guard condition to test the state of a reachable object [Object Path] **in** State 1 or [Object Path] **not in** State 2. The Object Path is needed to indicate the actual object to test.

The guard condition is placed after the event on the transition line. It is surrounded by square brackets. In Fig. 18.13, we are modeling a part of a library that has two categories of **Books**: circulating and noncirculating (e.g., reference, rare, expensive, or fragile books). Only if a **Book** is a circulating book (isCircBook = true), does a request to borrow a ShelvedBook cause the **Book** to transition to the BorrowedBook state. If isCircBook is False, the transition does not fire, and the state of the **Book** stays the same.

Continuing this example, we allow circulating Books to be reserved. If a Book is on the shelf and then reserved, it is placed in a Reserved Book section, where it can be picked up by the book reserver to be borrowed. If the

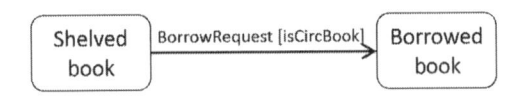

FIGURE 18.13
Guarded transition.

Book is already borrowed when it is reserved, it is placed in the Reserved Book section when it is returned.

In Fig. 18.14, you can see how the same event (Returned) and the same starting state (BorrowedBook) can still yield a different target state based on differences in the Guard Condition (no Reserve vs ReserveOpen).

It should also be mentioned that a guard is only evaluated once when the event arrives. Over time, if the guard were to be periodically reevaluated, different results might occur. Once the guard evaluates as false, it is not reevaluated unless a new triggering event arises.

In some circumstances, the state machine rules are easier to see when presented in a State Transition Table format as shown in Table 18.3.

Especially when you see it in the table format, the commonality of the response in the Borrowed Book state to the Returned event is a bit more apparent. It can be (reverse) factored out to make the diagram easier to understand. In Fig. 18.15, we factored the two Returned transitions into one that leaves the Borrowed Book and goes to the JUNCTION PSEUDOSTATE (*bullet*) where the guard conditions determine the direction to continue. The guard conditions are evaluated before the combined Returned branch is entered, yielding the same results as in Fig. 18.14. This Junction is called the STATIC CONDITIONAL BRANCH because the branch taken is determined beforehand and not reevaluated dynamically.

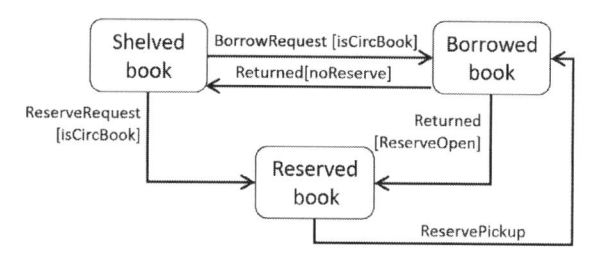

FIGURE 18.14
Borrow and reserve model.

Table 18.3 State Transition Table

Current State	Incoming Event	Guard Condition	New State
Shelved Book	Borrow Request	[isCircBook]	Borrowed Book
	Reserve Request	[isCircBook]	Reserved Book
Borrowed Book	Returned	[no Reserve]	Shelved Book
		[ReserveOpen]	Reserved Book
Reserved Book	Reserve Pickup		Borrowed Book

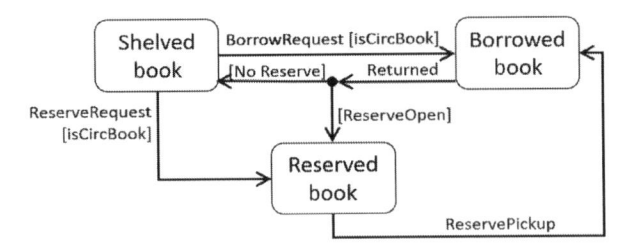

FIGURE 18.15
Use of junction pseudostate.

If more than one guard is evaluated to be true, the results are unpredictable.[8] If none is true, you can use an [Else] guard to indicate where to go.

18.2.4 Transition Effect

A transition may also have behavior associated with it.[9] In UML 1.x, this behavior was called an ACTION and was similar to the actions of Activity Diagrams. In the State Machine Diagrams, an action was limited to be noninterruptible and atomic at the current time scale. The reason for this limitation was that the action has to execute during the transition between the states. If it were to be interrupted, it would leave the state machine in some undefined state. In UML 2.x, we call this a TRANSITION EFFECT or a TRANSITION BEHAVIOR and do not enforce the atomic restriction. However, if the effect was to be interrupted, the consequences are still undefined. Following the UML 1.x restrictions on the behavior may be a good idea for the general case.

A transition effect may be a call to an operation, a sending of a signal, or some direct execution of opaque code, as long as it is understood by the model readers or code generation engine of the modeling tool. The effect is also listed on the transition where it is preceded by a "/." The "/" prevents confusion of the transition *event* with the transition effect.

In Fig. 18.16, we defined a new property of the **Book** class, an integer-typed attribute named #res, to capture the number of outstanding reservations on the **Book**. It is used in two guard conditions [#res = 0] and [#res > 0] that determine which direction to go from Borrowed **Book** when a Returned event occurs. It is also used in four transition effects. Once to initialize #res = 1 on the first reservation, twice to increment the number of reserves, #res++, and

---
[8]Usually a path associated with one of the true guards will be taken, but the choice may not be predictable or repeatable.
[9]Having a behavior associated with a transition, which depends on the previous state and the incoming event, is characteristic of Mealy state machines.

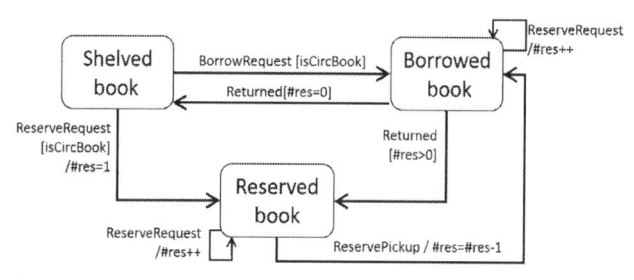

FIGURE 18.16
Borrowing with reserve counting.

once to decrement the number of reserves, #res = #res-1, when there is a reserved pickup for borrowing.

In the two self-transitions (aka reflexive transitions), the transition arrow exits and then enters the same state. In such situations, the transition effect still occurs (and any guard condition would apply). In both of the above diagram's reflexive transitions, the number of reserves is incremented by one.

If there is only one term on the transition line, examine it for a "/," a slash. If the term is not near a slash or precedes a slash, the term represents an event. If the term follows a "/," the term represents a behavior (an action). If the term is contained within square brackets, it represents a guard condition.

18.2.5 Transition Syntax

Using the Backus–Naur form (BNF) syntax, the format of a transition is as follows:

[<trigger> ["," <trigger>]* ["[" <guard> "]"] ["/" <behavior-expression>]]

POINTS TO REMEMBER

- A transition is a change in state
  - It is represented by an arrow connecting the source state and the target state
    - The source and target state can be same, in a reflexive or self-transition
  - A transition has an optional label, consisting of three optional pieces
    - The trigger, the event(s) that the state machine is sensitive to.
    - The guard condition that if evaluated to true, lets the trigger fire. It is always surrounded by square brackets []
    - The behavior expression (effect) that executes when the trigger fires before the next state is reached. If it appears it is always preceded by a "/" (slash)

18.2.6 Ongoing Behavior

As mentioned previously, while an object is in a state, it also can be busy. We can indicate the behavior being performed by the object by showing the behavior in the state body.[10]

18.2.6.1 Implicit Behavior

One type of behavior common within a state is active waiting as an ongoing step in the process. We can usually identify this situation by naming the state with the name of the ongoing behavior. Such states are typically named, as "Waiting," "Cruising," or "Illuminating." They are usually named with the gerund form of the verb (ending in "ing") or in some similar manner. Such states can transition to another state by either receiving an incoming event that triggers a transition or by finishing their behavior(s). When a transition is sensitive to the completion of the ongoing behavior, the transition arrow does not have a triggering event listed, though a guard condition and effect may still appear. This implied trigger is an example of a COMPLETION EVENT, an event capable of triggering a transition without an explicit event on the transition. We call these transitions COMPLETION TRANSITIONS, though they are often referred to as AUTOMATIC TRANSITIONS as they appear to start without an event.

There can be many completion transitions from the same state if they each have different guard conditions. If more than one guard evaluates to true, it is unpredictable which transition would be taken and the diagram is considered ill-formed.

18.2.6.2 Do Behavior

Often, we would like to be specific about what behavior is ongoing in a state. To do this, we specify "do/behavior" in the body of the state. We replace the word "behavior" with a reference to the operation or activity that represents the behavior we want. This allows the modeler explicitly to connect the state with some behavior or activity that is available on the object. This is the preferred method of indicating ongoing behavior.

If the object is still in the state when the behavior finishes, a completion event is issued. A completion transition would then be taken if one was available with guards evaluating as true.
In Fig. 18.17, we see a small piece of a state machine with one event trigger (the top one) and one completion trigger (the bottom one). If the sleeper finishes sleeping before the alarm, s/he attempts to traverse the completion trigger to the Wash Up state. However, if this happens more than 10 minutes

---

[10]Having behavior associated with the current state, and which only depends on the current state, is characteristic of Moore state machines.

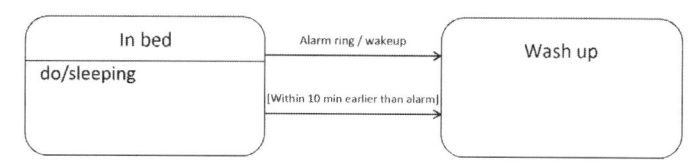

FIGURE 18.17
Example with guarded completion transition.

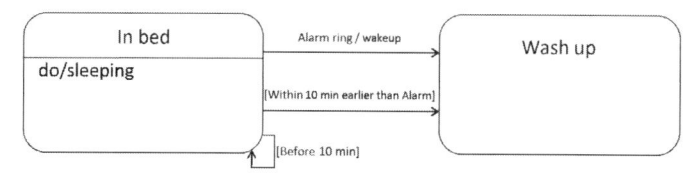

FIGURE 18.18
Restarting state with completion transition.

before the alarm time (i.e., too early), the guard would be false, and the sleeper must stay within the In Bed state until the alarm rings. The sleeper will not be allowed to traverse the completion transition even during the 10 minutes that would otherwise be allowed (i.e., if the sleeper had not attempted to traverse too early). Because a guard on a trigger is only evaluated one time, if the guard fails (i.e., evaluates to false), it fails and remains false. It will not be reevaluated unless the triggering event occurs again. For completion events, this would only happen if the state was restarted.

In Fig. 18.18, which is very similar to Fig. 18.17, we have added a reflexive transition (self-transition) that is also a guarded completion transition. Can you find that transition?[11]

With this change, if you finish sleeping early (before 10 minutes of the alarm) instead of hanging out in the In Bed state until the alarm finally rings, we reenter the In Bed state where we start the state all over again. In this case, as with entering the state from scratch, the do/behavior is restarted from the top. So if you now wake again, both guard conditions are retested. If you do not wake on your own, some time within the last 10 minutes, you will eventually wake with the alarm.

18.2.7 State Setup and Teardown

Besides the do/behavior within a state, we have the ability to specify *entry* and *exit* behavior. These behaviors are always executed as the state is entered

---

[11] It is the transition with the guard condition [before 10 minute] of the wakeup time.

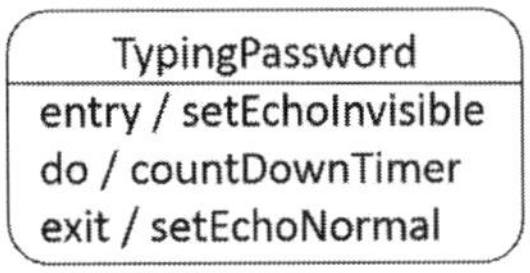

```
┌─────────────────────────┐
│     TypingPassword      │
│ entry / setEchoInvisible│
│ do / countDownTimer     │
│ exit / setEchoNormal    │
└─────────────────────────┘
```

FIGURE 18.19

Entry, do, & exit behaviors. *Modified from UML 2.5 Fig. 14.6.*

Table 18.4 Internal Behaviors

entry/ behavior	When the state is entered or reentered, this atomic behavior must be executed as the first thing after any behavior on the transition
do/ behavior	After the entry behavior finishes, any available do/behavior(s) will start. This behavior can finish normally raising a completion event, or an interrupting event may force it to stop
exit/ behavior	When the state is exited for any reason, this atomic behavior must be executed as the last thing, before the exit transition behavior can start

or exited. They are typically used to initialize state conditions or variables and to restore them after the state is finished. See Fig. 18.19. In the figure, we see the use of entry and exit combined with do/behavior previously discussed. These are INTERNAL BEHAVIORS and are often placed in their own compartments (Table 18.4).

All three words, "entry," "do," and "exit," are reserved words and cannot be used as the name of events that might appear elsewhere. Because events can also be used on Activity, Sequence, and Timing diagrams, it is best to avoid using them in any way that could be inconsistent with their reserved use in State Machine diagrams.

18.2.8 Exit/Entry Action Equivalents

When there is more than one transition into a state, they all take the entry/behavior after they execute their transition-specific behavior. It is not possible to bypass the common behavior indicated by the entry/behavior. This reveals the major use of entry/behavior, to identify and specify the common behavior needed to set up or initialize the state, as it is executed on of any of the ways in. For example, entry/behavior is often used to initialize state attributes. If you use the entry/behavior in this way, you will need to (1) check that it belongs on all entry transitions and (2) remove the behavior from the transitions (you do not want them to execute twice).

In Fig. 18.20, there are three ways of getting into State 1. We summarize these in Table 18.5.

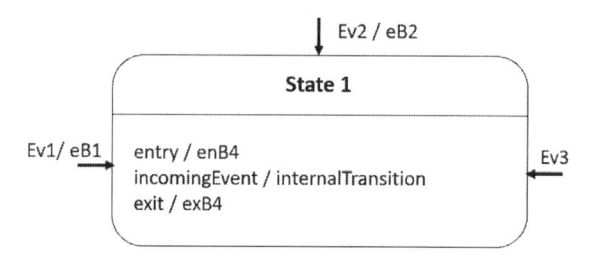

[FIGURE 18.20 diagram: State 1 with Ev2/eB2 entering from north, Ev1/eB1 entering from west, Ev3 entering from east; internal compartment shows entry / enB4, incomingEvent / internalTransition, exit / exB4]

FIGURE 18.20
Entry events.

Table 18.5 Multiple Ways of Getting Into a State

Direct from	From Ev1 (west side)	From Ev2 (north side)	From Ev3 (east side)
Behavior executed	eB1 then enB4	eB2 then enB4	enB4

18.2.9 Completion

As soon as a state finishes its entry/behavior, if there no do/activity for the state, the state is *complete*. If it has some do/activity to perform, it is not *complete* until the do/activity is done. When the state is finally complete, if there is a completion transition on the state whose guard is met, it will then execute its exit/behavior. Then it will take the completion transition. This can appear to be instantaneous, especially in these PASSTHROUGH STATES. See Fig. 18.21. BTW, what is the value of x when the diagram is finished?[12]

Remember a completion transition is a transition missing the triggering event. Using BNF, a completion transition looks like the following:

["[" <guard> "]"] ["/" <behavior-expression>]]

18.2.10 Internal Transitions

An internal transition follows the format of a transition [event (guard)/ behavior] but does not have a start or end state. It is placed inside the body of the state, sometimes in a separate compartment. In Fig. 18.22, the two lines at the bottom of the state represent internal transitions. If the char event arrives, the countDownTimer may be considered to suspend; then the handleChar behavior is invoked, and the countDownTimer is restarted with no

---

[12] It is hard to keep track, but I get $x = 19$. You should also note that the guard condition is evaluated before the effect is executed.

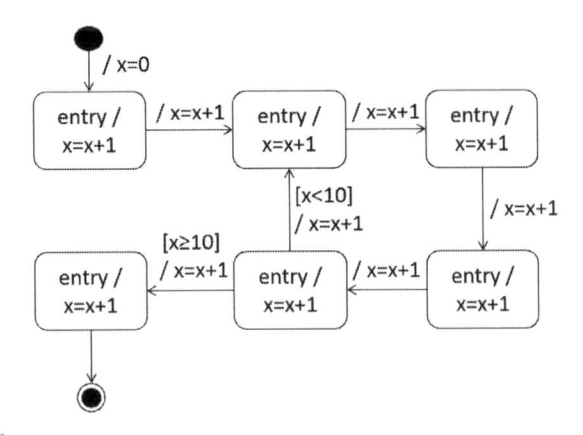

FIGURE 18.21
Empty or passthrough states (states with no internal do/activity).

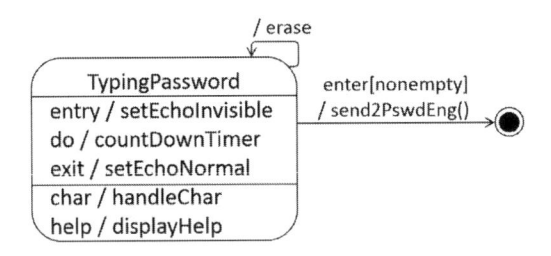

FIGURE 18.22
State with internal behavior and final state.

noticeable impact. If the `help` event arrives, the `countDownTimer` is also suspended, the `displayHelp` behavior is invoked, and the `countDownTimer` is resumed where it left off. In a multiple threaded environment, the suspension of the `countDownTimer` needs not occur as the `countDownTimer` runs concurrently with the transition's behavior.

If the `countDownTimer` expires naturally, the automatic transition (completion transition) is taken. It is the transition marked "/erase." As this transition is a self-transition, the erase behavior (erasing whatever is in the password buffer) executes, and the `TypingPassword` state starts all over from the top. The order of this behavior is

1. (do) `countDownTimer` expires
2. (exit) `setEchoNormal`
3. (completion transition behavior) `erase`
4. (entry) `setEchoInvisible`
5. (do) `countDownTimer` expires

If instead of the timeout, the user now presses enter (and the password buffer is not empty), the following behavior occurs:

6. (incoming event) enter [nonempty]
7. (do) `countDownTimer` is canceled
8. (exit) `setEchoNormal`
9. (transition behavior) `send2PswdEng`
10. (Final State) The diagram ends (at this level). If there is a completion transition at the next higher level, it will be attempted.

POINTS TO REMEMBER

- An entry/action is a behavior (either an opaque expression or method call) that is automatically invoked as soon as a state is entered, without exception
  - Commonly used to set up a state, such as to initialize local variables
- A state may use a do/Activity to indicate ongoing behavior that is started after the entry/Action is finished
  - This behavior may be interrupted by any incoming event causing an external transition
  - When the do/Activity is finished, a completion event is raised, possibly triggering a completion transition—an unlabeled transition
- An exit/Action is a behavior (either an opaque expression or method call) that is automatically invoked as soon as a state is being exited, without exception
  - Commonly used to tear down a state, such as to release unneeded memory

18.3 STATE MACHINE PROCESSING

18.3.1 Run-to-Completion

UML State Machines follow a `Run-to-Completion (RTC)` paradigm.[13] A UML state machine completes processing of each event before it can start processing the next event.

In this approach, the system processes events in discrete, atomic RTC steps. New events cannot interrupt the processing of the current event and must be stored (in an EVENT POOL) until the state machine becomes idle again. What this means is that each state machine continues processing until it reaches a WAIT POINT, when it is eligible to accept new events.

Many mistakenly believe that RTC means that a state machine has to monopolize the CPU until the RTC step is complete. The prohibition on preemption only applies to the busy state machine. In a multitasking/multiprocessing environment, other state machines can be running, possibly preempting the currently executing state machine.

---

[13] The UML 2.5 specification calls this the run-to-completion paradigm. Other literature calls it run-to-completion Semantics.

At a wait point, all processing in the state machine has been completed, except perhaps for do/behaviors. Once a wait point is reached, the events in the EVENT POOL are evaluated to see if the state machine is currently waiting on them for some transition. (The pool is usually thought of as an EVENT QUEUE).

If an enabled event is there, the state machine accepts the event and processes the transition. It then stops at the next wait point, where the cycle continues again. The sequence of behaviors between wait points is called a State Machine STEP.

This processing flow is an alternation of being *in transit* or *in state*. It is in transit when an event is dispatched that matches at least one of its associated triggers. While in transit, it may execute some behaviors associated with the path it is taking (e.g., entry, exit, transition). Even when in a stable state (at a wait point), there could be behaviors being executed. These arise from the do/Activity behaviors.

Events that are not processed off the pool are generally dropped. They will need to be resent to the state machines for them to be considered. The order the events are examined from the pool is not specified, though the pool is usually considered an EVENT QUEUE. However, because completion events have priority, they will be dispatched ahead of any other events in the pool.

In Fig. 18.23, we can trace the RTC Steps and Wait Points based on arriving events. We show the trace in Table 18.6. The Step and Wait Point terminology is proper UML, but not common. The key thing to understand from this is the sequence of uninterruptible behaviors during a Step, where the Wait Points are, and what happens inside of them.

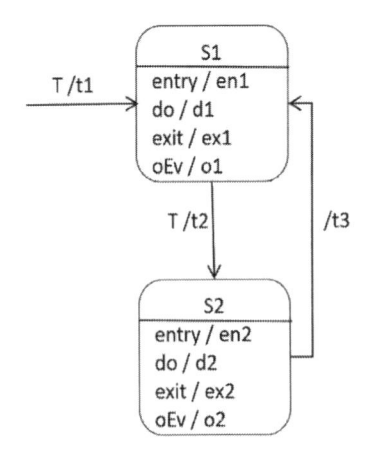

FIGURE 18.23
RTC and steps.

Table 18.6 RTC, Steps, and Events

Event	Label	Behaviors
T	Step 1	Run t1
		then en1
	Wait Point 1	Start d1
		enable oEv,
		enable T, and
		enable d1 completion
T	Step 2	Cancel d1 if still running
		run ex1
		then t2
		then en2
	Wait Point 2	Start d2
		enable oEv and
		enable d2 completion
d2 completion	Step 3	Run ex2
		then t3
		then en1
	Wait Point 3	Start d1
		enable oEv,
		enable T, and
		enable d1 completion
oEv	Step 4	Run o1[a]
	Wait Point 4	Re-enable oEv and
		enable T

The order of the running during the Steps is as specified. The order of enabling during the Wait Points is only notional. An enabled event is one the state will be awaiting.
oEv stands for other-Event. This would be an internal transition.
[a]*Technically o1 runs without impact to d1. That is, there is no interference between the do/activity and the internal event/action. In practice, a do/activity may need to suspend and resume if this is on a single threaded machine.*

18.3.2 States and Pseudostates

A UML State Machine can be described as a directed graph of VERTICES that an object (or behavior) can traverse over time. So far, we have only discussed states as possible vertices. However, besides states, there are also PSEUDOSTATES. Pseudostates are transient, in that the state machine cannot rest at one of these vertices, based on the RTC rules. They generally indicate control and flow information on a State Machine (Tables 18.7 and 18.8).

In Fig. 18.24, we see two uses of the Choice Pseudostate. As this is the Dynamic Conditional branch, it will evaluate the guards only when it gets to

Table 18.7 Pseudostates on the First Exam

Name	Symbol	Description	Comments
INITIAL PSEUDOSTATE	●	This symbol indicates the start of a state machine An arrow points from the symbol to the INITIAL STATE of the machine, but it is not a state itself See Fig. 18.12	Normally, these are not labeled and may not have any guard or event on the arrow pointing to the initial state There can be only one per region The symbol is also used to indicate the start of Activity Diagrams
JUNCTION PSEUDOSTATE	●	a. May be used to join several transitions into one b. May be used to split a complex transition into several guarded alternatives See Fig. 18.15	Called a STATIC CONDITIONAL BRANCH This Junction Pseudostate does not change the interpretation from individual transitions. Before the first part of the transition is attempted, the guards are evaluated in all parts of the transition and remembered If no path with only true guards is available, the transition is not entered. An [else] branch may help as it will be taken if no other path is ok, though the junction would not be entered if there were no way out A path with no guard is evaluated as [true]
CHOICE PSEUDOSTATE	◇	May be used to split a transition into several guarded alternatives, where each guard is evaluated as needed when reached See Fig. 18.24	Called a DYNAMIC CONDITIONAL BRANCH This Choice may take a different alternative than the Junction because it dynamically evaluates the guards If no path with only true guards is available, the transition may be stuck at the diamond, as there is no way of going on. This produces a malformed model. An [else] branch may help as it will be taken if no other path is true, preventing the State Machine from becoming stuck A path with no guard is evaluated as [true]

Table 18.8 Additional States on the First Exam

Name	Symbol	Description	Comments
Final State	●	A real state (not a pseudostate), this node indicates that no more events will be accepted by this state machine and no more change of states will occur It is also used to indicate the end of a substate See Fig. 18.22	There can be 0..* Final states. Reaching a final state indicates a completion event at the next higher level

FIGURE 18.24
Two uses of the choice pseudostate.

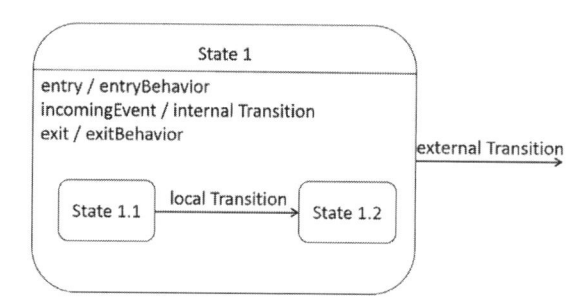

FIGURE 18.25
Types of transitions.

the diamond. This allows the behavior of `recalcX` to change the value of X intentionally. The left and right versions are the same. However, the right version takes advantage of a shortcut that is allowed when the guards all involve the same term. Here, we place the common term X in the center of the diamond and eliminate the X from the guards, but retaining the same meaning.

18.3.3 Types of Transitions

UML supports three major types of transitions: external, internal, and local. See Fig. 18.25.

External Transition: Leaves the containing state and executes the exit behavior of the containing state (exitBehavior in Fig. 18.25).

Local Transition: Leaves a substate but does not execute the exit behavior of the containing state, though it will execute any exit behavior of the substate it came from.

Internal Transition: Does not leave any state nor does it execute any exit behavior.

POINTS TO REMEMBER

- Both a junction pseudostate (the ball) and the choice pseudostate (the diamond) can split a decision so that it can be made at different points in the transition
  - The junction/ball just splits the decision diagrammatically. This is a static decision that is evaluated before the processing reaches the ball, and cannot be changed. If no path is clear, the decision structure will not be entered
  - The diamond allows for a dynamic decision. The decision to take a path is dynamically decided only when the processing gets to the diamond branch point
    - The dynamic decision can cause blocked/stuck processing if no guards are true
  - Use of an [else] branch can guarantee that the processing is not stuck. It can be used in both the choice and the junction decisions
- The RTC (run-to-completion) semantics used by UML means that no UML event can interrupt an object's processing until a *step*, where the object is awaiting a new event to be dispatched from the event pool
  - do/Activity behavior may be interrupted by any incoming event causing an external transition
  - When the do/Activity is finished normally, a completion event is raised, possibly triggering a completion transition—an unlabeled transition

18.3.4 State Diagrams and Machines

When all of an object's initialization is complete, it will start its state machine (if any). It will start at the topmost level of the state diagram and enter the state pointed to by the Initial Pseudostate (solid ball). This is the initial transition. It is normally unlabeled. However, it may be labeled with the Event type of the occurrence that created the object, and otherwise, it must be unlabeled. However, if there is only one state at the topmost level of the diagram, usually it is interpreted, as that state is the initial state, even without the Initial Pseudostate pointing toward it. If there was no Initial Pseudostate and there are multiple states in the topmost region of the diagram, the behavior is unspecified; generally, we would consider the model to be an ill-formed model.

There can only be one Initial Pseudostate per region. The topmost state machine diagram is a region. The transition from the Initial Pseudostate cannot have a trigger or guard, though it may have a behavior. Only one transition is allowed from the Initial Pseudostate.

The header for the state machine diagram is the same pentagonal shape that the other diagrams use. The diagram-kind field is **stm**, indicating a **state machine**. A state machine diagram can only have one state machine inside it. See Fig. 18.26.

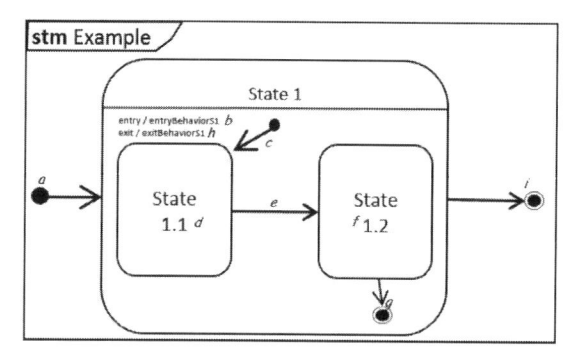

FIGURE 18.26
Top of state hierarchy/state diagram.

The second field in the **stm** header indicates the name of the classifier or behavior that follows the contained state machine. This is normally a class, though it can be a use case or operation.

18.3.5 Hierarchy of States

As shown in several previous figures, such as Fig. 18.25, a state can have substates of its own. In Fig. 18.26, we see that the State Machine **Example** has a State 1 made of two states, State 1.1 and State 1.2. Even though we are not explicitly being shown the substate decomposition indicator (which looks sort of like eyeglasses), we know that when the behavior of State 1.1 is completed, the state machine will transition to State 1.2. We can see this because there is an unlabeled completion transition from States 1.1 to 1.2 (item *e*).
In turn, when the behavior of State 1.2 is completed, the state machine will transition to the final state (that looks like a bull's eye) (item *g*). Again, we see this by the completion transition to final state within State 1. This is followed by the execution of the exit behavior for State 1, exitBehaviorS1 (item *h*).

Moreover, this will cause the state machine for the entire State 1 to complete and follow a transition out of the State 1 (on the right side), ending the state machine (item *i*).

At a lower level, the initial pseudostates and the final states work in the same way.
In the inside of State 1, of Fig. 18.27, we see that the initial pseudostate of State1 (item *a*) works to start the behavior, by first triggering the entry action entryBehaviorS1 (item *b*) and starting State 1.1 (on the left). Inside State 1.1,

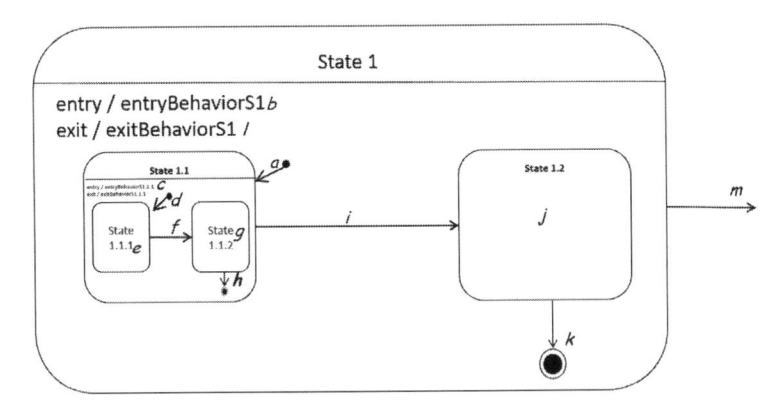

FIGURE 18.27
Lower level of hierarchy.

the initial pseudostate works to start the behavior of State 1.1 by starting the entry behavior (item *c*) and State 1.1.1 (item *d*). When the behavior of State 1.1.1 completes, processing automatically transfers (item *f*) to State 1.1.2 (item *g*). When State 1.1.2 finishes, processing transfers to the final state of State 1.1. As this is a final state, all behavior within State 1.1 is now complete, causing State 1.1 to complete and to perform the exit behavior (`exit BehaviorS1.1.1`) and undergo the automatic completion transition (item *i*) to State 1.2 (item *j*), where the processing can continue.
When State 1.2 finishes, the final state is reached (item *k*) and the `exitBehaviorS1` is executed (item *L*). Finally, the automatic transition to the subsequent state (item *m*) is traversed.

The key idea here is that reaching a final state at the $N + 1^{th}$ lowest level causes a completion event and transition on the Nth level. For example, reaching item *h* is followed by traversing item *i*. Entering a state from an initial pseudostate can cause a transition from an initial pseudostate at the next lower level. For example, item *a* is followed by item *d*. This continues up and down for as many levels as are documented.

18.3.6 States Contours

Occasionally, we see a simplified version of the above structures. The physical boundary of a state (the roundtangle) is often called a CONTOUR. A transition going inside a state, i.e., crossing a contour, to reach to another substate, still, executes all the entry behavior of all of the intermediate containing states. A transition going outside and crossing contours still executes all the exit behaviors of all the intervening containing states. In Fig. 18.28, we should see the transitions going directly through some of the contours. The effect

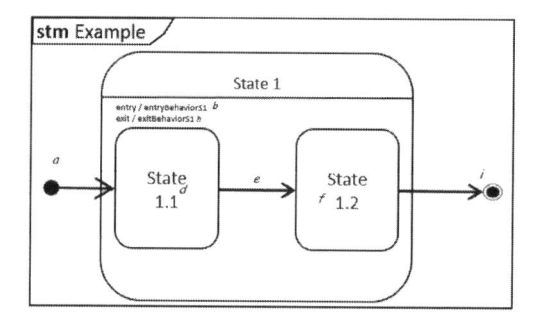

FIGURE 18.28
Going in through the contour.

Table 18.9 State vs Activity Diagram Semantics

	More than One Entering Edge		**More than One Exiting Edge**		**A Reflexive Edge**
Activity Diagram	All edges must be populated with tokens[a]	These are mandatory input parameters to the behavior. An "and"	All outgoing edges will be populated with tokens[a]	These are the output parameters from the behavior	A behavior cannot logically use its own output as an input
State Diagram	One edge must be triggered by an event to transition into the state	An "or"	One edge must be triggered by an event to transition to the next state		Not a problem

[a]Advanced Activity notation allows the parameters to be optional or to have different multiplicities.

should be the same as in Fig. 18.26. For example, even though transition a goes through the contour of state 1 directly into state 1.1, the entry action of state 1 (item b) is still executed. In the same manner, the outwardly crossing transition going to the final state (item i) still causes the exit action (of item h) to be invoked.

POINTS TO REMEMBER

A State machine diagram uses "stm" as the diagram namespace kind

A State machine diagram has exactly one state machine inside

Bypassing the contour still invokes the entry or exit actions of all the intervening states

Reaching a final state at the $N + 1^{th}$ level causes a completion event and transition on the Nth level

Entering a state from an initial pseudostate can cause a transition from an initial pseudostate at the next lower level

18.4 STATE VS ACTIVITY SEMANTICS

As we discussed in Chapter 17, Questions for Chapter 16, on Activity Diagrams, we mentioned that one of the changes to Activity Diagrams was to drop State Diagram processing semantics and replace them with Petri-net-like semantics. Practically, the change is captured in Table 18.9.

CHAPTER 19

Questions for Chapter 18

1. Which symbol is used to start a UML 2.5 State Machine Diagram?

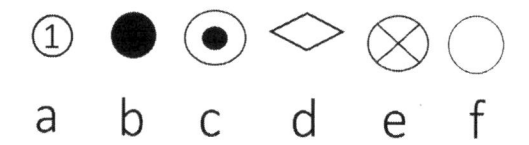

   a   b   c   d   e   f

   A. a
   B. b
   C. c
   D. d
   E. e
   F. f

2. Examine the State Machine Diagram fragment below. What state will the State Machine be in after the events e1, e2, e3, and e1 occur (in that order)?

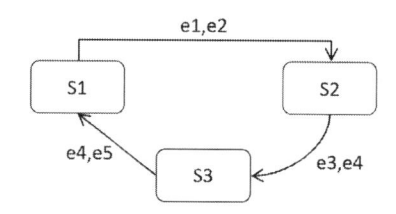

   A. It is not possible to tell.
   B. S1
   C. S2
   D. S3
   E. The diagram is not a valid State Machine Diagram.

3. Which list completely identifies the possible features of a transition?
   A. trigger
   B. trigger, guard
   C. trigger, guard, state
   D. trigger, guard, state, effect
   E. trigger, constraint, effect
   F. trigger, guard, effect
   G. trigger, guard, effect, return
4. What type of behavior should a system exhibit to be most appropriate for using a State Machine to help in understanding the manifest behavior of the system?
   A. Continuous and self-adjusting behavior
   B. Cooperating identical peer instances
   C. Genetic Evolving Algorithms with feedback
   D. Discrete Event-driven behavior
   E. Time-based Schedule driven behavior
5. Which statement best describes how a higher priority event interrupts the processing of a lower priority event in a UML state machine?
   A. The events are taken from the event pool in strict priority order. Thus, a newly arriving high priority event can interrupt ongoing behavior.
   B. There is no possibility for interrupting events because of Run-to-Completion Paradigm (RTC).
   C. The UML 2.5 Specification does not allow for State Machine-mediated interrupts. However, changes to the priority of an object's thread and changes to the resources available to the thread may cause a particular thread to be suspended and others to be enabled.
   D. Higher priority events may be taken before lower priority events by an unspecified algorithm, causing effective interrupts.
   E. The UML 2.5 Specification indicates that completion events are of higher priority than other events. This ordering causes completion events to be examined before external events, leaving interrupts in their wake.
6. A State Machine Diagram has at least one Final State at the top level (at the State Machine diagram level), with more than one incoming edge. When does the State Machine finish?
   A. The State Machine finishes when all the incoming edges to the Final State have supplied at least one token.
   B. The State Machine finishes with the first transition to a top-level (diagram) Final State.
   C. The State Machine finishes when the majority of incoming edges have transitioned to a top-level Final State.

D. The State Machine finishes when every top-level (diagram level) Final State has had a transition into it.
7. In a UML 2.5 State Machine, an expression may be surrounded by square brackets, [ ]. What does this mean?
   A. An "invariant constraint" is surrounded by square brackets. The modelers state their intention that the model will enforce these constraint expressions to be true.
   B. The use of square brackets announces that the expression is an "opaque expression", whose meaning is context dependent.
   C. Such expressions are "guard conditions" or "guard expressions", that only allow passage when the contained condition is evaluated to be "true".
   D. The string inside the square brackets identifies a "behavior effect" that invokes an action by the same name on the state machines' object.
   E. The square brackets highlight an error in the original state machine. It is related to the use of Latin, *sic* (so, thus) to flag errors in the original material in the text.
8. In UML 2.5, when might it be useful to use an exit action in a state machine?
   A. An exit action might be useful when all of the possible ways of leaving a state must execute a common behavior or sequence of behaviors.
   B. Upon leaving an exit state.
   C. Upon entering a final state.
   D. An exit action might be useful when most of the possible ways of leaving a state execute a common behavior or sequence of behaviors. The behavior may be an opaque behavior if necessary.
   E. There is no such thing as an exit action in UML 2.5 State Machines. It indicates an exit condition.
9. What symbol is used to indicate that substates have been elided?

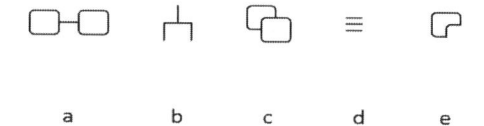

   a   b   c   d   e

   A. a
   B. b
   C. c
   D. d
   E. e

10. After this state machine completes, what is the value of X?

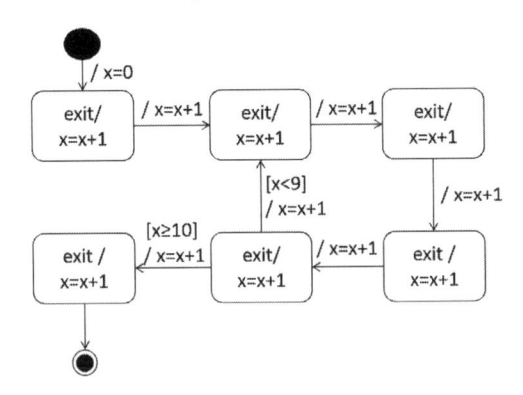

   A. 11
   B. 10
   C. The state machine never ends
   D. 17
   E. 20
   F. 19
11. Which of the following statements is true about UML State Machines?
    A. Every State must have possible transitions in and possible transitions out.
    B. Every State Machine diagram must have a final state.
    C. The star-shaped state indicates concurrency.
    D. Every transition is from one state to another different state.
    E. A completion transition is triggered by the completion of the activity within its state.
12. Given the following State Machine fragment for an object of Class X, what is the minimum number of behaviors that have to be implemented inside Class X for the diagram to be correct?

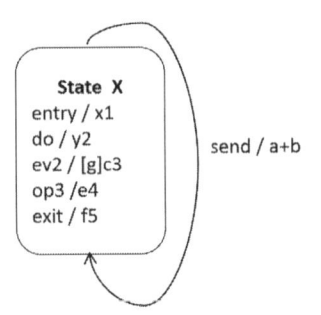

State X
entry / x1
do / y2
ev2 / [g]c3
op3 /e4
exit / f5

send / a+b

A. 0
B. 5
C. 6
D. 7
E. 8

13. In the STM diagram fragment below, we see five transitions marked with italic letters. Which one can't have a guard condition added?

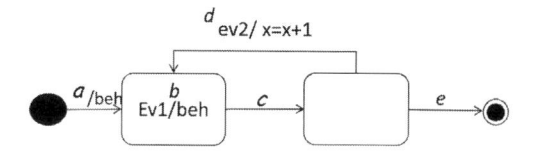

d ev2/ x=x+1

a /beh   *b* Ev1/beh   *c*   *e*

A. *a*
B. *b*
C. *c*
D. *d*
E. *e*

14. Assume the below state machine fragment is in State S1.1 when the do activity b4 finishes. What is the sequence of behaviors that then follows?

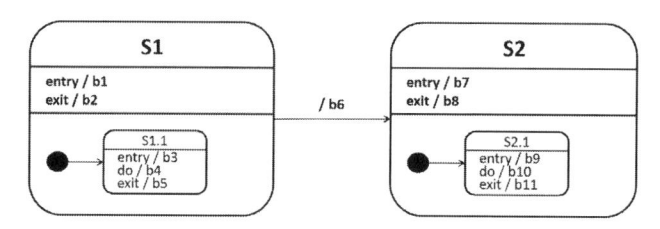

S1
entry / b1
exit / b2

/ b6

S2
entry / b7
exit / b8

S1.1
entry / b3
do / b4
exit / b5

S2.1
entry / b9
do / b10
exit / b11

A. b1, b2, b3, b4, b5, b6, b7, b8, b9, b10, b11
B. The diagram is malformed.
C. b5, b2, b7, b9
D. b5, b2, b7, b9, b10
E. b2, b5, b6, b7, b9, b10
F. b5, b2, b6, b7, b9, b10

15. Examine the following diagram fragment. What statement properly describes the fragment?

348 CHAPTER 19: Questions for Chapter 18

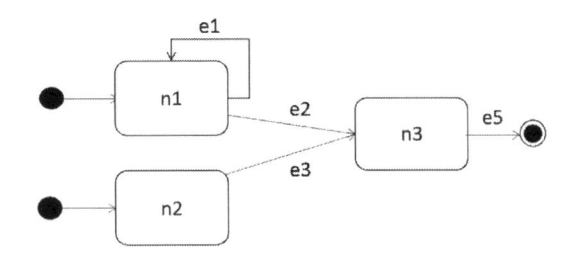

```
        e1
        ↓
    ┌──────┐
 ●─→│  n1  │        e2    ┌──────┐    e5
    └──────┘ ─────────→  │  n3  │ ─────→ ●
                   ↗      └──────┘
               e3
    ┌──────┐
 ●─→│  n2  │
    └──────┘
```

A. A valid state diagram
B. An invalid activity diagram
C. A valid but not executable activity diagram
D. Both a valid state or an activity diagram

ANSWERS FOR CHAPTER 18

1. Which symbol is used to start a UML 2.5 State Machine Diagram?

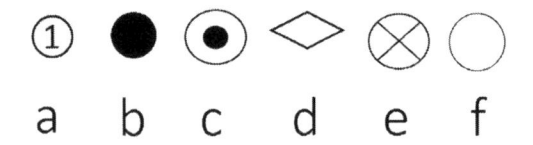

① ● ⦿ ◇ ⊗ ○
a   b   c   d   e   f

A. a
B. **b**
C. c
D. d
E. e
F. f

Discussion:
A—No. While it often used to indicate the start of thing, e.g., a path on a map, it has no use in UML.
B—Yes, the solid ball is used in both Activity Diagrams and State Machines Diagrams to indicate the start of execution. In UML state machines, it is called the Initial Pseudostate. The ball symbol is also used as a Junction Pseudostate.
C—No, this symbol indicates a Final State.
D—No, this symbol indicates a Choice Pseudostate in UML state machine diagrams.
E—No, this symbol indicates a Terminate Pseudostate. It allows the modeler to produce a named exit point for a state. It is also used as a

connection point reference on the boundary of a state, to refer to the named exit point by the same name. These usages are not tested on the Foundation exam.

F—No, this symbol indicates a named entry point in UML State Machine diagrams. It is also used as a connection point reference on the boundary of a state, to refer to the named entry point by the same name.

2. Examine the State Machine Diagram below. What state will the State Machine be in after the events e1, e2, e3, and e1 occur (in that order)?

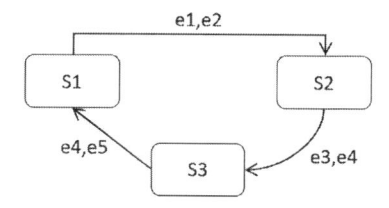

A. It is not possible to tell.
B. S1
C. S2
D. **S3**
E. The diagram is not a valid State Machine Diagram.

Discussion:

Possible Starting State	After event e1 next State	After Event e2 Next State	After Event e3 Next State	After Event e1 Next State
S1	S2	S2	S3	**S3**
S2	S2	S2	S3	**S3**
S3	S3	S3	S3	**S3**

No matter which state you start with, you wind up in S3.

3. Which list completely identifies the possible features of a transition?
   A. trigger
   B. trigger, guard
   C. trigger, guard, state
   D. trigger, guard, state, effect
   E. trigger, constraint, effect
   F. **trigger, guard, effect**
   G. trigger, guard, effect, return

Discussion:
States, Constraints, and Returns are not possible features of a transition. This leaves, A, B, and F as possible answers. F is the complete answer.

4. What type of behavior should a system exhibit to be most appropriate for using a State Machine to help in understanding the manifest behavior of the system?
   A. Continuous and self-adjusting behavior
   B. Cooperating identical peer instances
   C. Genetic Evolving Algorithms with feedback
   D. **Discrete Event-driven behavior**
   E. Time-based Schedule driven behavior

   Discussion:
   A and C—No. Self-adjusting and evolving algorithms cannot easily be captured in a predictable event-based response approach in a state-like manner.
   B—No, cooperating peers usually work best in an agent-based approach. In any case, understanding how an individual responds will not give direct insight into the manifest or emergent system properties.
   D—Yes, UML State Machines are best using for discrete event-driven behavior.
   E—No, Time and scheduling algorithms may use state machines to process the time alarms, but the entire picture of the system is not appropriate for state machines.

5. Which statement best describes how a higher priority event interrupts the processing of a lower priority event in a UML state machine?
   A. The events are taken from the event pool in strict priority order. Thus, a newly arriving high priority event can interrupt ongoing behavior.
   B. There is no possibility for interrupting events because of RTC.
   C. **The UML 2.5 Specification does not allow for State Machine-mediated interrupts. However, changes to the priority of an object's thread and changes to the resources available to the thread may cause a particular thread to be suspended and others to be enabled.**
   D. Higher priority events may be taken before lower priority events by an unspecified algorithm, causing effective interrupts.
   E. The UML 2.5 Specification indicates that completion events are of higher priority than other events. This ordering causes completion events to be examined before external events, leaving interrupts in their wake.

Discussion:
Because of the RTC, no direct state machine mechanism allows for interrupts. Thus, A, D, and E are incorrect. They do not describe interrupts as no ongoing behavior is stopped. Though the facts they say about event processing order are correct, just the selection of a higher priority event before a lower priority event does not allow for interrupts with RTC, as every event's processing still runs to its end. This leaves B and C as possible correct answers.

However, as completely banning interrupts may produce priority inversion problems, UML 2.5 allows for thread and resource-based prioritization to order the execution of different instances over time. The mechanisms for accomplishing this are not specified within UML. However, within a state machine, no incoming UML-defined event can interrupt the ongoing processing.

6. A State Machine Diagram has at least one Final State at the top level (at the State Machine diagram level), with more than one incoming edge. When does the State Machine finish?
   A. The State Machine finishes when all the incoming edges to the Final State have supplied at least one token.
   B. **The State Machine finishes with the first transition to a top-level (diagram) Final State.**
   C. The State Machine finishes when the majority of incoming edges have transitioned to a top-level Final State.
   D. The State Machine finishes when every top-level (diagram level) Final State has had a transition into it.

   Discussion:
   A—No, token arrival is not considered in State Machine Diagrams. Token arrival is part of UML 2.5 Activity Diagrams.
   B—Yes, once a top-level final state has been reached the diagram, and the State Machine is done.
   C—No, there is no concept of voting.
   D—No, once any top-level final state is reached the diagram is done.

7. In a UML 2.5 State Machine, an expression may be surrounded by square brackets, [ ]. What does this expression mean?
   A. An "invariant constraint" is surrounded by square brackets. The modelers state their intention that the model will enforce these constraint expressions to be true.
   B. The use of square brackets announces that the expression is an "opaque expression", whose meaning is context dependent.
   C. **Such expressions are "guard conditions" or "guard expressions", that only allow passage when the contained condition is evaluated to be "true".**

D. The string inside the square brackets identifies a "behavior effect" that invokes an action by the same name on the state machines' object.
   E. The square brackets highlight an error in the original state machine. It is related to the use of Latin, *sic* (so, thus) to flag errors in the original material in the text.

   Discussion:
   A—No. In UML, constraints are surrounded by squiggly brackets {}.
   B—No, though the contents may be opaque expressions, they are called "guard expressions" and have a specific purpose.
   C—Yes. A guard expression can be used as path annotations when multiple paths may appear. When a guard expression is false, that path is prohibited. If more than one guard expression is true (which should not be), processing will follow one of the true conditions.
   D—No, a behavior effect follows the "/" on a transition. It is possible that the guard expression is an opaque Boolean expression or a query operation on the object.
   E—No, we do not repeat errors in UML. If we need to flag an error, we would use comments.

8. In UML 2.5, when might it be useful to use an exit action in a state machine?
   A. **An exit action might be useful when all of the possible ways of leaving a state must execute a common behavior or sequence of behaviors.**
   B. Upon leaving an exit state.
   C. Upon entering a final state.
   D. An exit action might be useful when most of the possible ways of leaving a state execute a common behavior or sequence of behaviors. The behavior may be an opaque behavior if necessary.
   E. There is no such thing as an exit action in UML 2.5 State Machines. It indicates an exit condition.

   Discussion:
   An exit action is a UML 2.5 mechanism to provide a mandatory common behavior or sequence of behavior (an action) for all the possible ways of leaving a state. It is not necessary to use.
   An exit condition is not a UML term. If we needed such a thing, we would use a Guard condition. Many modelers confuse exit action and exit condition.

9. What symbol is used to indicate that substates have been elided?

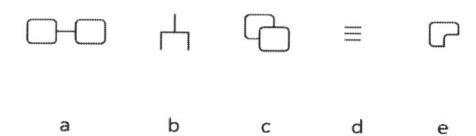

       a   b   c   d   e

A. a
B. b
C. c
D. d
E. e

Discussion:
The symbols used to indicate a decomposition hierarchy looks like a stylized example of the model type being decomposed. The exact format is left to the modeling tool, though the UML specification gives examples.
A—Yes, this looks like the symbol used. In some places, the nodes look more like circles
B—No, this is the *rake* symbol used in static diagrams. BTW, at the time of this writing, the SysML Revision Task Force is debating adding the rake symbol as a possible indicator of the decomposition hierarchy of all model elements. Even if accepted by the SysML RTF, this does not change the rules for UML
C—No. This symbol is not used in UML.
D—No. This is the hamburger icon that is used in some user interfaces to indicate that selecting it will produce a menu of pages or options.
E—No. This symbol is not used in UML.

10. After this state machine completes, what is the value of X?

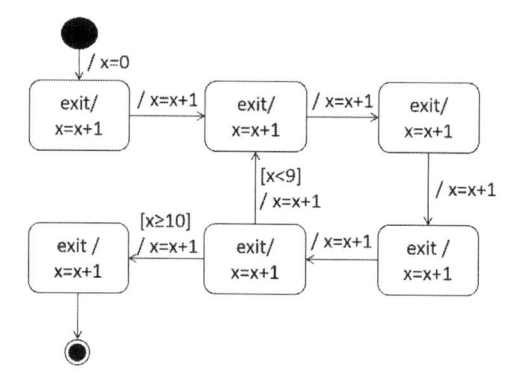

A. 11
B. 10
C. The state machine never ends.
D. 17
E. 20
F. <u>19</u>

Discussion:
The [guard condition] is evaluated to determine if the transition should be taken. If the transition causes an exit to be taken, then the exit action is performed on the way out. This is followed by the transition and the associated action.
In this type of question, a good strategy would be to count it twice. If you get the same answer, go with it. If not, come back to the question with a fresh mind.
F—The correct answer is 19.
In some situations, it may be considered that such values are undefined after the machine ends.

11. Which of the following statements is true about UML State Machines?
    A. Every State must have possible transitions in and possible transitions out.
    B. Every State Machine diagram must have a final state.
    C. The star-shaped state indicates concurrency.
    D. Every transition is from one state to another different state.
    E. **<u>A completion transition is triggered by the completion of the activity within its state.</u>**

    Discussion:
    A—No. A Final State may not have any transitions out.
    B—No. Some State Machines are not intended to end. Consider a light switch.
    C—No. There is no star-shaped pseudostate.
    D—No. It is possible for a transition to lead back to the original state.
    E—Yes. That is the definition of a completion transition.

12. Given the following State Machine fragment for an object of Class X, what is the minimum number of behaviors that have to be implemented inside Class X for the diagram to be correct?

A. 0
B. 5
C. 6
D. 7
E. 8

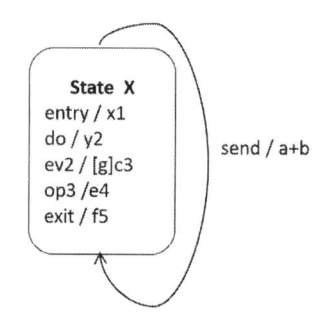

Discussion:
This is a tricky question because Class X need not implement any behavior. It could be a subclass of a group of Super classes that implement the required behaviors. Therefore, the correct answer is
A—0
However, if you believe this is too tricky the correct answer is (give yourself half credit)
B—5
Remember the [g] is a guard condition that could be implemented as a behavior, but need not be.
Send is the name of the incoming event, not a behavior.
A + B is an opaque behavior, but not required to be implemented by X.

13. In the STM diagram fragment below, we see five transitions marked with italic letters. Which option cannot have a guard condition added?

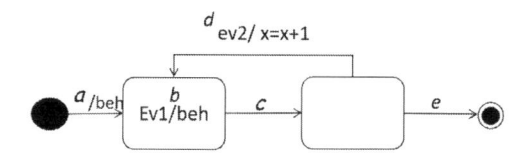

A. *a*
B. *b*
C. *c*
D. *d*
E. *e*

Discussion:
A—Correct. This is an initial transition. As a pseudostate, it is not allowed to have an event nor a guard because processing must not stop there. It can have an effect (behavior or action).
B—Incorrect. This is an internal transition. It can have a trigger, guard, and effect.
C—Incorrect. This is a completion (automatic) transition. It can have guard and effect but no trigger.
D—Incorrect. This is a normally triggered transition. It can have a trigger, guard, and effect.
E—Incorrect. This is a final transition. It can have a trigger, guard, and effect.

14. Assume the below state machine fragment is in State S1.1 when the do activity b4 finishes. What is the sequence of behaviors that then follows?

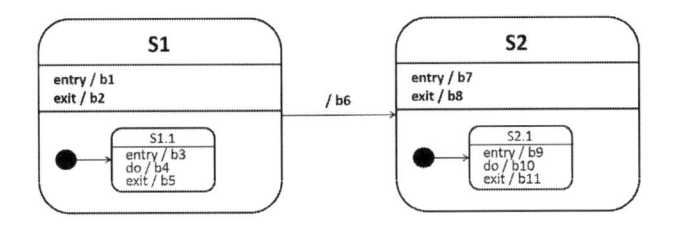

```
       S1                              S2
  entry / b1                      entry / b7
  exit / b2         / b6          exit / b8
    ┌─S1.1──┐                       ┌─S2.1──┐
  ● │entry/b3│                    ● │entry/b9│
    │do / b4 │                      │do / b10│
    │exit/b5 │                      │exit/b11│
    └────────┘                      └────────┘
```

A. b1, b2, b3, b4, b5, b6, b7, b8, b9, b10, b11
B. The diagram is malformed.
C. b5, b2, b7, b9
D. b5, b2, b7, b9, b10
E. b2, b5, b6, b7, b9, b10
F. **b5, b2, b6, b7, b9, b10**

Discussion:
A—Incorrect. This is just the list of possible behaviors is collating order.
B—Incorrect. The diagram is valid. For example, the transition between the states is a completion transition and needs no explicit trigger.
C—Incorrect. The list of behaviors is missing b6. This is executed during the transition between S1.1 and S2.1. It is also missing the do activity behavior b10.
D—Incorrect. The list of behaviors is still missing b6. This is executed during the transition between S1.1 and S2.1.
E—Incorrect. The order of the behaviors is incorrect. When leaving states, the exit behaviors are done *inside out*. That is, the exit behavior

from the lowest state that is exited is executed first, and the exit behavior from the highest state is executed last.

F—Correct. Note that when entering states, the entry behaviors are done *outside in*. That is, the entry behavior from the highest state is executed first, and the entry behavior from the lowest state is executed last.

15. Examine the following diagram fragment. What statement properly describes the fragment?

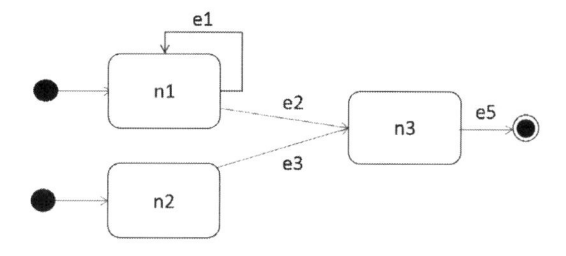

A. A valid state diagram.
B. An invalid activity diagram.
C. **A valid but not executable activity diagram.**
D. Both a valid state or an activity diagram.

Discussion:
This question requires you to be sensitive to the differences between an activity and state diagram.
A—Incorrect. A state diagram may only have one Start Pseudostate.
B—Incorrect. The diagram is valid. However, see the next answer.
C—Correct. The syntax is correct. However, because node n1 requires e1 to be available before it starts and as e1 is an output of node n1, it is not logically possible for the start condition to occur.
D—Incorrect. It is not a legal state diagram.

Index

Note: Page numbers followed by "*f*" and "*t*" refer to figures and tables, respectively.

".", member scope resolution operator, 100
"∷ = ", definition, 71
" < > ", a user-supplied field, 70
" « » ". *See* Guillemets
∷ operator, 136
"#", Protected visibility, 103. *See also* Visibility
"⊙"
   Activity Final, 272*t*
   Final State, 336*t*
"⊗". *See* Flow Final node
"Δ". *See* Generalization; Inheritance
"*". *See* Unbounded Multiplicity
"∷", package scope resolution operator, 71
"∷ = " assignment statement, 71
":", the type of the preceding element, 62–63
": <Type > ", 95
"^". *See* Inherited flag
"{ }", constraint delimiters, 73
"~", package visibility indicator, 103, 133*t*. *See also* Visibility
"-", private visibility indicator, 103, 133*t*. *See also* Visibility
" + ", public visibility indicator, 101, 103, 133*t*. *See also* Visibility
"⊕", package containment, 129–131
"◇". *See* Aggregation; Decision Node; Merge Node
"●". *See* Initial Node on Activity Diagrams; Initial Pseudostate; Junction Pseudostate
"©". *See* Composition
«Actor» stereotype, 211

«modelLibrary», 147
⊕ symbol, 129–131

A

AACR. *See* Anglo-American Cataloging Rules (AACR)
AB. *See* Architecture board (AB)
Abstract
   class, 186
   operation, 186
   syntax, 25, 58–60
AbstractDataType (ADT), 102
Abstraction, 24, 39, 102–103
Access, 143, 143*f*, 144*f*
Accessioning, 90–91
Action behavior, 326
Action Roundangle, 272, 272*t*
Activation, 252
Activity, 272
Activity diagrams, 271–277, 272*t*, 273*f*, 292–295. *See also* Sequence diagram (sd); State machine diagram
   activities, 293
   advanced topics
      local pre/postconditions, 291–292, 292*f*
      send/receive messages/events, 290–291
      stream, 289–290
      weights, 289
   with alternate flows, 274*f*
   calling operation, 294–295, 295*f*
   with concatenated ifs, 276*f*
   concurrent diagrams, 278–281
   consuming tokens, 281–283
   with Do While loop, 276*f*
   with If Then ElseIF EndIF, 276*f*
   invoking activity, 294, 294*f*
   joining at action, 283–284, 284*f*
   loop antipattern, 275*f*
   with merge and decision nodes indicating do until loop, 274*f*
   object flows/edges, 287–289, 287*f*
   of OMG standard process, 27*f*
   questions and answers, 297–312
   shape, 293*f*
   single token diagrams, 277–278
   in standard UML form, 293*f*
   timers and timing events, 284–286
Activity edges, 272, 272*t*
Activity Node, 272
Acton Language for Foundational UML (Alf), 6
Actors, 207, 210–214, 210*f*, 212*f*, 245
   adornments on, 212*t*
   alternative Actor symbol, 211*f*
   database Actors, 214
   external system Actors, 214
   human Actors, 212–213
   multiple Actors for single Use Case in package, 213*f*
Admin Actor, 218
Adornment, 97, 104, 107
ADT. *See* AbstractDataType (ADT)
ADTF. *See* Analysis & Design Task Force (ADTF)
"Advanced UML" training courses, 5
Aggregation, 40, 179–183
   AggregationKind, 174, 181
   physical *vs.* catalog composition, 182–183

359

Index

Alf. *See* Acton Language for Foundational UML (Alf)
Alias, 141
Analog systems, 29–30
Analysis & Design Task Force (ADTF), 26, 28
Analysis, 31–32
　domain, 31–32
　Requirements, 32
　Use Case, 32
Anglo-American Cataloging Rules (AACR), 175–176
Annexes, 55–56
　UML 2.5 specification, 57*t*
Architecture, 33
　models, 33
Architecture board (AB), 26
Argument multiplicity, representing, 167–168, 167*f*, 168*f*
arguments "()", 95
Associations, 172–183
　attribute and role adornments, 172–175, 173*f*
　　book-person-score, 175*f*
　　properties for attributes, 173*t*
　　properties on role ends, 174*t*
　book-person, 172*f*
　composition and aggregation, 179–183
　and datatypes, 178, 178*f*
　descriptions, 58
　line formats, 172*f*
　links and instances, 179, 179*f*
　reading, 175–178
　　association with reading direction, 177*f*
　　bidirectional associations, 175*f*
　　more than one associations between classes, 177*f*
　　named association, 176*f*
　　properties for association, 177*t*
Asynchronous
　messages, 244*f*, 247
　operation call, 245, 246*t*
At least one, 8, 334
Attributes, 59, 62–64, 89, 93–94, 129, 137
　representing multiplicity of, 163–167, 166*f*
　　alternate form, 165*f*
　　book allowing zero authors, 165*f*
　　book with multivalued attribute, 164*f*
　　book with specific room reserved for additional authors, 164*f*
　　constraint and optional, 166*f*
　　multiplicity and constraint, 167*f*
Author attribute, 164
Automatic code generation, 34
Automatic transitions, 328

B

Backus–Naur Form (BNF), 59, 73
Bag, 169
Base Use Case, 219–220
Behavior, 328–329
　activity diagrams, 271–296
　diagrams, 68, 69*t*
　do behavior, 328–329
　example with guarded completion transition, 329*f*
　implicit behavior, 328
　internal behaviors, 330*t*
　restarting state with completion transition, 329*f*
　sequence diagrams, 243–258
Beta review and criteria, 15–16
Beta test, 15
Bill of materials (BOMs), 20
Bill-of-Materials, 181
Biological systems, 29–30
BNF. *See* Backus–Naur Form (BNF)
BOMs. *See* Bill of materials (BOMs)
Booch method, 22, 22*t*
Boolean expression, 324
"Bootstrapping" technique, 60
Borrow and reserve model, 325, 325*f*
Borrowing, 92
Borrowing Large Print Material, 218
Brain dumping, 10
byRef ("&"), 95
byVal ("*"), 95

C

Calling operation, 294–295, 295*f*
Car Hailing App, Package structure for, 138, 139*f*
Cardinality value, 163
Case/switch pattern, 274
Catalog composition, 182–183, 182*f*
Causality, 248
CDR. *See* Critical Design Review (CDR)
Certification Program, 2
Cheating, 9–10
Choice Pseudostate, 335–337, 336*t*, 337*f*
Circulation system, 244
Clashing names, 129
Class diagram, 14*f*, 65, 92
Classes, 129
　assigning value, 109–113
　　expressions, 111–113
　　instance specifications, 110–111
　　literals, 109
　　value assignments, 112*f*
　and classifiers, 137
　finding, 89–97
　　attributes, 93–94
　　book class with operations, 95*f*
　　operations, 94–95
　　referring to member feature, 96
　　static features, 96–97
　four views of same class, 94*f*
　and instance, 109*f*
　modifiers, 104–108
　　default value, 105–106
　　derived properties, 104–105
　　parameter direction, 107–108
　　protecting from change, 106–107
　questions and answers, 115
　types, 97–103
　　class *vs.* datatype, 98
　　DataTypes, 101–103, 101*f*
　　enumerations, 99–101
　　primitive types, 98–99, 98*f*
　　UML visibility notation, 100*t*
Classification, 40–41, 91
Classifier descriptions, 56–57
Clauses, 55–58
Clock. whatTimeIsIt() query, 316
CM. *See* Configuration management (CM)
Collection types, 168–170
Comments, 73
Communication, 35–37
Compartment, 62–63
Compartment, 247
Completion, 331
　completion event, 328
　completion transitions, 328

Index

Composition, 40, 60, 179–183, 180f, 181f
Compound Structure, 186–187
Conceptualization, 33
Concrete class, 67, 186
Concurrency, 277–278
Concurrent diagrams
  explicit token creation, 278–280
  forking *vs.* spawning, 280–281
  implicit token creation, 280, 280f
  multiple forks, 280, 280f
Configuration management (CM), 132
Connectable elements, 243–244, 255
Constraints, 58, 73–74, 101, 102f
Contour, 340–342
Control Flow, 272, 272t
Control node, 272, 272t
countDownTimer, 331–333
Coverage map, 10–11
Critical Design Review (CDR), 145
Crossed messages, 249
Cruising State, 317
Cut score, 16

D

Database Actors, 214, 214f
DataTypes, 101–104, 101f, 178, 178f
  abstraction, 102–103
  class *vs.*, 98
  and instance, 111f
  user-defined dataTypes, 104f
Debugging, 35
Decision Node, 272, 272t, 274
Decisions, 277
Declarative Sentence, 60
Default value, 174
  for arguments/parameters, 106
  for attributes/properties, 105–106
Design
  Detailed Design, 33–34
  in UML Modeling, 32–33
Diagram(s), 147–148. *See also* Activity diagrams; Sequence diagram (sd)
  fragment, 70, 73
  frame and header, 70–71
  Kind, 71–72
  UML, 65–74
    behavior diagrams, 68, 69t

  general diagram features, 68–74
  structure diagrams, 67–68, 68t
  UML 2.5 specification annexes, contents, and, 57t
  UML 2.5 specification clauses, contents and, 57t
Direct simulation or execution, 34
displayHelp behavior, 331–332
Distinguishable names, 137–138
Distractors, 11–13
Divide-and-conquer approach, 214
Do behavior, 328–329, 330f
do-until loop, 274–275
do-while loop, 276
Documentation, 36–37
Domain, 31–32
  analysis, 31–32
Domain Technology Committee, 26

E

Element(s), 129–131, 243
  descriptions, 59
  import, 141–142, 142f
  from Packages, 140–144
    access, 143, 143f, 144f
    comparison of Package *vs.* Element import, 141–142
    Element import, 141
    Package dependencies and cycles, 144
    Package import, 141
    Package merge, 144
Elide, 39
Ellipsis, 94
Encapsulation, 39
Encrypted cipher text, 289
Entry action equivalents, 330, 331f
Entry behavior, 329–330, 330f
Enumerations, 99–101
  inherited enumerations, 100f
  literal, 99–101
  UML visibility notation, 100t
Environmental systems, 29–30
Event pool, 334
Events, 244, 313–314, 321–322
Executable node, 272, 272t
Execution Specification, 253–254, 254f, 255f
Exit action equivalents, 330
Exit behavior, 329–330, 330f
Explicit token creation, 278–280
  actions and control nodes, 279t

  fork node inducing concurrency, 279f
  initial nodes inducing concurrency, 279f
EXPRESS (modeling language), 20
Expressions, 111–113
Extend, 220–223
  «extend» notation, 221–222
  using extension, 221
  extension points, 222–223
Extension, 221
  points, 222–223, 223f
  Use Case, 220
External system Actors, 214
External Transition, 337

F

Factorial function (!), 60–61
Feature, 184–186. *See also* General diagram features
FIFO, 287
Figure Manager class, 188
FigureManager. getDiagramArea(), 188
"Fill Out Survey", 221
Filtering criteria, 15
Final Node, 272–273, 272t
Final State, 313
Finalization Task Force (FTF), 27
Finding States, 319–321
Flow final node, 283
Flows, 271
Fork, 280–281
  control node, 278–279
Foundation Exam, 10–11, 14f
  topic areas on, 10t
Frame, 70
Framework, 147
FTF. *See* Finalization Task Force (FTF)
Full lock-step approach, 282–283
fUML. *See* Semantics of Foundational Subset for Executable UML Models (fUML)

G

General diagram features, 68–74
  comments, 73
  constraints, 73–74
  diagram frame and header, 70–71

General diagram features (*Continued*)
  Diagram Kind, 71–72
  namespace, 72
  package with class and an object, 72f
  relationship between model and diagram elements, 69f
  views, 69–70
Generalization, 24, 40–41, 65, 183–189, 217–218
  of actor and use case, 219f
  actor inheritance, 217f
  diagram of UML diagrams, 184f
  polymorphism, 187–189
  process, 187
  reflexive structures using generalization, 186–187
  use case, 218f
Grammar, 60
Guard conditions, 324–326
Guards, 274
Guillemets, 64

H
"Hail a Ride", 221
handleChar, 331–332
Head of lifeline, 245
Header, 70–71
Hierarchy of states, 339–340
Human Actors, 212–213, 213f
Humans, communication to, 35

I
IDEF. *See* Integration Definition (IDEF)
Identity, 98
Idle State, 317
if-then pattern, 274
ILL. *See* Interlibrary loan (ILL)
Implicit behavior, 328
Implicit token creation, 280, 280f
Import, 140–141
In state, 334
In transit, 334
Include, 219–220, 220f
Included Use Case, 219–221, 220f
Information hiding, 39
Information hiding and simplicity, 38–39
Inheritance, 24, 183–189, 185f
Inherited flag, 173

Initial Node, 272–273, 272t
Initial Pseudostate, 323–324, 336t, 338
Initial State, 313
Initial value. *See* Default value
Instance(s), 179, 179f
  class and, 109f
  specification, 62–63, 110–111
Integer Literals, 109
Integration Definition (IDEF), 20–21
Interaction, 243, 255
  Diagrams, 255
Interlibrary loan (ILL), 67–68
Internal behaviors, 329–330, 330t
Internal transitions, 331–333, 337–338
International Telecommunication Union-Standardization (ITU-T), 243
Interval, 102
ISO, 56
isOrdered, 168–169
isUnique, 169
Itinerary, 169
ITU-T. *See* International Telecommunication Union-Standardization (ITU-T)

J
Join node, 281
  with two tokens/edges, 281f
Joint Technical Committee on Information Technology 1 (JTC-1), 28
Junction pseudostate, 325, 326f, 336t

L
Layered approach, 139
Layered metamodel, 60–65
Leibniz's Law, 90–91
Letter of Intent (LOI), 26
Library Circulation System, 215
Library of Congress (LOC), 175–176
Library Patron, 89
Library system, 207
Lifeline, 244
LIFO, 287
Links, 179, 179f
Literals, 109
  values in UML, 109t

LOC. *See* Library of Congress (LOC)
Local pre/postconditions, 291–292, 292f
Local Transition, 337
LOI. *See* Letter of Intent (LOI)
Loops, 274
Lower-bound, 164–165

M
Machine Readable Cataloging (MARC), 175–176
Mass noun, 91
Members, 95, 129
  feature, 96
  Namespace, 129–130
  package member visibility, 133–134
  Package with, 131f
Merge Node, 272, 272t, 274–275
Merges, 277
Message Sequence Charts (MSC), 243
Messages, 245–247
  asynchronous, 244f, 247
  lifeline occurrences, 246t
  synchronous, 245–247
Meta Object Facility-based languages (MOF-based languages), 58
Metamodel, 25, 163, 181f
Mixed-level diagram, 64
Model databases, 132–133
Model Interchange SIG, 37
"Model-a-little code-a-little" approach, 34–35
ModelLibrary, 147
Modes, 315
  enumerations, 315f
Modifiers, 104–108
  default value, 105–106
  derived properties, 104–105
  parameter direction, 107–108
  protecting from change, 106–107
MOF-based languages. *See* Meta Object Facility-based languages (MOF-based languages)
MSC. *See* Message Sequence Charts (MSC)
Multi-Token diagrams, 278–281
Multiple forks
  concurrent diagrams, 280, 280f
  consuming tokens, 281–283

Index

flow final and activity final, 283*f*
free running and asynchronous ending, 282*f*
fully lockstep, 282*f*
join node with two tokens/edges, 281*f*
Multiplicity, 60, 163–171, 211
  of attributes, 163–167
  discontinuity, 170–171
  properties and collection types, 168–170
    bag, 169
    ordered set, 168–169, 169*f*
    sequence, 169–170, 170*f*, 171*t*
    set, 168
    unique, 169
  representing argument, 167–168
Multivalued, 164–165, 168, 169*f*

N

Name Authority File (NAF), 175–176
Name collision, 141
Named Element, 129–130, 145
Namespace, 72, 137–138, 255
Naming states, 317
Naming Use Cases, 208–210, 208*f*, 209*f*
Natural language, 289
Navigability, 177*t*
Noncountable noun. *See* Mass noun
Nonobject-oriented modeling techniques, 24
Normative document, 55–56
Notation, 21, 59, 281
Note-symbol, 73
Notional diagram, 249–250

O

Object Constraint Language (OCL), 58, 96
Object flows/edges, 287–289, 287*f*
  action
    with alternative format pins, 288*f*
    and control nodes, 288*t*
    with pins, 288*f*
Object Management Group (OMG), 1–2, 23, 26–29
  Activity Diagram of OMG standard process, 27*f*

history of UML, 28–29
standards-making process of, 26–28
Object Modeling Technique (OMT), 22
Object-oriented modeling languages, 21
Object-oriented programing languages (OOPL), 90
Object-Oriented Software Engineering (OOSE), 22
Object-oriented theory, 95
Object(s), 89
  assigning value, 109–113
    expressions, 111–113
    instance specifications, 110–111
    literals, 109
    value assignments, 112*f*
  creation, 250–251
  destruction, 245, 246*t*
  finding, 89–97
    attributes, 93–94
    operations, 94–95
    referring to member feature, 96
    static features, 96–97
  flows, 272
  modifiers, 104–108
    default value, 105–106
    derived properties, 104–105
    parameter direction, 107–108
    protecting from change, 106–107
  questions and answers, 115
  types, 97–103
    DataTypes, 101–103, 101*f*
    enumerations, 99–101
    primitive types, 98–99, 98*f*
    UML visibility notation, 100*t*
Occurrences, 244, 247–253
OCL. *See* Object Constraint Language (OCL)
OCL-like expressions, 320
OCUP. *See* OMG Certified UML Professional (OCUP)
OMG. *See* Object Management Group (OMG)
OMG Certified UML Professional (OCUP), 1
  certification examinations, 2–3
  OMG, 2
OMG Certified UML Professional 1 (OCUP 1), 1
  certification program, 55

OMG Certified UML Professional 2 (OCUP 2), 1–2
  certification program, 55
  exam structure, 12–13
  Foundation Exam, 11
  Foundation Level icon, 7*f*
  levels, 3–6
    advanced level, 6
    foundation level, 4–5
    intermediate level, 5
    state machine diagram for passing exams and certifications, 4*f*
  OMG Certified Professionals Directory, 6
  preparation, 8–11
    cheating, 9–10
    coverage map, 10–11
    topic areas on foundation exam, 10*t*
  printed examination results report, 6
  question structure, 13–14
  signing up for exam, 7–8
  UTI, 12
  writing examinations, 14–16
    beta review and criteria, 15–16
    review process and criteria, 15
    team, 14–15
OMT. *See* Object Modeling Technique (OMT)
ON/OFF states, 322–323
ON/OFF/ON state, 323–324
OOPL. *See* Object-oriented programing languages (OOPL)
OOSE. *See* Object-Oriented Software Engineering (OOSE)
Opaque action, 273–274
Opaque expression, 111
Operation call, 245, 246*t*
Operation call, 245
Operations, 137
Ordered bag, 171*t*
Ordered set, 168–170, 169*f*, 170*f*, 172, 188
Ordering
  methods, 287
  rules, 248
Organization of UML
  abstract syntax, 59–60
  diagrams, 65–74
    behavior diagrams, 68, 69*t*

Index

Organization of UML (*Continued*)
  general diagram features, 68–74
  structure diagrams, 67–68, 68*t*
  language definition–clauses, 56–58
  layered metamodel, 60–65
  levels of metamodeling, 61*t*
  questions and answers, 75–88
  subclauses, 58–59
  taxonomy of UML diagrams, 66*f*
  UML 2.5 specification, 55–56
Outer names, 135–137, 136*f*
Overlapping states, 317–319
Owned Elements, 129–130
Owners, 223–224, 224*f*
Ownership, 145

P

Package, 129
  and contents, 138–144
  dependencies, 140
  diagram, 132, 147
  elements from, 140–144
  import, 141–142, 142*f*
  member visibility, 133–134
    notation and packages, 134*f*
    of package elements, 135*t*
    UML visibility notation in packages, 133*t*
    visibility in packages, 134*f*
  MyPackage, 130–131
  notation, 129–133
    diagrams of packages, 131–132, 131*f*
    packages and contents, 129–131, 130*f*
    URI, 132–133
  questions and answers, 149
  stereotypes, 144–148
  and visibility, 133–138, 133*t*
Package stereotypes. *See also* Stereotypes
  miscellaneous stereotypes of Packages
    Diagrams, 147–148
    Framework, 147
    ModelLibrary, 147
    Profiles, 147
  packages and models, 144–146, 146*f*, 146*t*
Packageable element, 129–130
Packaged Elements, 138
Parameter direction, 107–108
  ParameterDirectionKind, 107*t*, 108*f*

Parameters, 246
Part, 180–181
Partial ordering, 248
Participants, 243
PAS process. *See* Publicly Available Specifications process (PAS process)
Passthrough states, 331, 332*f*
Patron, 244
Patron Actor, 218
PDR. *See* Preliminary Design Review (PDR)
Pearson Vue, 10, 12, 15
  OMG site, 7
Petri nets, 28, 271
Physical composition, 182–183, 182*f*
Platform Technology Committee and Industry, 26
Polymorphism, 187–189, 188*f*
Potential Passengers, 207
Practical sequence diagrams, 256–257
Preliminary Design Review (PDR), 145
Primary Actor, 211
Principles of UML modeling, 37–41
  classification and generalization, 40–41
  information hiding and simplicity, 38–39
  risk mitigation, 38
  sample risks mitigated by modeling, 38*t*
  whole-part relationships, 40
Problem Statement, 91, 94
Profiles, 147
Protecting from change, 106–107
Pseudostates, 335–337, 336*t*
Psychometricians, 15
Publicly Available Specifications process (PAS process), 28
Python, 18

Q

Qualified name, 136
Qualifier, 174, 174*t*
Queries, 106–107
  operation, 107*f*
Question structure, 13–14

R

Rational Unified Process (RUP), 22–23
Reading direction, 176–177, 177*f*

ReadOnly, 106
ReadSensor action, 285–286
Receive messages/events, 290–291
Receptions, 247, 250
Reference Book, 92
Reflexive structures using generalization, 186–187
Reification, 90, 92
Relationship, 163, 174–176, 179–181, 183–184
Request for Proposal (RFP), 26, 28–29
Requirements analysis, 32
"Return Book", 221
Reverse engineering, 34
Review process and criteria, 15
RFP. *See* Request for Proposal (RFP)
Risk mitigation, 38
Role adornments, 172–175
Role names, 172, 177–178, 180*f*, 185, 243
Round trip modeling, 34–35
RTC paradigm. *See* Run-to-Completion paradigm (RTC paradigm)
Rumbaugh, Jim, 22
Run-to-Completion paradigm (RTC paradigm), 333–334, 334*f*, 335*t*
RUP. *See* Rational Unified Process (RUP)

S

SA/SD diagram. *See* Structured Analysis/Structured Design diagram (SA/SD diagram)
SCs. *See* Subcommittees (SCs)
sd. *See* Sequence diagram (sd)
SDL. *See* Specification and Description Language (SDL)
SDR. *See* System Design Review (SDR)
Searching State, 317
Secondary Actor, 211
Semantics, 58–59
Semantics of Foundational Subset for Executable UML Models (fUML), 6
Send messages/events, 290–291
Sending lifeline, 245
Sequence, 169–170, 170*f*, 171*t*
Sequence diagram (sd), 65, 243, 255. *See also* Activity diagrams; State machine diagram
  borrowing book scenario, 256*f*

Execution Specification, 253–254, 254f
lifelines, 243–245, 244f
messages, 245–247
practical sequence diagrams, 256–257
principal parts of, 256f
questions and answers, 259–270
time & occurrences, 247–253
UML sequence diagram showing email processing, 19f
Set, 89, 168
Signal, 247
SIGs. *See* Special Interest Groups (SIGs)
Simple state machine, 322–324
Simulation Program with Integrated Circuit Emphasis (SPICE), 29–31
Single Pole Single Throw (SPST), 322
Single-level diagrams, 64
Software development, 38
Software-intensive systems, 29
"Sort of", 65, 183
Source class, 178–179
Source side, 176
Spawning, 280–281
Special Interest Groups (SIGs), 26
Specialization, 40–41, 65, 183–189, 218
Specification (Spec), 55–56
Specification and Description Language (SDL), 243
SPICE. *See* Simulation Program with Integrated Circuit Emphasis (SPICE)
SPST. *See* Single Pole Single Throw (SPST)
SRR. *See* System Requirements Review (SRR)
Stack class, 102, 103f
Standards-making process of OMG, 26–28
Start node, 273
State machine diagram, 92, 313–321. *See also* Activity diagrams; Sequence diagram (sd)
  class diagram supporting widowed state, 315f
  differences between states, 316
  Finding States, 319–321
  naming states, 317
  overlapping states, 317–319

  for passing exams and certifications, 4f
  qualitatively different states, 316–317
  state machine processing, 333–341
  state *vs.* activity diagram semantics, 341t, 342
  states and modes, 315
  transitions, 321–333
State machine processing, 313, 333–341
  additional states on first exam, 336t
  diagrams and machines, 338–339
  hierarchy of states, 339–340
  lower level of hierarchy, 340f
  RTC paradigm, 333–334
  state diagrams and machines, 338–339
  states and pseudostates, 335–337
  states contours, 340–341
  top of state hierarchy/state diagram, 339f
  types of transitions, 337–338, 337f
State(s), 313, 315, 335–337
  class diagram supporting widowed, 315f
  contours, 340–341, 341f
  criteria based on attributes, 320t
  criteria based on navigation properties, 320t
  differences between, 316
  enumerations, 315f
  examples, 314f
  finding states, 319–321
  naming states, 317
  overlapping states, 317–319
  qualitatively different states, 316–317
  setup, 329–330
Static conditional branch, 325, 336t
Static features, 96–97
Static model
  associations, 172–183
  generalization, specialization, and inheritance, 183–189
  multiplicity, 163–171
  questions and answer, 191
Static scope, 173t, 174t
Statistical analysis of beta results, 15
Stem, 13–14

Stereotypes, 63, 133, 173t, 174t, 177t. *See also* Package stereotypes
Stream, 289–290, 290f
Structure class, 187
Structure diagrams, 67–68, 68t
Structured Analysis/Structured Design diagram (SA/SD diagram), 20
Subclass, 178–179, 184–188
Subclauses, 55–56, 58–59
Subcommittees (SCs), 26
Subject, 214–215, 216f, 225
  interlibrary loan Use Case, 215f
  phrase, 60
  relationship between Use Cases and, 215f
Substitute, 184
Substitution, 40–41, 71
Superclass, 184–188
Surface syntax, 59
Swimlanes, 271
Switch Turned Off events, 322–323
Switch Turned On events, 322–323
Synchronous messages, 245–247
SysML. *See* Systems Engineering Modeling Language (SysML)
System boundary, 225
System Class, 247
System Design Review (SDR), 145
System object, 315
System of Interest, 214
System Requirements Review (SRR), 145
Systems Engineering Modeling Language (SysML), 25, 29–31

T

Target classes, 177–178
Target side, 176
Task Forces (TFs), 26–27
Teardown, 329–330
Technology Committees (TCs), 26
Test Readiness Review (TRR), 145
Textual syntax, 59
TFs. *See* Task Forces (TFs)
Three Amigos, 22–24, 22t
Three-way switch, 323–324
Time, 247–253
Time Trigger event, 284–285, 285t
Timers, 284–286, 285t
Timing Diagrams, 244
Timing events, 284–286, 285t

Token, 271–272, 277
  flow final, 283
  multiple forks, 281–283
Trace, 248
Transitions, 313–314, 321–333
  behavior, 328–329
  borrow and reserve model, 325f
  borrowing with reserve counting, 327f
  completion, 331
  effect, 326–327
  events, 321–322
  exit/entry action equivalents, 330
  guard conditions, 324–326
  guarded transition, 324f
  internal transitions, 331–333
  multiple ways of getting into state, 331t
  simple state machine, 322–324
  simple switch, 322f
  SPDT with initial pseudostate, 323f
  state setup and teardown, 329–330
  state transition table, 325t
  state with internal behavior and final state, 332f
  state-dependent transitions, 323f
  states with, 321f
  syntax, 327
  transition behavior, 326
  transition effect, 326
TRR. *See* Test Readiness Review (TRR)
Two-way switch, 322
TypeName, 243

U

UML. *See* Unified modeling language (UML)
UML 1.x diagrams, 271
UML 2.5, 244
  development, 2
  specification, 9, 55–56
    annexes, contents, and diagrams, 57t
    clauses, contents, and diagrams, 57t
    document layout, 55–56
    semantic areas of, 58f
    target audience, 55
    UML diagram with <heading> and <contents area>, 70f

UML Revision Task Force (UML RTF), 23–24
UML Technology Institute (UTI), 12
"Unbounded (*)", 164
Unified modeling language (UML), 17, 131, 143f, 163, 220, 291
  development, 23
  diagram, 207
  history of, 28–29
  infrastructure document, 28–29
  kind of modeling, 29–30
  language, 17–18
  literal values in, 109t
  mapping written languages to, 18t
  model builders, 4–5
  model users, 4–5
  modeling language, 18–21
  object-oriented modeling languages, 21
  OMG, 26–29
  original goals, 23–24
  partners, 23–24
  principles of modeling, 37–41
    classification and generalization, 40–41
    information hiding and simplicity, 38–39
    risk mitigation, 38
    sample risks mitigated by modeling, 38t
    whole-part relationships, 40
  purposes for UML modeling, 30–37, 31t
    analysis, 31–32
    communication, 35–37
    design, 32–33
    implementation, 34–35
  questions and answers, 43–54
  sources, 22t
  specifications, 1
  State Machine, 335
  superstructure document, 28–29
  tool, 224
  UML sequence diagram showing email processing, 19f
  updated goals, 24–25
  version 1.3, 24–25
Uniform Resource Identifier (URI), 132
Unique, 169
Upper-bound, 164–165
URI. *See* Uniform Resource Identifier (URI)

Use Cases, 139, 207–217
  actors, 210–214
  analysis, 32
  diagrams, 224–225, 224f
  naming, 208–210
  question and answers, 259
  simplifying, 217–225
    extend, 220–223
    generalization, 217–218
    include, 219–220
    owners, 223–224
    use case diagrams, 224–225
  Subject, 214–215
User-defined dataTypes, 104f
User-interface Packages, 139
UTI. *See* UML Technology Institute (UTI)

V

Value assignments, 112f
Verb Phrase, 60
Vertex, 321, 335
Vertical diamond, 275
Views, 33, 69–70, 129, 137
Visibility, 173t, 174t
  packages and
    inner and outer names, 135–137, 136f
    namespaces and distinguishable names, 137–138
    package member visibility, 133–134
  signs, 133
VisibilityKind indicator, 100
Vision-Impaired Patron, 218
Voting-style error checking, 282–283

W

Wait for Time Event, 284–287, 285t, 290–291
Wait point, 333
Wakeup Signal, 247
Weights, 289
Whole-part relationships, 40, 60, 180
Wide diamond, 275

X

XML Metadata Interchange (XMI), 25, 37, 57t, 132

Printed in Great Britain
by Amazon